365 RACHAEL RAY :NO REPEATS

RACHAEL RAY
365: NO REPEATS

A Year of Deliciously Different Dinners

Clarkson Potter/Publishers
New York

Published in the United States by Clarkson Potter/Publishers, an imprint of the
Crown Publishing Group, a division of Random House, Inc., New York.
www.crownpublishing.com
www.clarksonpotter.com

Clarkson N. Potter is a trademark and Potter and colophon are registered
trademarks of Random House, Inc.

Library of Congress Cataloging-in-Publication Data
Ray, Rachael.
    Rachael Ray 365 : no repeats : a year of deliciously different dinners /
Rachael Ray—1st ed.
        p.   cm.
1. Quick and easy cookery.   I. 30-Minute meals (Television program)
II. Title.
    TX833.5.R387   2005   2005023361
    641.5'55—dc22

ISBN-13 978-1-4000-8254-4
ISBN-10 1-4000-8254-4

Printed in the United States of America

Design by Jennifer K. Beal

20

First Edition

For the two
hungriest girls
I've ever known—
Boo and Isaboo

thank you notes

Thanks to my family, especially my mom, Elsa, and my hubby, John, for loving me even when I am cranky and tired—as this is most of the time. Additionally, thanks for cooking for me when I am in this state as well.

Thanks to the fans of 30 Minute Meals—stay hungry!

Thanks to the crew of 30-Minute Meals at Food Network—especially Emily, for cracking the whip! Do you all have to be so organized?

Thanks to the gang at Clarkson Potter, especially Pam Krauss, for turning my confusing, gigantic files and piles of 366 recipes and notes into a user-friendly book.

Introduction

I don't know what my total lifetime limit is for new recipes, but 365 is definitely this cook's limit for one book. After 62 sleepless nights, 5 bottles of headache relief capsules, and 47 pounds of really good coffee I finally understand why so many people tell me "I'm in a rut. I just can't come up with any new ideas for dinner." I used to think smugly to myself "How could anyone run out of ideas? Food is limitless!" Now, I get it. Coming up with the recipes for this collection of 30-Minute Meals almost killed me!

So, why bother to create *365: No Repeats*? Well, aside from wanting to use that cute title (which I was totally hooked on) I did have a legitimate goal: I wanted to write a book that inspired people to become more creative and instinctual when they cook. I wanted to put together an assortment of 30-Minute Meals so broad it conveyed the idea that once you get the hang of it, cooking gets easier and easier—so easy that you could prepare dinner every single night for a year and never eat the same thing twice and still not have to spend your life in the kitchen.

The whole idea of 30-Minute Meals actually started as a cooking class in which I would teach 6 master recipes and 5 versions of each master recipe. After a couple of hours, participants would go home knowing how to make 30 different 30-Minute Mediterranean Meals. The class became so popular that the local news came to report on it. One thing led to another and, just like the master recipes multiplying out, the 30-Minute Meal concept grew to take on a life of its own—and eventually took over my life!

For this book I have brought back the concept that I started with in that first class: learn one and you get some. For instance, once you've made the Balsamic-Glazed Pork Chops with Arugula-Basil Rice Pilaf, just by trading chicken breasts for the pork and adding some smoked mozzarella, tomatoes, and garlic to the rice you can make Balsamic-Glazed Chicken with Smoked Mozzarella and Garlic Rice Pilaf.

One procedure, two entirely different tastes and meals. Once you learn the trick, you'll find yourself making new versions of your own "old standby" recipes, too. I love it when I can share a recipe that will become five or six other recipes just by swapping out a few ingredients. It just intensifies the payoff for everyone.

You'll notice that this book is not arranged in the conventional way, with chapters on chicken, meat, and pasta. I've mixed things up for a reason: I intended that you could just cook your way through this whole book (maybe marking one here and there that didn't grab you that particular night but you want to come back to) and never get bored. No more leftovers for you—every night can be full of new flavors! Of course I hope you won't be able to help yourself from returning to a few fast favorites now and again. And at least once, try one of the master recipes and one of its variations on two consecutive nights so you can taste for yourself how changing up even one ingredient can totally transform a dish and leave it unrecognizable. You'll see that when you've mastered one of these recipes, you've really mastered two or three! (If you're not in a skimming mood I have provided some lists on the pages that follow to help you zero in on what you might want to make tonight.)

I still feel the same excitement when people use my recipes today that I did 10 years ago teaching that first 30-Minute Meal class. Cooking is empowering. To watch someone discover their own talent by creating a meal, something that appeals to all five senses, for themselves or to share with the ones they love is magic!

So, here they are, 365 30-Minute Meals (and an extra Leap Year recipe for good measure!) all in one book. Chances are there will be a few ingredients you don't like and some recipes that just don't appeal to you, but even skipping those you should be able to get a good 9 or 10 months of meals outta here, minimum, no repeats. No more ruts for you! (But, can I ask you a favor? If you happen to pass me in the street, could you stop and give me a few of your recipes? I just can't come up with any new ideas for dinner!)

I wish you all a tasty year.

Yummo!

Rachael Ray

Some Notes About Measurements in This Book

If you've watched *30-Minute Meals* you probably already know that I'm not very big on measuring (that's why I'm not much of a baker!). Throughout this book you'll see I've listed ingredients in the usual ounces, tablespoons, and cups, but that I also encourage you just to eyeball the amount a lot of the time. In these cases, a smidge more or less either way won't make a big difference in the final dish, and using nature's best measuring tools—your hands and eyes—really saves on time *and* cleanup.

These are some of my favorite measuring shortcuts; once you get a good visual sense of what a tablespoon of salt looks likes like in your palm or how many handfuls of chopped parsley make a half cup you'll throw those measuring spoons to the back of the drawer for good!

Dry spices, finely chopped herbs	1 tablespoon equals a slightly mounded palmful; 1 teaspoon is ⅓ palmful
Grated cheese, breadcrumbs	1 handful equals ¼ cup; 3 generous or overflowing handfuls equal 1 cup
Rough chopped fresh herbs	2 generous handfuls unchopped equal ¼ cup chopped; 2 palmfuls chopped equal ¼ cup
EVOO	A thin stream of oil all the way around a 9- or 12-inch skillet equals about a tablespoon
Wine (or anything in a narrow-necked bottle)	A good "glug" from the inverted bottle equals ¼ cup

Perfect Pasta

4 Mac-n-Cheddar with Broccoli

#5 Mac-n-Smoked Gouda with Cauliflower

#6 Tex-Mex Mac-n-Cheddar with Beef and Peppers

#7 Smoky Chipotle Mac-n-Cheddar with Tomato and Chorizo

#22 Boo's Butternut Squash Mac-n-Cheese

#27 Pumpkin Pasta with Sausage and Wild Mushrooms

#28 Pasta with Spinach, Mushrooms, Pumpkin, and Hazelnuts

#36 BLT Pasta Bake: Bacon, Leeks, and Tomatoes

#39 Pasta with Roasted Eggplant Sauce and Ricotta Salata

#49 Pasta with Swiss Chard, Bacon, and Lemony Ricotta Cheese

#66 Chipotle Chicken Chili Mac

#70 Sardine and Bread Crumb Pasta with Puttanesca Salad

#79 Caprese Hot-or-Cold Pasta Toss

#88 Pesce Spada Pasta

#126 Spicy Shrimp and Penne with Puttanesca Sauce

#127 Frutti di Mare and Linguine

#137 Artichoke and Walnut Pesto Pasta

#147 Italian-Style Garlic Shrimp with Cherry Tomatoes and Thin Spaghetti

#153 Southwestern Pasta Bake

#154 Smoky Chipotle Chili Con Queso Mac

#176 Chicken in a Fresh Tomato and Eggplant Sauce with Spaghetti

#178 Seared Greens with Cheese Ravioli and Sage Butter

#183 Venetian Calamari with Spicy Sauce and Egg Fettucine

#188 Involtini all' Enotec'Antica with Gnocchi

#192 Ricotta Pasta with Grape Tomatoes, Peas, and Basil

#193 Ricotta Pasta with Sausage

#194 Ricotta Pasta with Zucchini, Garlic, and Mint

#195 Ricotta Pasta with Tomatoes al Forno

#196 Ricotta Pasta with Spinach

#198 White Beans, Pancetta, and Pasta

#204 Mini Chicken Sausage Meatballs with Gnocchi and Tomato Sauce

#239 Grilled Shrimp Scampi on Angel Hair Pasta

#241 Grilled Scallops, Scampi Style, with Angel Hair Pasta

#242 Tomato-Basil Pasta Nests

#243 Roasted Garlic and Eggplant Marinara Nests

#244 Beef and Mushroom Nests

#249 Pistachio Pesto

#250 Pecan and Arugula Pesto

#251 Walnut-Parsley-Rosemary Pesto

#268 Veal Polpette with Thin Spaghetti and Light Tomato and Basil Sauce

#270 Sausage Meatballs with Peppers, Onions, and a Side of Penne

#280 Pasta with a Lot of Mussel

#304 Zucchini and Bow Ties

#305 Springtime Bows with Asparagus, Ham, and Peas

#310 Mexican Pasta with Tomatillo Sauce and Meatballs

#328 Pasta with Mushroom Cream Sauce

#340 Gnocchi with Sausage and Swiss Chard

#366 Christmas Pasta

On the Light Side

#18 Turkey Saltimbocca Roll-Ups

#28 Pasta with Spinach, Mushrooms, Pumpkin, and Hazelnuts

#37 Warm Lemon Chicken Sandwich with Arugula and Pears

#57 Turkey Cutlet Parmigiano with Warm, Fresh Grape Tomato Topping, Pesto, and Mozzarella

#73 Spicy Shrimp and Bok Choy Noodle Bowl

#77 Swordfish Cutlets with Tomato and Basil Salad

#80 Sweet, Spicy, and Tropical: Crab Salad Lettuce Wraps

#83 Ginger Vegetable Chicken Noodle Bowl

#96 Piña Colada Shrimp

#130 Sliced Herb and Garlic Tagliata

#131 Baked Sole and Roasted Asparagus with Sesame

#139 Lettillas: Mix-n-Match Lettuce Tacos

#147 Italian-Style Garlic Shrimp with Cherry Tomatoes and Thin Spaghetti

#148 Spanish-Style Garlic Shrimp and Orzo

#151 French Salade Superb

#152 Baby and Big Bella Mushroom and Chicken Stew

#157 Warm Tangerine and Grilled Chicken Salad Served on Grilled Garlic Crisps

#161 Tex-Mex Grilled Chicken Caesar

#162 Orange and Herb Chicken Caesar

#175 Indian Tofu and Spinach over Almond Rice

#180 Swordfish Burgers with Lemon, Garlic and Parsley

#181 Scallop Burgers

#185 Salad Capricciosa

#186 30-Minute Chicken Under a Brick

#199 Lemon-Thyme Succotash with Garlic-Parsley Shrimp

#215 Chicken Breasts or Swordfish Steaks with Raw Puttanesca Sauce and Roasted Capers

#219 Sliced Chicken Breast Subs with Italian Sausage

#263 Grilled Swordfish Salad

#266 Grilled Halibut with Fennel, Orange, Red Onions, and Oregano

#288 Lime-and-Honey Glazed Salmon with Warm Black Bean and Corn Salad

#304 Zucchini and Bow Ties

#305 Springtime Bows with Asparagus, Ham, and Peas

#306 Incredible French Crunchy Salad

#319 Pancetta-Wrapped Shrimp Supper Salad

#336 Sweet Lemon Salmon with Mini Carrots and Dill

#360 Incredible French Endive Salad with Aged Herb Goat Cheese Toasts

Super Fast Suppers

#1 Scramblewiches

#25 Taco Chili-Mac

#38 Grilled Flank Steak Sandwich with Blue Cheese Vinaigrette—Dressed Arugula and Pears

#47 Couple-of-Minute Steaks and Potato Ragout

#110 Chicago Dog Salad

#149 Greek-Style Garlic Shrimp and Orzo

#151 French Salade Superb

#166 Sweet Pea Soup with Parmigiano Toast

#167 Creamy Spinach Soup with Fontina Toast

#168 Creamy Broccoli Soup with Cheddar and Chive Toast

#170 Turkey Cutlets with Sautéed Brussels Sprouts

#173 Greek Bread Salad with Grilled Shrimp

#177 My Mom's 15-Minute Tomato and Bean Stoup

#179 Fried Greens with Ham and Eggs

#180 Swordfish Burgers with Lemon, Garlic and Parsley

#181 Scallop Burgers

#187 Steak Sandwich . . . Knife and Fork Required

#197 About-15-Minute Soup with Spinach, Artichokes, and Tortellini

#209 Pumpkin Polenta with Chorizo and Black Beans

#210 Pumpkin Polenta with Italian Sausage and Fennel

#238 Sautéed Salmon with Spicy Fresh Mango-Pineapple Chutney

#263 Grilled Swordfish Salad

#298 Grilled Steak Sandwich . . . I Mean, Salad— No! Sandwich!

#309 Turkey Tacos

#318 Bacon-Wrapped Beef Supper Salads

#348 Turkey, Tomatillo, and Bean Burritos

#361 Tuna with Everything-but-the-Kitchen Sink

#362 Chopped Antipasto Stuffed Bread

#363 Quick Cassoulet Stuffed Bread Melts

#364 Nacho Bread Pizza

#365 Hamburger and Onion Stuffed Bread

MYOTO (Make Your Own Take Out)

#40 Mostly Green Curry Chicken over Coconut Jasmine Rice

#41 Mostly Green Curry Veggies and Tofu over Coconut Jasmine Rice

#63 Lion's Head (Pork Meatballs and Napa Cabbage)

#64 Whole Fish with Ginger and Scallions

#112 Indian Spiced Vegetables

#113 Ginger-Soy Chicken on Shredded Lettuce

#114 Thai Chicken, Pork, or Shrimp with Basil

#190 Crunchy Japanese Fish with Vegetable and Noodle Toss

#214 Thai-Style Shrimp and Veggies with Toasted Coconut Rice

#245 Five-Spice Burgers with Warm Mu Shu Slaw Topping

#338 Thai-Style Steak Salad

#339 Thai-Style Pork and Noodle Salad

#352 Asian Pinwheel Steaks with Noodle and Cabbage Sauté

#356 Honey Chicken over Snow Pea Rice

A Big Bowl

#11 Italian Sub Stoup and Garlic Toast Floaters

#20 Black Bean Stoup and Southwestern Monte Cristos

#24 Salsa Stoup and Double-Decker Baked Quesadillas

#31 Papa al Pomodoro

#32 Ribollita con Verdure

#45 Sausage and Fennel Ragout with Creamy Polenta

#55 Halibut Soup

#68 Chicken Cacciatore Stoup

#97 Chicken Tortilla Soup with Lime

#99 Chicken, Corn, and Black Bean Stoup

#118 Peasant Soup

#122 Chicken and Rice Stoup

#125 Swedish Meat Dumpling Stoup

#134 Seafood Newburg Stoup

#135 Crab and Corn Chowda

#142 Bacon-Makes-It-Better Corn Chowder with Tomato and Ricotta Salata Salad

#146 Spanish Fish and Chorizo Stoup

#166 Sweet Pea Soup with Parmigiano Toast

#167 Creamy Spinach Soup with Fontina Toast

#168 Creamy Broccoli Soup with Cheddar and Chive Toast

#177 My Mom's 15-Minute Tomato and Bean Stoup

#182 Chicken with White and Wild Rice Soup

#197 About-15-Minute Stoup with Spinach, Artichokes, and Tortellini

#202 Fall Minestrone

#220 Charred Tomato Soup with Pesto and Prosciutto Stromboli

#227 Eggplant, Mushroom, and Sweet Potato Indian-Spiced Stoup

#233 Chorizo and Butternut Soup with Herbed Tomato and Cheese Quesadillas

#275 Lamb "Stew" (Wink, Wink)

#277 Chorizo-Tomato Stew on Garlic Croutons

#307 Triple-Onion Soup with Triple-Cheese Toast

#308 Sausage, Fennel, and Tomato Soup with Triple-Cheese Toast

#311 Mexican Tomatillo Stoup with Chorizo

#327 Mushroom Bisque

Romantic Dinners

#58 Chicken with Sweet Raisins and Apricots on Toasted Almond Couscous

#62 Balsamic-Glazed Swordfish with Capers and Grape Tomato-Arugula Rice

#156 Sweet and Savory Stuffed Veal Rolls with a Mustard Pan Sauce

#158 Shrimp Martinis and Manhattan Steaks

#189 Veal Scallopine with Dijon Sauce, Asparagus, and Avocados

#265 Columbus's Pork Chops

#285 Golden Raisin and Almond Chicken

#292 Lemon and Brown Butter Fish Fillets with Seared Red and Yellow Tomatoes

#321 Sweet Sea Scallops in a Caper-Raisin Sauce

Burger Bonanza

#10 The T2: Turkey Chili–Topped Turkey Chili Burgers with Red Pepper Slaw and Funky Fries

#15 Super Tuscan Burgers and Potato Salad with Capers and Celery

#29 Beef and Chicken Fajita Burgers

#30 Paella Burgers and Spanish Fries

#67 Sirloin Burgers with Gorgonzola Cheese

#103 Salmon Burgers with Ginger-Wasabi Mayo and Sesame-Crusted French Fries

#115 Jambalaya Burgers and Cajun Corn and Red Beans

#116 Cacciatore Burgers

#117 Big Beef Burger Stack-Ups with Mushrooms, Peppers, and Onions

#159 Burly-Man-Size Chicken-Cheddar Barbecued Burgers and Spicy Coleslaw

#174 Chili Dog Bacon Cheeseburgers and Fiery Fries

#180 Swordfish Burgers with Lemon, Garlic, and Parsley

#181 Scallop Burgers

#191 Super Marsala Burgers and Arugula-Tomato Salad

#216 Chicken or Turkey Spanikopita Burgers

#245 Five-Spice Burgers with Warm Mu Shu Slaw Topping

#259 A Burger for Brad: Barbecue Burger Deluxe

#260 Buffalo Turkey Burgers with Blue Cheese Dressing

#281 Big Bistro Burgers

#320 Lamb and Scallion Burgers with Fried Asparagus

Good for a Crowd

#3 Lamb or Beef Goulash

#8 Mega Meatball Pizza and Zippy Italian Popcorn

#33 3 Beans and Some Chicken

#36 BLT Pasta Bake: Bacon, Leeks, and Tomatoes

#44 Ricotta Smothered Mushroom "Burgers" with Sweet Onion–Olive Topping, Prosciutto, and Arugula

#48 Sausage and Spinach Pastry Squares with Cherry Tomato–Arugula Salad

#71 BBQ Sloppy Chicken Pan Pizza

#72 Fajita Beef Pie

#74 Turkey or Chicken Croquettes with Spinach Mashers and Pan Gravy

#75 Cod Croquettes and Red Bell Pepper Gravy with Spinach Mashers

#81 Mashed Plantains with Oh, Baby! Garlic-Tomato Shrimp on Top, Grilled Flank Steak with Lime and Onions, and Quick Rice with Beans

#89 Lamb Patties with Garlic and Mint over Mediterranean Chopped Salad

#90 Grilled Turkey Cutlets with Warm Cranberry Salsa

#128 Shrimp and Crab Fritters with Chopped Salad

#138 Spinach and Artichoke Calzones

#150 German Potato Salad with Kielbasa

#157 Warm Tangerine and Grilled Chicken Salad Served on Grilled Garlic Crisps

#158 Shrimp Martinis and Manhattan Steaks

#160 Super-Grilled Steak Sandwich with Horseradish-Dijon Cream

#173 Greek Bread Salad with Grilled Shrimp

#184 Pizza Capricciosa

#201 Aussie Meat Pies, Made Quick

#203 Italian Sweet Chicken Sausage Patties with Peppers and Onions on Garlic Buttered Rolls

#212 Broccoli Frittata with Goat Cheese and BLT Bread Salad

#217 Spanikopizza

#222 Oven-Baked Corn Dogs with O & V Slaw

#224 White Pita Pizzas with Red and Green Prosciutto Salad

#229 Verdure di Primio Maggio con Polenta

#223 Chicken Sausage with Fennel and Onions

#234 Big Beef and Garlic Italian Stir-Fry

#237 Crispy Fried Sesame Shrimp, Zucchini, and Mushroom Caps with a Ginger-Soy Dipping Sauce

#252 Croque Monsieur with Greens

#253 Ham and Asparagus Tartines

#254 Italian Open-Face Sandwiches

#258 Chicken Fingers with Honey Mustard Dipping Sauce

#259 A Burger for Brad: Barbecue Burger Deluxe

#264 Warm and Cold Bordeaux Salad, Lamb Loins with Red Wine

#272 Mushroom Sauté on Charred Polenta and Seared Spicy Ham

#279 Everything-Crusted Chicken Rolls Stuffed with Scallion Cream Cheese

#291 Spinach and Goat Cheese Chicken Rolls in a Pan Sauce

#298 Grilled Steak Sandwich . . . I Mean, Salad— No! Sandwich!

#299 Chipotle Chicken Rolls with Avocado Dipping Sauce

#300 Turkey and Sage Rolls with Cranberry Dipping Sauce

#302 Wingless Buffalo Chicken Rolls with Blue Cheese Dip

#309 Turkey Tacos

#312 Boo-sotto

#313 Scotch and Wild Mushroom Risotto

#314 Lemon and Artichoke Risotto with Shrimp

#315 Cream Risotto with White Asparagus and Andouille

#317 Zucchini Pizza

#330 French Onion Sliced Steak Croissant Sandwich

#348 Turkey, Tomatillo, and Bean Burritos

#349 Pork, Chipotle, and Bean Burritos

To Serve 1 or 2

#12 Spiced Lamb Chops on Sautéed Peppers and Onions with Garlic and Mint Couscous

#16 Oregon-Style Pork Chops with Pinot Noir and Cranberries

#17 Honey Nut Chicken Sticks

#23 Boo's Smoky Chicken Patties on Buttered Toast

#46 Prosciutto, Garlic, and Herb Cheese-Stuffed Chicken with Tarragon Pan Sauce

#53 Eggs-traordinary Stuffed Toasty Baskets with Lemony Greens

#54 Eggs-traordinary Spanish-Style Stuffed Toasty Baskets with Lemony Greens

#60 Balsamic-Glazed Pork Chops with Arugula-Basil Rice Pilaf

#62 Balsamic-Glazed Swordfish with Capers and Grape Tomato–Arugula Rice

#69 Garlic and Mint Lamb or Chicken Patties on Lentil Salad

#77 Swordfish Cutlets with Tomato and Basil Salad

#86 Chicken Mamacello and Asparagus Tips

#93 Citrus Lover's Menu: Rosemary-Orange Pork Chops

#94 Sliced Grilled Steak on Blue Cheese Biscuits

#103 Salmon Burgers with Ginger-Wasabi Mayo and Sesame-Crusted French Fries

#106 Honey-Orange–Glazed Ham Steaks

#111 Pork Chops with Grainy Mustard and Raisin Sauce

#119 Boneless Rib-Eye Steaks with Killa' Chimichurri

#123 Steaks with Two Tapenades, Arugula Salad, and Crusty Bread

#124 Steaks with Horseradish Cream Sauce, Watercress Salad, and Crusty Bread

#132 Chicken, Veal, or Pork Schnitzel with Red Caraway Cabbage

#133 Fa-Schnizzel My Schnitzel

#147 Italian-Style Garlic Shrimp with Cherry Tomatoes and Thin Spaghetti

#163 Lamb Chops and Early Spring Salad

#164 London Broil with Mushroom Vinaigrette

#165 Pan-Roasted Garlic and Herb Chicken Breasts

#169 Cumin and Lime Roasted Pork Tenderloin with Spicy Creamed Corn

#172 Ham and Swiss Crepes with Chopped Salad

#179 Fried Greens with Ham and Eggs

#188 Involtini all' Enotec'Antica with Gnocchi

#200 Big Mussels with Chorizo and Saffron Rice

#206 Strip Steaks with a Side of Blue Cheese Spaghetti

#207 Olive-Butter–Slathered Broiled Lamb Chops with Caramelized Zucchini Orzo

#208 Olive and Anchovy–Slathered Beef Tenderloin Steaks

#212 Broccoli Frittata with Goat Cheese and BLT Bread Salad

#213 Seafood Frittata with Fennel, Orange, and Arugula Bread Salad

#218 Spanish-Style Pork Chops with Chorizo and Roasted Red Pepper Sauce and Green Beans

#221 Chunky Turkey, Potatoes, and Veggies in Red Wine Sauce

#223 Bacon-Wrapped Beef Tenderloin and Super-Stuffed Potatoes

#230 Sweet Prune and Sage Pork Chops with Potatoes

#231 Sweet Date, Apricot, and Sage Veal Chops with Chive Potatoes

#236 Cornmeal-Crusted Catfish and Green Rice Pilaf

#238 Sautéed Salmon with Spicy Fresh Mango-Pineapple Chutney

#262 Veal Saltimbocca with Spinach Polenta

#266 Grilled Halibut with Fennel, Red Onions and Oregano

#276 Veal Chops and Balsamic-Thyme Roasted Tomatoes and Mushrooms

#278 Anyone for Brunch? B, L, or D Adaptation

#283 Broiled Lamb Chops with Sweet Pea and Spinach Couscous

#287 Grilled Skirt Steak and Orzo with the Works

#289 Sage and Balsamic Pork Chops with Creamy Pumpkin Polenta

#292 Lemon and Brown Butter Fish Fillets with Seared Red and Yellow Tomatoes

#324 Pork Loin Chops with Golden Delicious Apples on Polenta with Honey

#326 Simple and Delicious Chicken with Potatoes and Asparagus

#329 Ham and Spinach Hash with Fried Eggs

#331 Rosemary Lemon–Pepper Pork Tenderloin

#333 Sweet and Spicy Pineapple Pork

#334 Chili-Spiced Grilled Halibut with Grilled-Corn Saucy Salsa

#351 Pork Chops in a Sweet Chili and Onion Sauce with Creamy Cilantro Potato Salad

#357 Crispy Turkey Cutlets with Bacon-Cranberry Brussels Sprouts

#359 Roast Crispy Mushrooms and Grilled Tenderloin Steaks with Green Onions

Fancy Fare

#76 Sicilian-Style Swordfish Rolls with Fennel and Radicchio Salad

#85 Flounder Francese with Toasted Almonds, Lemon, and Capers

#155 Indian-Asian Seared Cod with Cilantro-Mint Chutney and Sweet Pea and Coconut Jasmine Rice

#156 Sweet and Savory Stuffed Veal Rolls with a Mustard Pan Sauce

#231 Sweet Date, Apricot, and Sage Veal Chops with Chive Potatoes

#246 Cod in a Sack

#247 French Fish in a Sack

#248 Spanish Fish in a Sack

#301 Lamb and Feta Rolls with Cucumber-Mint-Yogurt Dipping Sauce

#331 Rosemary Lemon–Pepper Pork Tenderloin

Pick of the Chix

#13 Saucy BBQ Chicken Sammies

#17 Honey Nut Chicken Sticks

#23 Boo's Smoky Chicken Patties on Buttered Toast

#33 3 Beans and Some Chicken

#35 Sautéed Sweet Chicken Breasts with a Spicy Fresh Tomato Chutney and White Rice

#37 Warm Lemon Chicken Sandwich with Arugula and Pears

#42 Cider Vinegar Chicken with Smashed Potatoes

#43 Chicken in Spicy and Sweet Onion Sauce

#46 Prosciutto, Garlic, and Herb Cheese-Stuffed Chicken with Tarragon Pan Sauce

#50 Big, Thick, Hearty Thighs

#51 Big, Thick, Hearty Thighs Spanish Style

#52 Chicken with Wild Mushroom and Balsamic Cream Sauce

#56 Big Bird: Jumbo Chicken, Spinach, and Herb Burgers

#58 Chicken with Sweet Raisins and Apricots on Toasted Almond Couscous

#59 Chicken in a Horseradish Pan Sauce over Orange and Herb Couscous

#69 Garlic and Mint Lamb or Chicken Patties on Lentil Salad

#78 Sicilian-Style Chicken Cutlets with Chopped Caprese Salad

#84 Chicken Francese and Wilted Spinach

#86 Chicken Mamacello and Asparagus Tips

#87 Bel Aria Chicken and Pasta

#95 Island Bird: Pineapple-Rum Chicken

#102 Grilled Chicken Paillard with Grilled Red Onion and Asparagus Salad

#104 Garlic and Herb Chicken with Romesco Sauce

#105 Lemony Crispy Chicken Cutlets and Roasted Tomato Salad

#108 Park City Cashew Chicken

#109 Asian-Style Cashew Chicken

#120 Chicken Chimichurri Burgers

#121 Spring Chicken with Leeks and Peas Served with Lemon Rice

#144 Super Mashers with Chicken and Green Chili Hash

#152 Baby and Big Bella Mushroom and Chicken Stew

#153 Southwestern Pasta Bake

#161 Tex-Mex Grilled Chicken Caesar

#162 Orange and Herb Chicken Caesar

#165 Pan-Roasted Garlic and Herb Chicken Breasts

#171 Fruited Chicken Curry in a Hurry

#176 Chicken in a Fresh Tomato and Eggplant Sauce with Spaghetti

#182 Chicken with White and Wild Rice Soup

#186 30-Minute Chicken Under a Brick

#203 Italian Sweet Chicken Sausage Patties with Peppers and Onions on Garlic Buttered Rolls

#204 Mini Chicken Sausage Meatballs with Gnocchi and Tomato Sauce

#205 Chicken Sausage on a Roll with Egg and Fontina

#215 Chicken Breasts or Swordfish Steaks with Raw Puttanesca Sauce and Roasted Capers

#216 Chicken or Turkey Spanikopita Burgers

#225 Rosemary, Parmigiano, and Pine Nut Breaded Chicken Cutlets with Fennel Slaw

#226 Chicken and Sweet Potato Curry-in-a-Hurry

#228 Chicken in Puttanesca Sauce over Creamy Polenta

#235 Marinated Grilled Chicken Breasts with Zippy Chunky Salad

#256 Chicken Divan and Egg Noodle Bake

#257 Super Mashers with Chicken Cordon Bleu Hash

#258 Chicken Fingers with Honey Mustard Dipping Sauce

#267 Pretzel-Crusted Chicken Breasts with a Cheddar-Mustard Sauce

#279 Everything-Crusted Chicken Rolls Stuffed Scallion Cream Cheese

#284 For Neil Diamond: Tangy Cherry Chicken

#285 Golden Raisin and Almond Chicken

#286 For Almodovar: Spicy Spanish Raisin and Olive Chicken, Olé!

#291 Spinach and Goat Cheese Chicken Rolls in a Pan Sauce

#293 Chicken #14,752—Chicken in Mustard Sauce

#294 Chicken #14,753—Deviled Divan

#295 Chicken #14,754—Chicken Bustard

#296 Chicken #14,755—Chicken in Mustard-Tarragon Sauce

#297 Chicken #14,756:—Chicken in "Lighter" Mustard and Lemon Sauce

#299 Chipotle Chicken Rolls with Avocado Dipping Sauce

#302 Wingless Buffalo Chicken Rolls with Blue Cheese Dip

#325 Creamy Chicken and Asparagus on Toast

#326 Simple and Delicious Chicken with Potatoes and Asparagus

#335 Chicken Topped with Caponata and Mozzarella

#337 Mediterranean Chicken and Saffron Couscous

#353 Crispy Rosemary-Orange Chicken with Parmigiano String Beans

#354 Chicken Cutlets on Buttermilk-Cheddar-Chorizo Biscuits

#356 Honey Chicken over Snow Pea Rice

#358 Fresh Tomato and Basil Chicken over Super Creamy Polenta

Vegetarian Meals

#32   Ribollita con Verdure – *optional vegetarian version*

#129   Veggie Fritters and Asian Salad

#211   Vegetarian Pumpkin Polenta with Spinach and White Beans

#227   Eggplant, Mushroom, and Sweet Potato Indian-Spiced Stoup

#242   Tomato-Basil Pasta Nests

#243   Roasted Garlic and Eggplant Marinara Nests

#261   Baked Sesame Eggplant Subs with Fire-Roasted Tomato and Red Pepper Sauce

#271   Mixed Wild Mushroom Sauté on Toast Points with Gruyère

#273   Creamed Mushroom Sauté with Artichoke Hearts, Spinach, and Penne

#274   Creamed Mushroom Sauté with Hearts of Palm, Arugula, and Pappardelle

#304   Zucchini and Bow Ties

#306   Incredible French Crunchy Salad

#316   Spinach and Hazelnut Risotto

#317   Zucchini Pizza

#323   Mushroom-Veggie Sloppy Sandwiches

#347   Super Mushroom Polenta "Lasagna"

#360   Incredible French Endive Salad with Aged Herb Goat Cheese Toasts

Comfort Food

#2   Smoky Turkey Shepherd's Pie

#3   Lamb or Beef Goulash

#8   Mega Meatball Pizza and Zippy Italian Popcorn

#9   Turkey Noodle Casserole

#12   Spiced Lamb Chops on Sautéed Peppers and Onions with Garlic and Mint Couscous

#14   Fiery Hot Texas T-Bones with Chipotle Smashed Potatoes

#19   Rosemary Corn Cakes with Prosciutto and Chicken Sausages

#26   Florentine Meatballs

#34   Sweet Sausages Braised in Onions with Horseradish Smashed Potatoes

#65   Uptown Down-Home Chili

#82   Ropa Vieja Josés (Cuban Sloppy Joes)

#91   Fancy-Pants Bangers n' Mash

#92   London Broil with Parsley-Horseradish Chimichurri

#98   Ham and Cheese-Stuffed Pork Chops with Lot-o'-Mushroom Sauce

#100   Gravy-Smothered Cajun-Style Meatloaf Patties with Maple Pecan-Glazed String Beans

#101   Cheddar-Studded Tex-Mex Meatloaf Patties

#107   Turkey Club Super Mashers

#141   Crab Tortilla (Egg Pie) and Shredded Plantain Hash Browns

#143   Super Mash with Steak and Pepper Hash

#144   Super Mashers with Chicken and Green Chili Hash

#145 Super Mashers with Shrimp and Chorizo Hash

#223 Bacon Wrapped Beef Tenderloin and Super-Stuffed Potatoes

#255 Wild Cream of Mushroom Egg Noodle Bake

#256 Chicken Divan and Egg Noodle Bake

#257 Super Mashers with Chicken Cordon Bleu Hash

#269 Big Beef Balls with Bucatini

#290 Chili-Sweet Potato Hash with Fried Eggs and Fresh Tomato Salsa

#303 London Broil with Buttered Potatoes and Caramelized Zucchini and Mushrooms

#325 Creamy Chicken and Asparagus on Toast

#332 Bacon-Wrapped Meatloaf Patties with Pan Gravy and Sour Cream-Tomato Smashed Potatoes

#340 Gnocchi with Sausage and Swiss Chard

#341 Turkey Stroganoff Noodle Toss

#343 Sausage and Mushroom Polenta "Lasagna"

#344 Sweet and Savory Polenta "Lasagna"

#345 Sausage, Mushroom, and Olive Polenta "Lasagna"

#346 Sausage, Mushroom, and Pesto Polenta "Lasagna"

#347 Super Mushroom Polenta "Lasagna"

#350 Crispy Horseradish Battered-Fried Fish with Watercress-Cucumber Tartar Sauce

#354 Chicken Cutlets on Buttermilk-Cheddar-Chorizo Biscuits with Tomato-Olive Salsa Mayo

#355 Spinach and Spicy Ham Pasta Bake

#363 Quick Cassoulet Stuffed Bread Melts

#365 Hamburger and Onion Stuffed Bread

Your Faves

Okay, here goes—
366 all-new recipes.
Start here or jump around,
it's your call, but be sure to
check off the ones you
love—and the ones you
want to come back to
another day!

Scramblewiches

1 baguette (day-old is fine)

2 tablespoons unsalted butter

½ pound deli-sliced ham, smoked turkey, pastrami, or corned beef

8 large eggs
 A splash of milk

1 teaspoon hot sauce
 Salt and freshly ground black pepper

4 deli slices of Swiss cheese (halved lengthwise to fit bread), or 8 slices of Cheddar (2 squares per bread), or 6 slices of Provolone cheese (1½ slices per bread, cut to fit)
 Chopped fresh chives or flat-leaf parsley, to garnish

Preheat the oven to 200°F.

Crisp the bread in the low oven, split it lengthwise, and hollow it out. Cut each bread in half again, across, making 4 boats. Switch the broiler on.

Heat a large nonstick skillet over medium heat. Add the butter and melt it. When the bubbles stop, add the meat and cook, separating the pieces, for 3 minutes, or until brown at the edges. In a bowl, beat the eggs with the milk, hot sauce, salt, and pepper. Add to the meat and scramble, keeping the eggs a little soft. They will continue to cook in the oven.

Divide the eggs among the bread and cover with the cheese. Melt the cheese under the broiler. Take it out as soon as the cheese softens and melts. Do not brown or allow the cheese to bubble; there are eggs under there! Garnish with the chopped chives or parsley and serve.

4 SERVINGS

TRY THIS LATER

IT'S A KEEPER

2 MASTER RECIPE
Smoky Turkey Shepherd's Pie

Coarse salt

3 large Idaho potatoes, peeled and cubed

2 tablespoons extra-virgin olive oil (EVOO) (twice around the pan)

¼ pound bacon or turkey bacon, chopped

1 package (about 1⅓ pounds) ground turkey

1 tablespoon smoked paprika (available in small cans on the spice aisle of the market), or substitute 1½ teaspoons each of sweet paprika and cumin, plus a sprinkle
Coarse black pepper

2 tablespoons fresh thyme leaves (from 5 or 6 sprigs)

1 medium onion, chopped

2 carrots, diced

3 celery ribs from the heart, chopped

1 small red bell pepper, cored, seeded, and chopped

2 cups frozen peas

2 tablespoons all-purpose flour

2 cups chicken stock or broth

1 cup sour cream

1 large egg, beaten

3 tablespoons unsalted butter

10 to 12 fresh chives, chopped or snipped

Bring a medium pot of water to a boil, salt it, and cook the potatoes while you make the turkey filling.

Heat a deep, large skillet over medium-high heat. Add the EVOO to the skillet, then add the bacon and brown it up. Drain off the excess fat, then add the turkey to the pan and break it up with a wooden spoon. Season the turkey with the smoked paprika, salt, pepper, and thyme. When the turkey is browned, add the onions, carrots, and celery. Season the veggies with salt and pepper. Cook for 5 minutes, stirring occasionally, then add the red bell peppers and peas and cook for another 2 minutes. Stir in the flour and cook for 2 minutes. Add the stock and combine. Stir in ½ cup of the sour cream and simmer the mixture over low heat.

Preheat the broiler to high.

When the potatoes are tender (10 to 12 minutes), stir a ladle of the cooking water into the egg, then drain the potatoes. Return the potatoes to the warm pot to dry them out a little. Add the remaining ½ cup of sour cream, the butter, and salt and pepper. Smash and mash the potatoes, mashing in the beaten, tempered egg. If the potatoes are too tight, mix in a splash of milk.

Pour the turkey mixture into a medium casserole dish. Top with the smashed potatoes and spread evenly. Place the casserole 5 inches from the hot broiler. Broil until the potatoes are golden at the edges. Garnish the casserole with the chives and a sprinkle of smoked paprika.

4 SERVINGS

NOW TRY... Lamb or Beef Goulash

☐ TRY THIS LATER

☐ IT'S A KEEPER

OMIT

Potatoes

Peas

Egg

SWAP

2 pounds ground lamb or sirloin for the ground turkey

2 cups beef stock for the chicken stock

ADD

½ pound wide egg noodles

Follow the same method as for the Shepherd's Pie filling, swapping lamb or beef for the turkey and beef stock for the chicken stock. Serve the goulash over cooked egg noodles dressed with the butter and chopped chives.

4 SERVINGS

4 MASTER RECIPE
Mac-n-Cheddar with Broccoli

Coarse salt

1 pound elbow macaroni or cavatappi (corkscrew-shaped pasta)

2½ cups broccoli florets

1 tablespoon extra-virgin olive oil (EVOO) (once around the pan)

2 tablespoons unsalted butter

1 small onion, finely chopped

3 tablespoons all-purpose flour

½ teaspoon cayenne pepper

1 teaspoon paprika

3 cups whole milk

1 cup chicken stock or broth

3 cups grated sharp yellow Cheddar

1 tablespoon Dijon mustard

Freshly ground black pepper

Bring a large pot of water to a boil. Add salt to season the cooking water, then add the pasta. Cook for 5 minutes, then add the broccoli and cook for 3 minutes more or until the pasta is cooked al dente and the florets are just tender. Drain well and return to the pot.

While the pasta cooks, heat a medium sauce pot over medium-low heat. Add the EVOO and heat with the butter until it melts. Add the onions and cook for 3 to 5 minutes to sweat them out and turn the juices sweet. Raise the heat a bit, then whisk in the flour, cayenne, and paprika. Whisk together until the roux bubbles up, then cook for 1 minute more. Whisk in the milk and stock and raise the heat a bit higher to bring the sauce to a quick boil. Once it bubbles, drop the heat back to a simmer and cook until the sauce thickens, 3 to 5 minutes.

Add the cheese to the thickened sauce and stir to melt it, a minute or so. Stir in the mustard and season the sauce with salt and pepper. Pour over the broccoli and cooked pasta and toss to combine. Adjust the seasonings, transfer to a large platter, and serve.

4 SERVINGS

---

5 NOW TRY... Mac-n-Smoked Gouda with Cauliflower

SWAP

1 head of cauliflower, cut into florets, for the broccoli

Shredded smoked Gouda for the Cheddar

ADD

¼ cup (a generous handful) smoked almonds, chopped

Prepare as for the master recipe, #4. Sprinkle the finished dish with the smoked almonds.

4 SERVINGS

TRY THIS LATER

IT'S A KEEPER

4 **RACHAEL RAY**

OR TRY... Tex-Mex Mac-n-Cheddar
with Beef and Peppers

6

☐ TRY THIS LATER

☐ IT'S A KEEPER

OMIT

Broccoli

SWAP

Sharp white Cheddar for the yellow Cheddar

ADD

More EVOO

1 pound ground sirloin

1 red or yellow bell pepper, cored, seeded, and cut into thin strips

Preheat a medium nonstick skillet over medium-high heat. Add a drizzle of EVOO and the beef. Brown the meat, breaking it up with a wooden spoon. Add the peppers and cook together for 5 minutes, seasoning with salt and pepper to taste.

Prepare the Mac-n-Cheddar, without the broccoli, as in the master recipe, #4. Fold in the beef and bell peppers after combining the cheese sauce with the cooked pasta.

4 SERVINGS

- -

AND THEN TRY... Smoky Chipotle Mac-n-Cheddar
with Tomato and Chorizo

7

☐ TRY THIS LATER

☐ IT'S A KEEPER

OMIT

Broccoli

SWAP

Smoked Cheddar for the sharp Cheddar

ADD

2 chipotle peppers in adobo, chopped, or 1 tablespoon ground chipotle powder
EVOO

¾ to 1 pound chorizo, casings removed, diced

1 15-ounce can diced fire-roasted tomatoes, drained

Prepare as for the master recipe, #4, adding the chipotle in adobo or ground chipotle to the sauce pot when you add the onions.

Place a small nonstick skillet over medium-high heat and add a drizzle of EVOO and the chorizo. Brown the chorizo, then add the tomatoes and cook briefly, just to heat them through.

Add the smoked Cheddar to the thickened sauce as you would the sharp Cheddar. Add the chorizo and tomatoes to the drained pasta in the large pot when you add the cheese sauce. Stir to combine, and serve.

4 SERVINGS

8 Mega Meatball Pizza
and Zippy Italian Popcorn

PIZZA

Extra-virgin olive oil (EVOO), for drizzling,
plus 2 tablespoons

1 pizza dough, store-bought or from your
favorite pizza shop
A palmful of all-purpose flour or cornmeal

2 tablespoons finely chopped fresh rosemary
(a couple of sprigs)
Coarse salt

1½ pounds ground sirloin

1 medium onion, finely chopped

4 to 6 garlic cloves, finely chopped
Coarsely ground black pepper, to taste

1 3-ounce can tomato paste

½ cup grated Parmigiano-Reggiano
A handful of fresh flat-leaf parsley, chopped

½ teaspoon dried oregano

¾ pound fresh mozzarella or brick mozzarella,
sliced or grated

ZIPPY ITALIAN POPCORN

1 package reduced-fat natural-flavor
microwave popcorn

2 tablespoons unsalted butter

1 teaspoon garlic powder or granulated garlic

1 teaspoon dried oregano

1 teaspoon crushed red pepper flakes

⅓ cup grated Parmigiano-Reggiano (a handful)

Preheat the oven to 425°F.

Drizzle a round pizza pan or a rectangular baking sheet with EVOO. Dust the dough with flour or cornmeal, then spread out the dough to form your crust. Poke the pizza dough in several places with the tines of a fork. Drizzle the dough with EVOO, then season it with the rosemary and a little salt. Bake for 10 minutes.

Heat a large skillet over medium-high heat. Add the 2 tablespoons of EVOO (twice around the pan), then the meat. Brown and crumble the meat for a couple of minutes, then add the onions and garlic. Season the meat with salt and pepper, then work in the tomato paste using the back of a wooden spoon. Stir in the cheese, parsley, and oregano.

Remove the pizza crust from the oven and top with the meat mixture. Arrange the cheese over the pizza, working from the center to the outside edge. Return the pizza to the oven and bake until the cheese is golden, another 10 to 12 minutes.

Microwave the popcorn according to the package instructions. Place the popped corn in a bowl. Combine the butter and spices in a small cup or bowl and microwave for 10 to 15 seconds on High or until the butter melts. Stir and pour over the popcorn, then sprinkle it with grated cheese.

Cut the pizza into wedges and serve with the popcorn.

4 SERVINGS

Turkey Noodle Casserole

Serve with a green tossed salad.

Coarse salt
½ pound **extra-wide egg noodles**
1 tablespoon **extra-virgin olive oil** (EVOO) (once around the pan)
3 slices **bacon** or turkey bacon, chopped
1 package (about 1⅓ pounds) **ground turkey breast**
1 pound **white mushrooms**, wiped, trimmed, and sliced
1 medium **onion**, chopped
Freshly ground black pepper, to taste
2 teaspoons **ground thyme** or poultry seasoning
½ cup **dry white wine**
1 cup **chicken stock** or broth (eyeball it)
½ cup **heavy cream** (3 times around the pan)
¼ teaspoon **freshly grated nutmeg**
2 tablespoons **unsalted butter**, softened
2 cups grated **Gruyère cheese** (about an 8-ounce brick)
1 cup **plain bread crumbs**
2 to 3 tablespoons chopped fresh **flat-leaf parsley**

Bring a large pot of water to a boil for the egg noodles. When it boils, salt the water and cook the noodles al dente. Drain well and return to the pot.

Preheat a large, deep skillet over medium-high heat. Add the EVOO and the bacon. Cook for 2 to 3 minutes, until the fat is rendered and the bacon begins to brown at the edges. Add the turkey and brown it, crumbling it with a wooden spoon. Move the meat over to one side of the pan and add the mushrooms and onions to the opposite side. Cook the mushrooms and onions for 3 to 5 minutes, then stir the meat and veggies together. Season the mixture liberally with salt and pepper, and sprinkle in the ground thyme or poultry seasoning. Cook for another 5 minutes. Add the wine and deglaze the pan, using a wooden spoon to scrape up pan drippings and browned bits. Stir in the stock and bring to a bubble, then stir in the cream and reduce the heat to low. Add the nutmeg and stir. Taste and adjust seasonings if necessary.

Preheat the broiler to high. Combine the noodles with the turkey and sauce. Grease a casserole dish with a little softened butter. Transfer the turkey-noodle mixture to the dish and top with Gruyère cheese and then bread crumbs. Place the casserole 8 to 10 inches from the broiler and brown for 2 to 3 minutes, or until the cheese is melted and the crumbs are brown. Garnish the casserole with the parsley.

4 SERVINGS

10 The T2: Turkey Chili-Topped Turkey Chili Burgers
with Red Pepper Slaw and Funky Fries

1   sack (16 to 20 ounces) extra-crispy-style frozen French fries

¼   cup chili powder (3 palmfuls)

2   tablespoons ground cumin

2   tablespoons grill seasoning, such as McCormick's Montreal Steak Seasoning (a palmful)

¼   cup vegetable oil

2   packages (2 to 2⅔ pounds total) ground turkey breast

1   medium onion, finely chopped

2   tablespoons Worcestershire sauce (eyeball it)

1   8-ounce can tomato sauce

3   red bell peppers, ¼ of 1 pepper finely chopped, remaining peppers thinly sliced

4   garlic cloves, chopped

2   tablespoons hot sauce, such as Tabasco

6   ounces Cheddar or smoked Cheddar, cut into ¼-inch dice

3   tablespoons red wine vinegar (eyeball it)

1   tablespoon sugar

2   teaspoons coarse salt

1   sack (16 ounces) shredded red cabbage (available in the produce department)

1   small red onion, thinly sliced
    Coarse black pepper, to taste

3   tablespoons unsalted butter, cut into chunks

¼   cup finely chopped curly parsley

4   soft burger rolls

Preheat the oven to the temperature listed on the sack of fries.

Preheat a medium nonstick skillet over medium-high heat. Combine the chili powder, cumin, and grill seasoning in a small bowl. To the skillet add a tablespoon of the vegetable oil, once around the pan, and half of the turkey. Break up the turkey with the back of a wooden spoon, then season with half of the spice mixture. Combine to break up and brown the turkey for a couple of minutes, then add half of the chopped onions and cook for another couple of minutes. When the onions are translucent, add the Worcestershire sauce and tomato sauce; adjust the seasonings and simmer the chili sauce over low heat until ready to serve.

While the chili sauce is working, make the burgers. Place the remaining turkey in a bowl and add the remaining spice mixture, half of the remaining chopped onions, the finely chopped bell peppers, half the chopped garlic, and about a tablespoon of hot sauce. Mix well with your hands, then incorporate the diced cheese. Form the mixture into 4 inch-thick patties. Heat a second nonstick skillet over medium-high heat. Add a tablespoon of vegetable oil (once around the pan) and when hot, add the burgers. Cook the burgers for 6 minutes on each side.

When you place the burgers in the pan, the timing is right to add the fries to the preheated oven.

While everything is moving forward, throw together the slaw salad. In the bottom of a medium bowl, combine 1 tablespoon hot sauce—just eyeball it—with the vinegar, sugar, and 1 teaspoon of the salt. Add the red cabbage, red pepper strips, and red onions to the bowl and toss to combine. Season with black pepper.

On your cutting board add about a teaspoon of salt to the remaining chopped garlic and, using the flat of your knife blade, mash the garlic and salt into a paste. Scrape the paste into a small bowl with the butter and microwave on High for 20 seconds or so. Remove the fries from the oven and toss with the melted butter and the chopped parsley. Adjust seasoning to taste.

To serve, pile the chili-cheese burgers onto the buns, top with scoops of chili sauce, and a spoonful of the remaining chopped onions. Serve the burgers with piles of red pepper slaw and funky fries.

4 SERVINGS

Italian Sub Stoup and Garlic Toast Floaters

11

☐ TRY THIS LATER

☐ IT'S A KEEPER

Thicker than soup, thinner than stew, this stoup combines sausage, ham, pepperoni, veggies, and arugula. It tastes like a giant Italian sub!

STOUP

- 2 tablespoons extra-virgin olive oil (EVOO) (twice around the pan)
- ¾ pound (3 links) hot or sweet Italian sausage, removed from casings
- ¼ pound piece pepperoni, diced
- 1 ham steak, ½ to ¾ pound, diced
- 1 green bell pepper, cored, seeded, quartered, and sliced
- 1 medium yellow onion, quartered and sliced
- 1 28-ounce can diced tomatoes
  Salt and freshly ground black pepper
- 6 cups chicken stock or broth
- 1 cup gemelli pasta or other shaped pasta

CROUTONS

- ¼ cup EVOO
- 3 large garlic cloves, cracked from skins
- 5 cups crusty bread, cubed
- 1 teaspoon crushed red pepper flakes
- ½ teaspoon dried oregano
- ½ cup grated Parmigiano-Reggiano (a couple of handfuls)
- 4 cups arugula (2 bunches), trimmed and coarsely chopped

Place a soup pot on the stovetop and preheat to medium high. Add the EVOO and the sausage. Brown and crumble the sausage, drain off excess fat if necessary, then add the pepperoni and ham. Cook for 2 minutes, then add the bell peppers and onions and cook for 2 or 3 minutes more. Add the tomatoes and season with salt and pepper. Add the chicken stock and bring to a boil. Stir in the pasta and cook for 8 minutes.

While the pasta cooks, heat the ¼ cup of EVOO in a large skillet over medium heat. Add the garlic and cook for 1 minute. Add the bread cubes, toss, and toast the cubes for 5 or 6 minutes. Season the toasty cubes with the red pepper flakes, oregano, and grated cheese.

Stir the arugula into the stoup just before you serve it up. Float several bread cubes in each bowl.

4 SERVINGS

12 Spiced Lamb Chops

on Sautéed Peppers and Onions with Garlic and Mint Couscous

8 **lamb loin chops**
   Coarse salt and **coarse black pepper**
1 teaspoon **ground cumin** (⅓ palmful)
1 teaspoon **ground coriander** (⅓ palmful)
1 teaspoon **sweet paprika** (⅓ palmful)
4 tablespoons **extra-virgin olive oil** (EVOO)
2 **green bell peppers**, cored, seeded, and cut
   into 1-inch squares
1 large **yellow onion**, cut into 1-inch cubes
1 cup **grape** or **cherry tomatoes**
½ cup fresh **flat-leaf parsley** (a couple of
   handfuls), chopped
3 **garlic cloves**, finely chopped
1½ cups **chicken stock** or broth
1½ cups **couscous**
5 or 6 sprigs of fresh **mint**, finely chopped
   (about 3 tablespoons)
3 tablespoons **pine nuts**

Cover the chops with wax paper or plastic and whack each chop with the heel of your hand to flatten it out. Season the chops on both sides with salt and pepper. Combine the cumin, coriander, and paprika and sprinkle the mixture evenly over the chops. Pat the spices in place and wash up. Let the chops stand for 15 minutes.

Heat a large skillet over medium-high heat and add 2 tablespoons of the EVOO. When the oil is hot, add the peppers and onions. Season the vegetables with salt and pepper and cook together for 5 minutes, then add the tomatoes and continue to cook until their skins begin to burst. Add half of the parsley to the skillet and toss. Transfer the vegetables to a platter and cover loosely with foil to keep warm. Do not wash the skillet.

Place a tablespoon of the EVOO (just eyeball the amount) in a small pot for the couscous. Heat the oil over medium heat and add the garlic. Sauté for 1 minute, then add the chicken stock and bring it to a boil. Add the couscous, remove from the heat, and cover the pot. Let stand for 5 minutes.

Return the skillet you cooked the veggies in to the stove and add another tablespoon of EVOO, once around the pan. Add the lamb chops and sear for 2 to 3 minutes on each side for medium rare, 4 minutes on each side for medium well. Arrange the chops on top of the peppers and onions.

Fluff the couscous with a fork and stir in the mint, the remaining parsley, and the pine nuts. The couscous makes a nice bed for the veggies and lamb to catch all the juices.

4 SERVINGS

Saucy BBQ Chicken Sammies
with Pepper and Scallion Potato Salad

13

☐ TRY THIS LATER ☐ IT'S A KEEPER

2½ pounds small **potatoes**, such as baby Yukon Gold or red-skinned

2 ounces **jarred hot pepper rings**, drained and chopped, about 3 tablespoons (reserve the juice)

1 small **red bell pepper**, cored, seeded, and chopped

4 **scallions**, chopped

3 tablespoons **cider** or **wine vinegar** (eyeball it)

¼ cup plus 2 tablespoons **extra-virgin olive oil** (EVOO)

Salt and **freshly ground black pepper**

1 cup **chicken stock** or broth

1 cup **Mexican beer**

4 6-ounce boneless, skinless **chicken breast halves**

2 **garlic cloves**, chopped

1 medium **onion**, finely chopped

2 tablespoons **Worcestershire sauce** (eyeball it)

1 tablespoon **hot sauce**, such as Tabasco

2 tablespoons **grill seasoning** blend, such as McCormick's Montreal Steak Seasoning (2 palmfuls)

3 tablespoons **dark brown sugar**, packed

4 tablespoons **tomato paste**

1 large **sour pickle**, chopped

6 to 8 **sweet bread-and-butter pickle slices**, chopped

6 soft **sammy buns**, such as soft burger rolls

Chunk up the potatoes, cutting them into large bite-size pieces, and place them in a pot with water to cover. Bring to a boil, then simmer until tender, 10 to 12 minutes. Drain the potatoes and return them to the hot pot to dry them out. Add the hot peppers, bell peppers, and scallions to the pot, then dress everything with a splash of the hot pepper juice and the vinegar. Toss to combine, then drizzle with ¼ cup of the EVOO to coat the salad evenly. Season with salt and pepper.

While the potatoes work, bring the stock and beer to a simmer in a small or medium skillet. Slide in the chicken breasts and gently poach them for 10 minutes, turning once after 5 minutes.

While the chicken poaches, heat a second medium skillet over medium-low heat. To the hot skillet, add the remaining 2 tablespoons of EVOO, the garlic, and the onions and gently sauté until cooked through. Turn off the heat and set the pan aside.

Combine the Worcestershire, hot sauce, grill seasoning, brown sugar, and tomato paste in a medium bowl. Add 2 ladles of the poaching liquid to the bowl and mix well. Transfer the chicken breasts to the bowl, then use two forks to shred the meat, and combine it with the seasonings. Stir the shredded chicken into the pan of sautéed onions and garlic and combine well. Reheat together for 5 to 10 minutes, adding some more of the poaching liquid to make your chicken as saucy as you like.

Combine the sour and sweet pickles in a small bowl. Split the rolls and fill with scoops of shredded chicken. Top with pickle relish and serve with the potato salad.

6 SAMMIES

14 Fiery Hot Texas T-Bones with
Chipotle Smashed Potatoes and Hot and Sweet Pepper Sauté

3   whole jalapeños or 1 fresh ancho chili

3   bell peppers (choose 3 different colors)

2½   pounds small potatoes, such as baby Yukon Gold or red-skinned, coarsely chopped
     Coarse salt

2   slices bacon

2   tablespoons chipotle powder

1   small onion, chopped

1   cup sour cream

1   tablespoon dark chili powder

1   tablespoon ground cumin

2   tablespoons grill seasoning, such as McCormick's Montreal Steak Seasoning

2   large T-Bone steaks, 1½ inches thick (about 2½ pounds total)

3   tablespoons vegetable oil

¼   cup bourbon (eyeball it)

Seed and slice the hot and bell peppers and reserve.

Cover the potatoes with water and bring to a boil. Add salt to the boiling water. Cook the potatoes until tender, 8 to 10 minutes. Meanwhile, chop the bacon and brown over medium heat in a small skillet. Add a tablespoon of the chipotle powder and the onions, and cook over medium heat until the onions are tender, about 5 minutes. When the potatoes are done, drain them and return to the hot pot. Add the bacon mixture and the sour cream to the potatoes. Smash the potatoes and season with salt to taste.

While the potatoes are working, make a dry spice rub: Combine the chili powder, the remaining tablespoon of chipotle powder, the cumin, and grill seasoning. Rub the steaks liberally on both sides with the mixture. Heat a 12 to 14-inch skillet over high heat until screaming hot. Add 2 tablespoons of the vegetable oil, twice around the pan; it will smoke. Add the steaks and cook without turning for 6 minutes. Flip the steaks and cook for another 6 minutes for medium rare, or up to 10 minutes for well done. Remove the skillet from the heat and carefully add the bourbon. Return the steaks to the stove and flame the pan. When the fire goes out, transfer the steaks to a large serving platter and pour the pan juices over them. Let the meat rest for about 5 minutes so the juices can redistribute. Return the skillet to the heat and add the remaining tablespoon of vegetable oil. Add the hot and bell peppers and sauté for 5 minutes. Season with salt, then pile the peppers alongside the steaks.

Cut the meat from the T-bones and carve into 4 portions. Top each serving with some peppers and dollop some chipotle smashers alongside. Spoon the drippings and juices over the meat and serve.

4 SERVINGS

Super Tuscan Burgers and Potato Salad
with Capers and Celery

4 large Idaho potatoes
  Coarse salt
¾ pound ground pork
¾ pound ground veal
½ cup dry Italian red wine
¼ medium yellow onion, finely chopped
3 tablespoons chopped fresh sage leaves
  (from 5 or 6 sprigs)
4 garlic cloves, chopped
  Coarse black pepper
4 to 5 tablespoons extra-virgin olive oil
  (EVOO)
½ pound cremini (baby portobello)
  mushrooms, sliced
4 crusty rolls, split
8 ounces Italian sheep's-milk cheese, sliced
1 cup arugula leaves, trimmed of stems
3 tablespoons capers
4 celery ribs and their greens, from the heart
  of the stalk, chopped
½ medium red onion, finely chopped
  Zest and juice of 1 lemon
2 tablespoons red wine vinegar

Bring a medium pot of water to a boil while you peel and dice the potatoes. Add the potatoes to the boiling water and salt the water liberally. Boil the potatoes until tender, 12 to 15 minutes.

While the potatoes cook, prepare the burgers. Combine the pork and veal in a bowl with ¼ cup of the red wine (eyeball it); the yellow onions, sage, and garlic; and salt and pepper to taste. Form 4 large patties.

Preheat a large nonstick skillet over medium-high heat. Add a tablespoon of the EVOO, once around the pan, and set the burgers into the skillet, leaving a space in the center of the pan to pile in the mushrooms. Add the sliced mushrooms to the skillet with the burgers. Flip the burgers after 6 minutes and toss the mushrooms around as they brown at the center of the skillet. After the mushrooms begin to brown, season them with salt and pepper. (The color will be deeper and the mushrooms will remain firmer if you wait for them to brown before salting.) Cook the burgers for 5 minutes on the second side, then remove them from the pan and place them onto bottom halves of the rolls and arrange on a serving plate. Place the sliced cheese on the burgers, then spoon the hot mushrooms over the cheese. Cover the plate loosely with foil to slightly melt the cheese. Add the remaining ¼ cup of wine to the skillet and loosen the pan drippings. Dip the top halves of the rolls into the pan drippings to soak them up. Pile arugula on each burger, then set the top halves in place.

When the potatoes are cooked, drain them and return them to the warm pot to dry them out. Take the pot over to your cutting board and add the capers, celery, red onions, lemon zest and juice, red wine vinegar, and 3 or 4 tablespoons of the EVOO to the pot. Toss to combine the salad, then season the salad with salt and pepper. Transfer the salad to a serving dish. The potato salad can be served warm or cold.

4 SERVINGS

TRY THIS LATER

IT'S A KEEPER

16 Oregon-Style Pork Chops with Pinot Noir and Cranberries; Oregon Hash with Wild Mushrooms, Greens, Beets, Hazelnuts, and Blue Cheese; Charred Whole-Grain Bread with Butter and Chives

GO OREGONIAN!

Oregon on a plate: From Willamette Valley Pinot Noir to cranberry bogs and filbert trees, this menu celebrates one great state!

PORK CHOPS

- 4 boneless **pork loin chops**, $1\frac{1}{2}$ inches thick
  Salt and **freshly ground black pepper**
- 3 tablespoons **extra-virgin olive oil** (EVOO)
- 2 **leeks**
- 3 tablespoons **unsalted butter**

HASH

- 1 cup **hazelnut** or **filbert pieces**
- $\frac{1}{2}$ cup **dried sweetened cranberries**
- 1 cup **Willamette Valley Oregon Pinot Noir**
- 1 cup **chicken stock** or broth
- 1 tablespoon **EVOO**
- 1 tablespoon **unsalted butter**
- 2 **shallots**, thinly sliced
- 1 pound **cremini (baby portobello) mushrooms**, sliced
- $\frac{1}{2}$ pound **shiitake mushroom caps**, sliced
- 1 bunch of **kale**, chopped (4 to 5 cups)
- 1 15-ounce can **sliced beets**, drained
- 8 ounces crumbled **Oregon blue cheese**
- 1 loaf crusty **whole-grain bread**
- 1 tablespoon **unsalted butter**, softened
- 3 tablespoons chopped **chives**

Preheat a large skillet over medium-high heat. Season the chops with salt and pepper. Add 2 tablespoons of the EVOO to the hot skillet and then add the chops. Cook the chops for 3 to 4 minutes on each side. While they cook, split the leeks lengthwise, slice in $\frac{1}{2}$-inch half-moon pieces, and wash them vigorously under running water in a colander to release any sand. Shake to dry.

To make the hash, preheat a second large skillet over medium-high heat. Add the nuts to the skillet and brown for 2 to 3 minutes, then remove and set aside.

Remove the chops to a warm plate, tent with foil, and set aside. To the skillet, add another tablespoon of EVOO and the leeks. Cook the leeks until tender, about 5 minutes. Add the cranberries and Pinot Noir to the pan. Scrape up the pan drippings with a wooden spoon and stir in the chicken stock. When the sauce comes up to a bubble, add the chops back to the pan and reduce the heat to a simmer. Finish cooking the chops through, about 10 minutes.

To finish the hash: To the skillet used to toast the nuts, add the tablespoon of EVOO and 1 tablespoon of the butter. When the butter melts into the oil, add the shallots and mushrooms and cook for 5 minutes, then add the kale. Wilt the kale into the pan and season with salt and pepper to taste. When the kale is hot and wilted, add the beets and gently combine. Adjust the seasonings.

Preheat the broiler.

Pull the chops from their sauce and reserve on a clean, warm plate. Raise the heat and bring the sauce back to a bubble. Cut off 4 thick slices of the whole-grain bread. Char the bread under the broiler on each side while you finish the sauce. Add 2 tablespoons of butter to the sauce to give it gloss and weight, and turn off the heat. Spread the charred bread with the remaining tablespoon of butter and sprinkle liberally with chopped chives.

Pour the sauce over the chops. Serve the hash alongside the chops and toasts and top with crumbles of blue cheese.

4 SERVINGS

Honey Nut Chicken Sticks

17

TRY THIS LATER ☐ IT'S A KEEPER ☐

Serve with a green salad or vegetable sticks.

- 2   pounds **chicken tenders**
    Salt and **freshly ground black pepper**
- 1   cup all-purpose **flour**
- 3   **eggs**
    A splash of **milk**
- 2   cups **Honey Nut Corn Flakes**
- 1   cup **bread crumbs**
- 1   tablespoon **sweet paprika**
- 1   tablespoon **poultry seasoning**
- 2   tablespoons **grill seasoning**, such as McCormick's Montreal Steak Seasoning (2 palmfuls)
- ¼   cup **vegetable oil** (eyeball it)

Preheat the oven to 400°F.

Season the chicken tenders with salt and pepper. Place the flour in a large, shallow dish. Coat the chicken in the flour. Beat the eggs and milk in a shallow dish. Combine the cereal, bread crumbs, paprika, poultry seasoning, grill seasoning, and vegetable oil in a food processor. Transfer the breading to a shallow dish.

Place a nonstick baking sheet near the chicken breading station. In batches, dip the flour-coated chicken into the egg mixture and then in the breading and place on the nonstick cookie sheet. When all the tenders have been coated, bake them for 15 minutes, or until evenly browned and cooked through. Cool enough to handle and serve, or pack up for a picnic! This chicken may be served hot or cold.

4 SERVINGS

18 Turkey Saltimbocca Roll-Ups, Mushroom and White Bean Ragout, and Spinach with Pancetta and Onions

12 turkey cutlets, 1 to 1½ pounds in all

6 slices prosciutto di Parma, cut in half

12 whole fresh sage leaves plus 2 tablespoons finely chopped sage

4 tablespoons extra-virgin olive oil (EVOO), plus more for drizzling
   Salt and freshly ground black pepper

2 teaspoons poultry seasoning (⅔ palmful)

4 garlic cloves, chopped

½ teaspoon crushed red pepper flakes

1 pound cremini (baby portobello) mushrooms, wiped clean and sliced

1 15-ounce can cannellini beans, drained

2 tablespoons wine vinegar, white or red

2 cups chicken stock or broth

2 tablespoons unsalted butter

2 tablespoons all-purpose flour

½ cup dry white wine (eyeball it)

⅛ pound (3 slices) pancetta, chopped

1 medium onion, thinly sliced

1 pound triple-washed spinach, stemmed and coarsely chopped

¼ teaspoon freshly grated or ground nutmeg (eyeball it)

Using a meat mallet or a heavy, small skillet, pound the turkey between sheets of wax paper or plastic wrap to ⅛-inch thickness. Top each turkey cutlet with a half slice of prosciutto and a whole sage leaf. Roll up the cutlets and drizzle them with EVOO, then season with salt, pepper, and poultry seasoning. Heat a large nonstick skillet over medium-high heat. Add 1 tablespoon of the EVOO, once around the pan. Arrange the roll-ups seam side down and cook for 6 minutes, then turn and cook for 6 minutes more.

While the turkey cooks, make the mushroom and white bean ragout. Heat a medium skillet over medium heat. Add 2 tablespoons of the EVOO, twice around the pan, then add the garlic, red pepper flakes, and mushrooms and cook for 5 minutes to deepen the color. Stir in the beans and season up the mixture with salt and pepper. When the beans heat through, in a minute or two, add the vinegar and stir, then add ½ cup of the chicken stock to deglaze the pan. Turn off the heat.

After the turkey roll-ups have cooked on both sides, transfer to a platter and reserve. Add the butter to the skillet and reduce the heat to medium low. Add the flour to the melted butter and combine with a whisk. Whisk in the wine and cook it for about 30 seconds. Whisk in the remaining 1½ cups of chicken stock to make a gravy. Add the remaining chopped sage, then season with salt and pepper. Slide the roll-ups back into the gravy and simmer over low heat until ready to serve.

For the spinach, heat a medium skillet over medium-high heat. Add the remaining tablespoon of EVOO, once around the pan, then the chopped pancetta. Brown the pancetta for 1 minute, then add the onions and cook together for 5 minutes, or until they are just tender and the pancetta bits are crisp. Add the spinach to the pan and turn to wilt it while combining with the onions. Season the spinach with nutmeg, salt, and pepper.

Serve 3 roll-ups in gravy with a portion of the ragout and the spinach alongside.

4 SERVINGS

Rosemary Corn Cakes with Prosciutto and Chicken Sausages with Hot and Sweet Peppers

☐ TRY THIS LATER ☐ IT'S A KEEPER

This meal is good for B-L-D: breakfast, lunch, or dinner.

- 8 chicken sausages, any flavor or brand, such as sun-dried tomato or garlic
- 2 tablespoons extra-virgin olive oil (EVOO) (twice around the pan)
- 3 tablespoons unsalted butter
- 1 8 ½-ounce box Jiffy corn muffin mix
- 1 egg
- ¾ cup milk
- 2 to 3 tablespoons finely chopped fresh rosemary
- 4 slices prosciutto, chopped
  Coarse black pepper
- 2 large cubanelle peppers (long, light green Italian sweet peppers), seeded and thinly sliced
  Coarse salt
- 4 hot red cherry peppers from a jar, chopped (reserve the juice)
- ½ cup honey

Preheat a griddle or nonstick skillet over medium heat.

Prick the sausages with a fork and place in a large skillet, then add 1 inch of water to the pan. Add the EVOO to the pan and bring the water to a boil, then reduce the heat to medium. Let the sausages cook until the liquid evaporates, about 10 minutes.

Meanwhile, melt 2 tablespoons of the butter in the microwave on High for 15 seconds. In a medium bowl, combine the muffin mix with the egg, melted butter, milk, rosemary, prosciutto, and a few grinds of black pepper. Rub the griddle with the remaining 1 tablespoon butter nested in a paper towel to lightly coat the cooking surface. Form 4 small cakes, 2 to 3 inches in diameter, and cook until golden on each side, then repeat with the remaining mixture.

Check the sausages. When the liquid has evaporated, move the sausages off to one side of the pan to allow the casings to crisp and brown. Add the cubanelle peppers to the other side of the pan and let them cook until just tender. Season with salt and pepper, then add the hot peppers and toss. Douse the pan with a splash of pepper juice just before you serve the peppers.

Serve the sausages with the peppers on top and the cakes alongside. Drizzle the cakes with the honey.

4 SERVINGS

20 Black Bean Stoup and Southwestern Monte Cristos

A "stoup" is what I call a soup that is almost as thick as a stew. This one can be prepared as a vegetarian entrée as well by omitting the ham.

2 tablespoons **extra-virgin olive oil** (EVOO), (twice around the pan)

1 dried **bay leaf**

1 **jalapeño pepper**, seeded and chopped

4 **garlic cloves**, chopped

3 **celery ribs** with greens, chopped

1 large **onion**, chopped

1 **red bell pepper**, cored, seeded, and chopped

3 15-ounce cans **black beans**

2 tablespoons **ground cumin** (a couple of palmfuls)

1½ teaspoons **ground coriander** (⅓ palmful)
Salt and **freshly ground black pepper**

2 to 3 tablespoons plus 2 teaspoons **hot sauce**

1 quart **chicken** or **vegetable stock** or broth

1 15-ounce can **diced tomatoes**

8 slices **white sandwich bread**

½ cup **hot pepper jelly** or chili sauce, tomatillo or tomato salsa, or taco sauce—whichever you have on hand

8 slices **honey-baked ham** from the deli counter

8 slices **Pepper Jack cheese** from the deli counter

8 slices **smoked turkey** from the deli counter

2 **eggs**, beaten
A splash of **milk**

1 tablespoon **unsalted butter**

½ cup **sour cream**

2 to 3 **scallions**, chopped

Heat a medium soup pot over medium-high heat. Add the EVOO to the hot pot, then add the bay leaf, jalapeños, garlic, celery, and onions. Cook for 3 to 4 minutes, then add the bell peppers and continue to cook. Drain 2 cans of beans and add them. With the remaining can, pour the juice and half the beans into the pot. Use a fork to mash up the beans remaining in the can. Stir the mashed beans into the pot and season with the cumin, coriander, salt, pepper, and 2 to 3 tablespoons of the hot sauce. Add the stock and tomatoes to the stoup and bring to a bubble. Reduce the heat and simmer for 15 minutes over low heat.

While the stoup cooks, make the monte cristos: Spread the bread with a light layer of pepper jelly or chili sauce, salsa, or taco sauce, then build sandwiches using 2 slices each of ham, cheese, and turkey per sandwich. Beat the eggs with the milk and the remaining 2 teaspoons of hot sauce and season the mixture with a little salt. Heat a griddle pan or nonstick skillet over medium heat. Melt the butter in the skillet. Dip each sandwich in the egg coating and cook for 3 to 4 minutes on each side to melt the cheese and warm the meats through.

Ladle up the black bean stoup and top with sour cream and scallions. Cut the monte cristos corner to corner and serve alongside the stoup for dipping and munching.

4 SERVINGS

Citrus-Marinated Chicken and Orange Salad

3 **oranges**

3 **garlic cloves**, chopped

7 tablespoons **extra-virgin olive oil** (EVOO)

¼ teaspoon **cayenne pepper** (optional), plus a large pinch for the dressing
Salt and **freshly ground black pepper**

4 6- to 8-ounce boneless, skinless **chicken breast halves**

1 large head of **radicchio**

1 small **red onion**, thinly sliced

1 bunch of **arugula**, stemmed and thoroughly cleaned

3 sprigs fresh **oregano**, stripped of leaves then chopped

2 tablespoons **honey**

1 heaping tablespoon **Dijon mustard**

4 thick slices **crusty bread**

Preheat a grill pan or outdoor grill on high.

Zest 2 of the 3 oranges and put the orange zest in a large, shallow dish. Juice half an orange and add to the zest. To the zest and juice, add the garlic, 3 tablespoons of the EVOO, the ¼ teaspoon cayenne (if using), salt, and pepper and stir to combine. Add the chicken breasts, toss to coat thoroughly, and let marinate for 5 minutes.

While the chicken is marinating, with a paring knife cut the skin and white pith from the 2 remaining whole oranges, being sure to remove it all. Slice the oranges into disks and place in a salad bowl. Cut the radicchio in quarters through the core, cut the core off from each quarter, and then thinly shred the radicchio and add to the oranges. Add the red onions and arugula. To make the dressing, juice the other half orange into a small bowl and add the pinch of cayenne, the oregano, honey, and mustard. In a slow, steady stream, whisk in the 4 remaining tablespoons of EVOO.

Transfer the marinated chicken to the grill and cook on each side for 5 to 6 minutes, or until cooked through. Remove from the grill and let rest for a few minutes. Lightly toast the bread.

Thinly slice the grilled chicken on an angle, add to the salad, and then pour the dressing over. Toss to combine and serve with the toasted bread.

4 SERVINGS

22 Boo's Butternut Squash Mac-n-Cheese

I know it sounds odd, but my girl LOVED butternut squash! This dog might even go for it before a steak, especially if there were also pasta and cheese involved in the deal.

Coarse salt
1 pound macaroni with ridges, such as tubettini or mini penne rigate
1 tablespoon extra-virgin olive oil (EVOO) (once around the pan)
2 tablespoons unsalted butter
2 tablespoons chopped fresh thyme, plus a few sprigs for garnish
1/2 medium onion
3 tablespoons all-purpose flour
2 cups chicken stock or broth
1 10-ounce box frozen cooked butternut squash, defrosted
1 cup cream or half-and-half
2 cups (8 ounces) grated sharp Cheddar cheese
1/2 cup grated Parmigiano-Reggiano (a couple of handfuls)
1/4 teaspoon nutmeg (eyeball it)
Freshly ground black pepper, to taste

Heat a pot of water to boil for the pasta. Salt the water, then add the pasta and cook al dente, or with a bite to it.

While the pasta cooks, heat a medium heavy-bottomed pot over medium heat. Add the EVOO and butter. When the butter melts into the oil, add the thyme and grate the onion directly into the pot with a hand-held grater or Microplane. Cook the grated onions for a minute or 2, then add the flour and cook together for a minute or 2 more. Whisk in the stock, then add the butternut squash and cook until warmed through and smooth. Stir in the cream and bring the sauce to a bubble. Stir in the cheeses in a figure-eight motion and season the completed sauce with salt, nutmeg, and pepper. Taste to adjust seasonings.

Drain the cooked pasta well and combine with the sauce. Serve alongside chicken sammies or all on its own with a green salad. Garnish with thyme leaves. (Boo would also have a little extra sprinkle of that cheese, please!)

5 SERVINGS; BOO COUNTED FOR 2

BOO FOOD

Boo was my dog, my friend, and my test-kitchen eater for twelve years (eighty-four, to her) and about 2,700 recipes. These recipes are a tribute to all the flavors and foods Boo loved best. I was the luckiest girl in the world to share my life and so much good food with Miss Boo. When you make this meal, have a bite for her or for the special animal in your life.

Boo's Smoky Chicken Patties on Buttered Toast

23

TRY THIS LATER ☐   IT'S A KEEPER ☐

1½ pounds ground chicken breast

1 tablespoon smoked sweet Hungarian paprika, available on the spice aisle in small cans (a palmful)

1½ tablespoons grill seasoning, such as McCormick's Montreal Steak Seasoning (1½ palmfuls)

¼ to ⅓ cup chopped fresh flat-leaf parsley (a couple of handfuls of leaves)

½ medium yellow onion

4 garlic cloves, finely chopped

2 tablespoons extra-virgin olive oil (EVOO) (twice around the bowl)

8 slices sandwich white or whole-wheat bread

2 to 3 tablespoons unsalted butter, softened

2 cups chopped baby spinach, watercress, or arugula (Boo would skip the greens)

Heat a large nonstick skillet over medium-high heat.

Place the chicken in a bowl and add the smoked paprika, grill seasoning, and parsley. Using a hand-held grater or Microplane, grate the onion into the chicken (Boo liked onion juice and its flavor, but she did not like big pieces of onion). Add the garlic (Boo LOVED garlic!) and mix to combine. Make a mini patty, the size of a quarter, and cook it up, a minute on each side, to taste and check seasonings. If you want it really smoky, like Boo did, adjust the seasonings accordingly. Drizzle the chicken mixture with the EVOO and form 4 large, thin patties, then place them in the pan. Cook the patties for 5 minutes on each side. Toast the bread slices and spread liberally with softened butter. Serve the patties on the buttered toast with some chopped dark greens.

4 SERVINGS—BUT BOO COULD EAT IT ALL!

- -

Bonus Recipe: Boo's Vanilla Ice Cream
with Chunky Peanut Butter Sauce and Gingersnaps

TRY THIS LATER ☐   IT'S A KEEPER ☐

I won't count this one—it's a dessert, not a meal—but it has three Boo favorites in one dish.

1 cup chunky peanut butter (Boo preferred Skippy)

¼ to ⅓ cup milk or half-and-half (eyeball it)

¼ cup honey (eyeball it)

¼ teaspoon ground cinnamon

2 pints vanilla ice cream, softened

12 gingersnaps (Boo liked Midel brand because they were extra crunchy)

Place the peanut butter, milk, and honey in a small skillet and warm over low heat. Stir until smooth and season the sauce with a little cinnamon. Scoop the ice cream into dishes, top with peanut butter sauce, and jam the gingersnaps all around the bowl, getting the edges into the ice cream and sauce.

4 SERVINGS

24 MASTER RECIPE
Salsa Stoup and Double-Decker Baked Quesadillas

This spicy meal fills you up without filling you out!

2 tablespoons **vegetable oil** (twice around the pan), plus some for brushing the tortillas

2 **jalapeño peppers**, seeded and chopped

1 **green bell pepper**, cored, seeded, and chopped

1 large **onion**, chopped

3 **celery ribs**, chopped with greens

3 **garlic cloves**, chopped
Salt and freshly ground black pepper

1 28-ounce can **stewed tomatoes**

1 28-ounce can **crushed tomatoes**

2 cups **vegetable** or **chicken stock** or broth

3 tablespoons chopped fresh **cilantro**

6 6- to 8-inch **flour tortillas**

1 cup shredded **Cheddar**

3 **scallions**, chopped

1 cup shredded **Pepper Jack**
Sour cream, for garnish

Preheat the oven to 300°F.

Heat a medium soup pot over medium-high heat. Add the vegetable oil and the jalapeños, bell peppers, onions, celery, and garlic. Season with salt and pepper, then sauté the veggies for 5 minutes. Add all the tomatoes and stock and bring to a bubble. Reduce the heat to a simmer and stir in the cilantro.

Paint one side of 2 tortillas with oil and place them, oiled side down, on a large cookie sheet. Mix the Cheddar with the scallions and divide between the tortillas evenly. Top with another tortilla and top each of those with equal amounts of Pepper Jack cheese. Set the last tortillas on top and brush the tops with oil. Bake the quesadillas for 10 minutes, then cool for 5 minutes to set. Cut each into 6 wedges.

Serve each bowl of stoup with 3 wedges of quesadilla alongside and sour cream for topping either.

4 SERVINGS

25 NOW TRY... Taco Chili-Mac

ADD

1½ pounds **lean ground beef**

2 teaspoons **hot sauce**, such as Tabasco

1 tablespoon **Worcestershire sauce**

1 tablespoon **ground cumin**

2 tablespoons **chili powder**

1 pound **macaroni**, cooked al dente

Prepare the stoup as in the master recipe, #24, adding meat to the pot with the oil before you add the peppers. Cook over medium-high heat, crumbling the meat with a wooden spoon, then season with the hot sauce, Worcestershire, cumin, chili, and salt and pepper. Add the peppers and onions and proceed as above. Stir in the macaroni. Serve with the quesadillas.

6 SERVINGS

Florentine Meatballs

☐ TRY THIS LATER   ☐ IT'S A KEEPER

Serve with a green salad.

- 1 10-ounce box frozen **spinach**, defrosted
- 2 packages (2 to 2⅔ pounds) **ground turkey breast**
- 1 medium **onion**, finely chopped
- 3 **garlic cloves**, chopped
- 1 large **egg**
- 1¾ cups **milk**
- ¾ cup **bread crumbs** (3 handfuls)
- ½ cup grated **Parmigiano-Reggiano** (2 handfuls)
  Coarse salt and **coarse black pepper**
  Extra-virgin olive oil (EVOO), for drizzling
- 2 tablespoons **unsalted butter**
- 2 tablespoons all-purpose **flour**
- 1 cup **chicken stock** or broth
- 1 10-ounce sack **shredded Provolone cheese** or blend of Italian cheeses (available on the dairy aisle)
- ½ teaspoon freshly grated **nutmeg**
  A generous handful of chopped fresh **flat-leaf parsley**

TIDBIT

It's easy to thaw a frozen spinach block in the microwave. Just throw it in on High for 5 minutes. Let it cool a bit before wringing out the liquid.

Preheat the oven to 400°F.

Wring the defrosted spinach dry in a clean kitchen towel. Place the turkey in a large bowl and make a well in the center. Add the spinach, all but 3 table-spoons of the onions, all of the garlic, the egg, about ¼ cup of the milk, the bread crumbs, grated Parm cheese, salt, and pepper. Form into 12 large balls and drizzle with EVOO. Arrange on a nonstick cookie sheet and bake for 20 minutes.

While the meatballs are in the oven, heat a small sauce pot over medium heat. Add a drizzle of EVOO and the butter. When the butter is melted, add the reserved 3 tablespoons of chopped onions and cook for 2 min-utes. Whisk in the flour and cook for 1 minute, then whisk in the remaining 1½ cups of milk and the cup of stock. Bring to a boil, then stir in the shredded cheese. Season the sauce with salt, pepper, and nutmeg; turn the heat to the lowest setting and stir until the cheese melts. Keep warm.

Place 3 meatballs on each dinner plate and top with sauce, then garnish with parsley.

4 SERVINGS

MASTER RECIPE
Pumpkin Pasta with Sausage and Wild Mushrooms

Serve with crusty bread.

- 2 tablespoons **extra-virgin olive oil** (EVOO)
- 1 pound bulk **sweet Italian sausage**
- ¼ pound **shiitake mushroom caps**
- 2 **portobello mushroom caps**, halved and thinly sliced
- 3 **garlic cloves**, chopped
- 1 medium yellow **onion**, chopped
  Salt and **freshly ground black pepper**
- ½ cup **dry white wine** (eyeball it)
- 1 cup **chicken stock** or broth
- 1 14-ounce can **pumpkin purée**
- ½ cup **cream** (2 healthy turns of the pan)
- 2 to 3 tablespoons thinly sliced fresh **sage** leaves
- ½ teaspoon freshly **ground nutmeg**
  A pinch of ground **cinnamon**
- 1 pound **penne** or cellantani pasta
  Grated **Parmigiano-Reggiano** to taste
- ¼ cup finely chopped fresh **chives** (12 chives)

Bring a large pot of water to a boil.

Meanwhile, heat a deep skillet over medium-high heat. Add the EVOO (twice around the pan) and sausage. Brown the sausage and crumble it with a wooden spoon. Move the sausage to one side of the pan and add the mushrooms, garlic, and onions to the other side of the pan. Cook until the mushrooms brown, then season with salt and pepper. Combine the sausage and vegetables and deglaze the pan with the wine. Add the chicken stock and heat for 1 minute. Stir in the pumpkin and incorporate; it'll be thick. Stir in the cream, sage, nutmeg, and cinnamon and adjust the salt and pepper. Reduce the heat to low.

Add salt and the pasta to the boiling water and cook until al dente. Drain the pasta and add it to the pumpkin mixture. Top with the cheese and chives.

4 SERVINGS

- -

28
NOW TRY... Pasta with Spinach, Mushrooms, Pumpkin, and Hazelnuts

OMIT

Sausage

ADD

- 2 10-ounce boxes frozen **chopped spinach**, defrosted
- 1 cup chopped toasted **hazelnuts**

Wring out the spinach in a kitchen towel until dry. Start the pan with EVOO as in the master recipe, #27, and add the mushrooms, garlic, and onions. Cook until brown, then add the spinach, separating it with your fingertips as you add it to the pan. Combine and heat the mixture for 2 minutes, then add the wine and proceed as above. Top the pasta with cheese, chives, and the toasted hazelnuts.

4 SERVINGS

Beef and Chicken Fajita Burgers
with Seared Peppers and Onions

29

TRY THIS LATER · IT'S A KEEPER

Have one of each! Serve with spicy refried beans.

BEEF FAJITA BURGERS

- 1⅓ pounds ground sirloin
- 2 tablespoons Worcestershire sauce (eyeball it)
- 1 tablespoon chili powder (a palmful)
- 1½ teaspoons ground cumin (half a palmful)
- 2 to 3 tablespoons fresh thyme leaves (from several sprigs)
  Several drops of hot sauce
- 1 tablespoon grill seasoning, such as McCormick's Montreal Steak Seasoning
  Extra-virgin olive oil (EVOO), for drizzling

CHICKEN FAJITA BURGERS

- 1⅓ pounds ground chicken
- 1 tablespoon ground chipotle powder (a palmful)
- 2 to 3 tablespoons chopped fresh cilantro
  Several drops of hot sauce
- 1 tablespoon grill seasoning, such as McCormick's Montreal Steak Seasoning
  EVOO, for drizzling

SEARED PEPPERS AND ONIONS

- 1 tablespoon EVOO (once around the pan)
- 2 red and/or green bell peppers, cored, seeded, and thinly sliced lengthwise
- 1 medium yellow onion, thinly sliced lengthwise
- 2 garlic cloves, smashed out of the skin and chopped
- 1 jalapeño or serrano chili, seeded and chopped

- 2 cups prepared tomatillo salsa or chipotle-tomato salsa
- 8 crusty rolls, split

Heat a grill pan or large skillet over medium-high heat.

For the beef fajita burgers: In a large bowl, combine the ground meat, Worcestershire, chili powder, cumin, thyme, hot sauce, and grill seasoning. Divide the mixture into 4 portions and make 4 patties, 1 inch thick. Drizzle with EVOO. Cook the patties for 4 minutes on each side for medium, or until desired doneness.

For the chicken fajita burgers: In a large bowl, combine the ground chicken, chipotle powder, cilantro, hot sauce, and grill seasoning. Divide the meat into 4 portions and form 4 big patties, 1 inch thick. Drizzle the patties with EVOO and cook for 6 minutes on each side, or until the burgers are firm and cooked through.

To make the peppers and onions, heat a medium skillet over high heat. Add EVOO and the bell peppers and onions. Stir-fry the veggies, tossing them with tongs, to sear them at the edges. Add the garlic and jalapeños. Toss and turn the mixture for about 3 minutes, then add the salsa and toss for a minute longer. Place the burgers on each bun bottom and top with ⅛ of the pepper and onion mixture and bun top.

4 SERVINGS,
1 BEEF AND 1 CHICKEN BURGER PER PERSON

30 Paella Burgers and Spanish Fries
with Pimiento Mayonnaise

1 sack (16 to 18 ounces) extra-crispy–style frozen fries

1½ pounds ground chicken breast

1 cup fresh flat-leaf parsley leaves (3 or 4 handfuls)

7 garlic cloves, finely chopped

1 small yellow onion, finely chopped

4 teaspoons sweet paprika

4 teaspoons hot sauce

Zest of 2 lemons, 1 lemon cut into wedges after zesting

2½ tablespoons grill seasoning, such as McCormick's Montreal Steak Seasoning

Extra-virgin olive oil (EVOO), for drizzling

½ pound chorizo, casings removed, cut into 4 3-inch pieces and butterflied

4 jumbo shrimp (8 count per pound), peeled, deveined, and butterflied

Coarse salt

4 Portuguese rolls (slightly sweet rectangular crusty rolls), or other crusty bread or roll, split

1 cup pimiento peppers, jarred or canned, drained well

1 cup mayonnaise

3 tablespoons unsalted butter

2 cups chopped romaine lettuce

Preheat the oven and prepare the fries according to the package directions.

Preheat a large griddle or nonstick skillet over medium-high to high heat.

Place the chicken in a bowl. Set aside a handful of whole parsley leaves and finely chop the rest. Add half of the chopped parsley and a little less than half of the chopped garlic to the bowl with the chicken. Next, add the chopped onions, 2 teaspoons (⅔ palmful) of the paprika, about 2 teaspoons of the hot sauce, the zest of 1 lemon, and the grill seasoning. Pour a healthy drizzle of EVOO around the outside of the bowl. Combine the mixture and form 4 patties. Place the patties on the griddle and cook for 5 minutes on each side.

Place the chorizo on the griddle alongside the burgers. Try to weight down the chorizo to keep it from curling up by placing a plate or small skillet on the sausage and adding something heavy from your pantry, such as canned goods, to weight it down. Cook for just 2 or 3 minutes on each side. The chorizo is already fully cooked; you're just crisping the edges and heating it through. Transfer to a platter and keep warm.

Squeeze about 1 tablespoon of the lemon juice over the shrimp, then season them with a little coarse salt and drizzle them with EVOO. Grill the butterflied shrimp alongside the burgers, 2 minutes on each side, weighting them as you did the chorizo.

Remove the patties and shrimp and add to the chorizo, loosely tenting to keep warm. Drizzle the rolls with EVOO and place cut side down on grill. Weight the rolls down and press to toast and char them on both sides.

Place the pimiento peppers and mayo in a food processor and add the reserved whole parsley leaves, the zest of the second lemon, the remaining 2 teaspoons of hot sauce, and a few pinches of salt. Process together until the dressing is smooth.

Melt the butter together with the remaining chopped garlic over low heat until the garlic sizzles in the butter. Remove the fries from the oven and place in a large bowl. Add the remaining chopped parsley to the bowl and pour the melted garlic butter over the fries, then season with salt and toss.

Mound some chopped lettuce on the roll bottoms, then top with chorizo, chicken patties, and shrimp. Slather the bun top with pimiento mayo and set in place. Serve extra mayo with the fries for dipping.

4 SERVINGS

TIDBIT

To butterfly the chorizo chunks, cut into and across but not all the way through the sausage, then spread the meat, like wings. For the shrimp, cut along the incision used to devein the shrimp, then spread it open.

MASTER RECIPE
Papa al Pomodoro

TRY THIS LATER

IT'S A KEEPER

This thick soup is a ribollita (stale bread soup) made with tons of tomatoes. Torello (literally, "The Bull") from Florence makes his with tomatoes grown on his own land in Tuscany. At his restaurant, Il Latini, he taught me the manner—the *only* manner—in which one eats any type of ribollita: with chopped raw onions and a drizzle of EVOO on top. If you are not committed to this process or if you don't do raw onions, skip this recipe. You're not to eat it any other way. Torello will find out, and I'll be in for it!

3 tablespoons **extra-virgin olive oil** (EVOO) (3 times around the pan), plus some for drizzling
4 to 6 **garlic cloves**, chopped
1 medium to large **onion**, finely chopped
1 15-ounce can petite **diced tomatoes**
1 28-ounce can **crushed tomatoes**
   Salt and **freshly ground black pepper**
1 quart **chicken stock** or broth
4 cups chopped or torn **stale bread** (about ½ pound)
2 15-ounce cans **small white beans**, such as Goya brand (smaller than cannellini beans)
½ cup grated **Parmigiano-Reggiano**, to pass at the table
10 fresh **basil** leaves, torn (optional)

Heat a medium soup pot over medium heat. Add the 3 tablespoons of EVOO, the garlic and three fourths of the onions. Cook for 7 to 8 minutes, then add the diced and crushed tomatoes and season with salt and pepper. Add the stock and raise the heat to make the soup bubble. Reduce the heat to a simmer and add the bread and beans. Stir the soup as it simmers until it thickens to stew-like consistency. A wooden spoon should be able to stand upright in the pot.

Turn off the heat, adjust the seasonings and ladle the soup into shallow bowls. Top with grated cheese, an additional drizzle of EVOO, a spoonful of the reserved finely chopped raw onions, and torn basil. The basil, and only the basil, is optional.

4 SERVINGS

NOW TRY... *Ribollita con Verdure*

32

☐ TRY THIS LATER   ☐ IT'S A KEEPER

This bread soup has some vegetables in it, but it is made with beef stock. For a vegetarian version, use all vegetable or wild mushroom stock and skip the pancetta or bacon.

OMIT

Crushed tomatoes

SWAP

6 cups **beef stock** or broth for the quart of chicken stock

ADD

4 slices **pancetta** (not smoked) or bacon (smoked), chopped

2 medium **carrots**, diced

1 medium, skinny **zucchini**, cut into thin slices

½ cup **dry red wine**

4 cups chopped **kale** or chard

Prepare as for the master recipe, #31, adding the pancetta or bacon to the EVOO and rendering for 4 minutes. Add the garlic, three fourths of the onions, the carrots, and zucchini and season with salt and pepper. Saute for 7 to 8 minutes, then add the wine and deglaze the pot. Stir in the diced tomatoes and beef stock and bring up the heat. When the soup boils, reduce to a simmer and stir in the bread and beans. Pile the greens into the pot and wilt them into the soup. Simmer the ribollita for 5 minutes. Ladle into shallow bowls and top with EVOO and the remaining raw onions. Again, basil is an optional garnish.

4 SERVINGS

33 3 Beans and Some Chicken

I called this recipe "3 beans and some chicken" because I didn't want to put on any airs. If you're having people over for dinner and your guests inquire what you are serving, by all means posh it up and inform them that you are preparing "Lemon-Scented Sautéed Poulet with Legume Ragout." Snap!

Zest and juice of 1 **lemon**
3 tablespoons **extra-virgin olive oil** (EVOO)
2 tablespoons chopped fresh **thyme** leaves (from 4 sprigs)
Salt and **freshly ground black pepper**
4 6-ounce boneless, skinless **chicken breast halves**
¼ pound sliced **pancetta**, from the deli counter, chopped
1 large **yellow onion**, thinly sliced
½ teaspoon crushed **red pepper flakes**
¾ cup **dry white wine** (eyeball it)
1 cup **chicken stock** or broth
½ pound **green beans**, stemmed, then cut in half
½ pound **wax beans**, stemmed, then cut in half
1 15-ounce can **cannellini beans**, rinsed and drained
½ cup fresh **flat-leaf parsley** (a couple of generous handfuls), chopped

In a shallow bowl, combine the lemon juice, about 1 tablespoon of the EVOO, half of the thyme, and salt and pepper. Add the chicken and toss to coat, then let the chicken sit while you start the 3 beans.

Heat a medium-size skillet over medium heat. Add a tablespoon of the EVOO (once around the pan). Add the pancetta and cook until crisp, 2 to 3 minutes. Add the onions, red pepper flakes, salt, pepper, and the remaining chopped thyme. Cook, stirring frequently, for 5 minutes—you want the onions to get nice and brown. Add the white wine and stock and continue to cook until the liquids are reduced by half, 4 to 5 minutes. While the wine and stock reduce, start cooking the seasoned chicken.

Preheat a large nonstick skillet over medium-high heat with the remaining tablespoon of EVOO. Add the breasts and cook on each side for 5 to 6 minutes, or until cooked through.

Add the green beans and wax beans to the reduced chicken stock and wine, stir to combine, and cook for 2 to 3 minutes. Add the cannellini beans and cook until warmed through, 1 minute more. Finish the beans with the parsley and lemon zest. Taste and check for seasoning. Serve the chicken breasts whole or sliced on an angle over a serving of the beans.

4 SERVINGS

Sweet Sausages Braised in Onions
with Horseradish Smashed Potatoes

Serve with a green salad for a real meal.

- 2 pounds small **red potatoes**, cut into quarters
  Coarse salt
- 1 tablespoon **extra-virgin olive oil** (EVOO) (once around the pan)
- 8 links (about 2 pounds) **sweet Italian sausage**
- 2 medium **yellow onions**, thinly sliced
- 2 to 3 tablespoons chopped fresh **thyme** leaves (from 5 to 6 sprigs)
- 3 **garlic cloves**, chopped
  Coarse black pepper
- ¼ cup **balsamic vinegar** (eyeball it)
- 2 cups **chicken stock** or 1 14-ounce can chicken broth
- 2 tablespoons **honey**
- 2 tablespoons **unsalted butter**
- ¼ to ⅓ cup **sour cream**
- 1 rounded tablespoon **prepared horseradish**
- ¼ to ½ cup **milk**, depending on how you like your mashers
- ¼ cup fresh **flat-leaf parsley** (a couple of handfuls), chopped

For the smashed potatoes, place the potatoes in a pot and cover with water. Cover the pot with a lid and bring the water to a boil. Salt the water and potatoes. Take off the lid and boil the potatoes until tender, 10 to 12 minutes.

While the potatoes are cooking, start the sausages. Heat a large skillet over medium-high heat with the EVOO. Add the sausage links and brown on all sides, about 4 minutes. Remove the sausages from the skillet and reserve.

To the skillet, add the onions, thyme, and garlic, and season with salt and pepper. Cook the onions, stirring frequently, until they begin to brown, about 5 minutes. Add the balsamic vinegar, chicken stock, and honey. Bring the liquid to a simmer, then add the browned sausages back to the pan and braise the sausages until they are cooked through and the sauce has reduced by half, 8 to 10 minutes.

While the sausages are braising, drain the potatoes and return them in the hot pot to the warm stovetop to dry them out. Add the butter, sour cream, horseradish, and milk to the potatoes and smash to the desired consistency. Season the potatoes with salt and pepper to taste. Divide the horseradish smashed potatoes among 4 serving dishes. Add the chopped parsley to the sausages, then top each serving of potatoes with 2 sausages and some of the braising liquid.

4 SERVINGS

TRY THIS LATER ☐

IT'S A KEEPER ☐

35 Sautéed Sweet Chicken Breasts
with a Spicy Fresh Tomato Chutney and White Rice

2 14-ounce cans **chicken broth**

3 tablespoons **extra-virgin olive oil** (EVOO), plus a drizzle

2 cups **white rice**

6 **plum tomatoes**, quartered

1 teaspoon **ground cumin** (eyeball it in the palm of your hand)

2 teaspoons **ground coriander** (twice the amount of cumin)

1 **serrano** or **jalapeño pepper**, half of the seeds removed, then finely chopped

2 **shallots**, thinly sliced

2 **garlic cloves**, chopped
   Salt and **freshly ground black pepper**

3 tablespoons **sherry vinegar** (eyeball it)

3 tablespoons **brown sugar**, packed

¼ cup fresh **cilantro** leaves (a couple of palmfuls), chopped

3 **scallions**, finely chopped

¼ cup fresh **flat-leaf parsley** (a couple of palmfuls), chopped

1 tablespoon **honey** (a healthy drizzle)

4 6-ounce boneless, skinless **chicken breast halves**

Bring the chicken broth and a drizzle of EVOO to a boil in a medium pot. Add the rice, reduce to a simmer, and cover. Cook the rice covered, stirring occasionally, for 17 to 18 minutes, or until tender. Fluff with a fork.

While the rice cooks, work on the spicy fresh tomato chutney. Heat a medium-size skillet over high heat with a tablespoon of the EVOO (once around the pan). Add the quartered plum tomatoes, cumin, coriander, serrano peppers, shallots, garlic, and salt and pepper. Cook the mixture, stirring frequently, for 3 minutes. Add the sherry vinegar, brown sugar, and 1 cup of water. Turn down the heat to medium low and simmer for 10 to 12 minutes, or until the water has evaporated and the tomatoes have broken down and are slightly thickened. While the chutney is cooking, prepare the chicken.

In a bowl, combine the remaining 2 tablespoons of EVOO, the cilantro, scallions, parsley, honey, and a little salt and pepper. Add the chicken breasts and toss to coat. Heat a nonstick skillet over medium-high heat. Add the seasoned chicken breasts and cook for 5 to 6 minutes on each side, or until cooked through. Remove the chicken breasts from the pan to a serving platter. Top each chicken breast with some of the spicy fresh tomato chutney. Serve with the white rice.

4 SERVINGS

BLT Pasta Bake: Bacon, Leeks, and Tomatoes

36

☐ TRY THIS LATER   ☐ IT'S A KEEPER

Serve as is or with a simple green salad.

    Coarse salt
1 pound **elbow macaroni** or cavatappi (corkscrew-shaped pasta)
1 tablespoon **extra-virgin olive oil** (EVOO)
8 slices **bacon**, coarsely chopped
2 large **leeks**, trimmed of roots and dark green tops
    Coarse black pepper
3 tablespoons **unsalted butter**
3 tablespoons all-purpose **flour** (3 palmfuls)
1/2 teaspoon **cayenne pepper**
1 teaspoon **paprika**
3 cups whole **milk**
1 cup **chicken stock** or broth
3 1/2 cups grated **Gruyère cheese**
1 tablespoon **Dijon mustard**
1 pint **cherry tomatoes**
3/4 cup **plain bread crumbs**

Place a pot of water on to boil for the pasta. When the water reaches a boil, add some salt and the pasta and cook until al dente.

While the pasta cooks, heat a large skillet over medium heat. Add the EVOO and chopped bacon and cook until crisp. While the bacon is cooking, split the trimmed leeks in half lengthwise, lay the leeks cut side down, and thinly slice into half-moons. Fill a large bowl with water and mix the leeks into the water. Allow the water to settle and the dirt and grit to settle on the bottom of the bowl. Using your hands, draw the leeks from the water, taking care to not unsettle the dirt. Drain the cleaned leeks on a kitchen towel, pat dry, and then add to the pan with the bacon. Season the leeks with salt and pepper. Cook the leeks until tender, about 3 to 4 minutes.

To start the cheese sauce, heat a medium sauce pot over medium heat. Add the butter and melt, then add the flour, cayenne, and paprika and whisk together over the heat until the roux bubbles; cook for 1 minute more. Whisk in the milk and stock and raise the heat a little. Bring the sauce to a quick boil and simmer to thicken, about 5 minutes. Remove the sauce from the heat and whisk in 3 cups of the grated cheese and the mustard. Set aside

Add the cherry tomatoes to the leeks and continue to cook for 2 minutes. Remove from the heat and reserve.

Preheat the broiler.

Drain the pasta and add it back to the pasta pot. Combine the reserved leek mixture and the cheese sauce with the pasta. Season with salt and pepper to taste.

Transfer the pasta to a baking dish. Combine the remaining 1/2 cup of grated cheese with the bread crumbs. Top the pasta with the mixture. Place the dish under the broiler until the cheese melts and the bread crumbs are brown.

4 SERVINGS

TRY THIS LATER

IT'S A KEEPER

37 MASTER RECIPE
Warm Lemon Chicken Sandwich
with Arugula and Pears

2 lemons

2 tablespoons fresh thyme leaves (from about 4 sprigs), stripped and chopped

Salt and freshly ground black pepper

4 boneless, skinless chicken breast halves

1 tablespoon Dijon mustard

2 tablespoons white wine vinegar (eyeball it)

5 tablespoons extra-virgin olive oil (EVOO)

3 tablespoons grated Parmigiano-Reggiano (a small handful)

4 kaiser rolls, split

1 garlic clove, crushed

1 ripe Bartlett, Anjou, or Bosc pear

8 slices prosciutto di Parma

1 large bunch of arugula, cleaned and trimmed (2 to 2½ cups)

In a shallow bowl, combine the juice of 1½ lemons, the thyme, salt, and pepper. Add the chicken breasts and toss to coat. Marinate the chicken for 5 to 10 minutes.

In a small bowl, combine the Dijon mustard with the vinegar, salt, and pepper. Whisk in 3 tablespoons of the EVOO, then the Parmigiano. Toast the rolls. Rub the toasted cut sides with the garlic clove.

Preheat a nonstick skillet over medium-high heat. Add the remaining 2 tablespoons of EVOO, twice around the pan. Cook the chicken for 5 to 6 minutes on each side. Remove to a cutting board and tent with foil.

Thinly slice the pear, and toss in a salad bowl with the juice of the remaining half lemon. Slice the prosciutto into strips. Add the arugula leaves and prosciutto to the salad bowl and toss with the vinaigrette.

Thinly slice the cooked chicken. Layer half of the chicken slices onto the rolls and top with the arugula-pear salad. Add the remaining chicken and roll tops.

4 SERVINGS

TRY THIS LATER

IT'S A KEEPER

38 NOW TRY... Grilled Flank Steak Sandwich
with Blue Cheese Vinaigrette–Dressed Arugula and Pears

SWAP

1½ pounds flank steak for the chicken

¼ cup crumbled blue cheese for the grated Parmigiano-Reggiano

Preheat a grill pan or outdoor grill on high.

Grill the steak for 6 to 7 minutes on each side. Remove to a plate and loosely tent with foil to let the juices redistribute before slicing.

Thinly slice the steak against the grain and on an angle. Prepare the dressing, adding the blue cheese after you whisk in the EVOO. Assemble the sandwiches.

4 SERVINGS

Pasta with Roasted Eggplant Sauce
and Ricotta Salata

I love this dish, Pasta alla Norma. Traditionally, it is made with 1 whole cup of EVOO and lots of chopped baby eggplant. It's good, but if you don't find just the right eggplant to use, the dish can be greasy and bitter. The recipe below is a take-off on Norma that includes all the same elements, but it is never bitter and uses much less oil (making Norma's figure a little better!).

- 2 small, firm eggplant, peeled and cut into 1-inch cubes
- ½ cup plus 2 tablespoons extra-virgin olive oil (EVOO)
  Salt and freshly ground black pepper
- 6 garlic cloves, cracked from the skins
- 1 pound penne rigate pasta
- 1 medium yellow onion, finely chopped
- 1 28-ounce can crushed San Marzano or other variety canned plum tomatoes
- 1 cup fresh basil leaves (25 to 30), shredded or torn
- 2 cups ricotta salata cheese, crumbled

Heat the oven to 425°F. Place a large pot of water on to boil.

Place the eggplant on a cookie sheet. Pour about ½ cup EVOO into a dish. Brush the eggplant lightly with the EVOO. Season the eggplant with salt and pepper. Add the garlic to the cookie sheet and dab it with EVOO as well. Roast for 20 minutes or until both the garlic and the eggplant are tender.

When the water comes to a boil, salt it liberally and add the pasta. Cook the pasta al dente, with a bite to it.

Preheat a large skillet over medium heat. Add the remaining 2 tablespoons of EVOO and the onions and cook for 5 minutes. Place the cooked eggplant and the garlic in a food processor and process it into a smooth paste. Add the eggplant paste to the cooked onions then stir in the crushed tomatoes. Season the sauce with salt and pepper. Toss with the drained hot pasta and the shredded or torn basil. Top the pasta with lots of crumbled ricotta salata.

4 SERVINGS

40 MASTER RECIPE
Mostly Green
Curry Chicken over Coconut Jasmine Rice

TRY THIS LATER

IT'S A KEEPER

1½ cups **chicken stock** or broth

1 13½-ounce can **coconut milk**

1 cup **jasmine rice**

3 tablespoons **vegetable** or **canola oil**

4 6- to 8-ounce boneless, skinless **chicken breast halves**, cut into bite-size pieces
Salt and **freshly ground black pepper**

1 **green bell pepper**, cored, seeded, and thinly sliced

1 medium **yellow onion**, thinly sliced

3 large **garlic cloves**, chopped

1 small **jalapeño pepper**, cut in half and seeded
3-inch piece of fresh **ginger**, peeled and finely grated

2 cups **broccoli florets**
Zest and juice of 1 **lime**

¼ cup fresh **cilantro** leaves (a handful), chopped

3 **scallions**, thinly sliced

½ cup fresh **flat-leaf parsley** leaves (a couple of handfuls), chopped

1 cup frozen **peas**
Hot sauce, such as Tabasco, to taste (optional)

In a sauce pot, combine 1 cup of the chicken stock, 4 ounces (¼ cup) of the coconut milk, and the jasmine rice. Bring to a simmer, cover, and cook for 15 to 18 minutes. Turn the heat off and keep the rice covered until ready to serve.

While the coconut jasmine rice is cooking, preheat a large nonstick skillet over high heat with about 2 tablespoons of the vegetable oil. Season the chicken pieces with salt and pepper. Add the chicken pieces, spreading them evenly across the pan, and brown the chicken on all sides, about 3 to 4 minutes. Remove the browned chicken to a plate and reserve. Add the last tablespoon of vegetable oil to the pan. Add the green bell peppers, onions, garlic, jalapeños, ginger, and broccoli florets. Cook, stirring frequently, for 3 to 4 minutes, or until the veggies start to wilt. To the skillet add the remaining coconut milk and ½ cup chicken stock. Bring the mixture to a boil, then reduce the heat and simmer for 4 to 5 minutes. Add the chicken back to the skillet, and return it to a simmer for about 2 more minutes. Add the lime juice, lime zest, cilantro, scallions, parsley, and frozen peas. Stir to thoroughly combine. Simmer a minute more to heat the peas, taste, and adjust the seasoning. Add more salt or some hot sauce, if you like heat. Serve over the coconut jasmine rice.

4 SERVINGS

NOW TRY... **Mostly Green Curry Veggies and Tofu**
over Coconut Jasmine Rice

41

TRY THIS LATER

IT'S A KEEPER

SWAP

1½ cups **vegetable stock** for the chicken stock or broth

1 14-ounce container **firm tofu**, cut into 1½- to 2-inch pieces, patted dry, for the chicken

Prepare the tofu in the same way as the chicken in the master recipe, #40, browning it thoroughly on both sides. Remove the browned tofu from the pan and reserve. Follow the master recipe instructions for the veggies and liquids. When you are ready to add the lime juice and zest, add the reserved tofu back to the pan to warm it through. Serve over the coconut jasmine rice.

4 SERVINGS

TIDBIT

Hold on there! Before you tell me you can't make this because your grocery store doesn't carry coconut milk, I have a solution ready for you! For the coconut milk, in a small pot combine 1½ cups sweetened shredded coconut with 1½ cups chicken stock and bring it to a simmer. When it is time for adding the coconut milk, add this mixture and simply omit the ½ cup of chicken stock that you would have added if you had coconut milk.

42 MASTER RECIPE
Cider Vinegar Chicken with Smashed Potatoes
and a Watercress and Cucumber Salad

This recipe is an ode to my friend Leslie Orlandini's Cider Vinegar Chicken, which I have only heard tell about. Hey, Les! You get an ode and I'm still sittin' over here, hunched over my computer, open-mouthed, waiting for a taste of the real deal! HINT!

2 to 2¼ pounds small **red-skinned potatoes**
   Coarse salt

6 tablespoons **extra-virgin olive oil** (EVOO)

4 6-ounce boneless, skinless **chicken breast halves**
   Coarse black pepper

2 medium **yellow onions**, thinly sliced

2 tablespoons fresh **thyme** leaves, from 4 sprigs (leaves stripped and chopped)

3 tablespoons **honey** (eyeball it)

3 large **garlic cloves**, chopped

½ cup plus 2 tablespoons **apple cider vinegar**

2 cups **chicken stock** or broth

½ cup **half-and-half** or cream (eyeball it)

3 tablespoons **unsalted butter**, cut into pieces

1 tablespoon **Dijon mustard**

2 bunches of **watercress**, cleaned and trimmed

½ seedless **cucumber**, cut in half lengthwise then sliced into half-moons

Cut the potatoes in half and place in a pot, then cover with water. Cover the pot with a lid and bring the water to a boil. Salt the water and potatoes. Leave the lid off the pot and cook at a rolling boil until tender, 10 to 12 minutes.

Preheat a large skillet over medium-high heat. Add 2 tablespoons of the EVOO (twice around the pan). Season the chicken with salt and pepper and add to the hot skillet. Brown the chicken on both sides, 3 minutes per side. Remove and reserve the meat, covered with foil. Add another tablespoon of the EVOO, the onions, thyme, honey—3 good drizzles—and the garlic. Season the onions with salt and pepper and cook, stirring frequently for 7 to 8 minutes. You want the onions to get really brown and caramelized. Add ½ cup of the cider vinegar and the stock. Turn up the heat to high and bring the liquids up to a simmer. Once at a simmer, return the chicken to the skillet. Cook the chicken in the sauce for about 10 minutes, flipping the chicken over halfway through the cooking time. While the chicken is cooking, prepare the salad and finish the smashed potatoes.

Drain the potatoes and return to the hot pot. Add the half-and-half and the butter to the potatoes and smash with a fork or potato masher to the desired consistency. Season the potatoes with salt and pepper. Reserve the potatoes on the cook top, covered to keep warm.

For the watercress salad, in a bowl combine the Dijon mustard, the remaining 2 tablespoons of cider vinegar (a good glug) and salt and pepper. In a slow, steady stream, whisk in the remaining 3 tablespoons of EVOO. Toss the watercress and sliced cucumbers with the dressing.

Arrange the chicken breasts on dinner or serving plates. Pour a generous amount of sauce with the onions over the chicken breasts. (You will really enjoy dipping a little of those smashed potatoes in the sauce!) Serve the watercress and cucumber salad on the side.

4 SERVINGS

· ·

NOW TRY... Chicken in Spicy and Sweet Onion Sauce with Goat Cheese Smashed Potatoes and a Watercress and Cucumber Salad

43

☐ TRY THIS LATER

☐ IT'S A KEEPER

SWAP

½ cup white wine for ½ cup of the cider vinegar (you'll still need 2 tablespoons)

ADD

1 to 1½ teaspoons crushed red pepper flakes
½ to ¾ cup crumbled goat cheese

Prepare the chicken as in the master recipe, #42, add the crushed red pepper flakes when you add the onions to the skillet. Continue with the recipe as before.

Prepare the salad and potatoes as in the master recipe, adding the goat cheese to the potatoes at the same time that you add the butter.

4 SERVINGS

44 Ricotta Smothered Mushroom "Burgers"
with Sweet Onion-Olive Topping, Prosciutto, and Arugula

TRY THIS LATER

IT'S A KEEPER

¼ cup balsamic vinegar (eyeball it)

4 tablespoons extra-virgin olive oil (EVOO)
Salt and freshly ground black pepper

4 large portobello mushroom caps

1 large red onion, thinly sliced

2 large garlic cloves, chopped

1 rounded tablespoon tomato paste

1½ cups whole-milk ricotta cheese

3 tablespoons store-bought pesto sauce

½ cup chicken stock or broth

⅓ cup (a couple of handfuls) pitted kalamata olives, chopped

4 crusty kaiser rolls, split in half, toasted or not—it's up to you

8 thin slices prosciutto di Parma (optional)

1 small bunch of arugula, washed and trimmed of any thick stems

Preheat the oven to 450°F.

In a shallow bowl, combine the balsamic vinegar, about 2 tablespoons of the EVOO, salt, and pepper. Add the portobello mushrooms and toss to coat. Arrange the mushrooms on a cookie sheet, gill side up. Roast the mushrooms for 12 minutes or until tender and cooked through. While the mushrooms are roasting, prepare the caramelized onion topping.

Heat a medium-size skillet over medium-high heat with the remaining 2 tablespoons of EVOO (twice around the pan). Add the sliced red onions, garlic, tomato paste, salt, and pepper. Cook the onions, stirring frequently, for about 8 minutes, or until nice and brown. While the onions are caramelizing, prepare the ricotta cheese topping for the mushrooms.

In a bowl, thoroughly combine the ricotta cheese and the pesto. Once the mushrooms have roasted for 12 minutes, remove them from the oven and divide the ricotta mixture evenly among the 4 mushrooms, spreading it onto the gill side of the mushrooms with the back of a spoon. Return to the oven for about a minute, just to heat the cheese.

Add the chicken stock and chopped olives to the onions. Turn the heat to high and continue to cook until the stock has reduced almost completely.

Arrange one cheese-topped mushroom on the bottom of each split roll. Top the cheese with some of the caramelized onions. Top that with 2 slices of prosciutto and some arugula. Finish it off with a roll top. Eat and enjoy!

4 SERVINGS

Sausage and Fennel Ragout with Creamy Polenta

45

2 tablespoons extra-virgin olive oil (EVOO) (twice around the pan)

1 pound bulk sweet Italian sausage

1 large red onion, thinly sliced

1 large fennel bulb, cut in half lengthwise, cored, and thinly sliced

4 garlic cloves, chopped

2 tablespoons fresh thyme leaves (4 sprigs, stripped and chopped)
Salt and freshly ground black pepper

1 quart chicken stock or broth

1 cup milk

¾ cup dry white wine

¼ cup fresh flat-leaf parsley leaves (a generous handful), chopped

1 cup quick-cooking polenta (found in Italian foods or specialty foods aisles)

2 tablespoons unsalted butter

½ cup grated Parmigiano-Reggiano (a couple of healthy handfuls), plus some for garnish

Heat a large nonstick skillet over medium-high heat. Add the EVOO. Add the sausage, breaking it up with the back of a wooden spoon, and cook until browned, 4 to 5 minutes. Add the red onions, fennel, garlic, thyme, salt, and pepper. Continue to cook, stirring frequently, for about 4 minutes, or until the veggies wilt and the onions become translucent. While the veggies are cooking, start the polenta.

In a sauce pot combine 2½ cups of the chicken stock and 1 cup of milk. Season the liquid with salt and pepper. Place over medium-high heat and bring up to a simmer.

Once the veggies have wilted, add the white wine and the remaining 1½ cups of chicken stock to the skillet. Turn the heat to high and bring up to a simmer. Cook to reduce the liquids by half, about 4 to 5 minutes. Stir in the chopped parsley.

To the simmering chicken stock and milk add the polenta and whisk constantly until the cornmeal masses together. It's so cool how fast this happens—right before your eyes! Add the butter and grated cheese, stirring to combine. Keep in mind that polenta is very forgiving; if it becomes too thick, you can always add more warm chicken stock or milk.

Serve the polenta in a shallow bowl and top with a helping of the sausage and fennel ragout. Garnish with more grated Parmigiano-Reggiano.

4 SERVINGS

TIDBIT

Buy stock or broth in aseptic boxes rather than cans. They might cost a little more, but the stocks especially have great slow-cooked flavor that really makes fast-cooked food taste rich. Plus, whatever you don't use can go directly into the refrigerator, without having to transfer it from a can. If I know I am not going to use my remaining stock within the next few days, I will transfer it to a resealable plastic bag and freeze it flat. (I have had a small revolution of freezer storage space since embracing the freezing of things flat.)

46 Prosciutto, Garlic, and Herb Cheese–Stuffed Chicken
with Tarragon Pan Sauce

TRY THIS LATER

IT'S A KEEPER

Serve with a green salad.

4   6-ounce boneless, skinless chicken breast
    halves
    Large plastic food storage bags or
    wax paper
4   slices prosciutto di Parma
4   ounces (½ cup) garlic and herb cheese,
    such as Boursin
    Toothpicks
3   tablespoons extra-virgin olive oil (EVOO)
    (3 turns around the pan)
    Salt and freshly ground black pepper
2   tablespoons unsalted butter
2   tablespoons all-purpose flour
½   cup white wine (a couple of glugs; eyeball it)
1   cup chicken stock or broth
2   tablespoons fresh tarragon leaves (3 stems,
    stripped and chopped)

Place a chicken breast in the center of a plastic food storage bag or 2 large sheets of wax paper. Pound out the chicken from the center of the bag outward using a heavy-bottomed skillet or mallet. Be firm but controlled with your strokes. Repeat with the 3 remaining chicken breasts.

Place one slice of prosciutto on top of each pounded chicken breast. Place a quarter of the garlic and herb cheese on top of each prosciutto slice. Wrap and roll the chicken over the stuffing. Secure the meat with toothpicks. Preheat a nonstick skillet over medium-high heat with the EVOO. Season the stuffed and rolled chicken breasts with salt and pepper. Add the breasts to the pan and brown on all sides, cooking for 10 to 12 minutes. The meat will cook quickly because it is thin. Remove the breasts; add the butter to the pan, then the flour. Cook for a minute, whisk in the wine, and reduce for another minute. Whisk in the stock and tarragon and return the chicken to the pan. Reduce the heat and simmer until ready to serve. Remove the toothpicks. Serve the chicken breasts whole or sliced.

4 SERVINGS

Couple-of-Minute Steaks and Potato Ragout

47

4 minute steaks or cube steaks

3 tablespoons Worcestershire sauce (eyeball it)
Freshly cracked black pepper

4 tablespoons extra-virgin olive oil (EVOO)

2 medium-size baking potatoes, scrubbed clean and cut into ¼-inch dice
Coarse salt

4 sprigs of thyme, leaves removed, chopped

1 sprig of rosemary, leaves removed, chopped

1 small yellow onion, finely chopped

3 large garlic cloves, chopped

½ cup dry white wine (eyeball it)

1 cup chicken stock or broth

½ pint cherry tomatoes, cut in half

½ cup fresh flat-leaf parsley leaves (a couple of handfuls), chopped

2 tablespoons cold unsalted butter

Season the minute steaks with the Worcestershire sauce and some pepper. Let the steaks hang out while you start the potato ragout.

Preheat a large nonstick skillet over medium-high heat with about 2 tablespoons of the EVOO (twice around the pan). Add the diced potatoes to the skillet and spread them out in an even layer. Season the potatoes with salt and pepper and let them brown for about 2 minutes, resisting the urge to shake or stir the pan. Once browned on one side, go ahead and give the skillet a stir and a shake. Then leave it be for another 2 minutes. Add the thyme, rosemary, onions, and garlic and cook, stirring frequently, until the onions start to look translucent, about 3 minutes. Add the white wine and chicken stock, bring the mixture up to a simmer, and cook until the potatoes are tender, 5 to 6 minutes more.

Once the potatoes are almost tender, preheat another large skillet over high heat with the remaining 2 tablespoons of EVOO for the minute steaks. Season the steaks with salt and then add to the hot skillet. Sear the steaks for 1 to 2 minutes on each side.

While the steaks are cooking, add the cherry tomatoes and parsley to the potatoes. Toss and stir to incorporate. Heat the tomatoes for about 1 minute. Turn the heat off and add the cold butter, stirring constantly until the butter has melted. Serve the minute steaks with the potato ragout.

4 SERVINGS

48 Sausage and Spinach Pastry Squares
with Cherry Tomato–Arugula Salad

- 4 tablespoons extra-virgin olive oil (EVOO)
- 1 pound bulk sweet Italian sausage
- 1 small yellow onion, finely chopped
- 6 leaves fresh sage, chopped
  Salt and freshly ground black pepper
- 2 sheets frozen puff pastry, defrosted
  (recommended brand: Pepperidge Farm)
  1 box comes with 2 $9\frac{1}{2}$ x $9\frac{1}{2}$-inch sheets
- 4 tablespoons Dijon or spicy brown mustard
- 1 10-ounce box frozen chopped spinach, defrosted
  Zest and juice of 1 lemon
- 1 cup grated Parmigiano-Reggiano (a few large handfuls)
- 1 pint cherry tomatoes, halved
- 2 tablespoons red wine vinegar (eyeball it)
- 1 large shallot, finely chopped
- $\frac{1}{4}$ cup fresh flat-leaf parsley leaves (a generous handful), chopped
- 2 bunches of arugula, cleaned and trimmed of thick stems (about 4 cups)

Preheat the oven to 400°F.

Heat a medium nonstick skillet over high heat with 2 tablespoons of the EVOO (twice around the pan). Add the sausage, breaking it up with the back of a spoon, ensuring all the big chunks become small ones. Add the onions, sage, salt, and pepper. Cook, stirring occasionally, until the sausage is browned, 4 to 5 minutes. Once the sausage is brown, remove the skillet from the heat and drain the excess fat.

Cut each of the 2 sheets of puff pastry into 2 equal rectangles. With a pastry brush, paint the Dijon mustard on the top of each piece of pastry. Refrigerate the mustard-painted pastry until the sausage is ready.

Arrange the defrosted chopped spinach in the center of a kitchen towel, wrap the towel around the spinach, and squeeze out the excess liquid. Put the spinach in a mixing bowl, add the lemon zest and Parmigiano, and season with salt and pepper. Add the sausage mixture to the spinach and incorporate well.

Arrange the pastry rectangles on a cookie sheet. Place a quarter of the sausage-spinach filling on the bottom half of each piece of pastry. Fold the pastry over the filling, gently tugging at the pastry to cover the filling. Using a fork, firmly crimp the edges. With a sharp knife cut two inch-long slits in the top of each pastry. Bake for 12 to 15 minutes, or until the pastry is golden brown. While the sausage and spinach squares are baking, prepare the cherry tomato–arugula salad.

In a salad bowl, combine the cherry tomatoes, salt, pepper, the remaining 2 tablespoons of EVOO, the red wine vinegar, lemon juice, chopped shallots, and parsley. With a fork, lightly crush some of the cherry tomatoes.

Once the sausage and spinach squares are cooked, add the arugula to the tomatoes, then toss to coat. Serve the sausage and spinach squares right on top of a generous helping of the tomato–arugula salad.

4 SERVINGS

Pasta with Swiss Chard, Bacon, and Lemony Ricotta Cheese

In this dish, the hot pasta is served atop a mound of lemon-flavored ricotta cheese. The heat from the pasta will warm the cheese and send the lemony scent straight to your nose.

Coarse salt
1 pound cellantani (ridged corkscrew-shaped pasta) or other ridged short-cut pasta
Freshly ground black pepper
2 tablespoons extra-virgin olive oil (EVOO) (twice around the pan)
5 slices bacon, coarsely chopped
3 or 4 garlic cloves, chopped
1 small yellow onion, chopped
½ teaspoon crushed red pepper flakes
1 bunch of Swiss chard, cleaned and coarsely chopped
1 cup chicken stock or broth
1 cup whole-milk ricotta cheese
Zest and juice of 1 lemon
1 cup grated Parmigiano-Reggiano (a few handfuls), plus some to pass at the table

Bring a large pot of water to a boil for the pasta. When the water comes to a boil, add salt and cook the pasta al dente.

While the pasta cooks, preheat a large, deep skillet over moderate heat. Add the EVOO and bacon and cook until the bacon crisps, about 3 minutes. To the bacon add the garlic, onions, salt, pepper, and crushed red pepper flakes and cook, stirring frequently, for 5 minutes, or until the onions are lightly caramelized. Add the chopped Swiss chard, toss to coat, and wilt the chard down. Turn the heat up to high and add the chicken stock and a couple of ladles, about a cup, of the starchy, boiling water from the cooking pasta. When the liquid comes up to a boil, reduce the heat and simmer for 6 to 7 minutes.

In a small bowl, combine the ricotta with the lemon zest and season with salt and pepper. Place ¼ cup of the ricotta mixture in the bottom of each of 4 pasta bowls and reserve.

Add the lemon juice to the Swiss chard. Drain the pasta well and toss with the greens for a minute or so to let the juices absorb into the pasta. Turn the heat off and add the grated Parmigiano cheese to the pasta and greens and continue to toss to distribute. Serve the pasta immediately, dishing it up on top of the ricotta cheese. Stir the lemony ricotta up in your bowl to mix with the pasta.

4 SERVINGS

50 MASTER RECIPE
Big, Thick, Hearty Thighs . . .
and That's a Compliment!

Serve with an arugula or spinach salad.

- 2 tablespoons extra-virgin olive oil (EVOO) (twice around the pan)
- 8 boneless, skinless chicken thighs
  Salt and freshly ground black pepper
- 1 small yellow onion, thinly sliced
- 5 garlic cloves, chopped
- 1 tablespoon fresh thyme leaves (from a couple of sprigs), chopped
- 1 cup dry white wine
- 3 cups chicken stock or broth
- 3 medium to small red bliss potatoes, cut in half and then thinly sliced
- 1 cup frozen peas
  Zest and juice of 1 lemon
- ¼ cup fresh flat-leaf parsley leaves (a generous handful), chopped
  Crusty bread, to pass at the table

Preheat a large skillet or wide soup pot over medium-high heat and add the EVOO. Season the chicken thighs liberally with salt and pepper. Add the chicken to the skillet and brown on both sides for 3 minutes. Scoot the browned thighs to the edges of the pan, making some space in the center of the skillet. Add the onions, garlic, thyme, salt, and pepper. Cook, stirring frequently, for 2 minutes.

Add the wine and chicken stock, turn the heat up to high, and bring the mixture up to a simmer. Add the potatoes and stir everything together. Cover the pan with a lid or a piece of aluminum foil and simmer for 10 minutes.

Remove the lid and continue to cook for another 5 minutes. Add the peas, lemon juice, lemon zest, and parsley, and cook for 1 more minute to just heat the peas through. Serve with crusty bread.

4 SERVINGS

---

51 NOW TRY... Big, Thick, Hearty Thighs Spanish Style

ADD

- ⅓ pound chorizo, casings removed, thinly sliced
- 1 (8-ounce) jar roasted red peppers, drained, or 1 large freshly roasted red bell pepper, chopped

Prepare as for the master recipe, #50, but when you are adding the onions and garlic to the pan, add the sliced chorizo. Add the chopped roasted red peppers when you are adding the peas to the pan.

4 SERVINGS

Chicken with Wild Mushroom and
Balsamic Cream Sauce

52

☐ TRY THIS LATER ☐ IT'S A KEEPER

Coarse salt

½ pound orzo pasta

2 tablespoons extra-virgin olive oil (EVOO) (twice around the pan)

4 6-ounce boneless, skinless chicken breast halves

Coarse black pepper

2 tablespoons unsalted butter

12 cremini (baby portobello) mushrooms, sliced

12 shiitake mushrooms, stems removed and sliced

12 white mushrooms, sliced

2 large garlic cloves, chopped

1 tablespoon fresh thyme leaves (from a couple of sprigs), chopped

2 large shallots, thinly sliced

2 tablespoons all-purpose flour

1½ cups chicken stock or broth

1 tablespoon balsamic vinegar (eyeball it)

3 tablespoons heavy cream or half-and-half (a couple times around the pan)

¼ cup fresh flat-leaf parsley leaves (a generous handful), chopped

Heat a large pot of water to a boil. Salt the water and add the orzo. Cook until al dente.

Preheat a large nonstick skillet over medium-high heat and add the EVOO. Season the chicken liberally with salt and pepper and add to the hot skillet. Cook the chicken for 5 to 6 minutes on each side. Remove the chicken from the pan and cover with foil to keep warm.

Return the skillet to the heat, reduce the heat a bit, and add the butter. Once the butter melts, add the mushrooms and cook, stirring occasionally, for about 4 to 5 minutes. Once the mushrooms are brown, season with salt and pepper, then add the garlic, thyme, and shallots. Cook, stirring occasionally, for about 2 minutes, or until the shallots are wilted. Sprinkle the flour into the pan and cook for 2 minutes more. Whisk in the stock, balsamic vinegar, and cream. Turn the heat up to high and simmer for about 2 minutes, or until thickened. Slice the chicken on an angle. Add the chicken back to the skillet to heat up with the parsley, about 1 minute.

To serve, pile the orzo on dinner plates and top with the sliced chicken and sauce.

4 SERVINGS

TRY THIS LATER

IT'S A KEEPER

53 MASTER RECIPE
Eggs-traordinary Stuffed Toasty Baskets
with Lemony Greens

This is a B-L-D meal: good for Breakfast, Lunch, or Dinner.

    4 tablespoons extra-virgin olive oil (EVOO)
    4 slices bacon, chopped
    1 garlic clove, chopped
  ½ small onion, chopped
  ¼ teaspoon crushed red pepper flakes
      Salt and freshly ground black pepper
    4 slices soft white sandwich bread
    3 tablespoons melted unsalted butter
    1 vine-ripe tomato, chopped
    4 eggs
      Grated Parmigiano-Reggiano, for sprinkling
    1 tablespoon Dijon mustard
      Juice of 1 lemon
    6 cups mixed greens

Preheat the oven to 400°F.

Preheat a small skillet over medium heat, add 1 tablespoon of the EVOO (once around the pan) and the chopped bacon, and cook for 3 minutes, or until the bacon is crisp. Add the garlic, onions, crushed red pepper flakes, salt, and pepper. Cook until the onions start to turn translucent, about 3 minutes.

With a serrated knife, cut the crusts from the bread. With your fingertips or a rolling pin, flatten or roll out each slice of bread as thin as you can get it. Nestle each thin slice of bread into the cup of a nonstick standard ½-cup muffin tin, pushing the bread down on the bottom of the tin and pushing it up the sides of the tin. The bread will reach the top of each tin and be slightly above the rim. If the bread breaks or tears, just smoosh it together a little, it will still be fine. (If you do not have a nonstick muffin tin, liberally brush your muffin tin with some additional melted butter, then proceed with nestling the bread in each buttered cup.) Brush the bread with the melted butter.

Add the tomatoes to the bacon and onions. Turn the heat up and toss around to evaporate some of the tomato liquid, about 1 minute.

Working one at a time, crack the eggs into a small bowl and then carefully transfer to the bread-lined muffin tins. The goal is to not break the yolk. Sprinkle each egg with a little salt and pepper. Top each egg with one quarter of the tomato-onion mixture and then sprinkle each one with a little grated cheese. Place in the hot oven and bake for 15 minutes.

In a small bowl, combine the mustard with the lemon juice, salt, and pepper. In a slow, steady stream, whisk in the remaining 3 tablespoons of EVOO. In a salad bowl, toss the lemon dressing with the mixed greens.

To serve, use a butter knife to nudge the cooked toast and eggs out from each tin and onto a plate. Serve with the lemon-dressed salad.

4 SERVINGS

NOW TRY... Eggs-traordinary Spanish-Style
Stuffed Toasty Baskets with Lemony Greens

54

☐ TRY THIS LATER ☐ IT'S A KEEPER

SWAP

1 link of chorizo, casing removed, finely diced, for the bacon

ADD

3 tablespoons chopped green olives with pimiento

Cook the chorizo the same way you would have the bacon in the master recipe, #53, stirring frequently for about 3 minutes.

Assemble the menu as directed, garnishing the egg baskets with the chopped olives.

4 SERVINGS

Halibut Soup

55

☐ TRY THIS LATER ☐ IT'S A KEEPER

Serve the soup in shallow bowls and pass crusty bread for mopping.

2 tablespoons extra-virgin olive oil (EVOO)
½ pound chorizo or andouille sausage
1 large yellow onion, chopped
1 medium carrot, peeled, cut in half lengthwise, then sliced into half-moons
1 poblano pepper, seeded and chopped
4 garlic cloves, chopped
   Salt and freshly ground black pepper
1 cup dry white wine (3 or 4 glugs)
1 quart chicken stock or broth
1 15-ounce can hominy
1½ pounds fresh halibut, cut into 2-inch chunks
1 medium zucchini, cut in half lengthwise, then sliced into half-moons
¼ cup fresh flat-leaf parsley leaves (a generous handful), chopped
2 tablespoons chopped fresh cilantro (optional)
   Juice of 1 lime

Preheat a large soup pot over medium-high heat with the EVOO (twice around the pan). Remove the sausage casings and slice the sausage thinly. Add the sliced sausage to the pot and cook, stirring frequently, for 2 minutes. Add the onions, carrots, poblanos, and garlic, season with salt and pepper, and cook, stirring frequently, for 5 minutes. Add the white wine and cook for 3 minutes. Add the chicken stock, bring up to a simmer, and cook for 5 minutes. You want the soup to be at a gentle simmer before you add the fish so, if necessary, turn the heat down a little. Add the hominy, halibut, and zucchini. Gently simmer for 5 minutes. Finish the soup with the parsley, cilantro (if using), and lime juice.

4 SERVINGS

56 Big Bird: Jumbo Chicken, Spinach, and Herb Burgers
with Mushrooms and Swiss

1   10-ounce box frozen chopped spinach, defrosted

2   pounds ground chicken breast

1   shallot, finely chopped

2   tablespoons Dijon mustard, plus some for slathering on the rolls

10 leaves of fresh basil, shredded or torn

3   tablespoons fresh flat-leaf parsley (a handful), chopped
    Salt and freshly ground black pepper

2   tablespoons extra-virgin olive oil (EVOO), plus some for drizzling

20 white button mushrooms, thinly sliced

2   garlic cloves, chopped

½   cup dry white wine or chicken stock

4   slices Swiss cheese, from the deli counter

4   kaiser rolls or sandwich-size sourdough English muffins, split and toasted

4   red or green leaf lettuce leaves

1   vine-ripe tomato, thinly sliced

Preheat a large nonstick skillet over medium-high heat.

Arrange the defrosted chopped spinach in the center of a kitchen towel. Wrap the towel around the spinach and squeeze out the excess liquid. Put the spinach in a mixing bowl and combine with the chicken, shallots, 2 tablespoons of Dijon mustard, basil, parsley, salt, and pepper. Score the meat with the side of your hand to separate into 4 equal portions. Make 4 large patties, ¾ to 1 inch thick. Drizzle the patties with oil and place them in the hot skillet. Cook for 6 to 7 minutes on each side, until the chicken is cooked through.

Preheat a second medium-size skillet over medium-high heat with 2 tablespoons of EVOO, twice around the pan. Add the sliced mushrooms and garlic and cook, stirring occasionally, for 4 to 5 minutes, or until the mushrooms are nice and brown. Season the 'shrooms with salt and pepper. Add the wine or broth and cook until the pan is almost dry, about 2 minutes.

Top the big-bird burgers with the mushroom topping and the Swiss cheese. Fold each slice of cheese in half to fit the burger, if necessary. Cover loosely with aluminum foil. Turn off the pan and let the cheese melt, about 2 minutes.

Slather the tops of the buns or English muffins with a little mustard. Place the burgers on the bun bottoms and top with lettuce and tomato. Put the bun or muffin tops in place.

4 SERVINGS

Turkey Cutlet Parmigiano
with Warm, Fresh Grape Tomato Topping, Pesto, and Mozzarella

☐ TRY THIS LATER ☐ IT'S A KEEPER

2 tablespoons olive oil (lighter than EVOO), plus some for shallow frying

1 medium yellow onion, finely chopped

3 garlic cloves, chopped
Salt and freshly ground black pepper

3 to 4 tablespoons all-purpose flour

2 eggs

1 cup Italian bread crumbs (3 overflowing handfuls)

½ cup grated Parmigiano-Reggiano (a couple of handfuls)

¼ cup fresh flat-leaf parsley leaves (a generous handful), chopped

2 pounds turkey breast cutlets

1 pint grape tomatoes, red or yellow or a mix

½ cup dry white wine or chicken stock

1 cup store-bought, good-quality pesto sauce (the refrigerated stuff)

1 large ball fresh mozzarella cheese, thinly sliced or grated

For the grape tomato topping, preheat a medium-size skillet over medium-high heat with the 2 tablespoons of olive oil. Add the onions, garlic, salt, and pepper. Cook until the onions are translucent, 2 to 3 minutes.

While the onions are cooking, set up the breading station for the turkey cutlets. Place the flour in a shallow dish. In another shallow dish, thoroughly beat together the eggs with a splash of water. In a third shallow dish, combine the bread crumbs, Parmigiano, and parsley. Heat a thin layer of olive oil in a large skillet, just enough to coat the bottom of the pan, over medium to medium-high heat. Season the cutlets with salt and pepper on both sides and turn lightly in the flour. Thoroughly coat the cutlets in the eggs and then in the breading, and add to the hot oil. Cook the cutlets in a single layer, in 2 batches if necessary, for 3 or 4 minutes on each side, until the juices run clear and the breading is evenly browned. Remove the cooked cutlets to a plate lined with a paper towel.

To the skillet with the onions, add the grape tomatoes and white wine or stock. Cook, stirring occasionally, until the tomatoes start to burst and the wine has reduced by half.

Preheat the broiler.

Arrange the cooked cutlets on a cookie sheet. Top each cutlet with a little of the warm fresh grape tomato topping, top that with a little pesto, then top that with 2 slices of mozzarella cheese. Place the cookie sheet under the broiler and broil until the cheese warms and melts but has not browned. Serve immediately.

4 SERVINGS

58 Chicken with Sweet Raisins and Apricots
on Toasted Almond Couscous

3 tablespoons extra-virgin olive oil (EVOO)

4 6-ounce boneless, skinless chicken breast halves

Salt and freshly ground black pepper

1 tablespoon fresh thyme leaves (from a couple of sprigs), chopped

½ cup sliced almonds (2 2-ounce packages from the baking aisle of the market)

3½ cups chicken stock or broth, divided

1½ cups plain couscous

3 tablespoons chopped fresh flat-leaf parsley (a generous handful)

2 tablespoons unsalted butter

3 large shallots, thinly sliced

2 tablespoons all-purpose flour

12 dried, pitted apricots, halved

1 cup golden raisins

2 tablespoons cider or white wine vinegar (eyeball it)

Preheat a large nonstick skillet over medium-high heat. Add 2 tablespoons of the EVOO (twice around the pan). Season the chicken breasts with salt, pepper, and chopped thyme. Add the chicken to the hot skillet and cook on each side for 5 to 6 minutes.

Toast the nuts in the bottom of a medium sauce pot over medium heat until golden. Transfer the toasted nuts to a dish and reserve. Return the pot to the stovetop. Add 1½ cups of the chicken stock and the remaining tablespoon of EVOO, cover the pot, and raise the heat; bring the broth to a boil. Remove the pot from the heat. Add the couscous and parsley to the stock, then stir. Cover and let the couscous stand for 5 minutes. Fluff the cooked couscous with a fork and toss with the toasted almonds. Cover to keep it warm while you make the sauce for the chicken.

Remove the chicken from the skillet to a plate and cover with foil. Return the skillet to the heat and add the butter and shallots. Cook for about 2 minutes. Dust with the flour and continue to cook for 1 minute. Add the apricots, golden raisins, and cider vinegar. Whisk in the remaining 2 cups of chicken stock and turn the heat up to high. Simmer the mixture until thick. Add the chicken back to the skillet, coat in the sauce, and heat the chicken, about 1 minute. Serve the chicken and some sauce over the almond couscous.

4 SERVINGS

Chicken in a Horseradish Pan Sauce
over Orange and Herb Couscous

59

☐ TRY THIS LATER ☐ IT'S A KEEPER

- 3 tablespoons extra-virgin olive oil (EVOO)
- 4 6-ounce boneless, skinless chicken breast halves
  Salt and freshly ground black pepper
- 2¼ cups chicken stock or broth
- 1½ cups plain couscous
  Zest of 1 navel orange
- 3 tablespoons chopped fresh flat-leaf parsley (a handful)
- 1 medium yellow onion, finely chopped
- 2 tablespoons prepared horseradish
- 1 tablespoon fresh thyme leaves (from a couple of sprigs), chopped
- 1 tablespoon Dijon mustard
- ½ cup half-and-half

Preheat a large nonstick skillet with 2 tablespoons of the EVOO (twice around the pan) over medium-high heat. Season the chicken breasts with salt and pepper. Add the chicken to the hot skillet and cook for 5 to 6 minutes per side.

While the chicken is cooking, in a sauce pot combine 1½ cups of the chicken stock and the remaining EVOO, about 1 tablespoon. Cover the pot and raise the heat; bring the stock to a boil. Remove the pot from the heat, add the couscous, orange zest, and parsley, then stir. Cover and let the couscous stand for 5 minutes.

Remove the chicken from the skillet to a plate and tent with foil to keep warm. Return the skillet to the heat and add the onions, horseradish, and thyme. Cook, stirring frequently, for about 3 minutes. Add the mustard, about ¾ cup of the remaining chicken stock, and the half-and-half. Bring up to a simmer, and simmer until the liquids have reduced by half, 3 to 4 minutes. Return the chicken to the skillet to heat, about 1 minute.

Fluff the cooked couscous with a fork. Divide the couscous among 4 dinner plates, then top each portion with a chicken breast and some of the horseradish pan sauce.

4 SERVINGS

TRY THIS LATER   IT'S A KEEPER

60 MASTER RECIPE
Balsamic-Glazed Pork Chops
with Arugula-Basil Rice Pilaf

3   tablespoons cold unsalted butter
1   6-ounce box rice pilaf mix, such as Near East brand
3   tablespoons extra-virgin olive oil (EVOO)
4   1-inch-thick center-cut pork loin chops
    Salt and freshly ground black pepper
1   small onion, chopped
1   tablespoon fresh thyme leaves (from a couple of sprigs), chopped
1   sprig of fresh rosemary, chopped
3   garlic cloves, chopped
¼   cup balsamic vinegar (eyeball it)
2   tablespoons honey
1   cup chicken stock or broth
2   cups trimmed and chopped arugula (from 1 bunch)
15 to 20 fresh basil leaves, shredded or torn

In a medium pot over high heat, combine 1 tablespoon of the butter and 1¾ cups water. Cover and bring to a simmer. Add the rice and flavor packet to the water. Stir to combine, reduce the heat, and cook for 18 minutes, covered.

While the rice is cooking, heat a large skillet over medium-high heat for the chops. Add 2 tablespoons of the EVOO (twice around the pan). Season the chops with salt and pepper, then add to the hot skillet. Cook the chops for 5 minutes on each side.

Transfer the chops to a platter and cover with foil. Return the pan to the heat and add the remaining tablespoon of EVOO and the onions, thyme, rosemary, and garlic, then sauté for 4 to 5 minutes. Add the balsamic vinegar, honey, and chicken stock. Cook until the liquids have reduced by half.

While the glaze is reducing, finish the rice pilaf. Add the arugula and basil to the cooked rice, stirring with a fork to fluff the rice and combine the greens at the same time.

Once the balsamic glaze has reduced by half, turn off the heat and add the remaining 2 tablespoons of cold butter. Stir and shake the pan until the butter melts. Add the chops to the pan and coat them in the balsamic glaze. Serve the glazed chops alongside the arugula-basil rice pilaf.

4 SERVINGS

TIDBIT

The chicken with tomato, basil, and smoked mozzarella can be served cold as well, making this dish perfect for lunch or dinner buffet entertaining.

NOW TRY... Balsamic-Glazed Chicken
with Smoked Mozzarella and Garlic Rice Pilaf

SWAP

4 6-ounce chicken breast halves for the pork chops

ADD

2 minced garlic cloves
2 vine-ripe tomatoes, sliced
8 thin slices fresh smoked mozzarella, cut from a 1-pound ball
Extra EVOO, for drizzling

OMIT

Arugula

Do not chop or tear all the basil. Keep 8 leaves whole, then shred or tear the rest.

Prepare just as for the master recipe, #60, but when you start the rice, melt the butter in the saucepan and sauté the minced garlic for a minute or so, before adding the water. Finish as before.

Prepare the chicken exactly as you would the pork, giving an extra minute on each side. After you've glazed the chicken breasts top with alternating layers of tomato, whole basil, and smoked mozzarella, using 2 slices of each per breast. Drizzle EVOO over the tomato, basil, and cheese and season with salt and pepper.

4 SERVINGS

- -

OR TRY... Balsamic-Glazed Swordfish
with Capers and Grape Tomato–Arugula Rice

SWAP

4 1-inch-thick swordfish steaks for the pork chops

ADD

2 minced garlic cloves
$\frac{1}{2}$ pint grape tomatoes, red or yellow, halved
3 tablespoons capers, drained and coarsely chopped
2 to 3 tablespoons chopped fresh flat-leaf parsley (a handful)

Prepare just as for the master recipe, #60, but when you begin the rice, melt the butter in the saucepan, sauté the garlic for 1 minute before adding the water. Cook as directed. Add the grape tomatoes to the rice when tossing the rice with the arugula and basil.

Cook the swordfish as you would the chops but cook for 1 minute *less* on each side. When you remove the sauce from the heat and add the butter, add the capers and parsley, too.

4 SERVINGS

63 Lion's Head
(Pork Meatballs and Napa Cabbage)

The wonderful actress Ming Na taught me this recipe. It was handed down to her from her parents, who owned a successful Chinese restaurant for twenty-five years. It's not fair! Ming Na is gorgeous and talented *and* she can cook, too! But, we can console ourselves with these Chinese meatballs. The chopped cabbage is served in a pile, the meatballs in the middle: a head surrounded by a mane . . . a lion's head.

Ming uses mushroom-flavored thick soy sauce. I cannot find that product where I live, so I use finely chopped shiitakes and aged soy sauce.

　　　Coarse salt
　1　cup short-grain white rice
　　　Vegetable oil, for drizzling and frying
　½　pound shiitake mushrooms, stems removed and finely chopped
　6　garlic cloves, finely chopped
　2　pounds ground pork
　⅓　cup tamari (dark aged soy sauce found on the international aisle), plus more for serving
　1　egg, lightly beaten
　½　cup plus 1 tablespoon cornstarch
　1　teaspoon finely ground black pepper
　1　cup chicken stock or broth
　1　medium to large head of Napa cabbage, cut into large dice

Bring 2 cups of water to a boil. Add salt and the rice. When the water returns to a boil, reduce the heat to a simmer and cover the pot. Simmer for 20 minutes, or until the water is absorbed. Set aside.

Drizzle some oil in a small nonstick skillet preheated to medium-high heat, then cook the mushrooms and garlic for 3 to 4 minutes. Season with a little salt. Remove from the pan and cool for 5 minutes.

Pour 2 inches of the oil in the bottom of a large wok or wok-shaped skillet and heat over high heat.

Place the pork in a bowl. Add the mushrooms and garlic. Add the tamari, the egg, a few spoonfuls of the cornstarch, and the pepper. Use a pair of chopsticks to mix the meat, stirring only in one direction until combined. The mixture will be wet. Place all but one tablespoon of the remaining cornstarch on a plate. Form 10 to 12 large, soft meatballs and dust them lightly but evenly in the cornstarch.

When the oil smokes, add the balls and flash-fry them for 2 minutes on each side, or until deep golden in color. Drain the balls on paper towels.

In a deep pot heat the chicken stock to a bubble. Add half of the cabbage, then layer in all of the balls and the remaining cabbage. The pot should be filled to the top. Place a lid on the pot and simmer for 10 minutes. The cabbage will cook down and add to the broth. Remove a ladleful of broth to a small bowl and dissolve a tablespoon of cornstarch in it, then return it to the pot. Simmer with the lid off for a minute or two to thicken the broth. Serve with the rice and extra tamari.

4 SERVINGS

Whole Fish with Ginger and Scallions

Thanks again, Ming Na!

> Coarse salt
> 1 cup short-grain white rice
> 2 whole cleaned fish such as red snapper or small sea bass, each 1½ to 2 pounds
> 1 3-inch piece of fresh ginger, peeled and cut into matchsticks
> ½ cup vegetable oil (eyeball it)
> 1 bunch of scallions, cut into 3-inch pieces then thinly shredded into thin sticks
> ¼ to ⅓ cup tamari (dark aged soy sauce, found on the international aisle)

Bring 2 cups of water to a boil. Add salt and the rice. When the water returns to a boil, reduce the heat to a simmer and cover the pot. Simmer for 20 minutes, or until the water is absorbed. Set aside.

Place a steamer rack in a wok over a few inches of water. To make your own steamer, place a few inches of water in a deep skillet. Set a small bowl, inverted, into the water and use it as a pedestal. Bring the water to a boil and reduce the heat to a simmer.

Clean the fish under running water, making sure the inside cavity is completely clean. Cut off any fins left on the fish. Score the skin with a sharp knife, making 3 or 4 cuts into the skin along the side of the fish. Pat the fish dry inside and out and place half of the ginger in the cavity of each fish. Arrange the 2 fish on a plate and set the plate on the steamer rack or on top of the inverted bowl. Cover the pan and steam the fish until opaque and white, about 10 to 12 minutes for 2 whole fish, 8 to 10 for 1 fish. The ginger flavor will permeate the fish as it cooks. Remove the fish to a heat-proof platter.

Heat the oil in a small pot until it smokes.

Top the cooked fish with piles of shredded scallions. Pour a few tablespoons of tamari over the fish and scallions, then carefully drizzle on the hot oil. It will crackle and sizzle as it hits the scallions and the skin of the fish.

Carefully lift the fish off of the bones and serve the meat with the white rice.

4 SERVINGS

65 MASTER RECIPE
Uptown Down-Home Chili

3 tablespoons **extra-virgin olive oil** (EVOO)

2 pounds **ground sirloin**

2 tablespoons **grill seasoning**, such as McCormick's Montreal Steak Seasoning (2 palmfuls)

½ pound **baby portobello mushrooms**, chopped

¼ pound **shiitake mushroom caps**, sliced

1 medium **yellow onion**, chopped

3 **celery ribs**, chopped

1 large **red bell pepper**, cored, seeded, and chopped

4 to 6 **garlic cloves**, chopped

2 tablespoons **Worcestershire sauce**

2 canned **chipotle peppers in adobo**, chopped, with their juices, or 1 generous palmful ground chipotle chili powder (about 2 tablespoons)

1 tablespoon **ground cumin** (a palmful)

1 bottle **imported beer**, such as Stella Artois (imported just 'cause we're Uptown and that's all they drink here)

1 15-ounce can **black beans**, drained

1 15-ounce can **crushed tomatoes**

1 cup **beef stock** or broth

2 to 3 tablespoons fresh **thyme** leaves
8-ounce piece of **smoked Gouda**, shredded

1 small **white onion**, finely chopped

Heat a deep, large skillet or a pot over high heat. Add 2 tablespoons of the EVOO (twice around the pan) and the meat. Season it with the grill seasoning and sear it, browning and crumbling it, for 3 to 5 minutes. Transfer the meat to a plate and return the pot to the stove.

Reduce the heat to medium high and add the remaining tablespoon of EVOO. Add the mushrooms and begin to brown them before adding the other veggies. After 2 or 3 minutes the mushrooms will begin to shrink and soften. Push the mushrooms off to one side of the pot and add all the remaining veggies to the opposite side of the pot. Once the onions, celery, bell peppers, and garlic have been working for a few minutes, mix the veggies with the mushrooms. Return the meat to the pan, and season with the Worcestershire sauce, chipotle, and cumin. Add the beer to deglaze the pot, scraping up all the pan drippings. Reduce the beer by half, 2 minutes. Add the black beans, tomatoes, stock, and thyme to the chili and simmer for 10 minutes to let the flavors combine. Taste to adjust the seasonings. Top bowlfuls of the chili with shredded smoked Gouda and finely chopped raw onions.

4 SERVINGS

OMIT

Black beans

SWAP

Ground chicken for the ground sirloin
Chicken stock for the beef stock

ADD

1 pound cavatappi (corkscrew-shaped pasta)
or ridged macaroni
1 8-ounce sack shredded Cheddar cheese
A handful of cilantro, finely chopped

Preheat the broiler.

Prepare just as for the master recipe, #65, adding the chicken and chicken stock when you would the beef and beef stock. Omit the beans.

While the chili cooks, cook the pasta al dente, then drain and return it to the hot pot. Add the chili to the pasta and stir. Pour the chili-mac into a casserole dish and top with a mixture of smoked Gouda and Cheddar. Melt the cheeses under a hot broiler 6 inches from the heat until golden. Garnish the dish with finely chopped raw onions and chopped cilantro.

4 SERVINGS

TRY THIS LATER ☐   IT'S A KEEPER ☐

67 Sirloin Burgers with Gorgonzola Cheese
and Mediterranean Slaw

DRESSING

1 garlic clove, popped from its skin

4 ounces (½ cup) feta cheese crumbles
or ½ cup full-fat yogurt

¼ cup extra-virgin olive oil (EVOO) (pour to a
count of 4)
Juice of ½ lemon

2 teaspoons sugar

SALAD

3 heads of radicchio, shredded

½ medium red onion, thinly sliced

3 to 4 tablespoons chopped fresh dill
Coarse salt

1 teaspoon poppy seeds

2 teaspoons sesame seeds

BURGERS

1½ pounds ground sirloin

½ small yellow or white onion

1 teaspoon coarse salt (eyeball it in your palm)

2 teaspoons coarse black pepper (eyeball it)

3 to 4 tablespoons (4 or 5 leaves) fresh sage,
finely chopped
EVOO, for drizzling

¼ cup balsamic vinegar, aged 6 years or more

8 ounces Gorgonzola cheese

4 crusty sesame seed rolls, split

2 cups arugula or watercress leaves, stripped
from stems

In a food processor, combine the 5 ingredients for the dressing with a splash of water and process until smooth.

In a bowl, combine the radicchio, red onions, and dill. Coat the salad with the dressing and taste, adding salt if necessary. Top the slaw with the poppy and sesame seeds. Set aside while you prepare the burgers.

Preheat a nonstick skillet over medium-high heat. Place the sirloin in a bowl and hold a hand grater over the bowl. Grate the onion over the meat. Add the salt, pepper, and sage to the bowl. Drizzle the EVOO over the meat and mix gently. Do not overmix the meat or the burgers will be tough.

Pile the burger mix together in a flattened mound. Score the mound with the side of your hand into 4 equal quadrants so your patties will be uniform in size. Form 4 patties about 1 inch thick. Add the burgers to the pan and cook for 5 minutes on the first side, 2 minutes on the flip side. Add the vinegar to the skillet and turn the burgers as it cooks off, about 1 minute.

Turn off the heat and pile one quarter of the Gorgonzola cheese onto each burger. Tent the pan with foil and let the burgers stand for 4 to 5 minutes to melt the soft cheese and continue cooking the burgers with carryover heat. This will give you a medium cooked burger, still pink at the center. Add 2 minutes to the initial cook time for medium well to well done.

Place the burgers on the bottoms of the split buns and top with the arugula. Set the bun tops in the skillet to soak up any pan drippings, then set them in place atop the burgers. Serve with the slaw.

4 SERVINGS

Chicken Cacciatore Stoup

Stoup is what I call a meal that serves up thicker than a soup yet thinner than a stew. This hearty hunter's chicken stoup is a family favorite of ours, especially on chilly nights.

- 3 tablespoons extra-virgin olive oil (EVOO)
- 3 boneless, skinless chicken breasts (1 to 1⅓ pounds), diced
- 2 teaspoons grill seasoning or coarse salt and black pepper
- 1 teaspoon crushed red pepper flakes
- 2 large white potatoes, peeled and cut into 1-inch cubes
- 8 cremini (baby portobello) mushrooms, chopped
- 4 celery ribs from the heart, chopped
- 1 medium onion, peeled and quartered lengthwise, then thinly sliced
- 1 red bell pepper, cored, seeded, and quartered lengthwise, then thinly sliced
- 4 garlic cloves, chopped
- ½ cup dry Italian red wine (eyeball it)
- 1 15-ounce can diced tomatoes
- 1 28-ounce can crushed tomatoes
- 2 cups chicken stock or broth
- 3 tablespoons fresh rosemary, finely chopped (from 3 or 4 sprigs)
- 1 cup fresh basil, arugula, or baby spinach leaves—your choice, shredded or torn
  Grated Parmigiano-Reggiano or Romano cheese, to pass at the table
  Crusty bread, to pass at the table

Heat a deep skillet or a medium soup pot over medium-high heat. Add 2 tablespoons of the EVOO (twice around the pan) then add the chicken. Season with the grill seasoning and cook until evenly and lightly browned all over, 3 or 4 minutes.

While the chicken cooks, chop up the veggies.

Remove the cooked chicken to a plate and reserve. Add the remaining tablespoon of EVOO to the pan. Add the crushed red pepper flakes and potatoes. Cook for a couple of minutes, then add the mushrooms, celery, and onions and cook for another couple of minutes. Add the bell peppers and garlic and cook for another minute or two. Add the chicken back to the pan and toss it with the vegetables. Add the red wine to deglaze the pan, picking up any drippings. Add the tomatoes and stock to the stoup and stir to combine. Stir in the rosemary and reduce the heat to low. Cover and cook for 8 to 10 minutes.

Turn off the stoup and ladle it into shallow bowls. Top with basil, for a sweet finish and to balance the spice in the stoup; top with arugula for a peppery finish; or add spinach for a woodsy finish. At the table, pass grated cheese for sprinkling on top of the stoup and bread for mopping up the bowl.

4 SERVINGS

69 Garlic and Mint Lamb or Chicken Patties
on Lentil Salad

SALAD

Coarse salt
1 cup dried lentils
1 garlic clove, finely chopped
1 large shallot, finely chopped
2 teaspoons fresh lemon juice
2 tablespoons sherry vinegar or red wine vinegar (eyeball it)
1 teaspoon ground cumin (eyeball it in the palm of your hand)
3 tablespoons extra-virgin olive oil (EVOO) (eyeball it)
6 radishes, chopped
¼ cup chopped fresh flat-leaf parsley (a couple of handfuls)
Coarse black pepper, to taste

PATTIES

1½ pounds ground lamb or ground chicken
1 small yellow or white onion, finely chopped
2 tablespoons grill seasoning, such as McCormick's Montreal Steak Seasoning (2 palmfuls)
2 teaspoons ground cumin (eyeball it in the palm of your hand)
¼ cup chopped fresh mint leaves (a couple of handfuls)
¼ cup chopped fresh flat-leaf parsley (a couple of handfuls)
EVOO, for drizzling
4 flat breads or pita breads, plain or flavored, warm

Bring 2 inches of water to a boil and salt it. Add the lentils and cook for 22 minutes, or until tender. Drain the lentils. While the lentils cook, combine the garlic and shallots with the lemon juice and vinegar in a bowl and let stand for 10 minutes. Add the cumin and EVOO, then add the lentils, radishes, and parsley. Toss to dress the salad. Add the black pepper. Adjust the salt and pepper and reserve until ready to serve.

Preheat a nonstick skillet over medium-high heat.

While the lentils work, in a bowl, combine the ground lamb or chicken with the chopped onions, grill seasoning, cumin, mint, and parsley. Drizzle the meat with EVOO and mound the mixture together, then score it with your hand to divide the meat evenly. Form 8 small patties, 1 inch thick and 2 or 3 inches across, and add the patties to the hot skillet. Cook the mini lamb patties for 2 minutes on each side for medium doneness, 4 minutes on each side for fully cooked chicken patties.

Serve a mound of salad with 2 patties and 1 warm flat bread or pita per serving.

4 SERVINGS

Sardine and Bread Crumb Pasta
with Puttanesca Salad

1 pound linguine, fresh or dried, cooked al dente in salted water

4 vine-ripe tomatoes, seeded and chopped

½ red onion, chopped

3 tablespoons capers

½ cup kalamata olives, pitted and coarsely chopped

6 anchovies (1 tin of flat fillets), chopped

¾ cup fresh flat-leaf parsley tops (4 or 5 handfuls), divided; half coarsely chopped, half finely chopped
Juice of ½ lemon

¼ cup plus 3 tablespoons extra-virgin olive oil (EVOO), plus more for drizzling

12 to 15 fresh basil leaves, cut or torn into a chiffonade
Coarse salt and coarse black pepper, to taste

8 garlic cloves, chopped

1½ cups bread crumbs

2 4-ounce tins of sardines, drained and chopped

1 teaspoon crushed red pepper flakes

Bring a large pot of salted water to a boil. When the water boils, add the linguine and cook just until al dente. Drain well.

Combine the tomatoes, onions, capers, olives, anchovies, and the coarsely chopped parsley in a medium bowl. Dress with the lemon juice and a healthy drizzle of EVOO—enough to lightly coat the salad (1 to 2 tablespoons). Sprinkle in the basil and salt and pepper, toss again, and adjust the seasonings.

Preheat a large, deep skillet over medium heat. To the hot pan, add the ¼ cup of EVOO (4 times around the pan), and half the chopped garlic cloves. When the garlic speaks by sizzling in the oil, add the bread crumbs. Stir the bread crumbs until they are deeply golden in color. Add the finely chopped parsley and a liberal amount of salt and coarse black pepper. Transfer the bread crumbs to a dish and reserve.

Return the same skillet to the heat and add the 3 tablespoons of EVOO, 3 times around the pan. Add the remaining garlic, the sardines, and red pepper flakes to the pan and sauté over medium heat for 2 or 3 minutes. Add the hot, cooked pasta to the skillet and toss with the sardines. Add the bread crumbs to the pot and toss thoroughly to combine and evenly distribute the mixture. Taste to adjust seasonings and serve with the puttanesca salad alongside.

4 SERVINGS

71 MASTER RECIPE
BBQ Sloppy Chicken Pan Pizza

2 boxes corn muffin mix, such as Jiffy brand, 8½ ounces each

2 eggs

4 tablespoons unsalted butter, melted

1½ cups milk

1 cup frozen corn kernels

Extra-virgin olive oil (EVOO), for the pan

TOPPING

2 tablespoons EVOO (twice around the pan)

1 pound ground chicken breast

3 garlic cloves, crushed from their skins and chopped

1 medium yellow onion, chopped

1 small red bell pepper, cored, seeded, and chopped

Coarse salt and coarse black pepper

1 tablespoon chili powder (eyeball it in your palm)

1½ teaspoons ground cumin (half as much as chili powder)

2 teaspoons hot sauce, such as Tabasco

1 tablespoon Worcestershire sauce (eyeball the amount)

1 cup tomato sauce

3 tablespoons dark brown sugar

1 sack (10 ounces) shredded Cheddar cheese

3 scallions, chopped

2 to 3 tablespoons chopped fresh flat-leaf parsley or cilantro, your preference

Preheat the oven to 400°F.

In a large bowl, combine the 2 packages of corn muffin mix with the eggs, melted butter, and milk. Stir in the corn. Drizzle some EVOO into a large nonstick skillet with an oven-safe handle and wipe it around the pan with a folded paper towel. (Wrap the handle in a double layer of foil if it has a plastic or rubber handle.) Pour in the batter, place the pan in the center of the preheated oven, and bake until the cornbread becomes light golden in color, 12 to 15 minutes.

Place a second skillet over medium-high heat and add the 2 tablespoons of EVOO. Add the chicken and break it up with a wooden spoon. Once the chicken has crumbled and begins to brown, add the garlic, onions, and bell peppers and season with salt and pepper, chili powder, cumin, and hot sauce. Cook for 5 minutes, then add the Worcestershire, tomato sauce, and brown sugar. Stir to combine and reduce the heat to low. Simmer until the cornbread sets up and begins to brown. Adjust the seasonings to taste.

Remove the cornbread from the oven and cover it with the sloppy chicken mixture, then sprinkle with the cheese. Put the pan back in the hot oven and cook for 5 minutes longer to set the toppings and melt the cheese. Top with the scallions and chopped parsley or cilantro and serve from the skillet, cutting the pizza into 8 wedges.

4 SERVINGS, 2 SLICES EACH

NOW TRY... Fajita Beef Pie

Fajitas are fun, but a lot of work at the table. This recipe switches up a cornbread crust for the flour tortilla and ground beef for the usual sliced steak. Reinvent a fun food, tonight, with Fajita Beef Pie!

OMIT

Tomato sauce

SWAP

Ground sirloin for the ground chicken
8 ounces shredded jalapeño Pepper Jack cheese for the Cheddar cheese

ADD

½ bottle Mexican beer
2 to 3 tablespoons fresh thyme leaves (from 5 to 6 sprigs), chopped

Follow the instructions for the master recipe, #71, swapping beef for the chicken. When you would add the tomato sauce, add the beer and cook it off, 2 minutes. Stir in the fresh thyme. Taste and adjust the seasonings. Sprinkle on the Pepper Jack as you would the Cheddar. Delish!

4 SERVINGS

Spicy Shrimp and Bok Choy Noodle Bowl

3 tablespoons vegetable oil (3 times around the pan)
2 teaspoons crushed red pepper or chili flakes
4 garlic cloves, chopped
2-inch piece of fresh ginger, peeled and cut into very thin matchsticks or grated
½ pound shiitake mushroom caps, sliced (a couple of cups)
1 medium bok choy, trimmed and cut into 3-inch pieces, then cut lengthwise into sticks
Salt and freshly ground black pepper
1 quart chicken stock or broth
1 cup seafood stock or clam juice (available on soup aisle)
1½ pounds medium peeled and deveined shrimp

½ pound vermicelli (thin spaghetti)
4 scallions, cut into 3-inch pieces, then sliced lengthwise into thin sticks

Heat a medium soup pot over medium-high heat. Add the vegetable oil, crushed red pepper flakes, garlic, ginger, mushrooms, and bok choy, then season with salt and pepper. Add the chicken stock and seafood stock. Put a lid on the pot and bring the soup to a boil. Add the shrimp and noodles and cook for 3 minutes; add the scallions and cook for 2 minutes. Turn off the heat and let the soup sit for 2 to 3 minutes more. Adjust the seasoning and serve.

4 SERVINGS

74 MASTER RECIPE
Turkey or Chicken Croquettes
with Spinach Mashers and Pan Gravy

3 large starchy potatoes, peeled and cubed
  Coarse salt
1 package (about 1⅓ pounds) ground turkey
  breast or ground chicken
2 celery ribs and their greens, finely chopped
1 small yellow onion, finely chopped
2 teaspoons poultry seasoning (eyeball it in the
  palm of your hand)
3 tablespoons chopped fresh thyme
  (from 5 to 6 sprigs)
3 tablespoons chopped fresh flat-leaf parsley
  (a handful)
  Coarse black pepper
1 egg yolk
2 cups plain bread crumbs
¼ cup vegetable oil (eyeball it)
4 tablespoons unsalted butter
2 tablespoons all-purpose flour
2½ cups chicken stock or broth
½ cup cream or half-and-half
1 pound triple-washed baby spinach leaves
  Prepared whole-berry cranberry sauce,
  to pass at the table

Place the potatoes in a pot and cover with cold water. Put a lid on the pot and bring the water to a boil. Salt the water and cook the potatoes until tender, about 15 minutes.

While the potatoes cook, make the croquettes. Place the turkey or chicken in a bowl. Add the celery, onions, poultry seasoning, thyme, parsley, salt, pepper, and egg yolk. Combine and form 8 patties. Coat both sides of the patties in the bread crumbs. Heat the vegetable oil in a large nonstick skillet over medium to medium-high heat. Cook the patties for 5 minutes on each side. Remove the croquettes to a plate and cover loosely with foil to keep warm. Reduce the heat under the skillet. Add 2 tablespoons of the butter to the skillet and melt, then whisk in the flour. Cook the roux for a minute or two. Whisk in 2 cups of the chicken stock and bring to a bubble. Thicken for a minute or so and turn off the heat. Season the sauce with a little salt and pepper.

Drain the cooked potatoes and return to the hot pot. Add the remaining 2 tablespoons of butter, the remaining ½ cup of chicken stock, and the cream. Mash and season the potatoes with salt and pepper. Fold in the spinach leaves until they all wilt into the potatoes.

To serve, pile the spinach mashers on plates and top each portion with 2 croquettes and a spoonful of gravy. Pass the cranberry sauce at the table.

4 SERVINGS

NOW TRY... Cod Croquettes and Red Bell Pepper Gravy with Spinach Mashers

75

☐ TRY THIS LATER

☐ IT'S A KEEPER

OMIT

Cranberry sauce

SWAP

1½ pounds cod fish, cut into chunks, for the chicken or turkey

Old Bay Seasoning, available on the spice aisle or at the fish counter, for the poultry seasoning

ADD

1 lemon

½ red bell pepper, cored, seeded, and finely chopped

1 shallot, finely chopped

Bring ½ inch water to a simmer in a large nonstick skillet. Zest the lemon and reserve. Cut the lemon and season the fish with lemon juice and salt, then add the fish to the simmering water. Cover the pan and cook the fish for 8 minutes.

Remove the fish and flake it into a bowl. Discard the poaching water and wipe out the pan, returning it to the heat over a medium flame to heat up the ¼ cup vegetable oil. Add the reserved lemon zest, celery, onions, Old Bay, thyme, parsley, salt, and pepper to the fish. Add the egg yolk and 1 cup of the bread crumbs. Form 8 fish patties and coat in the remaining bread crumbs to set the patties.

Cook the patties for 4 to 5 minutes on each side until golden and reserve under a foil tent as with the meat croquettes. Return the skillet to the heat again and melt 2 tablespoons of the butter, then add the red bell peppers and shallots and cook for 2 to 3 minutes. Stir in the flour and cook for a minute more. Whisk in the stock to make a red pepper gravy. Season the gravy with a little salt and pepper.

Continue with the potatoes and serve as in the master recipe, #74.

4 SERVINGS

76 MASTER RECIPE
Sicilian-Style Swordfish Rolls
with Fennel and Radicchio Salad

I love the combination of a warm breaded cutlet with cool refrigerated salad. Here are three very different takes on this concept—plus a final variation that morphs the salad into a pasta topper!

- 2 pounds very thin swordfish steaks
  Coarse salt
- 2 cups Italian bread crumbs
- ½ cup fresh flat-leaf parsley leaves
- 4 large garlic cloves
- 1 lemon, zested, then cut into wedges
- 3 to 4 tablespoons extra-virgin olive oil (EVOO)
- 1 small red onion, thinly sliced
- 1 large navel orange, peeled and cut into thin half-moons
- 2 fresh fennel bulbs, trimmed of tops, quartered, cored, and thinly sliced lengthwise
- 2 medium heads of radicchio, shredded
- 2 tablespoons of red wine vinegar (eyeball the amount)
- 3 tablespoons EVOO
  Coarse black pepper
  2 tablespoons chopped fresh oregano (optional)

Pat the swordfish steaks dry and trim off the skin and dark connective tissue. Place the fish between sheets of wax paper and pound with a small skillet or a mallet, as you would chicken or veal cutlets, to a ¼-inch thickness. Cut the thin slices into several rectangular strips, about 2 inches by 4 to 5 inches. Season the fish strips with coarse salt.

Place the bread crumbs in a shallow dish. Pile a handful of the parsley, the garlic, lemon zest, and a little coarse salt on a cutting board. Finely chop the lemon-garlic mixture, then combine it with the bread crumbs. Gently press the fish slices into the bread-crumb mixture, coating both sides. Roll the coated fish strips tightly into small bundles.

For the salad, combine the onions, oranges, fennel, and radicchio in a bowl. Coarsely chop the remaining parsley and add to the salad. Dress the salad with about 2 tablespoons of vinegar and about 3 tablespoons of the EVOO; just eyeball the amounts. Season with salt, pepper, and oregano, if using.

Preheat a medium nonstick skillet over moderate heat and add 3 to 4 tablespoons of EVOO (3 to 4 times around the pan). Cook the rolls gently, 3 to 4 minutes on each side, until deep golden and firm. Remove from the pan and serve the swordfish rolls with lemon wedges and the fennel and radicchio salad.

4 SERVINGS

NOW TRY... Low-Maintenance Version for Two:
Swordfish Cutlets with Tomato and Basil Salad

This is an even easier meal, perfect for one or two tired souls with still-active taste buds. John and I make this one a lot—and even more as we grow older. We're getting a little slower, but our appetite and taste buds will clearly be the last to go! Sometimes, when we are really hungry, we serve a half-recipe of Aglio e Olio (page 121), garlic and oil pasta alongside.

OMIT

     All ingredients in the original salad

  1 cup bread crumbs

  1 garlic clove

FOR 2 SERVINGS

  2 1/2-inch-thick swordfish steaks, skin trimmed away

ADD (FOR TOMATO AND BASIL SALAD)

  3 small, firm (underripe) tomatoes, chopped

 1/2 small white onion, quartered and thinly sliced

  8 to 10 fresh basil leaves, shredded

     EVOO, for drizzling

     Salt and freshly ground black pepper

Pound the fish cutlets as in the master recipe, #76. Season the cutlets with salt and pepper. Mix the bread crumbs with the garlic, lemon zest, and half the parsley. (Save the rest for the salad.) Coat the fish as before then heat enough EVOO to coat the bottom of a large nonstick skillet over medium heat. Brown and cook the large cutlets for 4 minutes on each side.

In a medium bowl, combine the tomatoes with the onions, basil, the remaining parsley, salt, and pepper and just enough EVOO to lightly coat the salad. Toss the salad with your fingertips.

Serve the cutlets with a wedge of lemon. Top the cutlets with a little of the salad, serving the rest alongside.

2 SERVINGS

78 THEN TRY... Sicilian-Style Chicken Cutlets with Chopped Caprese Salad for Two

Adding bocconcini, bite-sized mozzarella balls, to the tomato-basil salad makes it a Caprese salad!

SWAP

2 6-ounce boneless, skinless chicken breast halves for the swordfish cutlets

ADD TO THE SALAD

6 bocconcini, drained and halved or chopped

Butterfly the breasts by cutting into and across each breast but not all the way through. Open the breast, like butterfly wings, and place between wax paper or plastic wrap and pound out to a ¼-inch thickness with a small skillet or mallet. Press the meat into the bread-crumb mixture, as you would the swordfish. Prepare as directed and serve with the wedges of lemon.

While the chicken cooks, make the tomato and basil salad as directed in the first variation, adding the mozzarella. Toss and serve the salad alongside the chicken.

2 SERVINGS

79 AND NOW TRY... Caprese Hot-or-Cold Pasta Toss

Now drop the cutlets, double up the salad ingredients, and add the pasta!

OMIT

Cutlet ingredients

ADD

Double the amounts of the Salad Capricciosa with bocconcini (#185)

1 pound penne rigate or other short-cut pasta

3 tablespoons EVOO (3 times around the pan)

3 garlic cloves, finely chopped

Cook the pasta in salted water until it is al dente.

While the pasta cooks, heat a large skillet over medium heat. Add the EVOO. When the oil is hot, add the garlic and the chopped onions and sauté for 5 minutes. Add the tomatoes, basil, and parsley to the pan and season with salt and pepper. Add the drained, hot pasta to the pan and toss. Add the bocconcini and toss again. Taste to adjust seasoning and serve, or chill and serve cold.

4 SERVINGS

Sweet, Spicy, and Tropical:
Crab Salad Lettuce Wraps

Choose your wrap: the Bibb will be soft, the iceberg will be crunchy. Like the difference between flour and corn tortillas.

1 serrano or jalapeño pepper, seeded and minced

2 rounded tablespoons sugar

3 tablespoons rice wine vinegar or white vinegar (eyeball it)

1 mango, peeled and diced

5 radishes, thinly sliced

1 celery rib, thinly sliced

½ red onion, finely chopped
  Juice of 1 lime

3 tablespoons mayonnaise, plain yogurt, or sour cream

3 tablespoons fresh cilantro leaves (a mounded palmful), chopped

3 tablespoons fresh flat-leaf parsley leaves (a mounded palmful), chopped

1 pound lump crabmeat, cleaned of bits of shell and cartilage
  Bibb or iceberg lettuce, for wrapping

In a small sauce pot, combine 2 tablespoons water with the hot peppers, sugar, and vinegar. Place over high heat and bring up to a simmer, then turn it off. Stir to ensure the sugar has dissolved completely. Remove from the heat.

Transfer the mixture to a mixing bowl and let stand for 5 minutes to cool. Add the mangoes, radishes, celery, red onions, lime juice, mayonnaise, cilantro, and parsley. Stir to combine. Gently fold in the crabmeat.

To serve, pile the crab salad in lettuce leaves. Roll the leaves around the crab salad to encase it.

4 SERVINGS

81

Mashed Plantains with Oh, Baby! Garlic-Tomato Shrimp on Top, Grilled Flank Steak with Lime and Onions, and Quick Rice with Black Beans

CUBAN VIA MIAMI FEAST

TRY THIS LATER

IT'S A KEEPER

Gloria Estefan taught me how to cook plantains in the microwave and her husband, Emilio, gave me the urban, updated idea of lightening up some Cuban-influenced dishes. The result is this menu, my interpretation of Metro-Retro Cuban cooking. This dinner is also delicious made with seasoned grilled thin-cut chicken breast, seasoned in the same manner as the steak.

7 tablespoons extra-virgin olive oil (EVOO), plus a little to drizzle
2 medium yellow onions, 1 finely chopped, 1 thinly sliced
1 tablespoon plus 2 teaspoons ground cumin
3 tablespoons fresh thyme (from 5 or 6 sprigs), chopped
3 cups chicken stock or broth
1½ cups uncooked white rice
1 15-ounce can black beans
   Coarse salt
2 pounds flank steak
2 tablespoons grill seasoning, such as McCormick's Montreal Steak Seasoning
1 lime, zested, cut into wedges
3 green plantains
   Wax paper
1 small green bell pepper, cored, seeded, and finely chopped
4 garlic cloves, finely chopped
1 pound small shrimp, peeled, deveined, and coarsely chopped

Coarse black pepper
Zest and juice of 1 lemon
1 8-ounce can tomato sauce
3 tablespoons finely chopped fresh flat-leaf parsley (a handful of leaves)
   Hot sauce, such as Tabasco, to taste

Heat a medium pot over medium heat. Add 1 tablespoon of the EVOO (once around the pan), and half of the finely chopped onions. Saute for 3 minutes, then season with 2 teaspoons of the cumin and the thyme leaves. Pour in 2½ cups of the chicken stock and raise the heat to bring to a boil. Add the rice and lower the heat to a simmer when a boil resumes. Cover the pot tightly. After 12 minutes, stir in the black beans and replace the cover. Cook for another 6 to 7 minutes. Turn off the heat, season the rice and beans with salt, and stir to combine, then let stand until ready to serve. While the rice cooks, make the plantains with shrimp and the meat.

Preheat a grill pan over high heat. The meat can also be prepared in a hot large cast-iron or nonstick skillet if you do not have a grill pan.

Place the flank steak in a shallow dish and drizzle with EVOO to coat—about 2 tablespoons. Mix the grill seasoning with the tablespoon of cumin (eyeball the measurement in your palm). Add the lime zest to the grill seasoning and cumin. Rub the mixture over the steak evenly. Place the steak on the hot grill or in the hot pan and cook for 4 to 5 minutes, then turn and cook for 3 minutes longer. Remove from the heat and let the juices redistribute for 5 minutes.

Slit the skins of the plantains from end to end to vent them for microwave cooking. Wrap each in wax paper, twisting the paper at the ends. Microwave the plantains for 4 to 5 minutes together or 90 seconds individually on High.

While the plantains and steak cook, place a medium nonstick skillet on the heat over a high flame. Add 2 tablespoons of the EVOO and the sliced onions. Sear the onions and heat through, but leave a bite to them. Place on a serving platter and cover with foil to keep them warm. Return the pan to the stove and reduce the heat to between medium high and medium. Add 2 tablespoons of the EVOO and the remaining finely chopped onions, the bell peppers, garlic, and shrimp.

Season with salt and pepper and add the lemon zest. Cook until the shrimp are firm and the peppers begin to soften, 4 minutes or so. Add half of the lemon juice, the tomato sauce, and parsley. Turn off the heat. Adjust the seasoning with salt, pepper, and lemon juice.

Peel and mash the steaming hot plantains with the remaining $1/2$ cup chicken stock and a drizzle of EVOO. Season the plantains with salt and pile on a platter or dinner plates, then top with garlicky shrimp and tomatoes. Very thinly slice the cooked steak on an angle, working against the grain. Squeeze lime juice over the meat and arrange over the reserved cooked sliced onions on the serving platter. Fluff up the rice and black beans a bit, transfer them to a bowl, and pass at the table.

4 SERVINGS

TIDBIT

Plantains look like green bananas and are available in the produce department.

GOSSIP

Gloria Estefan's favorite of her albums is one she shares with many great guest artists. It's called *Unwrapped*, and you might want to play it for mood music with this supper. It'll taste even better!

82 Ropa Vieja Josés (Cuban Sloppy Joes) with Smashed Yucca, Sliced Tomatoes, Plantain Chips, and Mojo Sauce

This recipe is for Gloria, Emilio, and Emily Estefan (or, as I call them, the Este-FUN Family). So, how Cuban did I get in 30 Minutes? XXOO, RR

2 pounds yucca root, peeled and cubed with a very sharp knife
Coarse salt

MOJO

10 garlic cloves, smashed from their skins
1 medium onion, coarsely chopped
2 teaspoons ground cumin (eyeball it in your palm)
Juice and zest of 1 lemon
1 cup extra-virgin olive oil (EVOO) (eyeball it)
1½ pounds ground sirloin
¼ cup green olives with pimiento, finely chopped
1 tablespoon paprika (eyeball it in your palm)
2 tablespoons Worcestershire sauce (eyeball it)
1 tablespoon hot sauce, such as Tabasco (eyeball it)
1 cup tomato sauce
A palmful of grill seasoning, such as McCormick's Montreal Steak Seasoning

4 crusty rolls (Look for Cuban or Portuguese rolls, which are slightly sweet, but good ole kaisers will work fine, too.)
2 large dill pickles, thinly sliced lengthwise
1 sack plantain chips, on the international aisle of the market, with Latin foods
2 beefsteak tomatoes, sliced

Place the peeled yucca in a small pot and cover with water. Cover the pot and bring to a boil. Salt the water and cook for 15 to 20 minutes, until tender. The yucca will not become as soft as a potato, just tender to the fork tines.

While the yucca cooks, make the mojo sauce. Place the garlic and onions in a food processor with the cumin, lemon zest, and lemon juice. Turn the processor on and stream in the EVOO and ¼ cup water.

Heat a medium nonstick skillet over medium-high heat. Add half the mojo. Heat for 15 seconds, then add the beef and begin to break it up. Brown and crumble the meat with the mojo for 3 minutes. Add the olives with pimientos, the paprika, Worcestershire, hot sauce, tomato sauce, and grill seasoning. Bring to a simmer and reduce the heat to low. Cook over low heat for 10 minutes.

TIDBIT

Yucca (you-kah) is yum-a! Cooked up, it tastes like a creamy, starchy cross between a turnip and a potato. You'll find it in the produce department near the root vegetables or in any Latin market. If your market does not carry yucca, cook up some peeled sweet potatoes and follow the method detailed above.

Split the rolls and pile the bottoms with hefty spoonfuls of the meat mixture. Cover the meat with sliced dill pickles and the tops of the rolls.

Drain the yucca and return it to the warm pot. Add half of the remaining mojo and mash. The yucca will break down a bit and become creamy and sticky but not smooth—like mashed potatoes with some soul. Season up the cooked yucca with salt and divide it among the dinner plates alongside the Sloppy Josés. Serve the plantain chips and sliced tomatoes alongside to finish your plates. Season the tomato slices with a pinch of salt and drizzle tiny spoonfuls of raw mojo sauce over the chips when passing out the plates.

4 SERVINGS

Ginger Vegetable Chicken Noodle Bowl

83

☐ TRY THIS LATER   ☐ IT'S A KEEPER

I love noodle bowls! What's not to like? This one makes plain chicken noodle soup seem, well, really plain. The next time you want either take-out Asian food or just a bowl of chicken noodle soup, make this instead. It rules!

2 tablespoons vegetable oil (twice around the pan)
1 pound boneless, skinless chicken tenders (white meat) or thighs (dark meat), cut into bite-size pieces
4 garlic cloves, finely chopped
1 2-inch piece of fresh ginger, peeled and cut into thin matchsticks or grated
1 cup shredded carrots (available in pouches in the produce department)
Salt and freshly ground black pepper
2 teaspoons ground cumin (eyeball it in your palm)
2 teaspoons Chinese five-spice powder (eyeball it)

6 cups chicken stock or broth
1/2 pound vermicelli (thin spaghetti)
4 scallions, trimmed and cut into 2 1/2-inch lengths, then cut lengthwise into matchsticks
2 cups fresh crisp bean spouts

Heat a medium pot over medium-high heat. Add the vegetable oil, then add the chicken and lightly brown it, about 3 minutes. Add the garlic and ginger, stir, add the carrots, season with salt and pepper, and add the cumin and five-spice powder. Add the stock and bring the soup to a boil. Add the vermicelli and reduce the heat to a simmer. Cook for 3 minutes, then add the scallions and bean sprouts and turn off the heat. Let the soup stand for 5 minutes, adjust the seasonings, and serve.

4 SERVINGS

TRY THIS LATER

IT'S A KEEPER

84 MASTER RECIPE
Chicken Francese and Wilted Spinach

1½ pounds **chicken breast cutlets**
 Salt and freshly ground **black pepper**
2 teaspoons **poultry seasoning** (half a palmful)
½ cup all-purpose **flour** (eyeball it)
2 large **eggs** plus 1 egg yolk
 A splash of **milk** or half-and-half
4 tablespoons **extra-virgin olive oil** (EVOO)
3 tablespoons **unsalted butter**
3 **garlic cloves**, 1 crushed, 2 chopped
½ cup **dry white wine** (a couple of glugs)
 A handful of fresh **flat-leaf parsley**, finely chopped
1 pound triple-washed **spinach**, tough stems removed, coarsely chopped
¼ teaspoon **grated nutmeg** (eyeball it)

Preheat a large nonstick skillet over medium to medium-high heat. Season the chicken cutlets with salt and pepper and poultry seasoning. Dredge the chicken in flour. In a small bowl, beat the eggs and egg yolk with milk or half-and-half and season with a lit-

tle salt. Add 2 tablespoons of the EVOO to the skillet (twice around the pan), then add 2 tablespoons of the butter, cut into small pieces. When the butter melts into the oil, add the crushed clove of garlic to the skillet. When the garlic speaks by sizzling in the oil, coat the chicken in the egg mixture, then add to the hot pan. Cook the chicken on both sides until just golden, 6 to 7 minutes total. Transfer the chicken to a plate and tent loosely with foil to retain the heat. Add the wine to the pan and deglaze by whisking up the drippings. Reduce the wine for 1 minute, then add the remaining tablespoon of butter and the parsley to the pan. Pour the sauce over the chicken.

Return the skillet to the heat. Add the remaining 2 tablespoons of EVOO, then add the chopped garlic and let it come to a sizzle. Wilt in the spinach, turning it to coat in the EVOO, and season it with salt, pepper, and nutmeg. Serve the spinach alongside the chicken francese. Pass crusty bread to mop up the sauce.

4 SERVINGS

TIDBIT

My mama loves an Italian liqueur called limoncello. Basically, it's a lemon vodka concoction; it's sweet and citrusy and too easy to drink! One night out in an opera-themed supper club, Mama was spied enjoying many encores of limoncello after the fat lady had sung! Ever since that night, Mama has been referred to as Mamacello. Limoncello is very affordable and is available in most liquor stores. If kept well chilled (I keep mine in the freezer), limoncello can stand alone as a great after-dinner treat, or try it drizzled over lemon sorbet or vanilla ice cream for a quick and spectacular dessert!

NOW TRY... Flounder Francese
with Toasted Almonds, Lemon, and Capers

85

OMIT

Chopped garlic (keep the crushed garlic)
Poultry seasoning

SWAP

4 flounder fillets for the chicken cutlets

ADD

Zest and juice of 1 lemon
3 tablespoons capers, drained
1 shallot, thinly sliced
2 ounces (¼ cup) sliced almonds, toasted

Prepare the fish as you would the chicken in the master recipe, #84, reducing the cooking time to 3 minutes on each side.

When preparing the sauce, after the white wine reduces, add the lemon zest to the pan, then the juice of the lemon and the capers. Continue as before, subbing the shallots for the garlic when preparing the spinach.

Top the fish with toasted almonds before serving.

4 SERVINGS

OR TRY... Chicken Mamacello and Asparagus Tips

86

OMIT

Spinach
Nutmeg

SWAP

¼ to ⅓ cup limoncello liqueur for the ½ cup
dry white wine

ADD

1 lemon
1½ pounds asparagus, cut just below the tender
tips (save the stalks for another use)

Cut off 2 or 3 pieces of lemon peel, then thinly slice the
lemon into disks. Remove the seeds.

Follow the chicken preparation in the master recipe, #84, swapping the limoncello for the wine.

Bring an inch of water to a boil in a medium skillet. Add salt and lemon peels. When the chicken is nearly done, cook the asparagus in the water with the lemon peels for 2 or 3 minutes; drain.

Add several thin slices of the lemon to the skillet the chicken cooked in. Spoon the sauce and lemon slices onto the finished chicken. Serve the asparagus tips alongside the chicken.

4 SERVINGS

TRY THIS LATER ☐

IT'S A KEEPER ☐

87 Bel Aria Chicken and Pasta

Related to my Chicken Mamacello story, this dish is all about singing for your supper. It is my at-home version of a chicken dish prepared at a fabulous opera café in New York City called Caffe Taci—the same café where Mama earned her nickname. The flavors in this dish are as big as Pavarotti's voice and it will have you, too, singing for an encore plateful!

Coarse salt
1 pound rigatoni pasta
3 tablespoons extra-virgin olive oil (EVOO)
3 tablespoons unsalted butter
1⅓ to 1½ pounds chicken tenders, cut into large bite-size pieces
Coarse black pepper
½ pound cremini (baby portobello) mushroom caps, thinly sliced, or 4 portobello caps, gills scraped out, halved and thinly sliced
4 garlic cloves, chopped
4 Italian hot red cherry peppers, drained and chopped, plus a splash of the pickling juices from the jar
½ cup dry white wine
½ cup grated Parmigiano-Reggiano (a couple of handfuls), plus more to pass at the table
A handful of fresh flat-leaf parsley, chopped
Crusty bread, to pass at the table

Bring a large pot of water to a boil for the pasta. When it comes to a boil, salt it and add the rigatoni. Heads up! Two ladles of the cooking water will be added to the sauce just before the pasta is drained.

While the pasta is working, heat a big, deep skillet over medium-high heat. Add 2 tablespoons of the EVOO (twice around the pan) and 1½ tablespoons of the butter. When the butter melts into the oil, add the chicken to the skillet, season with salt and pepper, and brown for 2 to 3 minutes on each side. Transfer the chicken to a plate. It will finish cooking through when added back to the sauce later.

Return the pan to the heat and add another tablespoon of EVOO, the remaining butter, then the mushrooms and garlic. Cook until the mushrooms are tender, 10 to 15 minutes. Salt and pepper the mushrooms after they brown. (If you salt them when they are first added to the skillet, the salt will draw out the liquids and slow the browning process.) Next, add the hot peppers and a splash of the pickling liquid to the pan. Add the white wine and scrape up the pan drippings with a wooden spoon. Cook the wine down for a minute, then slide the chicken back into the pan. Cook together for another couple of minutes to finish cooking the chicken through.

TIDBIT

If you want to add a salad, try *insalata tre colore* (three-color salad), a combination of chopped radicchio, endive, and romaine lettuce, dressed simply with balsamic vinegar or lemon juice, EVOO, salt, and pepper.

Just before you drain the pasta, add 2 ladles of starchy water to the skillet. The starchy water will help the sauce form and adhere to the pasta. Drain the pasta while it still has a strong bite to it, a little shy of al dente. It will continue to cook a little once it is combined with the sauce. Drain the rigatoni well and add it to the skillet. Turn off the heat and toss the chicken, mushrooms, and pasta together for a minute or two, sprinkling in 2 or 3 handfuls of grated Parmigiano cheese as you go, to allow the pasta to soak up the sauce and flavors. Garnish the pasta with lots of chopped parsley and pass extra cheese and crusty bread at the table.

4 SERVINGS

Pesce Spada Pasta

88

TRY THIS LATER ☐

IT'S A KEEPER ☐

Coarse salt
1 pound medium shell pasta
1¼ to 1½ pounds swordfish steak, trimmed of skin and dark connective tissue
¼ cup extra-virgin olive oil (EVOO) (4 times around the pan)
4 to 6 garlic cloves, chopped
1 medium zucchini, cut into short, thick matchsticks
1 pint grape tomatoes
6 scallions, chopped
¼ cup chopped fresh mint leaves (a handful)
¼ cup chopped fresh flat-leaf parsley (a handful)
½ cup dry white wine
Freshly ground black pepper

Bring a large pot of water to a boil. Add a couple of teaspoons of coarse salt to the boiling water, then add the pasta and cook for 8 or 9 minutes, until al dente.

Cut the swordfish into bite-size cubes.

Heat a large, deep skillet over medium-high heat. Add the EVOO, then the swordfish. Cook the fish until lightly browned on all sides. Remove with a slotted spoon to a plate, and cover loosely with foil to keep the fish warm.

Add the garlic, zucchini, and tomatoes to the pan and season with salt. Keep the veggies moving and cook for 3 minutes. Add the scallions. Cook for 2 minutes more to get the skins of the tomatoes to pop. Add the swordfish back to the pan and toss in the herbs. Douse the pan with the wine and scrape with a wooden spoon to lift the pan drippings. Add the hot drained starchy pasta and toss. Season with pepper and adjust the salt to taste, then transfer to a huge serving bowl or platter and serve.

4 SERVINGS

89 Lamb Patties with Garlic and Mint
over Mediterranean Chopped Salad

¾ cup fresh **flat-leaf parsley** leaves, divided

1¾ pounds **ground lamb**

5 to 6 **garlic cloves**, chopped

1 large **shallot**, chopped

¼ cup fresh **mint** leaves (a generous handful), finely chopped

2 teaspoons to 1 tablespoon **grill seasoning**, such as McCormick's Montreal Steak Seasoning (half a palmful)

2 teaspoons to 1 tablespoon **ground cumin** (half a palmful)

3 tablespoons **extra-virgin olive oil (EVOO)**, plus some for drizzling

½ seedless **cucumber**, chopped

1 **green bell pepper**, cored, seeded, and chopped

1 small **red onion**, chopped

3 **plum tomatoes**, chopped

1 cup pitted **kalamata olives**

1 cup **feta cheese crumbles** (⅓ pound)

8 **pepperoncini peppers**, chopped

Juice of 2 **lemons**

Salt and **freshly ground black pepper**, to taste

4 **pita breads**, any flavor or brand, warmed in the oven or toaster oven, then cut into halves or quarters

Coarsely chop the parsley. Set aside two thirds and finely chop the rest.

Heat a grill pan or a large nonstick skillet to medium-high heat. Place the ground lamb in a bowl with the garlic, shallots, mint, finely chopped parsley, grill seasoning, cumin, and a generous drizzle of EVOO. Mix the meat and score it into 8 portions. Form 8 patties, each 3 inches across and 1 inch thick. Add the patties to the skillet. Cook for 3 minutes on each side.

While the meat cooks, combine all the vegetables with the reserved coarsely chopped parsley, the olives, cheese, and hot peppers. Dress the salad with the juice of 2 lemons and about 3 tablespoons EVOO (3 times around the bowl). Season the salad with salt and pepper. Serve the salad with 2 patties of lamb on top and warm pita bread alongside.

4 SERVINGS

Grilled Turkey Cutlets with Warm Cranberry Salsa
and Sautéed Sweet Potatoes

3 tablespoons vegetable oil, plus some for drizzling

2 medium sweet potatoes, scrubbed clean, cut in half lengthwise, then thinly sliced into half-moons
Salt and freshly ground black pepper

1 large red onion, finely chopped

1 jalapeño pepper, seeded and minced

¼ cup cranberry juice

½ cup dried cranberries

1 cup chicken stock or broth

2 tablespoons honey or 1 tablespoon brown sugar

2 to 2½ pounds turkey breast cutlets

2 teaspoons poultry seasoning (eyeball it in the palm of your hand)

2 limes

2 tablespoons fresh cilantro leaves (a palmful), chopped

3 tablespoons cold unsalted butter

¼ cup fresh flat-leaf parsley leaves (a handful), chopped

Preheat an outdoor grill or a grill pan to high.

Preheat a large nonstick skillet over medium-high heat with 2 tablespoons of the vegetable oil (twice around the pan). Add the thinly sliced sweet potatoes and spread them out in an even layer across the surface of the pan. Liberally season the potatoes with salt and pepper and let the first side brown up, resisting the urge to stir for about 2 minutes. Give the pan a good shake and stir, then continue to brown and cook the sweet potatoes, stirring frequently, for 10 to 15 minutes, until the potatoes are browned and tender.

Preheat a small sauce pot over medium-high heat with the remaining tablespoon of vegetable oil. Add the red onions, jalapeños, salt, and pepper. Cook for about 2 minutes. Add the cranberry juice, dried cranberries, chicken stock, and honey. Bring the mixture to a simmer, turn down the heat to low, and simmer for 5 minutes, or until the liquids have reduced by half.

Season the turkey cutlets with salt, pepper, and poultry seasoning. Drizzle the cutlets with a little vegetable oil and add the cutlets to the hot grill. Grill the cutlets for about 5 minutes on each side, or until the turkey is cooked through. Squeeze the juice of 1 lime over the cutlets just before removing from the grill.

Remove the cranberry salsa from the heat, add the juice of the remaining lime and the cilantro, and stir to combine.

Once the potatoes are browned and tender, remove the pan from the heat and add the butter and parsley. Toss and stir the potatoes to melt the butter.

To serve, place a helping of the sweet potatoes on a dinner plate, arrange turkey cutlets on top of the sweet potatoes, and top them with a large dollop of the warm cranberry salsa.

4 SERVINGS

91 Fancy-Pants Bangers 'n' Mash

Bangers are a mild British pork sausage. If they are not available, any kind of mild pork, beef, or even chicken sausage will do the trick.

- 2 tablespoons extra-virgin olive oil (EVOO) (twice around the pan)
- 8 bangers or other sausages
- 2 pounds small red potatoes, cut into quarters
  Coarse salt
- 2 medium red onions, thinly sliced
- 1 tablespoon fresh thyme leaves (from a couple of sprigs), chopped
- 2 garlic cloves, chopped
  Coarse black pepper
- ½ cup dry red wine
- 1½ cups chicken stock or broth
- 2 tablespoons unsalted butter
- 2 tablespoons cream cheese
- 3 tablespoons fresh chives, chopped
- ½ cup milk
- ¼ cup fresh flat-leaf parsley leaves (a generous handful), chopped
  Juice of ½ lemon

Heat a large nonstick skillet over medium-high heat with the EVOO. Add the bangers and brown on all sides, about 3 to 4 minutes.

While the bangers are getting brown, start the mash by covering the quartered potatoes in water in a medium saucepan. Bring the water to a boil, salt it, and cook the potatoes until fork-tender, about 10 minutes.

Remove the bangers to a plate and reserve. Drain half of the fat from the skillet, then return the skillet to the stovetop. Add the red onions, thyme, garlic, salt, and pepper. Cook the onions, stirring frequently, for about 5 minutes, or until nice and brown. Add the red wine and chicken stock and bring up to a simmer. Add the browned bangers back to the skillet and cook until the sauce has reduced by half, about 5 minutes.

Drain the potatoes and return to the hot pan and warm stovetop to dry the potatoes out. Add the butter, cream cheese, chives, and milk to the potatoes and smash to the desired consistency. Season with salt and pepper.

Finish the bangers with the chopped parsley and the lemon juice. To serve, divide the mash among 4 shallow serving bowls. Top the potatoes with the bangers and sauce.

4 SERVINGS

London Broil with Parsley-Horseradish Chimichurri

Chimichurri is a South American herb condiment served with meats. This version, with horseradish, is my twist. Serve with steamed broccoli, broccolini, or green beans, your choice.

2-pound boneless shoulder steak or top round steak (often marked for "London Broil")

3 tablespoons Worcestershire sauce (eyeball it)

3 tablespoons extra-virgin olive oil (EVOO), plus some for drizzling
  Salt and freshly ground black pepper

2 tablespoons prepared horseradish

2 garlic cloves, finely chopped

2 tablespoons red wine vinegar (eyeball it)

½ cup fresh flat-leaf parsley leaves (a couple of generous handfuls), finely chopped
  Zest and juice of 1 lemon

Preheat a broiler on high and set the rack closest to the flame.

Coat the steak with the Worcestershire sauce, a drizzle of EVOO, salt, and pepper. Put the steak on a broiler pan and broil for 6 minutes per side. Remove the meat from the broiler and allow it to rest for 5 minutes, tented with a piece of aluminum foil. While the steak works, you can work on the chimichurri.

In a bowl, combine the horseradish, garlic, red wine vinegar, parsley, about 3 tablespoons of EVOO, the lemon zest and juice, salt, and pepper.

Slice the rested steak very thin, against the grain and on an angle, and serve it with the parsley–horseradish chimichurri.

4 SERVINGS

TIDBIT

The trick to great London broil is a sharp knife. How tender it is really depends on how thin you can slice it. It's that simple. The parsley-horseradish chimichurri is great with more than just steak. Leftovers can be saved in the refrigerator for 2 or 3 days and will taste great with chicken or pork or mixed into cooked, smashed potatoes.

TRY THIS LATER

IT'S A KEEPER

93 Citrus Lover's Menu: Rosemary–Orange Pork Chops
and Lemon-Butter Broccolini

Zest and juice of 1 navel orange

3 tablespoons light brown sugar

1 cup chicken stock or broth

2 sprigs of fresh rosemary, leaves removed and chopped

$\frac{1}{2}$ teaspoon crushed red pepper flakes

Salt and freshly ground black pepper

2 tablespoons extra-virgin olive oil (EVOO)

4 1-inch-thick center-cut pork loin chops

$1\frac{1}{2}$ pounds broccolini (3 bunches)

3 tablespoons cold unsalted butter

Zest and juice of 1 lemon

$\frac{1}{4}$ cup fresh flat-leaf parsley leaves (a generous handful), chopped

Crusty bread

In a medium sauce pot over high heat, combine the zest and juice of the orange, brown sugar, chicken stock, rosemary, crushed red pepper flakes, salt, and pepper. Bring the mixture to a boil, then lower the heat to a simmer and cook until reduced by half.

Heat a large skillet over medium-high heat with the EVOO (twice around the pan). Season the chops with salt and pepper, then add to the hot skillet. Cook the chops for 5 minutes on each side.

While the pork chops are cooking, trim the broccolini ends. Place the thin stalks into a skillet and cover with water. Cover the skillet and bring to a boil. Add salt and reduce the heat. Simmer the broccolini for 5 to 6 minutes, until tender and bright green.

Drain the broccolini and return the skillet to the stove over medium heat. Add the butter, lemon zest, and lemon juice. Add the broccolini to the skillet and stir and toss until the butter melts. Season the lemon-butter broccolini with salt and pepper.

Add the parsley to the reduced rosemary–orange glaze. Pour the glaze over the cooked pork chops. Toss to coat and transfer to a serving platter. Serve along with the lemon-butter broccolini and some crusty bread.

4 SERVINGS

Sliced Grilled Steak on Blue Cheese Biscuits
with Watercress, Sour Cream, and Sliced Tomatoes

94

☐ TRY THIS LATER ☐ IT'S A KEEPER

3   garlic cloves, finely chopped

2   tablespoons grill seasoning, such as McCormick's Montreal Steak Seasoning

1   tablespoon Worcestershire sauce (eyeball it)
    Salt and freshly ground black pepper

3   tablespoons extra-virgin olive oil (EVOO) (eyeball it)

2   pounds flank steak

1   8-ounce package buttermilk biscuit mix, such as Jiffy brand

½   cup blue cheese crumbles

1   vine-ripe tomato

1   small bunch of watercress, trimmed and cleaned

4   tablespoons sour cream

Preheat the oven to 450°F.

Preheat a grill pan or outdoor grill to high heat.

Mix together the garlic, grill seasoning, Worcestershire sauce, salt, and pepper. Whisk in the EVOO. Pour into a 9 x 13-inch glass dish or a sealable plastic bag. Add the flank steak and coat it evenly in marinade. Let stand for 10 minutes.

While the steak is marinating, prepare the biscuits. Place the biscuit mix in a bowl, add the blue cheese crumbles, and mix with a fork to distribute. Add water, according to the package directions. Once combined, dump the biscuit mix out on a cutting board. Using your fingertips, press out the mix into a 1-inch-thick square. Divide the square with a knife into 4 squares. Arrange the biscuits on a foil-lined cookie sheet and bake for 12 to 15 minutes, or until the biscuits are cooked through and the bottoms are golden brown. Remove from the oven and let cool.

Grill the flank steak for 6 to 7 minutes on each side or to your preferred doneness. Remove the flank steak from the grill and let the juices redistribute before slicing.

Thinly slice the tomato and coarsely chop the watercress; reserve.

To serve, thinly slice the rested meat on an angle, cutting against the grain. (To make easy work of the slicing, use a sharp knife.) Split each of the four biscuits in half. Arrange a slice or two of tomato on the bottom of each biscuit. Season the tomatoes with salt and pepper. Top the tomatoes with some of the sliced steak. Top that with a dollop of sour cream and a little of the chopped watercress. Set the biscuit top in place or slightly to the side. Wow! What a looker!

4 SERVINGS

95 MASTER RECIPE
Island Bird: Pineapple-Rum Chicken

1½ cups **jasmine rice**, any brand
1 whole **pineapple**, cored and peeled
3 tablespoons **vegetable oil**
1 small **yellow onion**, diced
2 **garlic cloves**, chopped
   Coarse salt
½ teaspoon crushed **red pepper flakes**
¼ cup (a 2-ounce nip) **spiced rum**, such as Captain Morgan's
2 cups **chicken stock** or broth
4 6-ounce boneless, skinless **chicken breast halves**
   Coarse black pepper
¼ cup fresh **flat-leaf parsley** leaves (a generous handful), chopped
2 tablespoons fresh **cilantro** leaves (a palmful), chopped

Cook the rice according to the package directions. While it cooks, make the chicken and sauce.

TIDBIT

You can often find whole pineapples already peeled and cored in pouches or tall plastic containers. Check the fresh produce section.

Cut the pineapple into bite-size chunks. Heat a medium saucepan over medium-high heat. Add 1 tablespoon of the vegetable oil, once around the pan. Add the onions, garlic, salt, and crushed red pepper flakes and cook for 2 minutes, stirring frequently. Add the pineapple chunks and the juice from the container, no more than ½ cup, and stir to combine. Remove the pan from the heat and add the spiced rum. Return the pan to the heat, keeping a little distance in case the pot flames up. You can flame it on purpose, if you want to look cool. Either way, let the alcohol cook away, 1 minute. Add the chicken stock and bring the mixture to a simmer, then cook until it reduces by half and has thickened slightly.

While the sauce is simmering, preheat a large nonstick skillet over medium-high heat with the remaining 2 tablespoons of vegetable oil. Season the chicken with salt and pepper and add to the hot skillet. Cook the chicken for 6 minutes on each side. For a smoky taste, grill the chicken on a grill pan or on an outdoor grill.

Slice the breasts and return to the large skillet. Pour in the pineapple and sauce and combine with a good shake of the pan. Add the parsley and cilantro to the pan and turn off the heat. Let stand for a minute or two. Serve up the jasmine rice and top with liberal ladles of the Island Bird.

4 SERVINGS

TRY THIS LATER ☐

OMIT

   1 cup of the chicken stock (you still need
      1 cup)

SWAP

 1½ pounds peeled, deveined shrimp for the
      chicken
   1 cup Coco López piña colada drink mix or
      coconut milk for 1 cup of the chicken stock

ADD

   1 cup shredded unsweetened coconut,
      available at health food stores

Make the sauce as in the master recipe, #95, adding the Coco López or coconut milk when you add the 1 cup of stock.

Toast the coconut in a skillet until evenly golden. Remove, return the pan to the heat, and cook the shrimp as you would the chicken, reducing the cooking time to 2 minutes per side, or until the shrimp are pink and firm. Add the sauce to the shrimp as you would the sliced chicken and serve over the rice. Sprinkle with the toasted coconut.

   4 SERVINGS

IT'S A KEEPER ☐

Chicken Tortilla Soup with Lime

97

TRY THIS LATER ☐

   2 tablespoons extra-virgin olive oil (EVOO)
 1½ pounds chicken tenders
      Salt and freshly ground black pepper
   3 garlic cloves, chopped
   1 green bell pepper, cored, seeded, and
      chopped
   1 large onion, chopped
   1 jalapeño, minced
   2 celery ribs, finely chopped
  ½ tablespoon ground cumin (half a palmful)
   1 tablespoon ground coriander (a palmful)
   2 cups yellow corn tortilla chips (about
      4 handfuls)

   2 teaspoons hot sauce, such as Tabasco
   1 quart chicken stock or broth
  ½ cup sour cream, for garnish
      Zest and juice of 2 limes
  ½ cup fresh cilantro leaves (a few handfuls),
      chopped
   4 scallions, white and green parts, thinly sliced

Preheat a medium soup pot over medium-high heat and add the EVOO (twice around the pan). Chop the chicken tenders into bite-size pieces. Season the chicken with salt and pepper and add to the hot soup pot. Lightly brown the chicken, 3 to 4 minutes, then add the garlic, bell peppers, onions, jalapeños, celery,

IT'S A KEEPER ☐

cumin, coriander, salt, and pepper. Continue to cook for 3 minutes, stirring frequently.

While that is cooking, place the tortilla chips in a food processor and process until well ground. If you don't have a food processor, place the chips in a sealable plastic storage bag and crush with a rolling pin. Add the ground tortilla chips to the soup pot and stir to combine. Add the chicken stock and bring the soup to a simmer. Simmer the soup for 15 minutes.

Ladle the soup into bowls and garnish with the sour cream. Pass the lime zest, chopped cilantro, and sliced scallions in shallow bowls for each person to add to taste.

4 SERVINGS

TRY THIS LATER

IT'S A KEEPER

98 Ham and Cheese-Stuffed Pork Chops
with Lot-o'-Mushrooms Sauce

Serve with broccoli or cauliflower, steamed and tossed in garlic butter.

- 4 1-inch-thick **pork rib chops** on the bone
  Salt and **freshly ground black pepper**
- 8 fresh **sage** leaves
- 4 ½-inch-thick slices **Gruyère cheese**
- 8 thin slices **Black Forest ham**
  Toothpicks
- 2 tablespoons **extra-virgin olive oil (EVOO)** (twice around the pan)
- 2 tablespoons **unsalted butter**
- 1 pound **white button mushrooms**, sliced
- 2 **garlic cloves**
- ½ teaspoon fresh **thyme** leaves, chopped
- 2 tablespoons all-purpose **flour**
- ½ cup **dry white wine**
- 2 cups **chicken stock** or broth
- 1 tablespoon **Dijon mustard**

Cut a large pocket horizontally to the bone of each chop, and open the pocket like a book. Season the inside with salt and pepper. Place 2 sage leaves on top of each slice of Gruyère. Wrap 2 slices of ham around each sage-cheese slice, creating a meat and cheese bundle. Tuck one bundle in each pork chop pocket and secure closed with a toothpick or two. Preheat a large skillet with the EVOO over medium-high heat. Season the outside of the chops with salt and pepper and add to the hot skillet. Cook on each side for 5 to 6 minutes. Remove the stuffed chops from the skillet to a platter, tent with foil, and allow the chops to rest for a few minutes.

While the chops are resting, add the butter, mushrooms, garlic, and thyme to the skillet. Sauté for 3 to 4 minutes, stirring frequently, then season with salt and pepper. Dust the mushrooms with the flour and continue to cook for 1 minute more. Whisk in the wine, stock, and mustard, and then simmer until thick, about 3 minutes.

Serve the stuffed chops with the mushroom sauce.

4 SERVINGS

Chicken, Corn, and Black Bean Stoup

99

☐ TRY THIS LATER ☐ IT'S A KEEPER

Here's another example of "stoup"; a meal in a bowl that's thicker than soup, thinner than stew.

- 2 tablespoons vegetable oil (twice around the pan)
- 2 pounds chicken tenders, cut into bite-size pieces
  Salt and freshly ground black pepper
- 1 tablespoon ground cumin (a palmful)
- 1½ tablespoons ground coriander (a heaping palmful)
- 1 chipotle chili pepper in adobo sauce (chopped)
- 1 large onion, chopped
- 4 ears of fresh corn, kernels cut from the cob
- 1 red bell pepper, cored, seeded, and chopped
- 3 tablespoons all-purpose flour
- 1 quart chicken stock or broth
- 1 15-ounce can black beans, drained
  Juice of 1 lime
- ¼ cup fresh cilantro leaves (a handful), chopped, plus some for garnish
  Hot sauce, such as Tabasco (optional)
  Sour cream, for garnish

Heat a large soup pot over medium-high heat with the vegetable oil. Add the chicken and season with salt, pepper, cumin, coriander, and chipotle chili pepper. Cook the chicken until lightly browned, about 3 to 4 minutes. Add the onions, corn kernels, and red bell peppers. Cook, stirring frequently, for about 3 minutes. Dust the chicken and veggies with the flour, stir, and continue to cook for 2 minutes. Turn the heat up to high and add the chicken stock. Bring the stew up to a simmer and then add the black beans. Simmer the stew for 15 minutes. Add the lime juice and cilantro, and stir to combine. Taste and check for seasoning; adjust with salt and pepper and a little hot sauce if you like the heat. Serve the stoup garnished with a little sour cream and a little bit of chopped cilantro.

4 SERVINGS

MASTER RECIPE
Gravy-Smothered Cajun-Style Meatloaf Patties
with Maple Pecan–Glazed String Beans

1 pound ground sirloin (90-percent lean
   ground beef)
⅓ pound ground pork
¼ cup plain bread crumbs
⅛ cup milk (a generous splash)
1 egg, lightly beaten
   Salt and freshly ground black pepper
3 tablespoons Worcestershire sauce (eyeball it)
¼ teaspoon ground or freshly grated nutmeg
   (eyeball it)
1 rounded tablespoon tomato paste
1 green bell pepper, cored, seeded, and finely
   chopped
1 large garlic clove, finely chopped
5 scallions, white and green parts, thinly sliced
2 tablespoons vegetable oil (twice around
   the pan)
½ cup pecan halves, chopped
1¾ cups chicken stock or broth
1½ pounds green beans, stem ends removed
4 tablespoons unsalted butter
¼ cup maple syrup
1 small onion, finely chopped
¼ teaspoon crushed red pepper flakes
2 tablespoons all-purpose flour
¼ cup heavy cream
¼ cup fresh flat-leaf parsley leaves
   (a generous handful), chopped

Place the meat in a large mixing bowl and create a well in the center of the meat. Fill the well with the bread crumbs and dampen them with the milk. Pour the egg over the bread crumbs and then add salt, pepper, the Worcestershire, nutmeg, tomato paste, green peppers, garlic, and scallions. Mix together and form into 4 large oval patties, ¾ inch thick. Preheat a large nonstick skillet over medium-high heat with the vegetable oil. Fry the meatloaf patties for 7 minutes on each side.

Preheat another large skillet over medium-high heat. Add the chopped pecans and toast them, stirring frequently, for about 3 minutes. Remove the toasted pecans from the pan and reserve. Return the skillet to the heat and add ¾ cup of the chicken stock; bring it up to a simmer. Add the trimmed string beans and spread out in an even layer. Cook the beans for about 3 minutes, or until almost tender. Add 2 tablespoons of the butter, the maple syrup, salt, and pepper to the skillet with the beans, turn the heat up to high, and cook until the liquid has evaporated and the beans are shiny and glazed, 2 to 3 minutes. Toss with the pecans.

Remove the meatloaf patties to a platter, tent with foil, and return the pan to the heat. Reduce the heat to medium and add the remaining 2 tablespoons of butter, the onions, and the red pepper flakes. Cook for about 2 minutes and then sprinkle the onions with the flour. Cook the flour for 1 minute and then whisk in the remaining cup of chicken stock and the heavy cream. Bring the gravy to a bubble. If the gravy is too thick, thin with additional stock. Taste and season with salt and pepper. Stir in the parsley and remove the gravy from the heat.

Slice the meatloaf patties and smother with the gravy. Serve with a pile of maple pecan–glazed string beans.

4 SERVINGS

NOW TRY... Cheddar-Studded Tex-Mex Meatloaf Patties, Scallion Smashed Potatoes, and Spicy Pan Gravy

101

OMIT

Ground pork

All green bean ingredients

¼ to ¾ cup of the chicken stock

2 tablespoons of the Worcestershire Sauce

Cheddar cheese

All but ¼ cup chopped onion

ADD

2 pounds small red potatoes, quartered

Coarse salt

Additional ⅓ pound ground sirloin

½ tablespoon ground coriander (half a palmful)

½ tablespoon ground cumin (half a palmful)

1 rounded tablespoon tomato paste

¼ pound sharp Cheddar cheese, cut into ¼-inch dice

½ cup sour cream

5 scallions, white and green parts, finely chopped

3 tablespoons fresh cilantro leaves (a small handful), chopped

Juice of ½ lime

For the scallion smashed potatoes, cover the potatoes in water in a medium saucepan. Bring the water to a boil, add a little salt, and cook the potatoes for 10 minutes, or until fork tender.

Mix the meatloaf patties as in the master recipe, #100. Form and cook as before.

Check on the potatoes. When they are tender, turn off the heat under the pan; drain the potatoes and return to the hot pan and warm stovetop to dry the potatoes. Add 3 tablespoons of the butter, the sour cream, and the scallions to the potatoes and smash to the desired consistency. Season the potatoes with salt and pepper.

Remove the meatloaf patties from the skillet and make the gravy as directed. Stir in the cilantro and lime juice, then remove the gravy from the heat.

Slice the meatloaf patties and drizzle with gravy. Pile scallion smashed potatoes alongside.

4 SERVINGS

102 Grilled Chicken Paillard with Grilled Red Onion and Asparagus Salad

6 tablespoons extra-virgin olive oil (EVOO),
  plus some for drizzling
2 large red onions, cut into ½-inch-thick disks
1 bunch of thin asparagus, trimmed of thick
  woody ends
  Salt and freshly ground black pepper
4 medium-size plastic food storage bags
4 6- to 8-ounce boneless, skinless chicken
  breast halves
  Juice of 1 lemon
1 tablespoon Dijon mustard
2 tablespoons white wine vinegar (eyeball it)
20 fresh basil leaves, coarsely chopped or torn
5 cups chopped romaine lettuce
½ pint grape tomatoes, cut in half
  Crusty bread

Preheat an outdoor grill or grill pan until very hot.

Drizzle EVOO over the onion disks and the asparagus and season with salt and pepper. Place the onions and asparagus on the grill. Grill the onions for 3 to 4 minutes on each side, or until charred and slightly tender. Grill the asparagus, turning frequently, for 2 to 3 minutes, or until tender. Coarsely chop the grilled onions and asparagus and reserve in a salad bowl.

While the veggies are grilling, prepare the chicken paillard. Sprinkle a little water in four medium-size food storage bags. Place 1 chicken breast in each bag and seal it up, pushing out any excess air. Using the bottom of a heavy pot or pan, pound each breast until flat and thin, just shy of bustin' out of the bag.

In a large shallow bowl, combine the lemon juice, 3 tablespoons of the EVOO, salt, and pepper. Add the pounded chicken breasts to the bowl and coat evenly. Transfer the seasoned chicken in a single layer to the hot grill and cook for 3 or 4 minutes on each side.

While the chicken is grilling, make the dressing. In a small bowl, combine the Dijon mustard, white wine vinegar, salt, and pepper. In a slow steady stream, whisk in the remaining 3 tablespoons of EVOO. To the salad bowl with the chopped grilled onions and asparagus, add the basil, chopped romaine lettuce, and grape tomatoes. Drizzle the dressing over the salad and toss to coat and combine. Serve the grilled chicken with the grilled red onion and asparagus salad and some crusty bread.

4 SERVINGS

Salmon Burgers with Ginger-Wasabi Mayo
and Sesame-Crusted French Fries

1 sack (16 to 18 ounces) crispy-style frozen French fries

4 tablespoons sesame seeds

1½ pounds fresh salmon fillet, pin bones and skin removed

2 garlic cloves, chopped
3-inch piece of fresh ginger, minced or grated

3 tablespoons tamari (dark aged soy sauce, found on the international aisle)

2 scallions, white and green parts, chopped

½ small red bell pepper, cored, seeded, and finely chopped

2 teaspoons sesame oil (eyeball it)

2 teaspoons grill seasoning, such as McCormick's Montreal Steak Seasoning, or 1 teaspoon coarse black pepper and ½ teaspoon coarse salt (eyeball it)
Coarse black pepper

1 tablespoon light-in-color oil, such as canola, safflower, or peanut oil

½ to ¾ cup mayonnaise

2 tablespoons wasabi paste
Juice of 1 lime

4 sesame kaiser rolls, split and toasted
Red leaf lettuce, for garnish

Preheat the oven according to the package directions for the fries.

Spread the French fries out on a cookie sheet and cook according to the package directions. Three minutes before the fries are finished cooking, remove them from the oven, sprinkle with the sesame seeds, toss with a spatula to coat, and return to the oven to finish cooking and to toast the sesame seeds.

Cube the salmon into bite-size pieces and place in a food processor. Pulse the processor to coarse-grind the salmon; it should take on the consistency of ground beef or turkey. Transfer the salmon to a bowl and combine with the garlic, three fourths of the ginger, the tamari, scallions, red bell peppers, sesame oil, grill seasoning, and black pepper. Form 4 large patties, 1½ inches thick. Drizzle the patties on both sides with the oil. Preheat a nonstick skillet over medium-high heat, add the salmon burgers, and cook for 5 to 6 minutes on each side for well done.

While the salmon burgers are cooking, prepare the ginger-wasabi mayo. In a bowl, combine the mayonnaise, wasabi paste, lime juice, and the remaining ginger.

Spread the ginger-wasabi mayonnaise on the buns. Top with a salmon burger and red leaf lettuce and set the bun tops in place. Serve with the sesame-crusted French fries.

4 SERVINGS

104 Garlic and Herb Chicken with Romesco Sauce
on Spicy Greens

5 garlic cloves

½ cup **extra-virgin olive oil** (EVOO)

¼ cup fresh **flat-leaf parsley** leaves (a generous handful)

Salt and **freshly ground black pepper**

½ tablespoon fresh **thyme** leaves

4 6- to 8-ounce boneless, skinless **chicken breast halves**

1 cup **sliced almonds**

1 slice **sandwich bread**

1 8-ounce jar **roasted red peppers**, drained, or 1 large freshly prepared roasted red bell pepper

¼ cup **red wine vinegar** (eyeball it)

1 **plum tomato**, cut into quarters

2 bunches of **arugula**, cleaned and trimmed (about 5 cups)

In a food processor, combine 3 of the garlic cloves, about ¼ cup of EVOO, the parsley leaves, salt, pepper, and the thyme. Process the ingredients to a somewhat smooth paste. Scrape the contents of the processor over the chicken breasts; coat the breasts in the mixture. Preheat a large nonstick skillet over medium heat, then add the seasoned chicken breasts to the skillet and cook on each side for 5 to 6 minutes. Remove the chicken from the pan and let rest for a few minutes covered with aluminum foil to keep warm.

While the chicken is cooking, toast the almonds in a medium skillet over medium heat until they are golden brown, about 3 to 4 minutes. Toast the slice of bread until golden brown. With your hands rip the toast into a few pieces and add to the bowl of the food processor. (There is no need to wash out the processor bowl after making the chicken coating. The flavors that remain in there will work in the Romesco sauce.) Add the toasted almonds, roasted red peppers, the remaining 2 garlic cloves, the red wine vinegar, plum tomato, salt, and pepper. Start processing and while the machine is running pour in the remaining ¼ cup of EVOO in a slow, steady stream. Process until all the ingredients are ground and the mixture is pretty smooth.

Arrange the arugula on the center of 4 serving plates. Slite each rested chicken breast on an angle, then place on top of the arugula. Top the chicken slices with a large dollop of the Romesco sauce.

4 SERVINGS

Lemony Crispy Chicken Cutlets and
Roasted Tomato Salad with Pine Nuts and Blue Cheese

105

☐ TRY THIS LATER

☐ IT'S A KEEPER

6 plum tomatoes, cut in half lengthwise
Extra-virgin olive oil (EVOO), for drizzling
½ tablespoon fresh thyme leaves, chopped
2 garlic cloves, minced
Salt and freshly ground black pepper
¼ cup pine nuts
½ cup all-purpose flour
2 cups Italian bread crumbs
Zest and juice of 1 lemon, plus 1 lemon cut into wedges
2 eggs
Vegetable oil, for shallow frying
2 pounds thin chicken cutlets
1 sack (12 ounces) baby spinach or ¾ pound from bulk bins, washed and patted dry
¾ cup crumbled blue cheese

Preheat the oven to 375°F.

Toss the tomatoes with a little drizzle of EVOO and season with the thyme, garlic, salt, and pepper. Arrange the seasoned tomatoes on a rimmed cookie sheet and roast for 20 minutes.

Preheat a small skillet over medium heat. Add the pine nuts and toast, stirring and tossing frequently, until lightly golden. Or you can toast the pine nuts in the oven on a rimmed cookie sheet until golden all over, about 10 minutes. Reserve the nuts.

Place the flour in a shallow dish. In another shallow dish combine the bread crumbs and lemon zest. Beat the eggs in a separate shallow dish with a splash of water.

Heat a thin layer of vegetable oil in a large skillet over medium to medium-high heat. Season the cutlets with salt and pepper on both sides and turn lightly in the flour. Coat the cutlets in the egg mixture, then in the breading, and add to the hot oil. Cook the cutlets in a single layer, in 2 batches if necessary, for 3 or 4 minutes on each side, until the juices run clear and the breading is evenly browned.

Remove the roasted tomatoes from the oven and coarsely chop, then transfer to a salad bowl. Add the baby spinach, the lemon juice, a drizzle of EVOO, the reserved toasted pine nuts, salt, and pepper. Toss together and let the heat of the tomatoes slightly wilt the spinach.

Serve the chicken cutlets with a generous portion of the roasted tomato salad; sprinkle the salad with the crumbled blue cheese. Arrange lemon wedges alongside.

4 SERVINGS

106 Honey-Orange–Glazed Ham Steaks
with Spicy Black Bean, Zucchini, and Corn Salad

Zest and juice of 2 oranges
1 tablespoon ground coriander (a palmful)
½ cup honey (eyeball it)
1 tablespoon chili powder (a palmful)
Salt and freshly ground black pepper
1½ cups chicken stock or broth
3 tablespoons extra-virgin olive oil (EVOO)
1 large red onion, chopped
3 large garlic cloves, chopped
1 jalapeño pepper, chopped
1 small zucchini, thinly sliced into disks
1 10-ounce box frozen corn kernels
2 large ham steaks, cut in half
1 15-ounce can black beans, drained and rinsed
Zest and juice of 1 lime
¼ cup fresh flat-leaf parsley leaves (a generous handful), chopped

In a small sauce pot over high heat, combine the orange juice, coriander, honey, chili powder, salt, pepper, and 1 cup of the chicken stock. Bring the mixture to a boil and simmer until reduced by half, about 5 minutes. Keep warm.

Preheat a medium skillet over medium-high heat with 2 tablespoons of the EVOO (twice around the pan). Add the onions, garlic, jalapeños, zucchini, salt, and pepper. Cook, stirring frequently for about 3 minutes, or until the onions start to turn translucent. Add the frozen corn, stir to combine, and continue to cook for 2 more minutes.

While the corn is cooking with the veggies, preheat another skillet over medium-high heat with the remaining tablespoon of EVOO. Add the ham steaks and heat through and brown slightly, about 2 minutes on each side.

To the corn and veggie mixture add the black beans and the remaining ½ cup of chicken stock and cook until the beans are heated through.

To the ham steaks, add the reduced honey-orange glaze. Flip the ham steaks around in the glaze and continue to cook for about 1 minute.

Add the orange zest, lime zest and juice, and parsley to the veggie and black bean mixture. Toss to combine. Serve the glazed ham steaks with a helping of the warm black bean, zucchini, and corn salad.

4 SERVINGS

Turkey Club Super Mashers

8   slices **applewood-smoked bacon**
4   large starchy **potatoes**, such as Idaho
    Coarse salt
1   package (1¼ to 1½ pounds) **turkey breast
    cutlets**
    Coarse black pepper
2   teaspoons **poultry seasoning**
2   tablespoons **extra-virgin olive oil** (EVOO)
    (twice around the pan)
2   tablespoons **unsalted butter**
2   tablespoons all-purpose **flour**
2   cups **chicken stock** or broth
2   to 3 tablespoons fresh **thyme** leaves, chopped
½   cup **sour cream** or reduced-fat sour cream
¼   to ½ cup **milk** or reduced-fat milk, depending
    on how soft you like your mashers
2   cups, stemmed and chopped **watercress**
    (1 bunch)
2   **plum tomatoes**, seeded and chopped, or, for
    extra-smoky mashers, use 1 14-ounce can
    diced fire-roasted tomatoes, drained, such as
    Muir Glen brand
4   **scallions**, chopped

Preheat the oven to 400°F. Arrange the bacon on a slotted broiler pan and bake it for 15 minutes, or until evenly crisp. Cool, chop, and reserve the bacon.

While the bacon cooks, peel the taters and cut them into small chunks. Place the potatoes in a pot and cover with cold water. Cover the pot and bring to a boil over high heat. Uncover, add salt, and cook until the potatoes are tender, about 15 minutes.

Heat a large nonstick skillet over medium-high heat. Season the turkey cutlets with salt, pepper, and poultry seasoning. Add the EVOO to the skillet. Add the cutlets and cook for 4 minutes on each side, or until evenly golden and firm but not dry. Transfer the cutlets to a platter and cover with foil. Return the skillet to the heat and melt the butter in it. Add the flour and cook together for 1 minute, then whisk in the chicken stock. Bring to a bubble and reduce the heat to simmer. Season the sauce with salt, pepper, and fresh thyme. The sauce will take about 5 minutes to become thickened gravy.

Drain the potatoes, then return them to the hot pot to evaporate some of the water content. Add the sour cream and start smashing away with a masher. Add enough milk to get the potatoes to the desired consistency. Season the super mashers with salt and pepper. Fold the bacon, watercress, and tomatoes ("BLT") into the smashed potatoes.

Pile up one fourth of the potatoes on each plate. Slice the cutlets and arrange the sliced turkey on the potatoes. Cover the meat with pan gravy. Top the turkey club super mashers with chopped scallions and serve.

4 SERVINGS

108 MASTER RECIPE
Park City Cashew Chicken

I was in an Albertson's grocery store in Park City, Utah, and picked up a sack of chipotle-coated raw cashews and started eating them while I was still shopping. WOW—were they ever good! I read the ingredients for the coating and used it to make a Western-style chicken and vegetable stir-fry.

3 tablespoons vegetable oil

1 tablespoon unsalted butter

1 large onion, ¼ finely chopped, ¾ thinly sliced

1½ cups brown rice

3 cups chicken stock or broth

1½ pounds chicken tenders; boneless, skinless chicken breasts; or boneless, skinless thighs, cut into 2-inch pieces

2 tablespoons grill seasoning, such as McCormick's Montreal Steak Seasoning

4 garlic cloves, chopped

1 red bell pepper, cored, seeded, and thinly sliced

3 tablespoons chipotle in adobo (available in cans on the international foods aisle), or 1½ tablespoons ground chipotle powder

1 tablespoon ground cumin (eyeball it in your palm)

2 tablespoons honey (2 healthy drizzles)

¼ cup real maple syrup

2 to 3 tablespoons chopped fresh cilantro or flat-leaf parsley, your preference

1 cup raw cashews

In a medium pot over medium heat, combine 1 tablespoon of the vegetable oil (once around the pan) and the butter. When the butter melts into the oil, add the chopped onions and cook for 2 minutes, then add the rice and cook for 3 minutes more. Add the stock and cover the pot. Raise the heat to bring the stock to a rapid boil. Once the stock boils, reduce the heat to low and cook, stirring occasionally, until the rice is tender, 17 to 18 minutes.

While the rice cooks, make the chicken. Heat a large skillet over high heat. Add the remaining 2 tablespoons of vegetable oil, then the chicken. Season the chicken with the grill seasoning. Lightly brown the chicken on both sides, then move off to one side of the pan. Add the remaining onions, the garlic, and bell peppers. Cook for 2 to 3 minutes, then mix the vegetables and meat together and add the chipotles and cumin. Toss to coat. Glaze the mixture with honey and maple syrup and turn off the heat. Add the chopped cilantro or parsley and the nuts.

Top the rice with the cashew chicken and serve.

4 SERVINGS

109

TRY THIS LATER

IT'S A KEEPER

OMIT

Chipotle
Cumin
Honey
Maple syrup

ADD

1 teaspoon crushed red pepper flakes
1 cup pea pods, chopped
2 cups bean sprouts
4 scallions, sliced on the diagonal in 2-inch lengths

⅓ cup tamari (dark aged soy sauce, found on the international aisle)
½ cup duck sauce (found on the international aisle)

Prepare the rice as for the master recipe, #108.

Cook the chicken as directed, adding the red pepper flakes to the hot oil before you add the chicken. Add the additional vegetables when you add the onions and red bell peppers. Season the stir-fry with tamari and duck sauce. Add the cashews and cilantro or parsley and serve over the brown rice.

4 SERVINGS

Chicago Dog Salad

SUPER SALAD SUPPER

110

TRY THIS LATER

IT'S A KEEPER

Eat well, eat more! I cut out the bun so I can have more dogs and veggies with less guilt. Chicago-style dogs are my favorites, with pickles, tomatoes, onions, mustard, and slaw on top. This salad reverses the order and piles the veggies up high underneath the dogs.

¼ cup yellow mustard
2 tablespoons vinegar (eyeball it)
1 rounded teaspoon sugar
4 tablespoons vegetable oil
1 small red onion, thinly sliced
½ sack (8 ounces) shredded cabbage blend for slaw salads

1 romaine lettuce heart, shredded
2 vine-ripe tomatoes, diced
3 large half-sour or garlic pickles, chopped
Salt and freshly ground black pepper
8 pork or beef hot dogs, cut on an angle into 1-inch-thick slices

In the bottom of a large bowl, combine the mustard, vinegar, sugar, and about 3 tablespoons of the vegetable oil. Add the onions, cabbage, romaine, tomatoes, and pickles and toss the salad, season with salt and pepper, adjust the seasonings, and reserve.

(continued on next page)

Heat a large nonstick skillet over medium-high heat. Add the remaining tablespoon of vegetable oil (once around the pan), then arrange the sliced dogs in a single layer. Sear them for a couple of minutes on each side.

Mound up the salad on plates and top with seared dogs and serve.

4 SERVINGS

111 Pork Chops with Grainy Mustard and Raisin Sauce

1½ cups **chicken stock** or broth
½ cup **dry white wine** (eyeball it)
1 cup **golden raisins**
4 tablespoons **extra-virgin olive oil** (EVOO)
4 1½-inch-thick boneless center-cut **pork chops**
1 tablespoon **paprika** (a palmful)
 Salt and freshly ground **black pepper**
1 medium **yellow onion**, chopped
1 tablespoon fresh **thyme** leaves, chopped (from 4 sprigs)
3 heaping tablespoons **grainy Dijon mustard**
¼ cup **heavy cream**
¼ cup fresh **flat-leaf parsley** leaves (a generous handful), chopped

Preheat the oven to 375°F.

In a small sauce pot over high heat, combine the chicken stock, wine, and raisins. Bring it to a simmer, then turn off the heat and let it sit. Heating the raisins in the liquids will make them tender and plump.

While the sauce pot with the stock and wine is coming to a simmer, heat a large skillet over medium-high to high heat with about 2 tablespoons of the EVOO (twice around the pan). Season the chops with paprika, salt, and pepper. Place the chops in the skillet and sear the meat on both sides to caramelize, about 2 minutes on each side. Transfer the chops to a rimmed cookie sheet and place in the oven to finish, 8 to 10 minutes, until the meat is firm to the touch, but not tough. Remove from the oven and let the chops rest, covered with a piece of aluminum foil, for a few minutes.

While the chops are in the oven, return their skillet to medium-high heat. Add the remaining 2 tablespoons of EVOO, the onions, thyme, salt, and pepper, and cook, stirring frequently, for about 3 minutes. Add the hot chicken stock, wine, and raisin mixture. Add the grainy mustard and heavy cream. Bring the mixture to a simmer and cook until slightly thickened, about 4 to 5 minutes. Finish the grainy mustard and raisin sauce with the parsley.

Serve the sauce over the rested pork chops.

4 SERVINGS

Indian Spiced Vegetables

☐ TRY THIS LATER ☐ IT'S A KEEPER

SPICE BLEND

1½ teaspoons turmeric (eyeball it in your palm)
1 teaspoon ground coriander (eyeball it)
1 teaspoon cumin seeds
1 tablespoon curry powder (about a palmful)
½ teaspoon cayenne pepper
2 pinches of ground cinnamon

3 large waxy white potatoes, peeled and diced
Coarse salt
1 head of cauliflower, cut into small florets
1 tablespoon vegetable oil (once around the pan), plus some for drizzling
2 tablespoons unsalted butter, cut into pieces
1 medium onion, chopped
3 garlic cloves, chopped
1 15-ounce can chick peas, drained
1 cup chicken stock or broth
1 cup frozen green peas
1 small head of iceberg lettuce, shredded
¼ cup sliced or slivered almonds
4 radishes, thinly sliced
3 tablespoons chopped fresh mint
3 tablespoons chopped fresh flat-leaf parsley or cilantro, your choice
Juice of 1 lemon

Combine the ingredients for the spice blend and reserve.

Place the potatoes in a pot and cover them with water. Cover the pot with a lid and bring to a boil. Take off the lid and add salt. Boil the potatoes for 6 to 7 minutes, then add the cauliflower to the same pot. Cook for 2 to 3 minutes longer, then drain. The potatoes and cauliflower should still be a little undercooked.

Heat a large skillet over medium heat. Add the vegetable oil, then the butter. When the butter melts into the oil, add in the onions and garlic and sauté for 5 minutes. Add the drained potatoes and cauliflower and the chick peas and combine. Stir the reserved spices into the vegetables and cook for a minute or two to develop the flavors. Stir in the stock and turn the vegetables to evenly distribute. The dish will turn a bright yellow. Cook over medium-low heat for 2 to 3 minutes longer. Add the peas and turn off the heat. The carry-over heat will warm them through. Taste to adjust the salt in the dish.

In a large bowl, combine the shredded lettuce with the almonds, radishes, mint, and parsley or cilantro. Dress the salad with the lemon juice, a drizzle of vegetable oil, and some salt. Pile the salad on plates, top with the hot vegetables, and serve.

4 SERVINGS

113 MASTER RECIPE
Ginger-Soy Chicken on Shredded Lettuce

Here's a low-carb-lover's delight! Have two servings —it's good for you!

- 3 tablespoons vegetable oil (3 times around the pan)
- 1¼ pounds chicken breast cutlets, cut into thin strips
  Salt and coarse black pepper
- 2-inch piece of fresh ginger, peeled and minced
- 4 large garlic cloves, chopped
- ½ teaspoon crushed red pepper flakes
- 6 scallions, cut into 2-inch lengths, then cut lengthwise into thin matchsticks
- ¼ cup tamari (dark aged soy sauce, found on the international aisle) (eyeball the amount)
- 3 tablespoons honey (3 times around the pan)
- 1 head of iceberg lettuce, core removed, shredded

Heat a large nonstick skillet over high heat. Add the vegetable oil. It should smoke up a bit. Add the chicken and season with a little salt and lots of black pepper. Stir-fry for a minute to sear the meat at the edges, then add the ginger, garlic, and red pepper flakes and cook for 2 minutes more. Add the scallions and stir-fry for another minute, then add the tamari and honey to form a sauce and glaze the chicken. Remove the pan from the heat. Cover a platter with shredded lettuce, top with the chicken, and serve.

4 SERVINGS

- -

114 NOW TRY... Thai Chicken, Pork, or Shrimp with Basil

It's amazing how different the master recipe above tastes with the addition of the peppers and basil. To make it even more different, make one of the swaps below.

SWAP

- 6 ¼-inch-thick pork loin chops, cut into thin strips, *or* 1½ pounds medium shrimp, peeled, deveined, and tails removed, for the chicken cutlets

ADD

- 1 red bell pepper, cored, seeded, quartered, and thinly sliced
- 20 fresh basil leaves, torn or shredded

Stir-fry the chicken, pork, or shrimp as directed in the master recipe, #113. Add the bell peppers to the pan when you add the ginger and garlic. Add the basil when you remove the stir-fry from the heat. Toss to wilt and combine. Serve over the shredded lettuce.

4 SERVINGS

Jambalaya Burgers and Cajun Corn and Red Beans 115

☐ TRY THIS LATER

☐ IT'S A KEEPER

1 package (1⅓ pounds) ground chicken or ground turkey breast

½ pound Cajun andouille sausage, casing removed, diced

3 celery ribs and their greens, finely chopped

1 green bell pepper, cored, seeded, and finely chopped

1 small onion, finely chopped

4 garlic cloves, finely chopped

3 tablespoons fresh thyme (5 or 6 sprigs), chopped

2 tablespoons hot sauce, such as Tabasco Salt and freshly ground black pepper

4 tablespoons extra-virgin olive oil (EVOO), plus more for drizzling

3 ears corn, from the cob, or 1 10-ounce box frozen corn kernels, defrosted

4 scallions, chopped

1 can red beans, drained

1 cup chili sauce, divided

½ cup mayonnaise (eyeball it)

¼ cup grainy mustard (eyeball it)

4 jumbo shrimp, peeled, deveined, and butterflied (cut almost all the way through)

1 tablespoon Old Bay Seasoning, at the seafood counter or on the spice aisle (eyeball the amount in your palm)

4 crusty rolls, split

4 green leaf lettuce leaves

1 large beefsteak tomato, sliced

Preheat a grill pan or large nonstick skillet over medium-high heat.

Place the chicken or turkey in a bowl. Add the sausage, half the chopped celery, half the chopped green bell peppers, the onions, half the garlic, the thyme, hot sauce, salt, pepper, and about 2 tablespoons of the EVOO. Combine the mixture and form 4 patties. Grill for 5 minutes on each side.

Heat a skillet over medium-high heat. Add 2 tablespoons of the EVOO (twice around the pan), the remaining bell peppers, remaining garlic, and the corn kernels, and season with salt and pepper. Cook the corn and bell peppers, stirring frequently, for 3 or 4 minutes, then add the scallions and red beans to the pan and heat through, 2 or 3 minutes. Add ½ cup of the chili sauce and cook for 1 minute more. Turn off the heat and let stand.

Combine the remaining chili sauce with the remaining celery, the mayo, and the grainy mustard and reserve.

Coat the shrimp with a little EVOO and the Old Bay Seasoning, salt, and pepper. Grill alongside the burgers, pressing the shrimp down with a small heavy skillet or a small skillet with a heavy can inside to prevent the shrimp from curling up. Cook for 2 minutes on each side.

Place the roll bottoms on plates and top with burgers, shrimp, lettuce, and tomato slices. Slather the bun tops with chili-mayo-mustard sauce and set in place. Serve the Cajun corn and beans alongside.

4 SERVINGS

TRY THIS LATER

IT'S A KEEPER

Extra-virgin olive oil (EVOO), for liberal drizzling, plus 4 tablespoons

1 package (1⅓ pounds) ground chicken or ground turkey breast

1 tablespoon Worcestershire sauce

4 garlic cloves, 2 cloves chopped, 2 cracked from skins and reserved

1 teaspoon crushed red pepper flakes

1 medium yellow onion, ¼ finely chopped, ¾ thinly sliced

A handful of fresh flat-leaf parsley, chopped

10 fresh basil leaves, shredded

A generous palmful of grated Parmigiano-Reggiano

Salt and freshly ground black pepper

2 portobello mushroom caps, thinly sliced

2 cubanelle (Italian light green) peppers, seeded and sliced

2 hot red cherry peppers, chopped, plus a splash of the pickling juice

4 slices Provolone cheese, deli sliced

4 crusty rolls, split

3 tablespoons unsalted butter

1 sack (12 ounces) prewashed mixed baby greens

2 tablespoons fresh thyme leaves, chopped

Juice of 1 lemon

1 sack of fancy chips, such as olive oil and rosemary flavor or Terra's garlic and onion Yukon Golds

Preheat a large nonstick skillet or grill pan to medium-high heat.

Drizzle some EVOO in a bowl and add to it the chicken, Worcestershire, chopped garlic, red pepper flakes, chopped onions, parsley, basil, Parmigiano, salt, and pepper. Combine to form 4 large patties and add to the hot skillet. Cook for 6 minutes, then flip the burgers. Cook for 5 minutes on the other side.

Heat a second skillet over medium-high heat. Add 2 tablespoons of the EVOO (twice around the pan). Add the mushroom caps with the sliced onions and cubanelle peppers. Season with salt and pepper and cook for 5 minutes, stirring frequently. Turn the heat off. Add the hot cherry peppers and a splash of their juice.

Place the Provolone over the burgers and turn off the heat in the pan. Tent the pan with foil to melt the cheese with carry-over heat.

Preheat the broiler to high. Toast the crusty rolls until golden. Melt the butter with the remaining cracked garlic in the microwave or over low heat in a small pan. Brush the garlic butter on the rolls.

Place the cheese-covered patties on the bottoms of the buns. Top with the peppers and onions and replace the top halves of the buns.

Toss the greens with the thyme, lemon juice, 2 tablespoons of the EVOO, salt, and pepper. Serve the greens alongside the cacciatore burgers with your chips of choice.

4 SERVINGS

Big Beef Burger Stack-Ups
with Mushrooms, Peppers, and Onions

117

SWAP

1⅓ pounds ground sirloin, for the ground chicken

3 tablespoons chopped fresh sage for the basil

2 small red bell peppers for the cubanelles
Sliced smoked Gouda cheese for the Provolone

Prepare the burgers, mushrooms, peppers, and onions as in the master recipe, #116. To assemble, stack the burgers covered with smoked Gouda on the bun bottoms and top with the sautéed mushrooms and red bell peppers and the garlic bun tops. Serve the burger stacks alongside the greens and chips.

4 SERVINGS

Peasant Soup

118

The restaurant La Tupina in Bordeaux, France, serves a soup that's slow cooked for four hours. The last few delicious spoonfuls are combined with red wine and swallowed back. These are my kind of people! This is an adaptation my way, minus three hours and thirty minutes. This peasant can't wait!

2 tablespoons extra-virgin olive oil (EVOO) (twice around the pan)

1 small ham steak, chopped

2 carrots, chopped

1 medium onion, chopped

1 celery rib with its greens, chopped

1 leek, cleaned and sliced into half-moons

4 garlic cloves, minced

1 large shallot, finely chopped

1 small head of cabbage, cut into large pieces

1 teaspoon sugar
Coarse salt

4 cups chicken stock or broth

1 15-ounce can cannellini beans
Coarse black pepper
Crusty bread

1 bottle red Bordeaux wine, for the chef and the last few swallows of soup!

Heat a soup pot over medium-high heat with the EVOO. Add the soup fixins to the pot as you chop them: ham, carrots, onions, celery, leeks, garlic, and shallots. Add the cabbage to the pot and sprinkle with the sugar and salt. Add 2 cups water and cover the pot. Steam the cabbage for 15 minutes. Uncover the pot and add the stock and beans. Crank the heat and bring to a boil. Reduce the heat and keep at a low simmer. Adjust the salt and pepper. Serve with crusty bread, and don't forget to down the last few swallows with your trusty Bordeaux!

4 SERVINGS

119

Boneless Rib-Eye Steaks with Killa' Chimichurri
and Mushrooms with Smoky Chipotle and Wilted Spinach

TRY THIS LATER □

IT'S A KEEPER □

4   10- to 12-ounce boneless rib-eye steaks,
    each about 1½ inches thick
    Extra-virgin olive oil (EVOO), for drizzling
2   tablespoons grill seasoning, such as
    McCormick's Montreal Steak Seasoning

CHIMICHURRI

4   stems fresh oregano, stripped of leaves
5   sprigs fresh sage leaves, stripped
6   stems fresh thyme leaves, stripped
1   generous handful fresh flat-leaf parsley
2   garlic cloves, popped from their skins
1   medium red onion, ½ finely chopped,
    ½ thinly sliced
    Zest of 1 lemon
3   tablespoons red wine vinegar (eyeball it)
⅓   cup EVOO

1   pound spinach leaves (stems removed)
3   tablespoons chipotle in adobo, chopped with
    the sauce, or 1 tablespoon chipotle chili
    powder
1½ pounds combined weight shiitakes and
    cremini (baby portobello) mushrooms,
    thinly sliced
    Salt and freshly ground black pepper
1   garlic clove, halved
4   slices crusty bread
    Worcestershire sauce

Pat the rib eyes dry and arrange on a broiler pan. Drizzle both sides with EVOO, then season them with the grill seasoning. Preheat the broiler to high.

Prepare the chimichurri: Pile the herbs together and finely chop. Coarsely chop 2 cloves of the garlic, reserving one whole clove. Add the chopped garlic to the herbs and mill them together, chopping even finer, then transfer to a small bowl. Add the finely chopped red onions and the lemon zest. Add the red wine vinegar, a splash of water, and about ⅓ cup of the EVOO and stir to combine.

Fill a sink or large bowl with cold water. Add the spinach and agitate to release the grit attached to the leaves. Repeat this process until they are free of sand. Dry in a salad spinner.

Heat a large nonstick skillet over medium-high heat. Add 2 tablespoons of the EVOO (twice around the pan), then add the chipotle in adobo, sliced onions, and mushrooms. If you are using powdered chipotle, add the onions and mushrooms first, then season with the powder. Cook the mushrooms and onions, stirring frequently, for 10 minutes. Do not add salt and pepper; the salt will draw liquid out of the mushrooms, slowing the browning process.

Place the steaks under the hot broiler and cook 6 inches from the heat for 6 minutes on side one, 4 minutes on the flip side, for medium rare to medium. Add 2 minutes for medium to medium well doneness. Once the steaks are cooked, let them rest for 5 to 10 minutes for the juices to redistribute.

Once the mushrooms are tender, coarsely chop the spinach and add it to the pan in bunches, folding it in until wilted and incorporated fully. Season the mixture with salt and pepper and remove from the heat.

Toast the bread and rub it with the cut garlic clove. Place the toasted bread on plates and top each slice with a whole steak. Top the steaks with a few shakes of Worcestershire and generous spoonfuls of chimi-churri. Serve "mountains" of smoky mushrooms and spinach alongside the steaks with lemon wedges to squeeze over all.

4 SERVINGS

NOW TRY... Chicken Chimichurri Burgers with Exotic Chips

120

☐ TRY THIS LATER   ☐ IT'S A KEEPER

If you make a double batch of chimichurri sauce one night you can make these burgers in a flash the next!

1 package (1½ pounds) ground chicken
1 cup chimichurri, see page 106
   Salt and freshly ground black pepper
2 cups shredded cabbage mix (available in sacks in the produce department)
1 small red bell pepper, cored, seeded, quartered lengthwise, and thinly sliced
1 large ripe tomato, sliced
4 crusty rolls, split
2 half-sour or crisp dill pickles, thinly sliced lengthwise
   Yellow mustard, for topping the burgers
1 sack Terra chips or other exotic root-vegetable chips

Heat a large nonstick skillet over medium-high heat. Place the chicken in a bowl and add half of the pre-pared chimichurri sauce, salt, and pepper. Combine and form the chicken mixture into 4 patties, then add them to the hot skillet and cook for 6 minutes on each side.

Pour the remaining chimichurri over the shredded cabbage blend and thinly sliced red bell peppers. Toss, then season the mixture with salt and pepper. Season the sliced tomato with salt, to taste.

Remove the burgers from the pan and place them on roll bottoms; top with sliced pickles, tomatoes, and piles of slaw; then slather the bun tops with yellow mustard and set them in place. Serve the completed burgers with chips alongside.

4 SERVINGS

121 MASTER RECIPE
Spring Chicken with Leeks and Peas
Served with Lemon Rice

Feel free to make this dish in all four seasons. I just call it "Spring Chicken" because it tastes light and crisp, like spring air, and because "Spring Chicken" sounds more appetizing than "Leeky Chicken," which was what I called an earlier version of this recipe.

2 cups chicken stock or broth
1 cup white rice
   Zest and juice of 1 lemon
3 tablespoons extra-virgin olive oil (EVOO)
1 tablespoon unsalted butter, cut into small pieces
1½ to 2 pounds chicken breast tenders, cut into large bite-size pieces, about 2 inches
2 medium leeks, trimmed of tough tops and roots
½ cup dry white wine (twice around the pan), or substitute chicken stock if you do not have wine on hand
1 10-ounce box frozen tender green peas
   Salt and freshly ground black pepper
   A handful of fresh flat-leaf parsley leaves, finely chopped

Bring the chicken stock to a boil in a small pot. Stir in the rice, lemon zest, and 1 tablespoon of the EVOO—eyeball the amount. Return to a boil, then reduce the heat to a simmer and cover the pot. Cook for 17 to 18 minutes, until tender.

Heat a large nonstick skillet over medium-high heat. Add the remaining 2 tablespoons of EVOO (twice around the pan), and the butter. When the butter melts into the oil, add the chicken to the pan and sauté until lightly golden on both sides, 4 minutes.

Cut the leeks in half lengthwise, then slice into ½-inch half-moons. Place the leeks in a colander and wash under cold running water, separating the layers and releasing all the grit. You can also place the sliced leeks in a large bowl of cold water and swish them around like a washing machine. The grit will fall to the bottom of the bowl. Drain the leeks well and add them to the chicken.

Cook the leeks with the chicken until they wilt down, 3 minutes or so. Add the white wine to the pan and scrape up any pan drippings. Add the peas and heat through, another minute or two. Turn off the heat and season with salt and pepper. Drizzle the lemon juice over the chicken and leeks. (Juice the fruit with the cut side facing up, keeping the seeds with the lemon rather than in the chicken.)

Fluff the rice with a fork. The zest in the cooking liquid will have infused the rice with lemon flavor. Add the parsley and toss the rice to combine.

Pile the chicken and leeks on dinner plates and top with a small mound of lemon rice.

4 SERVINGS

TIDBIT

I use an ice-cream scoop to serve rice.

NOW TRY... **Chicken and Rice Stoup**

122

TRY THIS LATER

IT'S A KEEPER

When it comes to this one-pot wonder, even Campbell's never made it *this* good! Use a large, deep-sided skillet or medium soup pot for this recipe.

OMIT

> Lemon
> White wine
> Green peas

ADD

- 1 bay leaf
- 1 cup shredded carrots, available in the produce section, or 1 large carrot, cut into matchsticks
- 2 celery ribs, chopped
- 3 tablespoons fresh thyme leaves (from 5 to 6 sprigs), chopped
- 1 quart chicken stock (6 cups total, including the 2 cups in the original recipe)
- ½ cup white rice (1½ cups total, including the 1 cup in the original recipe)

Prepare according to the master recipe, #121, skipping the first step of cooking the rice and starting by sautéing the chicken and leeks as before. When you add the leeks, also add the bay leaf, carrots, celery, and thyme. Add all 6 cups of stock and bring the stoup to a boil. Stir in the 1½ cups of rice and cook until the rice is just tender, 15 to 18 minutes. Stir in the parsley, adjust the salt and pepper, and serve. Leftovers will get really thick, and the rice will bloat. Add a combination of broth and water to reheat the stoup.

4 SERVINGS, WITH SECONDS

123 Steaks with Two Tapenades, Arugula Salad, and Crusty Bread

TAPENADES

- ½ cup pitted kalamata black olives
- 1 tin of flat anchovy fillets, drained (10 fillets)
- 3 tablespoons capers, drained
- 1 cup fresh flat-leaf parsley
- 2 lemons
- 3 jarred roasted red bell peppers, drained
- 3 rounded tablespoons prepared basil pesto

- 8 (1-inch-thick) medallions of beef tenderloin, or 4 New York strip steaks, 8 to 10 ounces each and 1 inch thick, at room temperature
  Extra-virgin olive oil (EVOO), for liberal drizzling
  Coarse salt and coarse black pepper
- 4 to 5 cups trimmed, washed, and dried arugula (2 bunches)
- 4 ounces Parmigiano-Reggiano, shaved with a vegetable peeler
  Crusty bread, warmed in a low oven until crisp

In a food processor, grind the olives with the anchovies, capers, ⅓ cup of the parsley, and the juice of ½ lemon. Scrape into a small ramekin or dish and wash and dry the processor bowl.

Preheat a heavy skillet over high heat.

Place the red peppers, pesto, the zest of 1 lemon, and ⅓ cup of the parsley in the processor bowl and grind. Scrape the red pepper paste into another ramekin.

Drizzle the steaks with EVOO and season with salt and pepper on both sides. When the skillet is screaming hot, cook the steaks for 2 minutes on each side for rare, 3 on each side for medium rare, 4 minutes on each side for medium to medium well. Let the meat stand for 5 to 10 minutes for the juices to redistribute in the meat.

Toss the arugula and the remaining ⅓ cup of parsley leaves with the juice of the zested lemon. Squeeze the lemon with the cut side up to keep the seeds from falling into the bowl. Drizzle the greens liberally with EVOO and season them with salt and pepper. Add the shaved cheese to the greens.

Serve the steaks with wedges of the remaining lemon half to squeeze over the top. Pass the tapenades at the table for topping the steaks. Serve the greens and warm, crusty bread alongside the steaks.

4 SERVINGS

124

NOW TRY... Steaks with Horseradish Cream Sauce, Watercress Salad, and Crusty Bread

☐ TRY THIS LATER

OMIT

Tapenade ingredients

Parmigiano-Reggiano

☐ IT'S A KEEPER

SWAP

Watercress leaves for the arugula

ADD (FOR THE HORSERADISH CREAM)

1 cup sour cream

1 shallot, minced

2 rounded tablespoons prepared horseradish

2 to 3 tablespoons snipped or chopped chives

Prepare the steaks as directed. Combine all ingredients for the horseradish cream in a bowl and season with salt. Serve the steaks with watercress dressed with lemon and EVOO, plenty of horseradish cream, and crusty bread to pass.

4 SERVINGS

125

Swedish Meat Dumpling Stoup

☐ TRY THIS LATER

This stoup is a one-pot Swedish meatballs and egg noodle supper, but soupier!

1 tablespoon extra-virgin olive oil (EVOO) (once around the pan)

2 tablespoons unsalted butter, cut into pieces

½ pound white mushrooms, thinly sliced

2 celery ribs, finely chopped

1 cup shredded carrots or 1 large carrot, cut into matchsticks

1 medium onion, thinly sliced

1 bay leaf

Salt and freshly ground black pepper

2 tablespoons all-purpose flour

2 cups beef stock or broth

☐ IT'S A KEEPER

1 quart chicken stock or broth

1 pound ground veal or meatloaf mix (ground beef, veal, and pork combined)

2 rounded teaspoonfuls Dijon mustard

1 egg, beaten

½ to ⅔ cup plain bread crumbs (about 3 generous handfuls)

½ teaspoon freshly grated or ground nutmeg

½ pound medium or wide egg noodles

1 cup sour cream

2 to 3 tablespoons chopped fresh chives or fresh dill, your choice

2 to 3 tablespoons chopped fresh flat-leaf parsley

(continued on next page)

Heat a medium soup pot over medium to medium-high heat. Add the EVOO and butter and when the butter melts into the EVOO, add the mushrooms, celery, carrots, onions, and bay leaf. Cook until the mushrooms are tender and the celery, carrots, and onions begin to soften, 7 to 8 minutes. Season with salt and pepper and add the flour. Cook for another minute. Whisk in the beef and chicken stock to combine. Cover the pot and bring to a boil.

While the soup comes to a boil, mix the veal with the mustard, egg, bread crumbs, nutmeg, salt, and pepper. Roll the meat into small balls, 1 inch in diameter, tops. Remove the lid from the soup and add the balls. The dumplings will cook in the soup. After 2 to 3 minutes, stir in the egg noodles and cook for 6 minutes

more. Turn off the heat and stir the sour cream into the stoup. Adjust the salt and pepper and fish out the bay leaf. Serve the stoup with a generous sprinkle of either chives or dill and chopped parsley.

4 SERVINGS

TIDBIT

I mix beef and chicken stock to make a flavor similar to veal stock for this soup. If you live near a market or kitchen store (such as Williams-Sonoma), you can buy and use 6 cups of veal stock for this recipe.

TRY THIS LATER

IT'S A KEEPER

126 MASTER RECIPE
Spicy Shrimp and Penne
with Puttanesca Sauce

Puttanesca is a sauce named after streetwalkers. The ladies would make pots of a fishy-smelling mixture of tomatoes, anchovies, and garlic and leave the pots in brothel windows to attract fishermen in like stray cats. After the business was done, the sauce was tossed with pasta and became their dinner, or breakfast. This is a very unappetizing story for such a delicious dish, so when I am asked what "it" means, I tell a slightly less descriptive version, which you can pass along: *Puttanesca* is the sauce of the ladies of the night because it's spicy, fast, and easy! (It still makes me blush, but at least I remain hungry.)

1 pound penne pasta
Coarse salt
1/4 cup extra-virgin olive oil (EVOO) (4 times around the pan)
8 garlic cloves, finely chopped
2 teaspoons crushed red pepper flakes (eyeball it in your palm)
8 to 10 whole anchovy fillets
1/2 cup cracked, pitted, good-quality black olives, such as kalamata, or 1/3 cup pitted oil-cured black olives (saltier taste), your choice, coarsely chopped
3 to 4 tablespoons capers, drained and coarsely chopped

1 14-ounce can crushed tomatoes
1 14-ounce can diced tomatoes
1 pound (24 count) peeled and deveined shrimp, tails removed
2 handfuls fresh flat-leaf parsley leaves, finely chopped

Place a large pot of water on to boil. When it comes up, add the penne pasta and salt.

While the pasta cooks, heat a large, deep skillet over medium heat. Add the EVOO, garlic, crushed red pepper flakes, and anchovies. Break up the fish with the back of a wooden spoon until they melt into the oil. The fish will develop a nutty, salty flavor; if you think you don't like anchovies, try this ONCE and you will! Add the olives, capers, and tomatoes. Bring the sauce to a bubble and add the shrimp, scattering them in a single layer. Cover the pan to cook the shrimp, 3 to 4 minutes. They will turn pink, opaque, and firm. Uncover the pan and add the parsley. Toss and adjust the seasonings to taste.

When the pasta is al dente, drain it well and add it to the sauce. Toss to combine and serve hot.

4 SERVINGS

NOW TRY... Frutti di Mare and Linguine 127

TRY THIS LATER ☐

IT'S A KEEPER ☐

OMIT

Olives
Capers

SWAP

1 pound linguine for the penne pasta
1 28-ounce can crushed tomatoes for the combination of diced and crushed tomatoes

REDUCE

Cut shrimp back to ½ pound and use smaller shrimp, 36 per pound (18 pieces total)

ADD

6 ounces lump crab meat, drained
Zest and juice of 1 lemon
1 pound mussels, scrubbed
3 tablespoons chopped fresh chives
1 cup fresh basil leaves, about 20, shredded or torn

Prepare the pasta and sauce as directed in the master recipe, #126, omitting the capers and olives and using 1 large can of crushed tomatoes rather than a mix of crushed and diced. Toss the shrimp with the crab meat and the lemon zest and juice. Season with salt, then add the whole mixture to the sauce in an even layer. Arrange the mussels in the pan. Cover the pot and cook for 5 to 6 minutes, or until the shrimp are pink and firm and the mussels are open. Discard any unopened mussels. Toss the sauce, adding the parsley and chives. Drain the linguine well, then add the hot pasta to the skillet and toss with the seafood to combine. Adjust the seasoning. Turn off the heat and let sit for a minute or two for the pasta to soak up a little sauce. Pile the pasta onto plates and garnish with shredded or torn fresh basil, then serve.

4 BIG PORTIONS

128 MASTER RECIPE
Shrimp and Crab Fritters with Chopped Salad
and Roasted Red Pepper and Pickle Vinaigrette

FRITTERS

Vegetable or other light-colored oil, for frying

2 cups complete pancake mix (the "just add water" type)

1/2 pound small cooked, peeled, and deveined shrimp, chopped

6 ounces lump crab meat, drained and checked for bits of shell

3 scallions, chopped

2 teaspoons hot sauce, such as Tabasco

1 tablespoon Old Bay Seasoning or other seafood seasoning blend, available at the fish counter

Coarse salt

VINAIGRETTE AND SALAD

3 tablespoons dill pickle relish

1 whole seeded roasted red pepper, drained (from a jar or from the bulk bins at the appetizer section of the market)

Juice of 1 lemon

2 to 3 tablespoons fresh flat-leaf parsley leaves

1/3 cup extra-virgin olive oil (EVOO) (eyeball it)

Salt and freshly ground black pepper

2 romaine lettuce hearts, chopped

3 celery ribs from the heart, chopped

1/2 red onion, chopped

1 lemon, cut into wedges, or malt vinegar, to pass at the table (optional)

Fill a deep, large skillet with about 1 1/2 inches vegetable or other light-colored oil. Heat the oil over medium heat until a 1-inch cube of bread browns to a deep golden color in a count of 40.

In a large bowl, stir together the pancake mix and 1 1/4 cups of water to combine. Then, add the shrimp and break up the crab into little bits as you drop it in. Add the scallions, hot sauce, and seafood seasoning and stir to combine. Use 2 tablespoons to drop 2-inch fritters into the pan. Cook small batches of fritters, no more than 6 at a time—do not crowd the pan or you will cause the temperature to drop too far, too fast. The fritters should cook for 2 to 3 minutes on each side to a deep golden color. Remove to a plate lined with paper towels to drain, and season with salt while they are hot. The recipe should yield 16 to 20 pieces, 4 or 5 fritters per portion, depending on the uniformity of size.

While the fritters are working, place the relish, roasted red pepper, lemon juice, and parsley in a food processor and turn it on. Stream in the EVOO to form the dressing, then stop the processor and season up the dressing with salt and pepper to taste.

Combine the chopped lettuce with the celery and onions and toss with the vinaigrette. Adjust the seasoning. Arrange the tossed salad on a platter or individual plates. Top the salad with the fritters or serve alongside. Pass the lemon wedges or malt vinegar at the table to squeeze or pour over the fritters, if you wish.

4 SERVINGS

129

☐ TRY THIS LATER ☐ IT'S A KEEPER

Some fritters (with a few changes), different salad—all new menu!

FRITTERS

OMIT

Shrimp
Crab
Old Bay Seasoning

ADD

1 cup shredded carrots or 1 large carrot, cut into matchsticks

1 10-ounce box frozen chopped broccoli, defrosted in microwave and squeezed dry in a kitchen towel

½ red bell pepper, cored, seeded, and finely chopped

2 tablespoons sesame seeds

ASIAN SALAD WITH SESAME DRESSING

3 tablespoons tahini (sesame paste), found on the specialty or whole foods aisle

2 tablespoons tamari (dark aged soy sauce)
Juice of 1 lime

3 tablespoons vegetable oil (eyeball it)

2 teaspoons hot sauce
Coarse salt

½ pound asparagus spears, blanched, then chopped

3 cups stemmed arugula or baby spinach leaves, chopped

½ seedless cucumber, chopped

6 radishes, thinly sliced

1 underripe Hass avocado, scooped from skin and chopped

To make the fritters, combine the pancake mix and 1¼ cups water, then stir in the veggies and sesame seeds as you would the seafood in the master recipe, #128. Cook the fritters using the same method and season with salt once they are removed from the oil.

In the bottom of a salad bowl, combine the tahini, tamari, and lime juice with a whisk and stream in the vegetable oil. Season the dressing with hot sauce and salt. Add the chopped asparagus, arugula, cucumber, radishes, and avocado to the bowl and toss gently to combine. Top the salad with the fritters and serve.

4 SERVINGS

TIDBIT

Sara Moulton has another cool method for testing oil temp: Place the handle of a wooden spoon into the oil and if bubbles form all around it, the oil is just right.

130 Sliced Herb and Garlic Tagliata   SUPER SALAD SUPPER
over Shaved Portobello, Celery, and Parmigiano-Reggiano Salad

Tagliata refers to Italian-style steaks that are cut thin and quickly cooked—all appealing to a 30-minute girl.

4 large garlic cloves, popped from the skins
2 lemons
2 to 3 tablespoons fresh rosemary leaves (from 2 stems)
8 fresh sage leaves
2 handfuls of fresh flat-leaf parsley leaves
3 to 4 tablespoons fresh thyme leaves (from 8 stems)
Coarse salt and coarse black pepper
Extra-virgin olive oil (EVOO), for liberal drizzling
4 thin cut (1/2-inch) boneless rib-eye or strip steaks (1 1/2 to 2 pounds)
1 celery heart, ends trimmed
4 portobello mushroom caps
1/3 pound Parmigiano-Reggiano
2 cups trimmed, washed, and dried arugula (1 bunch)
1 tablespoon Worcestershire sauce (eyeball it)

Preheat a grill pan, outdoor grill, or tabletop electric grill to high heat.

Chop the garlic and set to one side of the cutting board. Zest 1 lemon on the cutting board. Pile all of the rosemary, all of the sage, half of the parsley leaves, and all but 1 tablespoon of the thyme leaves on top of the lemon zest. Chop the herb pile together with the lemon zest, then add the garlic to the pile and continue until all the herbs, zest, and garlic are finely chopped and combined. Add about a teaspoon each of coarse salt and black pepper to the pile and mash it into the herbs and garlic using the flat of your knife and the palm of your hand.

Drizzle EVOO over the steaks liberally on both sides, then evenly smear the steaks with the good goop: garlic, herb, and zest mash. Grill the steaks for 2 minutes on each side for rare, 3 minutes on each side for medium to medium well. Let them rest for a few minutes before slicing.

Cut the celery on a very acute angle, very thinly slicing the greens and stalks. Cut the portobellos straight across but slice them as thin as possible as well. Shred the cheese using a vegetable peeler to make long, thin pieces of Parmigiano-Reggiano. In a large bowl, arrange and combine the celery with the mushrooms and cheese and arugula leaves. Coarsely chop the remaining parsley and thyme leaves and scatter over the salad. Dress the salad with the juice of the zested lemon. Cut the lemon in half across and squeeze the juice out with the cut side facing up. The juice will spill out and down over the sides. It's messy, but it keeps the seeds in the lemon and out of your salad. Generously drizzle the salad with some EVOO to coat and toss the salad lightly with your fingertips. Season with salt and pepper.

Cut the remaining lemon into wedges and squeeze a little juice over the cooked steaks. Slice the meat very thin against the grain and top with Worcestershire or lemon juice. Place a sliced steak on each dinner plate and top with mounds of the salad. YUMMO!

4 SERVINGS

Baked Sole and Roasted Asparagus with Sesame

131

TRY THIS LATER ☐   IT'S A KEEPER ☐

2 cups chicken stock or broth

1 tablespoon vegetable oil, plus some for drizzling

1 cup white rice

2-inch piece of fresh ginger, peeled and grated

4 tablespoons tamari (dark aged soy sauce, found on the international aisle)

2 garlic cloves, chopped

Juice of 1 lemon

6 scallions, thinly sliced

2 teaspoons toasted sesame oil

4 6- to 7-ounce sole fillets

2 pounds asparagus, trimmed to 4- to 5-inch tips

3 tablespoons sesame seeds (3 palmfuls)

Salt and freshly ground black pepper

Preheat the oven to 400°F.

Bring the stock and a drizzle of vegetable oil to a boil. Add the rice and stir. Return to a boil, then lower the heat, cover, and simmer for about 18 minutes, until tender.

In a shallow baking dish, combine the ginger, tamari, garlic, lemon juice, scallions, 1 teaspoon of the toasted sesame oil, and a drizzle of vegetable oil. Add the sole fillets to the shallow dish and coat in the mixture. Let the fish sit while you prepare the asparagus.

Place the asparagus on a rimmed cookie sheet and drizzle with the tablespoon of vegetable oil, the remaining teaspoon of sesame oil, the sesame seeds, salt, and pepper. Toss the asparagus around to make sure it is thoroughly coated. Transfer the fish and the asparagus to the oven and roast for 12 to 14 minutes, or until the fish is cooked through and the asparagus is tender.

When the rice is tender, fluff it with a fork and remove from the heat.

Serve the baked sole alongside the roasted asparagus with the white rice.

4 SERVINGS

TRY THIS LATER

IT'S A KEEPER

132 MASTER RECIPE
Chicken, Veal, or Pork Schnitzel
with Red Caraway Cabbage

2 pounds boneless, skinless chicken breast halves, or thin-cut boneless pork loin chops, or thin-cut boneless veal chops or cutlets (do not buy small scallops—size matters, here)
Salt and freshly ground black pepper

½ cup all-purpose flour

2 eggs beaten with a splash of milk or cream

2 cups plain bread crumbs

1 teaspoon freshly ground or grated nutmeg (eyeball it)
Vegetable oil or light-in-color olive oil, for frying, plus 2 tablespoons

CABBAGE

1 red onion, thinly sliced

1 green apple, peeled and chopped

½ red cabbage, chopped (about 4 cups)

1 teaspoon caraway seeds

2 tablespoons red wine vinegar

2 tablespoons light or dark brown sugar

2 teaspoons Worcestershire sauce

1 lemon, cut into wedges

If using chicken, butterfly each chicken breast and place between wax paper. For pork, place chops several inches apart between wax paper. For veal, if you have large, thin-cut pieces from the butcher, use as is. If the veal is more than ¼ inch thick, place it between wax paper. Pound the meat until very thin using a small heavy skillet or mallet.

Season the meat with salt and pepper and dust in flour. Beat the eggs and milk or cream in a large shallow dish. Combine the bread crumbs with the nutmeg and more salt and pepper and place on a large plate. Coat the meat in egg, then in crumbs. Heat a large nonstick skillet over medium to medium-high heat with just enough oil in it to thinly coat the bottom of the pan. When the oil gets wavy looking, add the meat in a single layer and cook until golden on each side, 3 minutes each. Transfer the meat to a plate and repeat, if necessary. Reserve the cooked schnitzel under a loose foil tent.

Meanwhile, heat a second, deep, large nonstick skillet over medium-high to high heat. Add about 2 tablespoons of the vegetable oil or light olive oil (twice around the pan). Add the onions, apples, and cabbage. Season the mixture with salt, pepper, and the caraway seeds. Toss and sear the mixture for 5 minutes, then add the vinegar, brown sugar, and Worcestershire and toss to coat and combine the cabbage evenly. Reduce the heat a bit and keep the cabbage going until the meat is all cooked.

Serve the schnitzels with the lemon wedges and a pile of seared red cabbage with caraway alongside.

4 SERVINGS

NOW TRY... *Fa-schizzel My Schnitzel:*
Cutlets with the Works! Breaded Meat with Mushroom
and Onion Gravy, Bacon, and Cornichons

ADD

8   slices center-cut bacon, chopped into 1-inch
     pieces
1   medium yellow onion, thinly sliced
½   pound white mushrooms, thinly sliced
2   tablespoons all-purpose flour
2   cups chicken stock or broth
2   to 3 tablespoons finely chopped fresh flat-leaf
     parsley leaves (a handful)
½   cup cornichon or baby gherkin pickles,
     chopped

Prepare the schnitzel and cabbage as directed in the master recipe, #132. When all of the schnitzels are cooked, wipe the skillet clean and return the pan to medium-high heat. Add the bacon and cook until crisp and brown. Drain on paper towels, reserving a tablespoon or so of the rendered fat in the pan. Add the onions and mushrooms and cook for 5 minutes. Season the veggies with salt and pepper. Add the flour and cook for a minute longer, then whisk in the stock and thicken a bit, 2 minutes. Add the parsley, adjust the seasonings in the gravy, and remove from the heat.

Top the schnitzel with lemon, the mushroom and onion gravy, crispy bacon bits, and chopped pickles and serve with the seared cabbage alongside. Pass rye or pumpernickel bread and sweet butter at the table.

4 SERVINGS

134 Seafood Newburg Stoup
with Cayenne–Chive-Buttered Corn Toasties

2 tablespoons extra-virgin olive oil (EVOO) (twice around the pan)

4 tablespoons unsalted butter

1 large starchy potato, peeled and chopped

2 celery ribs with their greens, chopped

1 medium yellow onion, chopped

1 bay leaf, fresh or dried
  Salt and freshly ground black pepper

1 tablespoon Old Bay Seasoning

3 tablespoons all-purpose flour

¼ cup dry sherry (eyeball it)

3 cups chicken or seafood stock

1½ pounds cod, scrod, or haddock, cut in chunks

1 pound medium shrimp, peeled and deveined, coarsely chopped

3 cups whole milk or half-and-half

½ teaspoon cayenne pepper

4 corn toaster pastries, such as Thomas' brand

2 tablespoons chopped fresh chives

Heat a medium soup pot over medium-high heat. Add the EVOO and the 2 tablespoons of cold butter, cut into small pieces. Add the veggies as you get them chopped, then season them with the bay leaf, salt, pepper, and Old Bay Seasoning. Cook for 5 minutes to begin to soften, then add the flour and cook for a minute longer. Next, add the sherry and cook for 1 minute. Whisk in the stock and bring it up to a bubble, then arrange the seafood in an even layer around the pan. Cover the pan and cook until the fish is opaque and the shrimp is pink, 4 minutes. Remove the lid and add the milk and cook for 2 to 3 minutes longer to thicken. Add about ¼ teaspoon cayenne pepper, then adjust the seasonings. Discard the bay leaf.

Melt the remaining 2 tablespoons of butter and ¼ teaspoon of cayenne pepper in a small cup. Toast the corn pastries, brush with cayenne butter, and sprinkle with the chopped chives. Serve alongside the stoup.

4 SERVINGS

135 NOW TRY... Crab and Corn Chowda

SWAP

12 ounces lump crab, for the fish and shrimp

ADD

1 10-ounce box frozen corn kernels

½ red bell pepper, finely chopped

Prepare as described in the master recipe, #134, but use the crab and corn rather than fish and shrimp—it tastes like a whole new thing! Add bell peppers with the celery and onions.

4 SERVINGS

Spaghetti con Aglio e Olio
with Tomato and Onion Salad

This meal and the next have appeared in other books of mine. I did not invent the dishes—they are classics. My take on these classics are my two favorite meals, ever. I simply could not have you (or me) live through a whole year without having these dishes in there somewhere. Enjoy these oldies-but-oh-so-goodies!

Coarse salt
1 pound spaghetti
Crusty bread, to pass at the table
1/3 cup extra-virgin olive oil (EVOO) (about 5 times around the pan), plus some for drizzling
8 garlic cloves, chopped
1 teaspoon crushed red pepper flakes (eyeball it in the palm of your hand)
8 to 10 flat anchovy fillets
1 cup fresh flat-leaf parsley leaves (3 fistfuls)
4 vine-ripe tomatoes or 6 Roma tomatoes, cut lengthwise, lightly seeded, then sliced into thin half-moons
1 small white or yellow onion, quartered lengthwise, then thinly sliced
Coarse black pepper

Preheat the oven to 200°F.

Heat a large pot of water to boil for the pasta. Salt the water and cook the pasta until al dente, 6 to 7 minutes or so.

Place the bread in a low oven to warm and crust it up.

While the pasta cooks, place a large, deep, nonstick heavy-bottomed skillet over medium-low heat. When the pan is warm, add the 1/3 cup of EVOO, the garlic, red pepper flakes, and anchovies.

While the sauce and pasta work, chop a fistful of the parsley and combine it with the tomatoes and onions in a shallow bowl. Dress the salad with a liberal drizzle of EVOO and season with salt and pepper. Finely chop the remaining parsley and set aside.

Drain the spaghetti really well but do not rinse it; rinsing will wash off the starch, and the starch helps the oil stick to the pasta. Pour the hot spaghetti into the skillet. Add the reserved parsley and toss the pasta together with the anchovies, garlic, and oil to coat evenly. Season the completed dish liberally with salt and pepper.

Serve the pasta with the tomato and onion salad and crusty bread alongside.

4 SERVINGS

TIDBIT

If you think you don't like anchovies, you're wrong. The anchovies will melt into the oil and break up completely. Help break them up with a wooden spoon as they cook. Once they melt into oil, the anchovies will no longer taste like fish but like salted, toasted nuts in garlic oil. Oh my God!

137 MASTER RECIPE
Artichoke and Walnut Pesto Pasta

Coarse salt

1 pound penne rigate pasta

4 ounces walnut pieces, toasted (about ⅓ cup)

1 15-ounce can artichoke hearts, drained

1 large garlic clove, cracked away from the skin

Zest of 1 lemon

A handful of fresh flat-leaf parsley leaves

½ cup grated Parmigiano-Reggiano (a couple of handfuls)

Coarse black pepper

¼ teaspoon grated or ground nutmeg (eyeball the amount)

⅓ cup extra-virgin olive oil (EVOO) (eyeball it)

3 cups coarsely chopped arugula (2 small bunches) or baby spinach leaves (half a sack)

Bring a large pot of water to a boil. Salt the water liberally, then add the pasta and cook al dente.

In the bowl of a food processor, combine the nuts, artichoke hearts, garlic, lemon zest, parsley, cheese, some pepper, and nutmeg and pulse the ingredients until chopped. Turn the processor on and stream in the EVOO in a slow stream until the pesto forms. It should be thick and pastelike in consistency.

Place the pesto in the bottom of a large serving bowl. Drain the pasta and add the hot pasta to the bowl. Add the arugula and toss to wilt the greens and evenly coat the pasta with the pesto. Adjust the salt and pepper and serve.

4 SERVINGS

NOW TRY... Spinach and Artichoke Calzones

138

OMIT

Pasta
Arugula or spinach

ADD

1 more garlic clove
4 cups ricotta cheese
2 10-ounce boxes frozen chopped spinach, defrosted in the microwave and wrung completely dry in a clean kitchen towel
2 balls or tubs of fresh pizza dough, any variety or brand
A sprinkle of flour, to dust hands for handling the dough
1 sack (10 ounces) shredded Italian cheese blend, shredded Provolone, or shredded mozzarella, your choice
A dab of EVOO to brush on the dough before baking

Preheat the oven to 400°F.

Make the pesto as in the master recipe, #137, adding the extra clove of garlic.

In a large bowl, combine the pesto and the ricotta. Add the spinach, pulling it apart as you add it to the bowl, then mix it through the ricotta and pesto. Taste the filling to adjust the salt and pepper.

Cut each ball of dough in half and with each half, dust your hands with flour, and form a 6- to 7-inch round crust. Pile one fourth of the ricotta filling on half of the round dough. Top with one fourth of the shredded cheese. Fold the dough over and seal at the edges. Brush the calzone lightly with EVOO and place on a cookie sheet. You should be able to fit all 4 on a large nonstick sheet. Bake for 15 to 18 minutes, until evenly deep golden and crisp.

4 SERVINGS

139 Lettillas: Mix-n-Match Lettuce Tacos

BEEF FILLING

1 tablespoon extra-virgin olive oil (EVOO)
1 pound ground sirloin
1 small yellow onion, chopped
2 garlic cloves, chopped
1/2 red bell pepper, finely chopped
2 tablespoons Worcestershire sauce
(eyeball it)
2 tablespoons chili powder (a healthy, rounded palmful)
Salt and freshly ground black pepper
1/2 cup tomato sauce

SHRIMP FILLING

2 tablespoons extra-virgin olive oil (EVOO)
2 garlic cloves, chopped
1 jalapeño or serrano pepper, seeded and finely chopped
1 pound small shrimp, peeled and deveined, tails removed
Salt and freshly ground black pepper
Zest and juice of 1 lime
A handful of chopped fresh flat-leaf parsley or 1 tablespoon chopped fresh cilantro, your choice

1 large head of iceberg lettuce, cored, then cut into quarters
1 sack (10 ounces) shredded Cheddar cheese
4 scallions, chopped
1 cup chopped green olives with pimientos (salad olives)

Prep all the ingredients for the fillings before you heat up the skillets at the stovetop so you can work two pans at once. Start the shrimp pan last; it takes just 5 minutes to cook. The meat filling takes double that time or more.

For the beef filling, add the EVOO (once around the pan) to a medium nonstick skillet over medium-high heat and brown the meat. Add the onions, garlic, and bell peppers and season with Worcestershire, chili powder, salt, and pepper. Cook the beef mixture for 5 minutes more, then add the tomato sauce, stir to combine, and turn off the heat.

For the shrimp filling, heat a medium nonstick skillet over medium-high heat. Add the EVOO (twice around the pan). Add the garlic, jalapeños, then shrimp and cook, stirring constantly, until the shrimp are pink and firm, 3 to 4 minutes. Season the shrimp with salt and pepper, lime zest and juice, and chopped parsley or cilantro.

Serve the fillings in bowls with the lettuce and toppings of cheese, scallions, and olives in smaller bowls all alongside. Take a piece of lettuce, place a heaping serving spoonful of filling on it, top with cheese, scallions, and olives, fold up the sides of the lettuce leaf, and eat.

4 SERVINGS

Beans and Greens Soup

Pancetta gives the soup its deep flavor. It is rolled cured pork that is similar to bacon, but not smoked. It is widely available at the deli counter in larger supermarkets or small Italian import shops.

- 1 loaf Italian semolina bread
- 3 tablespoons extra-virgin olive oil (EVOO) (3 times around the pan)
- ¼ pound pancetta, available at the deli, sliced the thickness of bacon, chopped
- 4 to 5 garlic cloves, chopped
- ½ teaspoon crushed red pepper flakes (eyeball it in the palm of your hand)
- 1 medium white or yellow onion, chopped
- 2 large heads of escarole, washed, dried, and coarsely chopped
- ½ teaspoon freshly grated or ground nutmeg Salt and freshly ground black pepper
- 1 quart chicken stock or broth
- 2 15-ounce cans white beans or cannellini Grated Parmigiano-Reggiano or Romano cheese, to pass at the table

Preheat the oven to 200°F.

Place the bread in the oven to heat and crust it up.

Heat a medium soup pot or a large, deep-sided skillet over medium-high heat. Add the EVOO, then add the pancetta, separating the pieces as you drop it in.

Brown the pancetta lightly, about 2 minutes or so, then add the garlic, red pepper flakes, and onions, and reduce the heat a bit. Cook for 3 to 4 minutes, then start turning and wilting piles of the greens into the pan. Once the greens are all in the pan, season them with nutmeg, salt, and pepper. Add the chicken stock and beans and turn the heat back up to medium high to bring the soup to a boil. Once the soup boils, reduce the heat back down to simmer and cook for 10 minutes. Adjust the salt and pepper and serve the soup in shallow bowls with lots of cheese and crusty hunks of bread for mopping up the bowl.

4 SERVINGS

141 Crab Tortilla (Egg Pie) and
Shredded Plantain Hash Browns

This is my at-home version of Chef José's crab omelet from the Floridian Diner in Fort Lauderdale, Florida. Hey, José, how did I do? Oh, and the inspiration for the hash browns comes from my love of latkes and my love of these crunchy treats called plantain spiders, which I had at La Casita Blanca in Puerto Rico. They are too delish!

2 cups pre-shredded hash brown potatoes, available in pouches on the dairy aisle, or 1 large starchy potato, peeled and shredded

2 celery ribs with greens, cut into chunks

2 small to medium onions, 1 peeled and cut into large cubes, 1 peeled and left whole

1 small green bell pepper, cored, seeded, and cut into chunks

$1/2$ cup extra-virgin olive oil (EVOO)
Salt and freshly ground black pepper

2 large green plantains, shredded

2 tablespoons all-purpose flour

6 eggs, beaten

$1/2$ cup cream or half-and-half

2 teaspoons hot sauce

12 ounces lump crab meat, broken into tiny pieces

1 tablespoon Old Bay Seasoning or other seafood seasoning blend

1 cup store-bought mango salsa or fruit chutney

Place the potatoes, celery, cubed onions and bell peppers in a food processor and process into a fine chop.

Heat an 8-inch skillet over medium heat. Add $1/4$ cup of the EVOO, then add the finely chopped veggies, season them with salt and pepper, and sauté for 5 minutes, or until they are just beginning to be tender.

Begin the plantain hash browns. Place the shredded plantains into a bowl and grate the whole onion over the bowl. Mix well, then sprinkle with the flour. Season with salt and pepper. Heat a large nonstick skillet over medium-high heat. Add the remaining $1/4$ cup of EVOO. Make 8 plantain hash brown rounds and place in the pan, trying not to crowd them. Each hash brown round should be about $2^{1}/_{2}$ to 3 inches across. Fry until golden on each side, 3 to 4 minutes per side.

Back to the fried "tortilla": Beat the eggs with the cream and hot sauce. Pour the eggs over the vegetables in the skillet and stir. Let the eggs begin to set up on the bottom, as for an omelet. Season the crab with the Old Bay Seasoning, then gently combine with the egg and veggie mixture. Use a heat-safe spatula to pull up the "skin" from the bottom and let more egg seep down. Once the eggs are almost totally set up, about 5 minutes, place a plate over the pan and invert it. The tortilla should slide out. Return the skillet to the heat and slide the tortilla back into the pan, uncooked side down. Fry for another couple of minutes. It should be evenly and deeply golden on both sides. Turn off the heat and let stand to cool and set a bit.

Cut the tortilla into 4 wedges. Serve 2 plantain hash browns alongside each wedge of crab tortilla. Pass the store-bought mango salsa or fruit chutney alongside.

4 SERVINGS

Bacon-Makes-It-Better Corn Chowder
with Tomato and Ricotta Salata Salad

142

☐ TRY THIS LATER   ☐ IT'S A KEEPER

1 quart chicken stock or broth

4 ears of fresh corn, shucked

5 tablespoons extra-virgin olive oil (EVOO)

6 slices bacon, chopped

2 tablespoons unsalted butter

1 large yellow onion, chopped

3 garlic cloves, chopped

1 tablespoon fresh thyme leaves, chopped

1 bay leaf

3 dashes hot sauce, such as Tabasco
   Salt and freshly ground black pepper

1 rounded tablespoon Dijon mustard

2 tablespoons red wine vinegar (eyeball it)

20 fresh basil leaves, torn or chopped

2 tablespoons all-purpose flour

1 cup heavy cream

½ small red onion, chopped

1 pint grape tomatoes, halved

1 seedless cucumber, cut in half lengthwise,
   then thinly sliced into half-moons

¼ cup fresh flat-leaf parsley leaves (a generous
   handful), chopped

6 ounces ricotta salata, crumbled (found in the
   specialty cheese case)
   Oyster crackers, for the chowda
   Crusty bread, to pass at the table

Place the chicken stock in a large pot over high heat; bring it to a boil while you prepare the corn. Cut the corn kernels from the cobs. Add the cobs to the stock and simmer for 8 to 10 minutes, to get every little bit of corn flavor in your chowder. (Cut the cobs in pieces if necessary to submerge them entirely.)

Preheat a soup pot over medium-high heat with 2 tablespoons of the EVOO (twice around the pan). Add the chopped bacon and cook until crisp, about 2 to 3 minutes. Remove the crispy bacon from the pot with a slotted spoon to a plate lined with a paper towel and reserve. Return the pot to the heat and add the butter. Once the butter melts, add the yellow onions, garlic, thyme, bay leaf, hot sauce, salt, and pepper. Cook, stirring frequently, for 4 minutes, or until the onions are starting to brown.

While the onions cook, in a small bowl combine the Dijon mustard, red wine vinegar, salt, and pepper. Whisk in the remaining 3 tablespoons of EVOO, then stir in the basil and reserve.

Add the reserved corn kernels to the onions in the soup pot and cook for 2 minutes. Dust the onions and corn kernels with the flour and cook for 1 minute more. Remove and discard the simmered cobs from the boiling stock. Whisk the hot stock into the onions and corn several ladlefuls at a time until incorporated. Add the cream, bring to a simmer, and cook for 8 to 10 minutes.

While the soup is cooking, in a large bowl combine the red onions, grape tomatoes, cucumbers, parsley, and crumbled ricotta salata cheese. Pour the reserved dressing over the salad and toss to coat. Season the salad with salt and pepper.

Serve the soup garnished with lots of the crispy bacon pieces and oyster crackers. Serve the tomato ricotta salata salad with some crusty bread alongside.

4 SERVINGS

143 MASTER RECIPE
Super Mashers with Steak and Pepper Hash

4 large starchy potatoes, such as Idaho
Coarse salt

3 tablespoons vegetable oil

2 tablespoons unsalted butter, cut into small pieces

4 garlic cloves, chopped

4 scallions, chopped

1⅓ pounds 1-inch-thick beef sirloin, trimmed and thinly sliced
Coarse black pepper

2 tablespoons Worcestershire sauce

1 red bell pepper, cored, seeded, and thinly sliced

2 Anaheim or poblano chilies, seeded and thinly sliced

1 medium red onion, thinly sliced

2 to 3 tablespoons fresh thyme leaves, chopped
Several drops of hot sauce, such as Tabasco, to taste (I add a couple of tablespoons!)
Juice of 1 lime

½ cup sour cream or reduced-fat sour cream

¼ to ½ cup milk or reduced-fat milk, depending on how soft you like your mashers

1 sack (10 ounces) shredded sharp Cheddar cheese

Peel the taters and cut them into small chunks. Place the potatoes in a pot and cover with cold water. Cover the pot and bring to a boil over high heat. Uncover, add salt to season, and cook until tender, about 15 minutes.

In a small pot over medium-low heat, add about 1 tablespoon of the vegetable oil—just eyeball it. Add the butter. When the butter melts into the oil, add the garlic. Sauté the garlic for 1 to 2 minutes, then add the scallions and remove the pan from the heat. Reserve.

Heat a large nonstick skillet over high heat. Season the sliced steak with salt and pepper, then heat 1 tablespoon of the vegetable oil (once around the pan). The oil will smoke—don't freak out, just add the meat and start searing it up. Brown the strips on all sides, hit it with some Worcestershire sauce, then push it off to one side of the pan and add the remaining tablespoon of vegetable oil to the pan. Add the peppers, chilies, and onions, season with salt and pepper, then toss them around, searing the edges, for another minute or two before combining all the meat and veggies together. Add the thyme and cook for another 2 to 3 minutes, keeping everything moving around like a stir-fry. Turn off the heat and drizzle some hot sauce and the lime juice over the steak and veggies. Adjust the seasonings.

Drain the potatoes, then return them to the hot pot to evaporate some of the water content. Add the reserved garlic and scallion mixture to the potatoes along with the sour cream and start smashing away with a masher. Add ¼ cup to ½ cup milk to get the potatoes to the desired consistency. Season the super mashers with salt and pepper.

Pile up one fourth of the potatoes on each plate. Top with a generous handful of Cheddar cheese. Pile up meat and veggies on top of the super mashers and serve. The heat of the meat and veggies will melt the cheese. YUMMO!

4 SERVINGS

NOW TRY... Super Mashers with Chicken and Green Chili Hash

144

OMIT

Worcestershire sauce
Hot sauce

SWAP

1 pound chicken breast cutlets, cut into thin strips, for the sirloin
Green bell pepper for the red

ADD

1 cup prepared green chili salsa (salsa verde, mild or medium heat level), available in the Mexican foods section of the market

Prepare the potatoes as directed as in the master recipe, #143. Prepare the chicken as directed for the beef, omitting the Worcestershire. Add the peppers, chilies, and onions at the same stage of the meal preparation. Leave out the hot sauce, but, after you add the lime juice, stir in the salsa, adding it to the cooked meat and vegetables.

Top the portions of mashers with a generous handful of shredded Cheddar cheese and the hot chicken, peppers, and chili salsa and serve.

4 SERVINGS

(variations continue on page 130)

TRY THIS LATER

IT'S A KEEPER

145

AND TRY... Super Mashers with Shrimp and Chorizo Hash

OMIT

Worcestershire sauce
Cheddar cheese

SWAP

1 pound medium shrimp, peeled and deveined, for the sirloin

ADD

½ pound diced chorizo, available in the packaged meats case of the market (kielbasa or andouille can be substituted)
Juice of 1 additional lime

Prepare the meal as in the master recipe, #143, adding the chorizo to the pan for 1 minute when you would add the steak. After the chorizo sears up for a minute or two, add the shrimp and cook for another 2 minutes, then move the sausage and shrimp to one side of the pan and continue the recipe with the peppers, chilies, and onions. Add the hot sauce, then use the juice of two limes rather than one.

Serve the mashers with the shrimp and chorizo mixture on top.

4 SERVINGS

TIDBIT

Chorizo is spicy pork sausage with lots of garlic and paprika.

TRY THIS LATER

IT'S A KEEPER

146

Spanish Fish and Chorizo Stoup

Food Network is located at Chelsea Market, in Manhattan. The Lobster Place is a great seafood shop within this huge market. I made up this meal one night during a run of taping for *30-Minute Meals*. I stopped into the market and took home pure white scrod, some tiny Manila clams, and a little pack of saffron powder as my inspiration. It was so delish that John and I ate it three nights in ten, sharing it with family and friends two of those evenings as the simplest, tastiest way we could think to entertain a crowd. Whether you're feeding one or some, make a whole pot of this stoup (thicker than soup, thinner than stew), as the leftovers get even better!

3 tablespoons extra-virgin olive oil (EVOO) (3 times around the pan)
½ pound chorizo, diced (available near kielbasa in the packaged meat section of the market)

1 large starchy potato, such as Idaho, peeled and chopped

4 large garlic cloves, chopped

3 celery ribs and the leafy greens, chopped

2 leeks, trimmed, halved lengthwise, cut into $1/2$-inch slices, then separated and washed to release dirt, and drained
Coarse salt and coarse black pepper

$1/2$ cup dry white wine or $1/3$ cup white vermouth (eyeball it)

1 14-ounce can diced tomatoes, drained

2 cups seafood stock (available on the soup aisle or at the seafood counter), or 1 cup each chicken stock and clam juice

1 envelope saffron powder, about $1 1/2$ grams, or a pinch of saffron threads

3 tablespoons fresh thyme leaves (from 5 to 6 sprigs), chopped

$1/4$ cup chopped fresh flat-leaf parsley (a couple of palmfuls)

$2 1/2$ to 3 pounds cod or scrod, cut into large bite-size chunks (buy thick pieces, cut from the center rather than the tail)
Juice of 1 lemon

1 to $1 1/4$ pounds small Manila clams
Crusty bread, for dipping

Heat a large, deep skillet with a tight-fitting lid over medium-high heat. Add the EVOO and chorizo, cook for a minute or two to darken and render the sausage a bit, then add the potatoes and garlic and coat in fat. Cook for 2 to 3 minutes. Add the celery and leeks and season the mixture with salt and pepper. Cook for 5 minutes, then add the wine, scraping up any bits from the bottom of the pan. Add the tomatoes and stock, saffron, thyme, and half of the parsley. Put the lid on the pan and bring the stoup to a boil. Season the fish chunks with lemon juice and salt. Arrange the fish in a single layer on top of the stoup and replace the lid. Cook for 3 minutes, or until the fish is opaque at all edges but still a bit undercooked in the middle and not yet firm. Add the clams in a single layer, replace the lid, and cook for 2 to 3 minutes more, until the clams all open. Discard any clams that refuse to open. Uncover the pan, dip into the stoup, and carefully spoon the sauce over the cooked seafood. Turn off the heat and let stand for 5 minutes. Ladle stoup into shallow bowls, garnish with the remaining parsley, and serve with lots of crusty bread.

4 VERY GENEROUS SERVINGS,
OR UP TO 6 SINGLE-BOWL SERVINGS

TRY THIS LATER

IT'S A KEEPER

147 MASTER RECIPE
Italian-Style Garlic Shrimp with Cherry Tomatoes and Thin Spaghetti

Coarse salt
1 pound thin spaghetti
1 pound small shrimp, deveined and peeled, tails removed
2 teaspoons lemon zest plus the juice of ¼ lemon
¼ cup extra-virgin olive oil (EVOO) (4 times around the pan)
6 garlic cloves, minced
1 pint cherry tomatoes, halved
4 scallions, thinly sliced on an angle
¼ cup white vermouth or ⅓ cup dry white wine (eyeball it)
2 handfuls fresh flat-leaf parsley, chopped
20 fresh basil leaves, torn or shredded
Coarse black pepper

Heat a large pot of water for the pasta. When the water boils, salt it and cook the pasta al dente.

Heat a large nonstick skillet over medium to medium-high heat. Season the shrimp with the lemon zest, lemon juice, and a little salt. Add the EVOO to the hot pan and then add the shrimp. Cook for a minute, then add the garlic, tomatoes, and scallions and toss, cooking for another minute or two until the shrimp are firm and pink. Add the white vermouth and the herbs. Turn off the heat. Drain the pasta well and add to the sauce. Toss and combine the sauce with pasta and season with salt and black pepper.

4 SERVINGS

148 NOW TRY... Spanish-Style Garlic Shrimp and Rice

TRY THIS LATER

IT'S A KEEPER

OMIT

Pasta
Basil

SWAP

Dry sherry for white vermouth

ADD

2 tablespoons EVOO
1 small white onion, chopped
1½ cups white rice
3 cups chicken stock or broth
½ cup jumbo green Spanish olives with pimientos, coarsely chopped

Start by making the rice. Place a medium pot over medium-high heat. Add the 2 tablespoons of EVOO and the onions. Cook for 2 to 3 minutes, then add the rice and lightly toast, 2 to 3 minutes. Add the chicken stock and cover the rice with a lid to bring the stock to a rapid boil. When the stock comes to a boil, reduce the heat to a simmer and cook, covered, stirring occasionally, for 17 minutes, or until tender.

Proceed as for the master recipe, #147, cooking the seasoned shrimp in the ¼ cup EVOO with the garlic, tomatoes, scallions, and parsley. Add the sherry when you would add the vermouth. Stir in the olives and remove from the heat.

Serve the shrimp over the rice.

4 SERVINGS

AND THEN TRY... Greek-Style Garlic Shrimp and Orzo 149

TRY THIS LATER   IT'S A KEEPER

Another variation on the master recipe.

OMIT

    Scallions
    Basil

SWAP

   ⅔ pound orzo (a little over half the box), for the thin spaghetti

ADD

   1 small red onion, chopped
   1 teaspoon crushed red pepper flakes
   ½ cup kalamata olives, pitted and chopped
   2 tablespoons chopped fresh oregano leaves (from 2 stems)
    Drizzle of EVOO
   8 ounces feta cheese, crumbled

Cook the orzo as directed for the spaghetti in the master recipe, #147, in salted water, until it is al dente.

Heat the ¼ cup of EVOO, then add the onions, red pepper flakes, and garlic. Cook for 2 minutes, then add the shrimp and cook for a minute more. Add the cherry tomatoes, parsley, olives, and oregano, and season with salt and pepper. Cook until the shrimp are pink and firm, then turn off the heat.

Drain the cooked orzo and drizzle with a touch of EVOO to keep it from sticking. Serve the orzo topped with the feta crumbles and the shrimp mixture.

   4 SERVINGS

150 MASTER RECIPE
German Potato Salad with Kielbasa

2½ pounds new red-skinned potatoes, quartered
    Coarse salt
8 slices thick center-cut bacon
3 tablespoons extra-virgin olive oil (EVOO)
    (eyeball it), plus some for drizzling
1 medium red onion, quartered and thinly sliced
4 cups coarsely chopped kale (1 small bunch)
3 tablespoons red wine vinegar
1 cup beef stock
¾ pound kielbasa, cut into half-moons
¼ cup fresh flat-leaf parsley, finely chopped
    Coarse black pepper

Preheat the oven to 400°F.

Place the potatoes in a pot and cover with water. Bring to a boil, add the salt, and boil the potatoes until just fork tender, 15 to 18 minutes.

Arrange the bacon on a slotted broiler pan and place in the middle of the oven. Bake the bacon until crisp, 10 to 12 minutes. Cool, chop, and reserve.

Heat a medium skillet over medium-high heat and add 2 tablespoons of the EVOO (twice around the pan). Add the red onion and sauté until just tender, 5 minutes. Add the kale in small bunches until all is wilted down. Add the vinegar and stock and turn off the heat.

Preheat a grill pan or a large nonstick skillet over medium-high heat. Drizzle the sliced kielbasa with a bit of EVOO and arrange on the preheated hot grill or in the preheated skillet. Cook for 2 minutes on each side, until hot through and crisp at the edges.

Drain the potatoes and return to the hot pot. Fold in the onion and kale mixture. Add the bacon, parsley, salt, and pepper, drizzle in the remaining tablespoon of EVOO, and fold in the cooked kielbasa.

4 SERVINGS

151 NOW TRY... French Salade Superb

OMIT

    Kielbasa

ADD

¾ pound fresh haricots verts (thin green
    beans) or trimmed green beans, halved
1 large head of frisée lettuce (pale lacy leaves,
    available in the produce department)

Prepare the potatoes, bacon, and onion-kale mixture as in the master recipe, #150. Cook the green beans in salted boiling water for 5 to 7 minutes; drain.

Combine the beans and potatoes in a large bowl with the kale mixture. Proceed as above, folding in the frisée last.

4 SERVINGS

Baby and Big Bella Mushroom and Chicken Stew

4 tablespoons extra-virgin olive oil (EVOO)

2 portobello mushroom caps, black gills scraped with a spoon, cut in half, and then thinly sliced

1 10-ounce container cremini (baby portobello) mushrooms, brushed clean and cut into quarters

4 boneless, skinless chicken breast halves cut into bite-size pieces
Salt and freshly ground black pepper

¼ cup all-purpose flour (3 rounded tablespoonfuls)

1 large yellow onion, chopped

4 garlic cloves, chopped

4 medium red bliss potatoes, thinly sliced

1 medium carrot, peeled and thinly sliced

1 celery rib with greens, thinly sliced

1 bay leaf, fresh or dried

1 tablespoon fresh thyme leaves, chopped (from 4 sprigs)

¾ cup dry white wine

1 quart chicken stock or broth

1 cup frozen peas

1 cup fresh flat-leaf parsley leaves (a few generous handfuls), chopped
Crusty, farmhouse-style bread

Preheat a large sauce pot over high heat. Add 2 tablespoons of the EVOO (twice around the pan). Add the portobello and cremini mushrooms and cook, stirring every now and then, for 5 to 6 minutes, or until all of the mushrooms are lightly brown. Remove the mushrooms from the pot to a plate, return the sauce pot to the heat, and add 2 more tablespoons of EVOO.

Season the chicken with salt and pepper, then sprinkle it with the flour. Add the chicken to the pot and cook for 3 to 4 minutes, then add the onions, garlic, potatoes, carrots, celery, bay leaf, thyme, salt, and pepper. Continue to cook for 5 minutes, stirring frequently. Add the wine, cook for 1 minute, then add the chicken stock, bring it up to a simmer, and return the mushrooms to the sauce pot. Simmer for about 10 minutes. Add the peas and parsley and simmer for 1 minute more. Fish out the bay leaf and discard. Serve the stew with some crusty bread.

4 SERVINGS

153 MASTER RECIPE
Southwestern Pasta Bake

Coarse salt

1 pound penne rigate (ridged penne) or cavatappi (ridged corkscrew pasta)

2 tablespoons vegetable oil (twice around the pan)

4 6-ounce boneless, skinless chicken breast halves, cut into bite-size pieces

1 tablespoon ground cumin (1 palmful)

1 tablespoon ground coriander (1 palmful)

2 tablespoons chili powder (2 palmfuls)
Coarse black pepper

1 large yellow onion, chopped

3 garlic cloves, chopped

1 jalapeño, seeded and chopped

2 tablespoons unsalted butter

2 tablespoons all-purpose flour (2 palmfuls)

2 cups milk

¾ pound sharp yellow Cheddar cheese, shredded (about 2½ cups)

¼ cup fresh cilantro leaves (a generous handful), chopped

½ cup fresh flat-leaf parsley leaves (a few handfuls), chopped

Preheat the broiler to high and position the rack 8 inches from the heat.

Bring a large pot of water to a boil. Salt the boiling water and cook the pasta until slightly undercooked—a little chewy at the center.

While the water is coming up to a boil, preheat a large skillet over medium-high heat with the vegetable oil. Season the chicken with cumin, coriander, chili powder, salt, and pepper. Add the seasoned chicken to the hot skillet and cook until lightly brown, about 4 to 5 minutes. Add the onions, garlic, and jalapeños and continue to cook for 5 minutes. While the chicken is cooking with the onions, make the Cheddar sauce.

In a medium sauce pot, melt the butter and add the flour to it. Cook for 1 to 2 minutes over moderate heat, then whisk in the milk. When the milk comes to a bubble, stir in the cheese, cilantro, and parsley with a wooden spoon. Season with a little salt and pepper and remove the cheese sauce from the heat.

Once the pasta is cooked, drain it and add it back into the large pot, add the contents of the chicken skillet and all of the Cheddar sauce, and stir to combine. Transfer to a baking dish and place under the broiler to lightly brown.

4 SERVINGS

SWAP

1½ pounds ground beef sirloin for the chicken
Ground chipotle powder for the chili powder

2½ cups shredded smoked Cheddar for the regular Cheddar

ADD

1 14-ounce can diced fire-roasted tomatoes (such as Muir Glen brand), drained

4 scallions, chopped, for garnish

Brown the beef, seasoned as you would the chicken in the master recipe, #153, swapping the chipotle powder for the chili powder. Continue with the recipe, swapping the smoked Cheddar for the Cheddar.

Stir the tomatoes into the cheese sauce once the cheese has melted. Garnish bowlfuls of chili con queso mac with chopped scallions.

4 SERVINGS

☐ TRY THIS LATER

☐ IT'S A KEEPER

155 Indian-Asian Seared Cod with Cilantro-Mint Chutney and Sweet Pea and Coconut Jasmine Rice

Remove the seeds from only half the jalapeño pepper. The heat lives in the seeds and this dish is a balance of heat with sweet.

        4   tablespoons vegetable oil
        1   small yellow onion, chopped
        2   large garlic cloves, crushed
            Salt and freshly ground black pepper
        1   cup jasmine rice
        1   cup sweetened shredded coconut
    1½   cups chicken stock or broth
        1   cup frozen peas
        4   8-ounce portions cod fillet
       ½   tablespoon ground coriander (half a palmful)
        1   cup fresh cilantro, stems and leaves
       ½   cup fresh mint leaves
        5   scallions, trimmed of roots, coarsely chopped
            2-inch piece of fresh ginger, peeled and cut
            into large chunks
        1   jalapeño, halved and seeds removed from
            one half
       ½   tablespoon ground cumin (half a palmful)
        2   tablespoons sugar
            Zest and juice of 1 lemon

Preheat the oven to 375°F.

Heat a sauce pot over medium-high heat with about 2 tablespoons of the vegetable oil (twice around the pan). Add three fourths of the onions, 1 of the crushed cloves of garlic, and salt and pepper. Cook for 2 minutes, then add the jasmine rice and stir to coat in the oil. Add the coconut and chicken stock and bring up to a simmer. Cover the rice with a tight-fitting lid and cook for 18 minutes, or until all the liquid has evaporated. Add the peas for the last 5 minutes of the cooking time.

Heat a large, nonstick, oven-safe skillet over high heat with the remaining 2 tablespoons of vegetable oil. Season the fish with the coriander, salt, and pepper. Add the fish to the pan and sear on the first side for 2 minutes.

While the fish is searing, start preparing the cilantro-mint chutney. Place the remaining one fourth of the onions in a food processor with the cilantro, mint, scallions, ginger, the remaining clove of garlic, the jalapeño halves, cumin, sugar, lemon zest and juice, and a splash of water. Puree until smooth.

Flip the seared cod over in the pan, cover with a piece of aluminum foil, transfer to the oven, and bake for 5 minutes. Add the chutney and return to the oven until the fish is firm to the touch and cooked through, another 3 to 5 minutes.

Stir the cooked rice with a fork to distribute the peas in the rice, and remove the crushed garlic clove. Serve the fish with some warm chutney over the pea and coconut jasmine rice.

4 SERVINGS

Sweet and Savory Stuffed Veal Rolls
with a Mustard Pan Sauce

156

☐ TRY THIS LATER   ☐ IT'S A KEEPER

Serve with a green salad and crusty bread.

$1/2$ cup pine nuts, toasted

12 large green olives, pitted, coarsely chopped

$1/4$ cup golden raisins (a generous handful)

$1/2$ cup fresh flat-leaf parsley (a couple of generous handfuls), chopped
Grated zest of 1 lemon

2 tablespoons grated Parmigiano-Reggiano (a rounded palmful)

$1/2$ cup shredded mozzarella cheese
Salt and freshly ground black pepper

$1\frac{1}{3}$ pounds (8 pieces) veal shoulder scallopini

8 slices prosciutto di Parma
Toothpicks

2 tablespoons extra-virgin olive oil (EVOO) (twice around the pan)

1 tablespoon unsalted butter

2 garlic cloves, chopped

1 tablespoon fresh thyme leaves, chopped (from 4 sprigs)

1 rounded tablespoon tomato paste

$1/2$ small yellow onion, chopped

1 heaping tablespoon Dijon mustard

$3/4$ cup chicken stock or broth (eyeball it)

To make the filling, in a medium bowl, combine the pine nuts, olives, raisins, parsley, lemon zest, Parmigiano, and mozzarella. Season with a little salt and pepper. Taste and adjust the seasoning; this is your last chance to make sure the filling is up to par.

Lay the 8 pieces of scallopini out on the cutting board without overlapping any of the pieces. Season the meat with a little salt and pepper. Lay 1 slice of prosciutto on top of each scallopini. If necessary, fold the prosciutto so that it fits the veal pieces without an overhang. Place about 1 heaping tablespoon of the filling on the lower half of each slice. Starting at the point closest to you, roll each portion away from you into a cigar shape. Secure each veal roll with a toothpick.

Heat a large nonstick skillet over medium-high heat. Add the EVOO and the butter. Once the butter is no longer foaming, add the 8 veal rolls. Brown on all sides, 2 to 3 minutes. Move the veal rolls over a little, clearing a spot in the skillet to add the garlic, thyme, tomato paste, and onions. Season with salt and pepper and cook for 1 minute. Add the mustard and chicken stock and continue to cook for 4 minutes. Serve the rolls with the sauce poured over them.

4 SERVINGS

TRY THIS LATER   IT'S A KEEPER

157 Warm Tangerine and Grilled Chicken Salad
served on Grilled Garlic Crisps

Zest and juice of 2 tangerines

2 sprigs of fresh rosemary, leaves removed and finely chopped

3 garlic cloves, chopped

¼ cup fresh flat-leaf parsley leaves (a generous handful), chopped

6 tablespoons extra-virgin olive oil (EVOO)
Salt and freshly ground black pepper

1½ pounds chicken cutlets

1 pint red grape tomatoes, halved

1 pint yellow grape tomatoes, halved

1 fennel bulb, quartered, cored, and thinly sliced (chop and reserve a handful of fronds)

12 kalamata olives, pitted and coarsely chopped

12 large green olives, pitted and coarsely chopped

4 scallions, thinly sliced

2 large white or whole-wheat pitas

¼ cup grated Parmigiano-Reggiano (a generous handful)

Preheat a grill pan or outdoor grill over high heat.

In a shallow dish, combine the juice of 1 tangerine, the rosemary, 2 of the chopped garlic cloves, the parsley, 2 tablespoons of the EVOO, salt, and pepper. Add the chicken cutlets and marinate for 5 minutes.

Place the tomatoes, fennel, fennel fronds, olives, and scallions in a large bowl; add the juice of the remaining tangerine and all of the tangerine zest. Season the salad with salt and pepper and drizzle with about 2 tablespoons of the EVOO, then stir to combine. The salt will start drawing the liquids from the tomatoes and that will become part of the dressing.

Separate the 2 pita breads into 4 round disks. Combine the remaining garlic with the remaining 2 tablespoons of EVOO. Brush both sides of the pitas with the garlic oil and season with a little salt and pepper. Place on the grill and cook until well marked on the first side, flip, and then sprinkle with a little Parmigiano. Cook until the second side is well marked. Remove the pita from the grill and reserve.

Place the chicken cutlets on the grill and cook on each side for 3 to 4 minutes, or until the chicken is cooked through. Remove from the grill to the cutting board. Let the meat rest for a minute, then cut into thin strips and add to the bowl with the tomatoes and fennel. Toss to combine.

To serve, arrange the grilled garlic crisps on 4 serving plates. Top each crispy pita with a generous pile of the warm tangerine and grilled chicken salad.

4 SERVINGS

Shrimp Martinis and Manhattan Steaks

158

TRY THIS LATER

IT'S A KEEPER

I usually make the shrimp martinis while the steaks cook, but if you prefer you can make the shrimp first and let them chill in the fridge.

Zest of 1 lemon plus 1 tablespoon lemon juice
1 celery rib, very finely chopped
Several drops of Tabasco, to taste
2 cups prepared cocktail sauce
¾ cup good-quality, well-chilled vodka
Salt and coarse black pepper
1 head of broccoli, cut in spears
4 1- to 1¼-inch-thick New York strip steaks or porterhouse steaks, each 10 to 12 ounces
2 tablespoons extra-virgin olive oil (EVOO)
3 tablespoons grill seasoning, such as McCormick's Montreal Steak Seasoning
2 tablespoons unsalted butter
1 large shallot, chopped
1 shot sweet vermouth (1½ ounces)
3 shots rye whiskey (4½ ounces)
4 slices white bread, toasted and cut into points
2 tablespoons finely chopped fresh flat-leaf parsley
20 cooked jumbo shrimp, cleaned and deveined

In a small pitcher, combine the lemon zest, celery, hot sauce, cocktail sauce, and vodka and season with salt and coarse black pepper. Place the sauce in the refrigerator to chill.

Drizzle the steaks with EVOO on both sides and coat them evenly with the grill seasoning. Heat a large nonstick skillet or heavy cast-iron skillet over high heat. Cook the meat for 5 minutes on each side for medium

rare, 7 minutes per side for medium well, and remove to a platter to allow the meat to rest and the juices to redistribute. Loosely tent the steaks with foil to keep in some heat.

Bring 1 inch of water to a boil in a saucepan. Season the boiling water liberally with salt. Add the spears and simmer the broccoli for 5 minutes, until just fork-tender but still bright green.

Return the skillet to the stove and reduce the heat to medium. Add 1 tablespoon of the EVOO (once around the pan), plus 1 tablespoon of the butter and melt together. Add the shallots and cook for 2 minutes. Add the vermouth and whiskey and ignite to burn off the alcohol (don't you look impressive doing this!). Once the flame dies, turn off the heat, add the remaining tablespoon of butter, and gloss up the reduction of, essentially, a Manhattan cocktail and the steaks' pan drippings. Place the toast points on dinner plates. Serve the steaks on the toast points and spoon the pan sauce over the meat. Garnish with parsley, and place broccoli spears alongside the steaks.

Chill 4 martini glasses by filling them with ice. Rinse the shrimp in cold water and pat dry. Squeeze the lemon juice over them and season with a bit of salt. Pour out the ice in the glasses and hook the shrimp, 5 per glass, over the edge of the martini glasses, tails hanging on the outside of the rim. Go get the chilled sauce, fill the glasses to the rim. Serve with the steaks for a very unusual Surf 'n Turf!

4 SERVINGS

159 Burly-Man-Size Chicken–Cheddar Barbecued Burgers with Spicy Coleslaw

Serve with waffle-cut frozen fries, cooked to package directions, or fancy specialty chips.

- 1 cup mayonnaise, plain yogurt, or prepared ranch-style dressing—your pick
- 1 tablespoon hot sauce, such as Tabasco (eyeball it)
  Juice of 1 lime
- ½ cup fresh flat-leaf parsley leaves (a couple of generous handfuls), chopped
- ¼ cup fresh cilantro leaves (a generous handful), chopped
  Salt and freshly ground black pepper
- ½ small red cabbage, halved, cored, then thinly sliced
- 1 red bell pepper, cored, seeded, and thinly sliced
- 6 scallions, thinly sliced
- 2 pounds ground chicken
- ½ cup of your favorite prepared barbecue sauce
- ⅓ pound sharp Cheddar cheese, cut into ¼-inch dice
  Extra-virgin olive oil (EVOO), for drizzling
- 4 kaiser rolls, split

For the spicy coleslaw, in a bowl combine the mayonnaise, hot sauce, lime juice, parsley, cilantro, salt, and pepper. Add the sliced cabbage, red bell peppers, and half of the scallions, stir to coat the cabbage, and reserve the spicy slaw for topping the burgers.

In a mixing bowl, combine the ground chicken, barbecue sauce, Cheddar dice, reserved scallions, salt, and pepper. Mix thoroughly. Score the meat with your hand to mark 4 equal portions. Form each portion into a 1-inch-thick patty. Preheat a nonstick skillet over medium-high heat. Drizzle EVOO over the patties and place them in the hot skillet. Cook for 5 to 6 minutes per side, or until the patties are firm to the touch and cooked through.

While the burgers are cooking, toast the kaiser rolls. Transfer the burgers to the bottoms of the toasted rolls, pile some spicy coleslaw on top, and then replace the roll tops.

4 SERVINGS

TIDBIT

The colder the cheese is the easier it will be to dice. Pop it in the freezer while you prep everything else and you will find that dicing it up will be a freezer-breeze-r!

Super-Grilled Steak Sandwich
with Horseradish–Dijon Cream and Spicy Greens

2 pounds flank steak

¼ cup Worcestershire sauce (eyeball it)

3 garlic cloves, chopped

Salt and freshly ground black pepper

Extra-virgin olive oil (EVOO), for drizzling

4 plum tomatoes, sliced into thirds lengthwise

1 large red onion, sliced into ½-inch-thick disks

1 baguette

1 cup whole or reduced-fat sour cream (eyeball it)

3 tablespoons prepared horseradish

1 heaping tablespoon Dijon mustard

¼ cup fresh flat-leaf parsley leaves (a generous handful), chopped

1 bunch of arugula or watercress, cleaned and trimmed (a couple of cups)

Preheat a grill pan or outdoor grill on high.

Season the steak with 2 tablespoons of the Worcestershire, the garlic, salt, and pepper, drizzle with some EVOO, and marinate for 5 minutes.

Drizzle the tomatoes and red onion slices with a little EVOO, the remaining 2 tablespoons of Worcestershire, and some salt and pepper. Place on the grill and cook until well marked on both sides, 2 to 3 minutes. Remove from the grill and reserve.

Grill the flank steak for 6 to 7 minutes on each side. Remove the steak from the grill to a cutting board to rest for 5 minutes.

Split the baguette lengthwise without cutting it all the way through, then cut into 4 equal sub-style rolls. Drizzle EVOO over the inside and season with salt and pepper. Place the open-faced cut rolls on the grill, oiled insides exposed. Place a heavy pan atop the bread to keep it flat on the grill. Grill until well marked, 1 to 2 minutes.

In a bowl, combine the sour cream, horseradish, mustard, and parsley and season with salt and pepper.

Thinly slice the flank steak on an angle, cutting the meat against the grain.

To assemble the sandwiches, slather the inside of the grilled bread with the horseradish–Dijon cream. Divide the sliced steak, grilled red onions, and tomatoes among the 4 grilled baguette rolls. Pile some arugula or watercress on each sandwich and serve.

4 SERVINGS

TIDBIT

When measuring out Worcestershire sauce, pop that jigger-safety-trigger, annoying plastic thing-a-ma-bob off the top of the bottle before you pour, or you will shake your arm off trying to come up with ¼ cup!

Tex-Mex Grilled Chicken Caesar

TRY THIS LATER ☐

IT'S A KEEPER ☐

2 tablespoons chili powder

1 teaspoon ground cumin ($\frac{1}{3}$ palmful)

About $\frac{1}{2}$ cup extra-virgin olive oil (EVOO)
Coarse salt

1$\frac{1}{2}$ pounds boneless, skinless thin cut chicken breasts

5 garlic cloves, 1 clove cracked from skin, 4 cloves finely chopped

3 cups cubed sourdough bread (half a round loaf)

1 cup grated Parmigiano-Reggiano (a few large handfuls), divided

3 anchovy fillets, drained, finely chopped

$\frac{1}{2}$ teaspoon crushed red pepper flakes

1 ripe avocado
Zest and juice of 2 limes

1 tablespoon Dijon mustard

2 teaspoons Worcestershire sauce (eyeball it)

2 tablespoons chopped fresh cilantro leaves (small handful)
Coarse black pepper

2 large romaine lettuce hearts, coarsely chopped

Preheat the oven to 375°F. and preheat a grill pan or outdoor grill on high.

In a shallow dish, combine 1 tablespoon of the chili powder (a palmful), the cumin, 2 tablespoons of the EVOO, and some salt. Add the chicken cutlets and coat in the seasoning. Transfer the cutlets to the grill and cook for 3 to 4 minutes on each side. Remove from the grill and slice into very thin strips.

While the chicken is grilling, rub the inside of a salad bowl with the cracked clove of garlic. Set aside. Then, place the cubed bread in a clean bowl with the garlic clove and drizzle about 3 tablespoons of the EVOO and the remaining tablespoon of chili powder over the cubed bread. Toss with about $\frac{1}{2}$ cup of the grated Parmigiano and toss to coat thoroughly. Spread the croutons evenly on a rimmed baking sheet and bake until crisp and golden, 10 to 15 minutes.

To make the dressing, place the remaining $\frac{1}{4}$ cup of EVOO in a small pan with the anchovies, red pepper flakes, and the finely chopped garlic. Stir together over very low heat until the anchovies melt. Remove from the heat and cool.

To prepare the avocado, cut all around the circumference of the ripe avocado, lengthwise and down to the pit. Twist and separate the halved fruit. Remove the pit with a spoon, then scoop the flesh out in one piece from both halves and cut into bite-size pieces.

In the bottom of the reserved salad bowl, combine the lime zest and juice, mustard, Worcestershire, cilantro, salt, and pepper. Whisk in the cooled EVOO with anchovies and garlic. Add the romaine to the bowl, followed by the croutons, avocado, and the remaining $\frac{1}{2}$ cup of grated Parmigiano. Toss the salad to coat, adjust the salt and pepper, and pile the salad onto plates. Top with sliced chicken.

4 SERVINGS

Orange and Herb Chicken Caesar

162

OMIT

Avocado

SWAP

2 tablespoons fresh thyme leaves, chopped, for the chili powder

1 sprig fresh rosemary, leaves removed and chopped, for the ground cumin

Zest and juice of 1 orange for the limes

2 tablespoons fresh flat-leaf parsley leaves, chopped, for the cilantro

Prepare the salad as for the master recipe, #161, making the substitutions listed above.

4 SERVINGS

Lamb Chops and Early Spring Salad

163

2 small racks of lamb, cut into chops
  Salt and freshly ground black pepper

1 large garlic clove, cracked out of its skin

1 fennel bulb, quartered, cored, and thinly sliced

1 cup fresh flat-leaf parsley leaves (a few big handfuls), coarsely chopped

½ cup fresh mint leaves (a couple of handfuls)

6 radishes, thinly sliced

6 scallions, chopped

4 celery ribs from the heart with leafy greens, chopped

1 romaine lettuce heart, shredded

1 head of radicchio, shredded

⅓ pound ricotta salata cheese, crumbled
  Zest and juice of 2 lemons
  Extra-virgin olive oil (EVOO), for generous drizzling
  Crusty bread, to pass at the table

Preheat the broiler to high.

Arrange the chops on a slotted broiler pan and season with salt and pepper on both sides.

Rub a large salad bowl with the cracked garlic. Toss in the fennel, parsley, mint, radishes, scallions, celery, lettuce, and radicchio. Sprinkle the cheese over the top, then dress with the lemon zest and juice and a generous drizzle of EVOO. Season the salad with salt and pepper to taste.

Broil the lamb chops for 2 minutes on each side for rare, up to 4 minutes on each side for well done.

Serve the chops alongside piles of salad and pass the crusty bread.

4 SERVINGS

164 London Broil with Mushroom Vinaigrette

Serve with baby spinach salad dressed with oil and vinegar or blue cheese dressing, your choice.

2-pound boneless shoulder steak or top round steak

3 tablespoons Worcestershire sauce (eyeball it)

5 tablespoons extra-virgin olive oil (EVOO), plus some for drizzling
Salt and freshly ground black pepper

1 10-ounce package cremini (baby portobello) mushrooms, brushed clean, quartered

1 large yellow onion, chopped

3 garlic cloves, chopped

1 tablespoon fresh thyme leaves, chopped (from 4 sprigs)

¼ cup sherry vinegar

2 heaping tablespoons Dijon mustard

½ cup fresh flat-leaf parsley leaves (2 generous handfuls), chopped

Preheat the broiler on high and set the rack closest to the flame.

Coat the steak with the Worcestershire sauce, a drizzle of EVOO, salt, and pepper. Marinate the steak for 5 minutes. Transfer the marinated steak to a broiler pan and broil for 6 minutes per side. Remove from the broiler and allow the meat to rest for 5 minutes, tented loosely with a piece of aluminum foil.

While the steak is working, heat a large skillet over medium-high heat with 2 tablespoons of the EVOO (twice around the pan). Add the mushrooms and brown for 5 minutes, stirring every now and then. Turn the heat down to medium and add the onions, garlic, and thyme and season with salt and pepper. Cook for 3 to 4 minutes, or until the onions become tender and translucent. Add the sherry vinegar and mustard and stir to combine. Turn off the heat. Some liquid will evaporate. Whisk in about 3 tablespoons more of EVOO, add the parsley, and reserve the vinaigrette while you slice the steak.

Slice the rested steak very thin, against the grain and on an angle. Serve the sliced meat topped with some of the mushroom vinaigrette.

4 SERVINGS

TIDBIT

Shoulder steak is often labeled as "London Broil" in the meat case.

Pan-Roasted Garlic and Herb Chicken Breasts
with Chopped Salad and Creamy Caper Dressing

4 garlic cloves, finely chopped
1 cup fresh flat-leaf parsley leaves (a few large handfuls), chopped
1 teaspoon hot sauce, such as Tabasco (eyeball it)
6 tablespoons extra-virgin olive oil (EVOO)
   Salt and freshly ground black pepper
4 6- to 8-ounce boneless, skinless chicken breast halves
4 tablespoons mayonnaise, plain yogurt, or sour cream
3 tablespoons capers, drained, coarsely chopped
2 tablespoons red wine vinegar (eyeball it)
3 tablespoons fresh dill, chopped
1 tablespoon Dijon mustard
1 pint yellow cherry or grape tomatoes, halved
1 large head of radicchio, thinly sliced
6 scallions, thinly sliced
1 seedless cucumber, cut in quarters lengthwise, then sliced into bite-size pieces
   Crusty bread, sliced and toasted

Preheat the oven to 400°F.

In a shallow dish, combine the garlic, parsley, hot sauce, 3 tablespoons of the EVOO, salt, and pepper. Add the chicken breasts and coat in the mixture; marinate for 5 minutes.

While the chicken is marinating, in a bowl combine the mayonnaise with the capers, red wine vinegar, dill, mustard, and some pepper. In a slow, steady stream, whisk in the remaining 3 tablespoons of the EVOO.

Preheat a large nonstick oven-safe skillet over medium-high heat. Add the chicken to the hot pan and brown on each side for 2 to 3 minutes. Transfer the skillet to the oven and roast the chicken for about 15 minutes, or until it is cooked through.

While the chicken is roasting, in a salad bowl combine the cherry tomatoes, radicchio, scallions, and cucumbers. Pour the creamy caper dressing over the chopped veggies and toss to combine.

Serve the chicken breasts whole or sliced with some of the dressed chopped salad and the toasted bread.

4 SERVINGS

TRY THIS LATER   IT'S A KEEPER

2 tablespoons extra-virgin olive oil (EVOO) (twice around the pan)

4 slices bacon, chopped

1 large yellow onion, chopped

3 garlic cloves, chopped

1 tablespoon fresh thyme leaves (from 4 sprigs), chopped
Salt and freshly ground black pepper
A couple of dashes of hot sauce, such as Tabasco

2 10-ounce boxes frozen peas

1 quart chicken stock or broth

1/2 cup heavy cream or half-and-half

8 slices baguette

1/2 cup grated Parmigiano-Reggiano (a few handfuls)

1/4 cup fresh flat-leaf parsley (a generous handful), chopped
Zest and juice of 1 lemon

Heat a large soup pot over medium-high heat with the EVOO. Add the bacon and cook until crisp, about 3 to 4 minutes. Remove the crispy bacon from the pan with a slotted spoon to drain on a paper towel. Add the onions, garlic, and thyme to the pot and season with salt, pepper, and a few dashes of hot sauce. Cook, stirring frequently, for 4 to 5 minutes, or until the onions are tender. Add the frozen peas and continue to cook until the peas are defrosted and heated through, 2 to 3 minutes. Transfer the onions and peas to a blender or food processor with 1/2 cup of the chicken stock and puree until smooth. Add the pureed peas back to the soup pot and stir in the remaining 3 1/2 cups of chicken stock and the cream, bring up to a simmer, and cook for about 8 to 10 minutes.

While the soup is simmering, toast the baguette slices until golden brown in the broiler or toaster oven. In a bowl, mix the Parmigiano with the reserved crispy bacon and the parsley. Once the toast is nice and golden, sprinkle the bacon–Parmigiano mixture over the bread and return to the broiler or toaster oven to melt and lightly brown the cheese.

To finish the soup, add the lemon zest and juice, stir to combine, and transfer the soup to serving bowls. Float 2 Parmigiano toasts on top of each soup bowl and serve immediately.

4 SERVINGS

NOW TRY... Creamy Spinach Soup with Fontina Toast 167

SWAP

3 10-ounce boxes frozen chopped spinach, defrosted and squeezed out dry in a kitchen towel, for the frozen peas
1 cup Fontina cheese, shredded, for the grated Parmigiano

Prepare as directed for the master recipe, #166, making the substitutions listed.

4 SERVINGS

☐ TRY THIS LATER

☐ IT'S A KEEPER

OR TRY... Creamy Broccoli Soup with Cheddar and Chive Toast 168

SWAP

2 10-ounce boxes frozen chopped broccoli, defrosted, for the frozen peas
1 cup shredded sharp Cheddar for the Parmigiano
3 tablespoons chopped fresh chives for the parsley

Prepare as directed for the master recipe, #166, making the substitutions listed.

4 SERVINGS

☐ TRY THIS LATER

☐ IT'S A KEEPER

169 Cumin and Lime Roasted Pork Tenderloin
with Spicy Creamed Corn

2¼ pounds **pork** tenderloin (sometimes sold 2 tenderloins per package)

Juice of 2 **limes**

4 tablespoons **extra-virgin olive oil** (EVOO)

2 tablespoons **ground cumin** (2 palmfuls)

1 tablespoon **ground coriander** (1 palmful)

Salt and **freshly ground black pepper**

6 **garlic cloves** (4 cloves cracked and 2 cloves chopped)

2 tablespoons **unsalted butter**

1 large **yellow** onion, chopped

2 **jalapeño** peppers, seeded and chopped

1 small **red bell pepper**, cored, seeded, and finely chopped

2 10-ounce boxes frozen **corn kernels**, or kernels cut from 5 ears of fresh corn

1 tablespoon **all-purpose flour**

1½ cups **chicken** stock or broth

½ cup **heavy** cream

¼ cup fresh **flat-leaf parsley** leaves (a generous handful), chopped

2 tablespoons chopped fresh **cilantro** leaves (a small handful)

Preheat the oven to 500°F.

Trim the silver skin or connective tissue off the tenderloins with a very sharp, thin knife.

Place the tenderloins on a rimmed nonstick cookie sheet and coat them with the lime juice, rubbing the juice into the meat. Drizzle EVOO over the tenderloins,

just enough to coat, about 2 tablespoons. Season the meat with the cumin, coriander, salt, and pepper. Cut small slits into the meat and disperse chunks of the cracked garlic cloves into the slits. Roast for 20 minutes. Remove from the oven and let rest for a few minutes, tented loosely with foil.

While the pork is cooking, preheat a skillet over medium-high heat with 2 tablespoons of the EVOO (twice around the pan) and the butter. Add the onions, jalapeños, bell peppers, chopped garlic, corn kernels, salt, and pepper. Cook for 4 to 5 minutes, or until the onions are tender. Sprinkle with the flour, and continue to cook for 1 minute. Whisk in the chicken stock and heavy cream. Bring the corn up to a simmer and then lower the heat to medium low and cook until it is thick and creamy, about 5 minutes. Finish the spicy creamed corn with the parsley and cilantro. Taste and adjust the seasoning with salt and pepper.

Slice the rested roasted pork and serve alongside the spicy creamed corn.

4 SERVINGS

TIDBIT

If you like the heat, only remove the seeds from half of the jalapeños.

Turkey Cutlets with Sautéed Brussels Sprouts
with Pancetta and Balsamic Vinegar

10   fresh sage leaves, thinly sliced
1   cup fresh flat-leaf parsley leaves (a few large handfuls), chopped
    Juice of 1 lemon
6   tablespoons extra-virgin olive oil (EVOO)
    Salt and freshly ground black pepper
2   pounds turkey breast cutlets
6   slices pancetta, chopped
1   large onion, chopped
3   garlic cloves, chopped
2   pints Brussels sprouts, thinly sliced
3½   cups chicken stock or broth
2   tablespoons balsamic vinegar (eyeball it)
2   tablespoons unsalted butter
2   tablespoons all-purpose flour

Preheat the oven to 375 F.

In a shallow dish, combine the sage, half of the parsley, the lemon juice, 2 tablespoons of the EVOO, salt, and pepper. Add the turkey cutlets, coat thoroughly, and marinate for 5 minutes.

Heat a large skillet over medium-high heat with 2 tablespoons of the EVOO (twice around the pan). Add the pancetta and cook until crisp, about 4 minutes.

Add the onions and garlic, season with salt and pepper, and cook, stirring occasionally, for 2 to 3 minutes. Add the sliced Brussels sprouts, ½ cup of the chicken stock, and the balsamic vinegar, stir to combine, and continue to cook for 4 to 5 minutes, or until the Brussels sprouts are tender.

While the Brussels sprouts are cooking, heat a large skillet over medium-high heat with the remaining 2 tablespoons of EVOO. Add the turkey cutlets and brown on each side. Transfer the cutlets to a shallow baking dish and add 1 cup of the chicken stock to keep the meat moist. Transfer the cutlets to the oven, loosely tented with foil, for 6 to 7 minutes, or until cooked through. To the skillet that you browned the cutlets in, add the butter and melt it over medium heat. Add the flour and cook for 1 minute. Whisk in the remaining 2 cups of chicken stock and allow it to thicken up, 3 to 4 minutes. Season the gravy with salt and pepper and finish with the remaining parsley.

Serve the turkey cutlets with the gravy and the sautéed Brussels sprouts.

4 SERVINGS

171 Fruited Chicken Curry in a Hurry

2 cups basmati rice

3 tablespoons vegetable oil (3 times around the pan)

4 6-ounce boneless, skinless chicken breast halves, cut into ½-inch slices across the width of the breast
Coarse salt and coarse black pepper

4 garlic cloves, chopped
2-inch piece of fresh ginger, peeled and grated

2 tablespoons ground coriander (2 palmfuls)

1 large yellow onion, chopped

1 large green apple, peeled and diced

2 tablespoons all-purpose flour

2 cups chicken stock or broth

2 tablespoons curry paste, mild or hot

¼ cup golden raisins (a generous handful)

8 pitted dates or 6 pitted prunes, chopped

MIX-AND-MATCH TOPPINGS

4 scallions, thinly sliced

1 cup toasted shredded coconut

½ cup sliced almonds or Spanish peanuts

1 cup prepared mango chutney

¼ cup finely chopped fresh cilantro leaves (a handful)

Prepare the rice according to the package directions.

Preheat a large, deep nonstick skillet over medium-high heat with 2 tablespoons of the oil. Add the chicken, season with salt and pepper, and lightly brown. Remove the chicken and reserve on a plate. To the same pan, add the garlic, ginger, coriander, onions, apples, and remaining tablespoon of oil and sauté together for 3 to 5 minutes. Add the flour and cook for 1 minute more. Add the chicken stock to the pan and bring to a bubble. Add the curry paste, golden raisins, and dates. Reduce the heat to medium low. Add the chicken pieces back to the pan. Simmer the curry for 8 to 10 minutes.

Assemble the toppings in small dishes. Serve the curry in shallow bowls with scoops of basmati rice. Garnish with any or all of the toppings.

4 SERVINGS

TIDBIT

For a Vegetarian Fruited Curry in a Hurry, swap a 14-ounce container of firm tofu, cut into 1½-inch-thick slices and patted dry, for the chicken, and vegetable broth for the chicken stock. Brown the tofu as you would the chicken and follow the same method above.

Ham and Swiss Crepes with Chopped Salad

½ cup all-purpose flour
  Coarse salt

3 eggs, beaten

¾ cup milk

2 tablespoons brandy (purchase a 2-ounce nip if you don't want a large bottle)

2 tablespoons melted unsalted butter

1 pint red cherry tomatoes

1 pint yellow cherry tomatoes

10 fresh basil leaves, chopped

½ cup fresh flat-leaf parsley leaves (a handful)

2 tablespoons balsamic vinegar (eyeball it)

3 tablespoons extra-virgin olive oil (EVOO)
  Coarse black pepper

½ seedless cucumber, quartered lengthwise and chopped into bite-size pieces

1 bunch of watercress, stemmed and coarsely chopped

1 small red onion, thinly sliced
  Vegetable oil, for cooking crepes

2 cups shredded Swiss cheese (from an 8-ounce brick)

½ pound thinly sliced Black Forest ham, chopped into ribbons

For the crepe batter, combine the flour and a pinch of salt in a bowl and make a well in the center. Add the eggs, milk, and brandy to the well and whisk to combine. Stir in the melted butter. Cover the batter and set aside for 20 minutes.

While the batter is resting, halve the red and yellow cherry tomatoes and add them to a salad bowl. Add the basil, parsley, balsamic vinegar, EVOO, salt, and pepper. Toss to coat. Add the cucumbers, watercress, and onions.

Preheat a 10-inch nonstick skillet over medium-low heat with a drizzle of vegetable oil. Cover the bottom of the skillet with just enough batter to coat, lifting and shaking the skillet to help the batter along. Let the crepe cook and lightly brown on one side, just about 1 minute. Turn the crepe with a rubber spatula, lifting up the edges, then use a toothpick or your finger to flip it over. Once it is flipped, scatter some of the cheese and ham on top. Season with a little salt and pepper, then fold the crepe over and continue to cook until the cheese starts to melt. Transfer the crepe to a plate and cover with foil to keep warm. Repeat this 7 more times to serve 2 crepes per person.

Divide the 8 crepes among 4 serving plates; serve some salad next to the crepes.

4 SERVINGS

173 Greek Bread Salad with Grilled Shrimp

If you don't groove on the shrimp, use 1½ pounds of chicken tenders, 20 large sea scallops, or even 8 pieces of calamari, 2 per person, and grill in the shrimps' place.

20 jumbo shrimp, peeled and deveined
¼ cup extra-virgin olive oil (EVOO), plus more for liberal drizzling
1 teaspoon dried oregano, crushed in the palm of your hand
1 tablespoon grill seasoning, such as McCormick's Montreal Steak Seasoning (a palmful)
2 pitas, split open
1 large garlic clove, minced and mashed to a paste with some coarse salt
Zest of 1 lemon and juice of 2 lemons
1 seedless cucumber, halved lengthwise, then sliced into half-moons
4 vine-ripe tomatoes, cut into thin wedges
1 small red onion, thinly sliced
½ cup fresh flat-leaf parsley leaves (a couple of generous handfuls), coarsely chopped
¼ cup fresh mint leaves (a handful), coarsely chopped
3 celery ribs, thinly sliced on an angle
1 cup pitted kalamata olives, coarsely chopped
Coarse salt and coarse black pepper
1 ¾-pound brick of Greek feta cheese, drained and sliced into 12 thin wedges

Heat a grill pan or outdoor grill to high.

Toss the shrimp with enough EVOO to coat, and season with the oregano and grill seasoning.

Grill the split pita halves for a minute or two to char on the grill. Remove when crisp, break or tear into large pieces, and reserve.

Combine the garlic with the zest of 1 lemon and the juice of 1½ lemons in the bottom of a large, shallow bowl. Add the cucumbers, tomatoes, red onions, parsley, mint, celery, olives, and the reserved bread. Add the ¼ cup of EVOO (4 times around the bowl) and lots of salt and coarse black pepper, then toss the salad with your hands to combine well.

Grill the shrimp on the screaming hot grill pan or outdoor grill. Cook for 2 to 3 minutes on each side, until pink and firm. Transfer to a plate and top with the juice of the remaining ½ lemon.

Pile the salad into large, shallow bowls and top with the grilled shrimp and wedges of feta.

4 SERVINGS

Chili Dog Bacon Cheeseburgers and Fiery Fries

Serve with veggie sticks or oil-and-vinegar–dressed slaw.

- 8 slices center-cut or other lean, thick-cut smoky bacon
- 1 sack (16 to 20 ounces) crispy-style frozen French fries
- 1 pound lean ground beef
- 2 beef or pork hot dogs, diced
- 2 tablespoons chili powder (2 palmfuls)
- 1 tablespoon grill seasoning, such as McCormick's Montreal Steak Seasoning
- 2 teaspoons Worcestershire sauce (eyeball it)
- 1 tablespoon plus 1 teaspoon hot sauce (eyeball it)
- 2 tablespoons ketchup
  Vegetable oil, for drizzling
- 4 slices deli sliced Cheddar cheese
- 2 tablespoons unsalted butter
- 3 garlic cloves, finely chopped
- 3 tablespoons chopped chives (a handful)
  Coarse salt, to taste
- ½ cup chili sauce
- 4 kaiser rolls, split

Preheat the broiler to high.

Place the bacon on a slotted broiler pan. Cook the bacon 10 inches from the heat for 3 to 4 minutes on each side, until crisp, and remove to a plate. Adjust the oven to bake, setting at the temperature recommended on the package of fries, and bake the fries.

While the fries cook, make the burgers. Preheat a large nonstick skillet over medium-high heat. Mix the beef with the chopped hot dogs, chili powder, grill seasoning, Worcestershire, 1 teaspoon of the hot sauce, and the ketchup. Form 4 large patties. Add a drizzle of oil, once around the skillet, and add the patties. Cook the burgers for 6 minutes on each side, then top each with 2 slices of bacon and 1 slice of Cheddar. Turn the heat off, cover the pan with a loose foil tent, and let the cheese melt for a minute or two.

When the fries are extra crisp remove them from the oven. Place the butter, the remaining tablespoon of hot sauce, and the garlic in a small dish and microwave on High for 20 seconds, then transfer the fries to a large bowl. Toss the fries with the butter mixture and chives and season with salt.

Slather chili sauce on the tops of the split kaiser rolls. Place the bacon-chili-cheeseburgers on the bun bottoms and set the tops in place. Pile fries alongside and serve.

4 SERVINGS

175 Indian Tofu and Spinach over Almond Rice

I really do not get tofu, but some of my friends do. This is for them.

2 cups basmati rice

3 tablespoons vegetable oil (3 times around the pan)

1 14-ounce container firm tofu, patted dry and cut into 1½-inch dice
Salt and freshly ground black pepper

4 garlic cloves, chopped
3-inch piece of fresh ginger, peeled and grated

1 large yellow onion, chopped

1 teaspoon ground cumin (⅓ palmful)

1 tablespoon ground coriander (1 palmful)

2 10-ounce boxes frozen chopped spinach, defrosted, squeezed dry of excess liquid in a kitchen towel

2 tablespoons all-purpose flour

2 cups vegetable stock or broth

2 tablespoons curry paste, mild or hot

¼ cup prepared mango chutney

1 15-ounce can chick peas

1 cup sliced almonds

Prepare the rice according to the package directions.

Preheat a large, deep nonstick skillet over medium-high heat with the vegetable oil. Add the tofu, season with salt and pepper, and lightly brown, 2 to 3 minutes per side. Remove the tofu from the skillet and reserve on a plate. To the same skillet, add the garlic, ginger, onions, cumin, and coriander. Sauté together for 4 to 5 minutes, or until the onions are tender. Add the spinach and continue to cook for 2 minutes. Add the flour and cook for 1 minute. Add the vegetable stock and bring to a bubble. Add the curry paste, mango chutney, and chick peas, then return the browned tofu to the skillet, reduce the heat to medium low, and simmer the curry for 8 to 10 minutes.

While the curry is simmering, toast the almonds in a small dry skillet over medium heat until golden. Once the rice is cooked, fluff it with a fork, add the toasted almonds, and stir with the fork.

Serve the curry in shallow bowls with scoops of almond rice on top. (Rice on the bottom gets too mushy.)

4 SERVINGS

Chicken in a Fresh Tomato and Eggplant Sauce
with Spaghetti

176

☐ TRY THIS LATER ☐ IT'S A KEEPER

Coarse salt

1 pound spaghetti

5 tablespoons extra-virgin olive oil (EVOO)

3 baby eggplant or 1 small, firm eggplant, cut into 1/2-inch dice

1 1/3 pounds chicken tenders (2 small packages), cut into small bite-size pieces

1 medium yellow onion, chopped

4 garlic cloves, chopped

Coarse black pepper

1 teaspoon crushed red pepper flakes

1/2 cup dry white wine (a couple of glugs; eyeball it)

1 1/2 cups chicken stock or broth

1 pint red cherry or grape tomatoes

1 cup fresh flat-leaf parsley leaves (a few generous handfuls), chopped

1 cup grated Parmigiano-Reggiano (a few overflowing handfuls)

Crusty bread, to pass at the table

Bring a large pot of water to a boil. Once it is boiling, salt the water and cook the pasta al dente. Heads up: you will need to reserve 1/2 cup of the pasta cooking water before draining.

Preheat a large nonstick skillet over medium-high heat with 3 tablespoons of the EVOO (3 times around the pan). Add the eggplant and cook, stirring occasionally, until brown, about 5 to 6 minutes. Remove the eggplant from the skillet to a plate and cover with aluminum foil to keep warm; return the skillet to the stove. Add the remaining 2 tablespoons of EVOO. Add the chicken and cook to lightly brown, about 4 to 5 minutes.

Add the onions and garlic and return the eggplant to the skillet, season with salt, pepper, and crushed red pepper flakes, and continue to cook for 3 to 4 minutes. Add the white wine and chicken stock, bring up to a simmer, and cook for 3 to 4 minutes more. Add the cherry tomatoes and the reserved pasta cooking water and cook until the tomatoes begin to burst. Add the parsley and the cooked pasta, toss to coat, and cook for 1 to 2 minutes, or until the sauce tightens up around the pasta. Turn the heat off and add the grated Parmigiano cheese.

Toss to coat the spaghetti, then serve it up. Scoop up any sauce left in the pan and divide it atop the pasta. Pass the crusty bread.

4 SERVINGS

177 My Mom's 15-Minute Tomato and Bean Stoup

One rainy day I called my mom from the road. I was getting a cold and I really wanted soup for supper. She said she didn't know what she had on hand, but she'd come up with something. This was it. (And you don't have to be sick to enjoy it.)

2 tablespoons extra-virgin olive oil (EVOO) (twice around the pan)
3 garlic cloves, chopped
½ teaspoon crushed red pepper flakes
1 medium onion, chopped
2 carrots, peeled and thinly sliced
2 celery ribs, chopped
1 small zucchini, sliced
2 cups vegetable or chicken stock or broth
1 15-ounce can diced tomatoes
1 15-ounce can tomato sauce
1 10-ounce box frozen cut green beans
1 10-ounce box frozen cut yellow beans
Salt and freshly ground black pepper
1 cup fresh basil leaves, torn or shredded
Grated Parmigiano-Reggiano or Romano cheese, to pass at the table
Crusty bread

Add the EVOO to a soup pot over medium-high heat. Add the garlic and crushed red pepper flakes, stir, then add the onions, carrots, celery, and zucchini. Cook for 10 minutes, then add the stock, tomatoes, tomato sauce, and beans. Bring the stoup up to a bubble and season with salt and pepper. Simmer for 5 minutes. Turn off the heat and wilt the basil into the stoup. Ladle up the stoup and serve with the grated cheese and the crusty bread.

4 SERVINGS

· ·

178 Seared Greens with Cheese Ravioli and Sage Butter

Coarse salt
1 pound cheese ravioli
3 tablespoons extra-virgin olive oil (EVOO) (3 times around the pan)
3 garlic cloves, chopped
2 shallots, thinly sliced
2 heads of Belgian endive, halved, trimmed, and sliced lengthwise
2 heads of radicchio, quartered, cored, and shredded
1 large bunch of arugula, trimmed and coarsely chopped
4 tablespoons finely chopped fresh sage leaves (from several sprigs)
3 tablespoons unsalted butter
Coarse black pepper

Bring a large pot of water to a boil. Salt it and add the ravioli; cook according to the package directions.

Heat a large nonstick skillet over medium-high heat. Add the EVOO, garlic, shallots, and greens and cook, stirring frequently, for 2 to 3 minutes. Transfer to a platter, return the pan to the stove, and reduce the heat to medium low. Add the sage and the butter and cook until the butter begins to brown. Drain the ravioli and toss in the sage butter to coat. Season with salt and pepper, scatter the pasta over the greens, and serve.

4 SERVINGS

Fried Greens with Ham and Eggs

179

TRY THIS LATER ☐ IT'S A KEEPER ☐

Here's another meal that's good for B, L, or D: Breakfast, Lunch, or Dinner. This one is for my gran'pa.

- 5 tablespoons extra-virgin olive oil (EVOO) (5 times around the pan), plus some for drizzling
- 4 large slices prosciutto di Parma, deli sliced but not too thin (you need to handle it)
- 6 garlic cloves, minced
- 1/2 teaspoon crushed red pepper flakes
- 1 tin of flat anchovy fillets, (8 to 10 fillets), drained (optional, but highly recommended)
- 1 1/2 pounds dandelion greens, trimmed and halved or torn across
  Coarse black pepper
  Freshly grated or ground nutmeg
- 4 large eggs
  Coarse salt
- 2 scallions, finely chopped

Heat a large nonstick skillet over medium heat. Add the 5 tablespoons of EVOO and fry the sliced prosciutto for 5 minutes, until crisp. Remove the prosciutto with tongs, reserving the oil. Cool the prosciutto and crumble it into pieces. Set aside.

Preheat a griddle or second large nonstick skillet over medium heat.

To the oil in the first skillet, add the garlic, crushed red pepper, and anchovies. Melt the anchovies into the oil, 2 minutes, breaking them up with a wooden spoon. Once melted, the anchovies will taste nutty rather than fishy. Add the greens to the pan and wilt. Season the greens with pepper and nutmeg to taste. The anchovies should provide enough salt.

Drizzle EVOO on the hot griddle pan and fry the eggs as you like: sunny side up, over easy, or over hard.

Pile one fourth of the greens on each plate and top with bits of crisp prosciutto and a fried egg. Season the egg with salt and pepper, garnish with chopped scallions, and serve.

4 SERVINGS

180 MASTER RECIPE
Swordfish Burgers with Lemon, Garlic, and Parsley

Serve with oil-and-vinegar-dressed slaw and specialty chips such as Terra brand's Yukon Gold onion and garlic chips.

    2 pounds swordfish steaks, trimmed of skin
       and dark connective tissue, cut into chunks
    4 garlic cloves, minced
    1 large shallot, finely chopped
  ¼ cup fresh flat-leaf parsley (a generous
       handful), chopped
       Zest of 1 lemon
       Coarse salt and coarse black pepper
       Extra-virgin olive oil (EVOO), for drizzling
       Crusty rolls, split and toasted
       Juice of ½ lemon
       Romaine lettuce leaves
  ½ red onion, very thinly sliced
    1 navel orange, pith and peel removed, sliced
       into thin disks

Preheat a large nonstick skillet over medium-high heat. Preheat the broiler to high.

Place the swordfish in a food processor and pulse to coarsely grind the fish, then transfer to a bowl. Add the garlic, shallots, parsley, lemon zest, salt, pepper, and a healthy drizzle of EVOO. Form 4 large patties, 1 inch thick, and cook in the preheated skillet for 4 minutes on each side until firm but not tough.

Char the buns under the broiler and drizzle with EVOO. Place the burgers on the bottoms of the buns and squeeze some lemon juice over each. Top with romaine, onions, and orange slices. Set the bun tops in place and serve with slaw and chips.

4 SERVINGS

181 NOW TRY... Scallop Burgers

OMIT

    Garlic
    Lemon zest

SWAP

  1½ pounds large sea scallops, patted dry, for the
       swordfish

ADD

       Zest of the navel orange (zest it before
       peeling and slicing)
    3 tablespoons chopped fresh chives
    2 teaspoons Old Bay Seasoning or other
       seafood seasoning blend (⅔ palmful)

Grind the scallops as you would the fish for the master recipe, #180, and mix with the shallots, parsley, orange zest, chives, Old Bay, salt, pepper, and a drizzle of EVOO. Mix and form patties ¾ to 1 inch thick and cook in a hot nonstick pan over medium-high heat for 3 minutes on each side, or until just firm but with a bit of a give left. The patties should be evenly caramelized on both sides.

Serve the burgers on charred rolls drizzled with EVOO and top the patties with lettuce, onions, and oranges.

Serve with chips and slaw.

4 SERVINGS

Chicken with White and Wild Rice Soup

182

1   5.5- to 7-ounce package white and wild rice blend, such as Near East brand, either chicken or herb flavor
2   tablespoons extra-virgin olive oil (EVOO) (eyeball it)
1   large yellow onion, chopped
3   garlic cloves, chopped
2   medium carrots, peeled and thinly sliced
2   celery ribs, thinly sliced
1   bay leaf
1   tablespoon fresh thyme leaves, chopped
    Salt and freshly ground black pepper
1   quart chicken stock or broth
2   pounds chicken tenders, cut into bite-size pieces
½   cup fresh flat-leaf parsley leaves (a few handfuls), chopped
¼   cup fresh dill (a generous handful), chopped
    Juice of 1 lemon
    Hot sauce, such as Tabasco

Cook the rice according to the package directions.

Preheat a large soup pot over medium-high heat with the EVOO. Add the onions, garlic, carrots, celery, bay leaf, and thyme, season with salt and pepper, and cook, stirring frequently, for 5 minutes. Add the chicken stock, bring up to a simmer, and cook for 5 minutes. Add the chicken and continue to cook for 10 minutes. Add the parsley, dill, the lemon juice, and hot sauce to taste. Remove the bay leaf.

Divide the cooked white and wild rice among 4 serving bowls; ladle the soup over the rice, making sure to distribute the chicken and veggies evenly among the bowls.

4 SERVINGS

☐ TRY THIS LATER   ☐ IT'S A KEEPER

Venetian Calamari with Spicy Sauce
and Egg Fettuccine

1 pound calamari, cut into thin rings
2 tablespoons extra-virgin olive oil (EVOO)
  (twice around the pan)
4 garlic cloves, chopped
1 teaspoon crushed red pepper flakes
½ cup dry white wine
1 14-ounce can chunky-style crushed tomatoes
1 teaspoon curry powder
  Pinch of ground cinnamon
  Salt and freshly ground black pepper
  A handful of chopped fresh flat-leaf parsley
¾ pound egg fettuccine, cooked al dente
10 fresh basil leaves, shredded or torn

Pat the calamari dry. Heat a large skillet over medium-high heat. Add the EVOO and calamari and cook for 3 minutes, turning frequently. Add the garlic and red pepper flakes and cook for 2 minutes more. Add the wine and cook off, 30 seconds. Add the tomatoes, curry, cinnamon, salt, pepper, and parsley. Toss the pasta with the calamari and sauce and turn out onto a large platter. Cover with the basil and serve.

4 SERVINGS

Pizza Capricciosa

Some great flavors, two entirely different ways to serve them.

2 tablespoons all-purpose flour or cornmeal, to work with the dough
1 pizza dough, bought from your market or favorite pizzeria
  Extra-virgin olive oil (EVOO), for drizzling
  Coarse salt
½ cup tomato sauce
10 fresh basil leaves, torn or shredded
½ to ¾ pound fresh mozzarella, very thinly sliced
6 cremini or white mushrooms, thinly sliced
1 14-ounce can quartered artichoke hearts, drained and chopped
¼ pound prosciutto di Parma, cut crosswise into 2-inch slices
½ cup frozen green peas (a generous handful)
2 hard-boiled eggs (from the salad bar section of the market), chopped

Preheat the oven to 425°F.

Dust the dough with the flour or cornmeal and stretch out to a 12- to 13-inch pizza. Place the dough on a pizza tray and pierce it with the tines of a fork. Drizzle with EVOO, season with a little salt, and bake for 10 minutes.

Remove the crust from the oven and top with the tomato sauce, basil, a thin layer of the mozzarella, the mushrooms, and artichokes. Bake for another 10 minutes, or until the cheese bubbles and the crust is crisp. In the last 5 minutes of baking time, add the proscuitto, peas, and eggs and another drizzle of EVOO.

4 SERVINGS

Salad Capricciosa

Eat well, eat more! Chew this one until you bust!

- 2 romaine lettuce hearts, shredded
- 1 14-ounce can quartered artichoke hearts, drained
- 1 cup marinated mushrooms, chopped or sliced
- 1 small red onion, chopped or sliced
- 1 tub (1 pound) bocconcini (bite-size fresh mozzarella), drained and halved
- 1 pint grape or cherry tomatoes, halved
- 20 fresh basil leaves, shredded or torn
- 2 handfuls of fresh flat-leaf parsley, chopped
- 1 cup frozen peas, defrosted
  Zest and juice of 1 lemon
- 3 tablespoons prepared store-bought pesto
- 3 tablespoons extra-virgin olive oil (EVOO) (eyeball it)
  Salt and freshly ground black pepper, to taste
- ½ pound prosciutto di Parma, cut crosswise into 2-inch ribbons

In a salad bowl, combine the lettuce, artichoke hearts, mushrooms, onions, bocconcini, tomatoes, basil, parsley, and peas. In a small bowl, mix together the lemon zest, lemon juice, pesto, and EVOO. Dress the salad and toss to combine, then season with salt and pepper. Pile the salad onto dinner plates, and top with a generous layer of prosciutto di Parma, and serve.

4 SERVINGS

TIDBIT ....

Bocconcini are bite-size balls of fresh mozzarella cheese. They are available in the specialty cheese case of the market.

186 30-Minute Chicken Under a Brick

TRY THIS LATER

IT'S A KEEPER

4 bone-in, skin-on chicken breast halves

4 fresh bay leaves

8 garlic cloves, cracked away from their skins

3 tablespoons extra-virgin olive oil (EVOO), plus more for liberal drizzling
A pile of a few sprigs each of fresh flat-leaf parsley, sage, rosemary, and thyme, finely chopped

2 tablespoons grill seasoning, such as McCormick's Montreal Steak Seasoning
Zest and juice of 1 lemon

2 romaine lettuce hearts, chopped

1 head of radicchio, shredded

½ cup mixed fresh herbs, whatever you have on hand, loosely packed and coarsely chopped

2 tablespoons honey

2 teaspoons grainy mustard
Salt and freshly ground black pepper
Crusty bread, to pass at the table

Preheat a heavy-bottomed skillet over medium-high to high heat and preheat the oven to 400°F.

Loosen the skin on the breasts with your fingers and place a bay leaf and some of the cracked garlic between the skin and the breast. Drizzle the breasts with a liberal amount of EVOO. Mix the finely chopped herbs with the grill seasoning and lemon zest, then coat the breasts liberally with the mix. Place skin side down in the skillet and top with another, smaller skillet. Weight the pan with a brick (or with a heavy can). Cook to crisp the skin, 6 to 8 minutes. Transfer the pan to the hot oven and roast for another 15 minutes, or until done.

Combine the greens and coarsely chopped herbs in a bowl. In a small bowl, whisk together the honey, mustard, and lemon juice, stream in the 3 tablespoons of EVOO, and season the dressing with salt and pepper. Dress the salad and toss.

Serve the salad and crusty bread alongside the chicken.

4 SERVINGS

Steak Sandwich . . . Knife and Fork Required

187

☐ TRY THIS LATER ☐ IT'S A KEEPER

1 sheet of puff pastry, defrosted, kept chilled (recommended brand: Pepperidge Farm)
Salt and freshly ground black pepper

1½ to 2 pounds beef skirt steaks

2 tablespoons extra-virgin olive oil (EVOO), plus some for drizzling

2 garlic cloves, chopped

2 sprigs of fresh rosemary, leaves removed and finely chopped

1 small bunch of thin asparagus

½ cup crumbled blue cheese

1 large bunch of arugula, stemmed, cleaned, and coarsely chopped

3 tablespoons balsamic vinegar (eyeball it)

Preheat the oven to 400°F.

Preheat a grill pan or outdoor grill on high.

With a sharp knife, cut the thawed but chilled puff pastry sheet into 4 squares, arrange on a cookie sheet, and sprinkle with a little salt and pepper. Bake the puff pastry according to package directions, or until golden brown all over, about 12 to 15 minutes.

While the puff pastry is baking, season the skirt steaks with the 2 tablespoons of EVOO, garlic, rosemary, salt, and pepper. Grill the meat for 3 to 4 minutes on each side. Remove the meat and let it rest for 5 minutes to allow the juices to redistribute. While the steak is cooking, trim the woody ends off the asparagus. Drizzle with EVOO and season with salt and pepper. As soon as the steaks are off the grill and resting, add the asparagus to the grill.

Grill the spears, turning frequently, until the asparagus is tender, about 4 to 5 minutes. Remove the asparagus from the grill and cut into 2-inch lengths.

In a bowl, toss together the grilled chopped asparagus, crumbled blue cheese, and chopped arugula. Season the mixture with balsamic vinegar, salt, and pepper.

Slice the steak thinly across the grain. Top each golden-brown puff pastry square with some slices of steak. Top the steak with the asparagus salad and serve.

4 SERVINGS

188 Involtini all'Enotec'Antica with Gnocchi

TRY THIS LATER

IT'S A KEEPER

I had these mini versions of stuffed cabbage, meat-balls in radicchio, in Rome, near the Spanish Steps at Enotec'Antica (Ancient Wine Bar), which is a real haunt of mine when in the city. This is a total guess at their recipe, but it's really tasty—try it, soon! It's closer to you tonight than Rome is, I bet!

1¼ pounds ground sirloin

2 handfuls of grated cheese, such as Parmigiano-Reggiano or Romano cheese, plus more for sprinkling

A handful of fresh flat-leaf parsley, chopped

10 fresh basil leaves, shredded or torn

3 garlic cloves, chopped

1 egg, beaten

A couple of handfuls of Italian-style bread crumbs

Salt and freshly ground black pepper

1 tablespoon extra-virgin olive oil (EVOO), plus more for drizzling

1 tablespoon unsalted butter, cut into pieces

3 tablespoons all-purpose flour

½ cup dry red wine (eyeball it)

2 cups beef stock or broth

1 cup tomato sauce

1 head of radicchio, leaves separated

1 pound frozen gnocchi (potato dumplings)

Bring a large pot of water to a boil for the gnocchi.

Mix the beef with the cheese, parsley, basil, garlic, egg, bread crumbs, salt, pepper, and a drizzle of EVOO.

Preheat a large, deep skillet over medium heat. Add the tablespoon of EVOO and the butter. When the butter melts, add the flour and cook for 1 minute. Whisk in the wine and stock and bring to a bubble. Add the tomato sauce. Return the sauce to a bubble and reduce the heat to medium low.

Form about 20 large meatballs, slightly oval in shape, and wrap in the radicchio leaves. Set them into the hot sauce in an even layer. Spoon a little of the sauce over the tops. Cover and simmer for 10 to 12 minutes.

Drop the gnocchi into the boiling water and salt the water to season it. Cook until the gnocchi are tender and floating, 5 to 6 minutes or according to the package directions. Drain well.

Arrange 5 wrapped meatballs on each plate. Spoon a touch of sauce over each. Add the gnocchi to the remaining sauce in the skillet. Coat the gnocchi in the remaining sauce and season with a little grated cheese, salt, and pepper, then serve alongside the meatballs in red lettuce wraps.

4 SERVINGS

Lime-and-Honey Glazed Salmon with Warm Black Bean and Corn Salad

366 Christmas Pasta

Tomato-Basil Pasta Nests **242**

Ricotta Pasta with Grape Tomatoes, Peas, and Basil **192**

158 Shrimp Martinis and Manhattan Steaks

Above: **222** Oven-Baked Corndogs; below: **17** Honey Nut Chicken Sticks

24

**Salsa Stoup
and Double-Decker
Baked Quesadillas**

281 Big Bistro Burger
with Caramelized Shallots
on Grilled Bread with Beet and
Goat Cheese Salad

15 Super Tuscan Burger
and Potato Salad
with Capers and Celery

56 Big Bird: Jumbo Chicken,
Spinach, and Herb Burgers
with Mushrooms and Swiss

357 Crispy Turkey Cutlets and
Bacon-Cranberry Brussels Sprouts

337 Mediterranean Chicken

267 Pretzel-Crusted Chicken Breasts with a Cheddar-Mustard Sauce

299 Chipotle Chicken Rolls with Avocado Dipping Sauce

Veal Scallopine with Dijon Sauce, Asparagus, and Avocados

189

☐ TRY THIS LATER   ☐ IT'S A KEEPER

This dish is one buttery, delicious, edible ode to spring. (Also, the flavor is so sexy, it could bring on some serious birds-and-bees action!)

Coarse salt
1 lemon
1 pound very thin asparagus tips
2 ripe Hass avocados
Extra-virgin olive oil (EVOO), for drizzling, plus 2 tablespoons (twice around the pan)
1¼ pounds veal scallopine
Coarse black pepper
1 tablespoon all-purpose flour, plus more for dredging
3 tablespoons unsalted butter, cut into small pieces
½ cup dry white wine
1 cup chicken stock or broth
2 tablespoons chopped fresh thyme leaves
2 teaspoons Dijon mustard
⅓ cup cream or half-and-half
3 tablespoons chopped fresh chives

In a large saucepan, bring 1 inch of water to a boil. Salt the water. Add a couple of curls of rind from the lemon and the asparagus tips. Cook the tips for 3 minutes, then drain and reserve.

Cut into and all around the pits of the avocados. Scoop the flesh from the avocados, and slice. Dress the sliced avocados with a little lemon juice, a drizzle of EVOO, and a pinch of salt and reserve.

Preheat your largest skillet over medium heat. Season the veal with salt and pepper on both sides. Dredge the scallopine in a little flour. Add the 2 tablespoons of EVOO and 2 tablespoons of the butter to the hot skillet. When the butter melts into the oil, add the veal and cook for 2 minutes on each side, or until evenly light golden in color. Place the veal on a platter under a loose tent of foil.

Add the remaining tablespoon of butter and the tablespoon of flour to the skillet. Cook for 1 minute, then whisk in the wine and scrape up the pan drippings, with a wooden spoon. Whisk the stock into the wine and add the thyme, salt, pepper, and mustard. Stir in the cream, then remove from the heat.

Arrange the asparagus and sliced avocados over the veal and pour a line of sauce over the top. Garnish the dinner plates or platter with chopped chives and serve.

4 SERVINGS

190 Crunchy Japanese Fish with Vegetable and Noodle Toss

TRY THIS LATER ☐   IT'S A KEEPER ☐

No panko (Japanese bread crumbs)? No problem! I got a great recipe from an old JayCee/community cookbook in New England. One local mom made Rice Krispie fish fillets in the oven with melted margarine. What a great substitute for panko flakes! Crushed Krispies! Cool! Here's my take . . . with a side of No-Pain Vegetable Lo Mein.

- ½ pound thin spaghetti
  Coarse salt
- 2 pounds haddock fillets
- 2 pinches of cayenne pepper
  Zest and juice of 1 lemon
- 3 cups Rice Krispies cereal, half crushed, half left whole
- 3 tablespoons chopped fresh flat-leaf parsley
- 3 tablespoons chopped fresh chives
- ½ cup butter or margarine, melted

LO MEIN

- 3 tablespoons vegetable oil (3 times around the pan)
- 3 garlic cloves, chopped
  2-inch piece of fresh ginger, minced
- 1 cup shredded carrots, or 1 carrot, peeled and cut into matchsticks
- 2 cups bean sprouts
- 1 8-ounce can sliced water chestnuts, drained and chopped
- 1 red bell pepper, cored, seeded, and thinly sliced
- 6 scallions, thinly sliced on an angle
- ⅓ cup tamari (dark aged soy sauce) (eyeball it)

Preheat the oven to 400°F.

Bring a pot of water to a boil, add the pasta and salt the water. Cook the pasta until slightly undercooked. Drain.

While the pasta works, prepare the fish. Season the haddock with salt, cayenne pepper, lemon zest, and the juice of ½ lemon. Cut the remaining ½ lemon into wedges and reserve. Crush half the cereal in a sealable plastic bag, then combine with the whole cereal, parsley, and chives. Dip the fish in the melted butter or margarine, then coat evenly in the cereal coating and place on a nonstick cookie sheet. Bake for 17 to 18 minutes, until evenly golden and crisp.

After the fish goes in the oven, heat a large nonstick skillet over high heat. Add the vegetable oil, garlic, ginger, and carrots. Cook for 1 minute, stir-frying the mixture, then add the bean sprouts, water chestnuts, red bell peppers, and scallions. Stir-fry for another 2 minutes and add the drained, hot pasta. Add the tamari and remove from the heat. Toss for a minute for the pasta to absorb the tamari and vegetable juices, and divide the No-Pain Lo Mein among 4 plates. Serve with the crispy oven-fried fish. Pass the lemon wedges at the table.

4 SERVINGS

Super Marsala Burgers and Arugula-Tomato Salad

☐ TRY THIS LATER   ☐ IT'S A KEEPER

1¼ to 1⅓ pounds ground chicken or ground veal

1 large shallot, finely chopped

3 tablespoons fresh sage (from 4 to 5 sprigs), finely chopped
A handful of fresh flat-leaf parsley, finely chopped

3 garlic cloves, 2 finely chopped, 1 cracked away from the skin

1 tablespoon Worcestershire sauce

1 tablespoon grill seasoning, such as McCormick's Montreal Steak Seasoning (a palmful)

2 tablespoons extra-virgin olive oil (EVOO), plus more for liberal drizzling

⅓ pound Italian Fontina cheese, sliced

1 tablespoon unsalted butter, cut into small pieces

1 medium onion, quartered lengthwise, then thinly sliced

4 portobello mushroom caps, thinly sliced
Salt and freshly ground black pepper

½ cup good-quality Marsala (fortified Spanish wine)

3 cups arugula, chopped

3 small plum tomatoes, halved and thinly sliced

4 crusty rolls, split

1 package olive oil or onion and garlic-flavored chips, any brand

Heat a grill pan or large nonstick skillet over medium-high heat. Place the meat in a bowl and add the shallots, sage, parsley, chopped garlic, Worcestershire, grill seasoning, and a healthy drizzle of EVOO. Mix the meat gently. Score it into 4 quarters and form 1-inch-thick patties. Cook the patties for 5 to 6 minutes on each side. Place the cheese on top of the patties in the last 2 minutes of cooking time and loosely tent the pan with foil to melt the cheese.

Preheat the broiler.

While the burgers cook, heat a medium skillet over medium-high heat. Add the 2 tablespoons EVOO and the butter. To the melted butter and hot EVOO add three fourths of the sliced onions and the sliced mushrooms and cook until the mushrooms are deep brown, 8 to 10 minutes, stirring them frequently. Season the mushrooms with salt and pepper after they brown. Salting them before they brown will draw out the liquids, slowing the browning process. Add the Marsala to the pan and cook it down to glaze the mushrooms with its flavor. Remove the mushrooms from the heat.

In a salad bowl, toss the chopped arugula with the sliced tomatoes and reserved raw sliced onions and dress the salad with a drizzle of EVOO, then season with salt and pepper.

Brown the split rolls under the broiler and rub lightly with the cracked garlic. Drizzle the rolls lightly with EVOO and top with Fontina-covered burgers and a pile of Marsala mushrooms. Set the roll tops in place and serve the arugula and tomato salad alongside with a pile of fancy chips.

4 SERVINGS

192 MASTER RECIPE
Ricotta Pasta with Grape Tomatoes, Peas, and Basil

This dish can be made 100 ways. It's one of the first dishes you eat as an Italian kid: macaroni with butter and ricotta cheese. Once you grow up, you add stuff in, but the base remains the same. I'll try to limit myself and just give you my top five versions.

1 pound penne or ziti rigate
Coarse salt
2 cups ricotta cheese
2 tablespoons unsalted butter, cut into small pieces
½ cup Parmigiano-Reggiano or Romano cheese (a couple of handfuls)
2 tablespoons extra-virgin olive oil (EVOO) (twice around the pan)
1 medium onion, finely chopped
1 cup frozen green peas
A generous handful of fresh flat-leaf parsley, finely chopped
Coarse black pepper
20 fresh basil leaves, shredded or torn
1 cup halved grape tomatoes (½ pint)

Bring a large pot of water to a boil. Add the pasta and salt the water. Cook the pasta al dente, with a bite to it.

Place the ricotta, butter, and Parmigiano or Romano in a large bowl.

Heat a small skillet over medium heat. Add the EVOO and onions and cook for 5 minutes. Add the peas and parsley and cook for 2 minutes. Turn off the heat.

Drain the pasta. Add to the bowl with the cheeses. Toss to melt the butter and evenly coat the pasta with cheeses, then season with salt and pepper. Top the pasta with the peas, basil, and halved grape tomatoes. Season with a little salt. Toss and serve at the table.

4 SERVINGS

193 NOW TRY... Ricotta Pasta with Sausage

OMIT

Frozen peas
Grape tomatoes

ADD

1 pound bulk Italian sweet sausage

Prepare as for the master recipe, #192, browning the sausage in the EVOO before adding the onions. Continue as directed, sprinkling the pasta with the shredded basil.

4 SERVINGS

THEN TRY... Ricotta Pasta with Zucchini, Garlic, and Mint

194

OMIT

Frozen peas
Grape tomatoes

ADD

4 garlic cloves, minced
1 medium zucchini, diced
A generous handful of fresh mint leaves, slivered

Prepare as for the master recipe, #192, adding the garlic and zucchini to the skillet with the onions and cook for 7 to 8 minutes. Add the mint with the parsley.

Continue as directed, tossing the pasta with the onions and zucchini.

4 SERVINGS

OR TRY... Ricotta Pasta with Tomatoes al Forno

195

OMIT

Frozen peas
Grape tomatoes

ADD

1/2 cup additional Parmigiano-Reggiano or Romano cheese
3 garlic cloves, chopped
1 14-ounce can crushed tomatoes
1/2 pound fresh mozzarella, thinly sliced

Prepare as for the master recipe, #192, sautéing the garlic with the onions until soft, 8 minutes. Stir in the crushed tomatoes and parsley and season the sauce with salt and pepper. Simmer for 5 minutes, then turn off the heat.

Preheat the broiler to high and place the top rack 6 to 8 inches from the broiler.

Drain the pasta. Add it to the bowl with the cheeses. Toss to melt the butter and evenly coat the pasta with cheeses, then season with salt and pepper. Add the tomato sauce and the basil and toss again to combine. Transfer the mixture to a baking casserole, then evenly distribute the remaining 1/2 cup of Parmigiano cheese and the slices of fresh mozzarella over the top. Place under the broiler and crisp up the top and edges of the pasta, melting and browning the cheeses evenly.

4 SERVINGS

(variations continue on page 172)

196 AND ONE MORE... Ricotta Pasta with Spinach

OMIT

Frozen peas
Grape tomatoes

ADD

3 garlic cloves, chopped
2 10-ounce boxes frozen chopped spinach,
   defrosted and squeezed dry in a clean kitchen
   towel
½ cup dry white wine
   Freshly grated or ground nutmeg

Prepare as for the master recipe, #192, sautéeing the garlic with the onions until soft, about 8 minutes. Separate the dry, defrosted chopped spinach, add to the garlic and onions, and heat through. Add the wine and loosen up the spinach. Cook off the wine, 1 minute, then turn off the heat.

Continue as directed, adding the spinach after the pasta and cheeses are combined. Season the mixture with salt, pepper, and nutmeg.

4 SERVINGS

197 About-15-Minute Soup with Spinach, Artichokes, and Tortellini

2 tablespoons extra-virgin olive oil (EVOO)
   (twice around the pan)
6 cremini (baby portobello) or white
   mushrooms, sliced
1 medium onion, chopped
   Salt and freshly ground black pepper
1 can quartered artichoke hearts, drained
6 cups chicken stock or broth
1 12- to 16-ounce package fresh refrigerated
   tortellini, any variety or flavor
1 pound fresh triple-washed spinach, stems
   removed and leaves coarsely chopped
   Grated Parmigiano-Reggiano or Romano
   cheese
   Crusty bread, to pass at the table

Heat a medium soup pot over medium-high heat. Add the EVOO, mushrooms, and onions, and season with salt and pepper. Cook for 5 minutes, add the artichokes and stock, raise the heat and bring to a boil. Add the tortellini to the pot and return to a boil, then reduce the heat to a simmer. Cook for 5 to 6 minutes, until the tortellini floats and is cooked through. Fold in the spinach until it has all wilted into the soup. Turn off the heat and serve up the soup. Top shallow bowls of soup with cheese and pass bread at the table.

4 SERVINGS

White Beans, Pancetta, and Pasta

198

☐ TRY THIS LATER ☐ IT'S A KEEPER

This is a mix-up of pasta e fagioli and minestra. Again, my indecisiveness is at play.

3 tablespoons extra-virgin olive oil (EVOO) (3 times around the pan)
⅓ pound pancetta, chopped
½ teaspoon crushed red pepper flakes
4 garlic cloves, crushed
6 sprigs fresh thyme
3 sprigs fresh rosemary
2 carrots, chopped
1 medium yellow onion, chopped
2 celery ribs with greens, chopped
  Salt and freshly ground black pepper
½ cup dry white wine (a couple of glugs)
3 cups chopped fresh dandelion greens (1 small bunch)
1 head of escarole, chopped
2 15-ounce cans small white beans or cannellini, drained
1 15-ounce can diced tomatoes in juice, San Marzano variety if available
6 cups chicken stock or broth
2 cups penne pasta
  Grated Parmigiano-Reggiano or Romano cheese, to pass at the table

Heat a soup pot over medium-high heat. Add the EVOO and the pancetta. Cook the pancetta for 3 to 4 minutes, then add the red pepper flakes, garlic, and herb sprigs. Add the vegetables as you chop: carrots, onions, and celery. Season with salt and pepper and cook until the carrots begin to soften, 7 to 8 minutes.

Add the wine and deglaze the pan, scraping up any good bits. Wilt in the greens and escarole in bunches. Add the beans, tomatoes, and stock and place a lid on the pot, raise the heat, and bring to a boil. Add the pasta and cook for 6 to 7 minutes, until cooked al dente. Serve the very thick soup in shallow bowls with lots of cheese.

4 SERVINGS

199 Lemon-Thyme Succotash
with Garlic-Parsley Shrimp

4 tablespoons extra-virgin olive oil (EVOO)
1 medium onion, chopped
1 red bell pepper, cored, seeded, and chopped
2 celery ribs and greens, chopped
  Salt and freshly ground black pepper
2 tablespoons unsalted butter, cut into small
  pieces
6 garlic cloves, minced
1½ pounds medium shrimp, peeled and deveined
2 cups frozen corn kernels
1 15-ounce can cannellini beans, drained
3 tablespoons fresh thyme leaves
  (from 5 to 6 sprigs), chopped
1 lemon, zested and cut into wedges
⅓ cup chopped fresh flat-leaf parsley (a couple
  of generous handfuls)
½ cup dry white wine or ⅓ cup white vermouth
  (eyeball it)

Heat two skillets: one over medium heat, the other over medium-high heat. To the hotter pan, add 2 table-spoons of the EVOO (twice around the pan), then the onions, bell peppers, celery, salt, and pepper. Give the pan a shake.

To the second skillet, add the remaining 2 tablespoons of EVOO and the butter, melting it into the oil. Add the garlic and cook for 1 minute, then add the shrimp and season with salt and pepper. Sauté the shrimp, tossing them around in the garlic butter until they become pink and firm, 3 to 5 minutes.

Add the frozen corn and cannellini beans to the succotash in the first pan. Adjust the salt and pepper and add the thyme and lemon zest. Once the beans and corn have warmed through, turn off the heat.

Add the parsley and wine to the shrimp and toss for 1 minute. To serve, pile the succotash onto plates and top with the garlic-parsley shrimp. Pass the lemon wedges at the table. Squeeze lemon juice over the shrimp and succotash before eating.

4 SERVINGS

Big Mussels with Chorizo and Saffron Rice

This meal is a lazy-man's version of paella. (But we lazy, big-mouthed, big-appetite girls can dispatch this dinner pretty easily, too!)

- 2 cups chicken stock or broth
- 1 cup seafood stock or clam juice (available at the seafood counter or near the canned tuna)
- ¼ teaspoon saffron threads
- 2 tablespoons extra-virgin olive oil (EVOO) (twice around the pan), plus more for drizzling
- 1½ cups short-grain white rice
- ½ pound chorizo sausage, diced
- 3 garlic cloves, chopped
- 1 medium onion, chopped
- 1 red bell pepper, cored, seeded, and chopped
- 2 celery ribs with greens, chopped
- 1 bay leaf, fresh or dried
  Salt and freshly ground black pepper
- ½ cup dry white wine
- 1 14-ounce can diced tomatoes
- 2 pounds cleaned mussels (Pull off the hairy "beards" with your fingers.)
- ½ cup fresh flat-leaf parsley (a couple of generous handfuls)
- 1 cup frozen green peas, defrosted
  Crusty bread

In a medium saucepan, heat the combination of stocks and saffron to a boil, then add a generous drizzle of EVOO and the rice. Cover and cook until tender, stirring occasionally, about 17 minutes.

Heat a deep skillet over medium-high heat. Add the 2 tablespoons of the EVOO and the chorizo and cook for 2 minutes to render some of the chorizo's fat, then add the garlic, onions, bell peppers, celery, and bay leaf and season with salt and pepper. Cook the vegetables for 7 to 8 minutes, then add the wine and reduce for 1 minute. Add the tomatoes and stir. Add the mussels to the pan in an even layer, then cover the pan tightly. Cook for 3 to 4 minutes to open the mussels. Remove the lid and discard any unopened mussels. Also discard the bay leaf. Combine the parsley in the pan with a serious shake.

To serve, add the peas to the cooked rice and toss to combine. Arrange the cooked rice in shallow bowls or on a large, deep platter. Top with the mussels and sauce. Pass crusty bread for mopping.

4 SERVINGS

TIDBIT

Saffron powder is sometimes available in small, affordable envelopes near the fish counter. Saffron threads are more expensive, but a tin will last a long time—just remember to keep it in a cool place away from the heat of the stove!

201 Aussie Meat Pies, Made Quick

Australia has these cool meat pies made of pastry crust stuffed with a slowly simmered, finely ground meat mixture. The pies can be topped with ketchup, and man, are they good! They taste like a ritzy version of a sloppy Joe. This is my sped-up version of a down-under favorite.

Serve the pies with a green salad.

- 2 sheets frozen puff pastry, defrosted but kept chilled (recommended brand: Pepperidge Farm)
  Salt and freshly ground black pepper
- 1 tablespoon extra-virgin olive oil (EVOO) (once around the pan)
- 2 tablespoons unsalted butter, cut into pieces
- 1½ pounds ground beef
- 1 medium onion, finely chopped
- 2 tablespoons all-purpose flour
- 2 tablespoons Worcestershire sauce (eyeball it)
- 1 rounded tablespoon tomato paste
- 1 rounded tablespoon brown sugar
- 1 cup beef stock or broth
- 1 tablespoon grill seasoning, such as McCormick's Montreal Steak Seasoning
  Ketchup, for garnish
- 2 tablespoons chopped fresh chives

Preheat the oven to 400°F.

With a sharp knife, cut the thawed but chilled puff pastry sheets into 4 squares each, 8 squares total, and arrange on a cookie sheet. Season the squares with a little salt and pepper. Bake the puff pastry according to the package directions, or until golden brown all over, about 12 to 15 minutes.

Heat a medium skillet over medium-high heat. Let it get really hot so the meat will caramelize when it hits the pan. Add the EVOO, then the butter. When the butter melts into the oil, add the beef and really work at breaking it up as it browns—get the bits all nice and tiny. Add the onions and cook for 5 minutes. Stir in the flour. Cook the mixture a minute more. In a small bowl, combine the Worcestershire with the tomato paste and brown sugar, then stir in the stock. Whisk the seasoned stock into the pan. Stir into the meat and combine. Season the meat with the grill seasoning and reduce the heat to low.

When the pastry squares are ready, assemble the pies. Place a square of pastry in the bottom of a shallow bowl. Top with one quarter of the meat mixture and another square. Place a large dollop of ketchup in the center of the top pastry and sprinkle the "pies" with chives to garnish, then serve.

4 SERVINGS

TIDBIT

You could also use refrigerated pie crusts instead of puff pastry sheets.

Fall Minestrone

TRY THIS LATER

IT'S A KEEPER

More like fall-in-love-with soup.

 2 tablespoons extra-virgin olive oil (EVOO)
(twice around the pan)

 ¼ pound pancetta, cut as thick as bacon from
the deli counter, chopped

 ½ teaspoon crushed red pepper flakes

 4 garlic cloves, chopped

 3 portobello mushroom caps, chopped

 2 medium onions, chopped

 2 medium carrots, peeled and diced

 2 celery ribs, chopped with greens
Salt and freshly ground black pepper

 2 stems of fresh rosemary

 8 fresh sage leaves, thinly sliced

 1 medium zucchini, diced

 1 small bunch of kale or chard, trimmed of
tough ends and veins and coarsely chopped
(4 to 5 cups)

 1 15-ounce can cannellini beans, drained

 1 14-ounce can petite diced tomatoes or
chunky-style crushed tomatoes

 1 quart chicken stock or broth

 2 cups vegetable stock or broth
A piece of rind of Parmigiano cheese—buy a
hunk that has a piece of rind attached to it, cut
from the outside of the wheel

 1 cup ditalini pasta
Grated Parmigiano-Reggiano, to pass at the
table
Crusty bread, for mopping

Heat a medium soup pot over medium-high heat and add the EVOO. Add the pancetta and brown for 2 minutes. Add the red pepper flakes, garlic, mushrooms, onions, carrots, and celery. Cook for 5 to 6 minutes, until the mushrooms are lightly browned. Season with salt and pepper and add the rosemary stems and the sage to the pot. Add the zucchini and chopped greens and stir them into the pot until all the greens wilt down, 2 to 3 minutes.

Add the beans, tomatoes, stocks, and cheese rind, then place a lid on the pot and bring the soup to a boil. Uncover and add the ditalini pasta. Cook the soup for 7 to 8 minutes at a rolling simmer, uncovered, until the pasta is al dente, with a bite to it. Remove the pot from the heat. Remove the rind and the now bare rosemary stems (the leaves fall off into the soup as it cooks). Adjust the salt and pepper to taste.

Ladle the soup into shallow bowls and top with grated cheese. Pass the crusty bread at the table.

4 SERVINGS

TIDBIT

You can now find vegetable stock in cartons on the soup aisle next to the boxes of beef and chicken broth.

203
MASTER RECIPE
Italian Sweet Chicken Sausage Patties
with Peppers and Onions on Garlic Buttered Rolls

Serve with chopped raw vegetable salad and fancy store-bought chips of choice.

- 1½ pounds ground chicken
- 1 tablespoon grill seasoning, such as McCormick's Montreal Steak Seasoning
- 1 teaspoon (⅓ palmful) fennel seeds
- 4 garlic cloves, minced
- ¼ cup tender sun-dried tomatoes (available in pouches or tubs in the produce section)
- 10 to 12 fresh basil leaves
- 2 tablespoons extra-virgin olive oil (EVOO), plus some to drizzle
- 2 cubanelle peppers (long, light green peppers), seeded and sliced
- 1 medium onion, thinly sliced
  Salt and freshly ground black pepper
- 4 crusty kaiser rolls, split
- 2 tablespoons unsalted butter
- 4 deli-cut slices of Provolone cheese

Preheat a nonstick skillet over medium-high heat.

Place the chicken in a medium bowl with the grill seasoning, fennel seeds, and half of the garlic. Pile the sun-dried tomatoes on top of each other in small stacks, then slice into thin strips. Coarsely chop the thin strips and add to the bowl. Stack the basil leaves together, then roll them up into a log. Shred the basil by thinly slicing the log (this makes a chiffonade). Add the basil to the bowl. Drizzle EVOO over the bowl. Mix the ingredients together and form 4 patties, ³⁄₄ inch thick. Cook for 5 to 6 minutes on each side in the preheated skillet.

Heat a second skillet over medium-high heat and preheat the broiler, placing the top rack at least 6 inches from the heat.

To the hot skillet, add the 2 tablespoons of EVOO (twice around the pan), then the peppers and onions. Season the mixture with salt and pepper. Cook until just tender, about 6 to 7 minutes.

Toast the rolls on a broiler pan under the hot broiler. Place the remaining garlic and the butter in a small dish and microwave for 15 seconds on High to melt the butter. Brush the toasted roll tops with garlic butter and reserve. Leave the bun bottoms on the broiler pan.

Place the patties on the bun bottoms, then top with the peppers and onions and sliced Provolone cheese. Place the chicken sandwiches under the broiler again for 30 seconds to 1 minute to melt the cheese. Set the buttered tops in place and serve!

4 SERVINGS

TIDBIT

Trim a sliver off one side of the peeled whole onion to keep it stable as you slice it into disks: Give it "feet" for stability.

☐ TRY THIS LATER   ☐ IT'S A KEEPER

OMIT

Cubanelle peppers
Rolls
Butter
Provolone

ADD

1 pound gnocchi (potato dumplings) from the refrigerated or frozen foods section of the market
Crushed red pepper flakes
1 28-ounce can crushed tomatoes
1 8-ounce can tomato sauce
10 more leaves of fresh basil (1 cup or 20 leaves, total)
Grated Parmigiano-Reggiano or Romano cheese, to pass at the table

PREP CHANGE

Finely chop the onion rather than slice it

Preheat the oven to 400°F.

Make the chicken sausage as directed in the master recipe, #203, reserving the basil leaves whole. Rather than form patties, roll the mixture into mini balls, 1½ inches across, and arrange on a rimmed nonstick cookie sheet. Bake for 10 to 12 minutes, or until firm and lightly golden.

Bring a pot of water to a boil for the gnocchi. Season the water with salt, add the gnocchi, and cook according to the package directions. Drain.

Preheat a large skillet over medium heat. Add the 2 tablespoons of EVOO and the onions, remaining garlic, and crushed red pepper flakes. Cook for 6 to 7 minutes, stirring frequently. Stir in the tomatoes and tomato sauce and season with salt and pepper. Simmer over low heat. Stir in the basil leaves, whole or torn.

Toss the gnocchi and meatballs with the sauce and serve with grated cheese to pass at the table.

4 SERVINGS

(variations continue on page 180)

205 OR TRY... Chicken Sausage on a Roll
with Egg and Fontina

This menu is good for B, L, or D: Breakfast, Lunch, or Dinner

OMIT

$\frac{1}{2}$ pound of the ground chicken—the patties are thinner
Garlic
Sun-dried tomatoes
Basil
2 tablespoons EVOO
Cubanelle peppers
Onion

SWAP

$\frac{1}{3}$ pound Italian Fontina, thinly sliced, for the Provolone

ADD

2 tablespoons honey (a couple of generous drizzles)
$\frac{1}{4}$ cup raisins or golden raisins, finely chopped
A handful of fresh flat-leaf parsley, chopped
4 large eggs

Heat a large nonstick griddle pan or a large skillet to medium high. Preheat the broiler to high.

Mix the chicken with the grill seasoning, fennel seeds, honey, chopped raisins, parsley, and a drizzle of EVOO. Form four $\frac{1}{2}$-inch-thick patties. Cook for 5 minutes on each side and transfer to a plate. Cover with foil and keep warm. Reduce the heat on the griddle to low.

Grease the griddle with a touch of butter. Crack the eggs on the griddle carefully to fry. Season them with salt and pepper. Cook the eggs up or over, however you like 'em.

Place the rolls under the broiler to toast. Butter them lightly and top the bottoms with sausage, then egg, then lots of sliced Fontina. Melt the cheese under the broiler, then set the roll tops in place and serve.

4 SERVINGS

Strip Steaks
with a Side of Blue Cheese Spaghetti

206

☐ TRY THIS LATER

☐ IT'S A KEEPER

4 slices bacon
4 8-ounce New York strip steaks
   Coarse salt
   Coarse black pepper
5 tablespoons unsalted butter
2 tablespoons chopped fresh chives (a palmful)
4 garlic cloves, minced
1 pound spaghetti
2 tablespoons extra-virgin olive oil (EVOO) (twice around the pan)
2 shallots, finely chopped
2 tablespoons all-purpose flour
1 cup chicken stock or broth
½ cup heavy cream
8 ounces blue cheese crumbles
2 to 3 tablespoons chopped fresh sage
2 cups cleaned, trimmed, and shredded arugula (a small bunch)

Put a large pot of water on the stove to boil for the pasta.

Preheat the broiler to high. Arrange the bacon on a slotted broiler pan and cook until crisp on both sides.

Season the steaks with salt and pepper on both sides. Remove the bacon to a plate lined with a paper towel. Arrange the steaks on the broiler pan. Place under the broiler and leave the oven door ajar to limit flare-ups and smoke. (Note that some broilers won't go on with the door open.) Cook for 4 minutes on each side for medium rare, up to 7 minutes on each side for medium well.

Soften 4 tablespoons of the butter in the microwave on High for 15 seconds. Mix in the chives and half of the minced garlic and reserve.

Salt the water for the pasta and add the spaghetti to the pot. Cook al dente, with a bite to it.

Heat a large skillet over medium heat. Add the EVOO and the remaining tablespoon of butter. When the butter melts into the EVOO, add the remaining garlic and the shallots, sauté for 3 minutes, add the flour and cook for a minute more. Whisk in the stock, bring to a bubble for about 30 seconds, then stir in the cream. When the cream comes to a bubble, add the blue cheese and sage and a few grinds of black pepper. Turn off the heat. Stir until the cheese melts.

Remove the steaks from the oven and let rest for 5 minutes. Spoon one fourth of the chive and garlic butter on each steak to melt down over the meat as they rest.

Drain the pasta and toss with the blue cheese sauce to coat and combine evenly, then taste to adjust the seasoning.

Chop and crumble the cooked bacon.

Serve the steaks with heaping portions of blue cheese pasta alongside. Top the pasta with the shredded arugula and bacon crumbles to mix in as you eat.

4 SERVINGS

207 MASTER RECIPE
Olive-Butter–Slathered Broiled Lamb Chops
with Caramelized Zucchini Orzo

Coarse salt
1/2 pound orzo pasta
2 tablespoons extra-virgin olive oil (EVOO), plus some for drizzling
2 small to medium zucchini, cut into thin disks
1 small yellow onion, sliced
3 garlic cloves, chopped
Coarse black pepper
4 tablespoons unsalted butter, softened
3 tablespoons store-bought green or black olive tapenade, any brand
12 1/2- to 3/4-inch-thick loin lamb chops
Zest and juice of 1 lemon
1/4 cup fresh flat-leaf parsley (a generous handful), chopped
1/2 cup grated Parmigiano-Reggiano (a couple of overflowing handfuls)

Bring a large pot of water to a boil for the orzo. Add a generous amount of salt to the water and cook the orzo al dente, with a bite to it.

Preheat the broiler to high.

Preheat a large skillet over medium-high heat with the 2 tablespoons of EVOO (twice around the pan). Add the zucchini, onions, garlic, salt, and pepper. Cook, stirring occasionally, for about 10 minutes, or until the zucchini are lightly caramelized.

Combine the soft butter with the olive tapenade and reserve in the refrigerator.

Arrange the lamb chops on a slotted broiler pan. Drizzle EVOO over the chops and season with salt and pepper. Broil the chops for 3 minutes on each side for medium rare, 5 minutes for well done. Squeeze lemon juice over them.

Add the cooked drained orzo to the browned zucchini and onions, then stir in the lemon zest, parsley, and grated cheese. Toss to distribute.

Remove the chops from the broiler and the butter from the refrigerator. Top each chop with a little olive butter. Serve the chops with the caramelized zucchini orzo.

4 SERVINGS

Olive and Anchovy–Slathered Beef Tenderloin Steaks with Caramelized Onion Orzo and Sliced Tomatoes

208

OMIT

Zucchini
Lemon zest and juice

SWAP

2 medium to large yellow onions, chopped, for the sliced small onion

8 1-inch-thick beef tenderloin steaks for the lamb chops

ADD

¼ cup white vermouth or ½ cup dry white wine

2 rounded tablespoons anchovy paste from a tube (sold near the tomato paste in most markets)

2 beefsteak tomatoes, sliced and seasoned with salt

Follow the master recipe, #207, just as before but sautéing the onions and garlic until caramelized, 15 minutes or so, stirring occasionally. Deglaze with the vermouth or wine.

Combine the soft butter with the tapenade and anchovy paste and refrigerate.

Arrange the steaks on the broiler pan and cook for the same time and in the same manner as the chops. Top with the butter and let it melt while the steaks rest.

Combine the orzo with the onions, parsley, and grated cheese. Adjust the salt and pepper, then serve alongside the steaks with sliced tomatoes on the side.

4 SERVINGS

209 MASTER RECIPE
Pumpkin Polenta with Chorizo and Black Beans

1 tablespoon extra-virgin olive oil (EVOO) (once around the pan)

¾ pound chorizo, casing removed, chopped

1 medium onion, chopped

1 15-ounce can black beans, rinsed and drained

2 pimiento peppers or roasted red peppers, chopped

3 cups chicken stock or broth

2 tablespoons unsalted butter

1 14-ounce can pumpkin puree

1 cup quick-cooking or instant polenta (found in Italian foods or specialty aisles)

1 tablespoon chopped fresh thyme (from 4 sprigs)

Salt and freshly ground black pepper

1 cup shredded Manchego (Spanish sheep's-milk cheese) or sharp or smoked Cheddar

¼ cup fresh flat-leaf parsley (a generous handful), chopped

Heat a medium nonstick skillet over medium-high heat. Add the EVOO and chorizo. Cook for a minute or two, then add the onions and cook for 3 to 4 minutes. Add the black beans and pimientos and heat through for another minute or two.

In a large saucepan, bring the chicken stock and butter to a boil and stir in the pumpkin. Add the polenta and stir until it masses, about 2 minutes. Remove from the heat and add the thyme, salt, pepper, and cheese. Adjust the seasonings. Pour or spoon the polenta onto plates. Top with chorizo and beans and garnish with parsley, then serve.

4 SERVINGS

. . . .

210 NOW TRY... Pumpkin Polenta
with Italian Sausage and Fennel

OMIT

Black beans

Pimientos or roasted peppers

SWAP

1 pound bulk sweet Italian sausage for the chorizo

Pecorino (Italian sheep's-milk cheese) for the Manchego

ADD

Another tablespoon of EVOO

1 large fennel bulb, quartered, cored, then thinly sliced

½ cup dry white wine

¼ teaspoon freshly grated or ground nutmeg (eyeball it)

PREP CHANGE

Thinly slice the onion, rather than chop it

Brown the sausage in the 1 tablespoon of EVOO in a skillet and transfer to a plate lined with a paper towel. Place the pan back on the stove. Add another tablespoon of EVOO, the sliced onions, and the fennel. Sauté over moderate heat until tender but not brown. Add the wine to the skillet and add the sausage back. Cook the wine away, a minute or so.

Cook the polenta as directed in the master recipe, #209, and stir in the nutmeg when you add the thyme and Pecorino cheese. Top the cooked polenta with sausage and fennel and garnish with chopped parsley.

4 SERVINGS

OR TRY... Vegetarian Pumpkin Polenta with Spinach and White Beans

211

☐ TRY THIS LATER ☐ IT'S A KEEPER

OMIT

> Chorizo
> Pimientos or roasted red peppers

SWAP

> White beans (cannellini), rinsed and drained, for the black beans
> Vegetable stock for the chicken stock
> Pecorino (Italian sheep's-milk cheese) for the Manchego

ADD

> Another tablespoon of EVOO
> 2 garlic cloves, chopped
> 2 10-ounce boxes frozen chopped spinach, defrosted and wrung dry in a clean kitchen towel
> ¼ teaspoon freshly grated or ground nutmeg (eyeball it)

Heat both tablespoons of EVOO (twice around the pan), in a skillet over medium heat. Sauté the onions and garlic for 3 to 4 minutes. Stir in the beans and defrosted spinach and heat through. Season the beans and spinach with salt, pepper, and nutmeg.

Heat the vegetable stock as you would the chicken stock and make the polenta as directed in the master recipe, #209, stirring in the Pecorino when you would the Manchego. Top the polenta with the spinach and beans and serve.

4 SERVINGS

212

Broccoli Frittata with Goat Cheese
and BLT Bread Salad

This meal is another B, L, D: good for Breakfast, Lunch, or Dinner.

½ pound day-old chewy farm-style bread, cubed (3 cups)

7 tablespoons extra-virgin olive oil (EVOO)

2½ cups broccoli florets, available packaged in the produce department

1 tablespoon chopped fresh thyme leaves (from 4 sprigs)

½ teaspoon crushed red pepper flakes (eyeball it in your palm)

1 large red onion, finely chopped
Salt and freshly ground black pepper

8 slices bacon, chopped

1 pint grape tomatoes, halved

2 romaine lettuce hearts, chopped (about 5 cups)

3 to 4 tablespoons red wine vinegar (eyeball it)

12 eggs
A splash of cream or half-and-half
Zest of 1 lemon and juice of ½ lemon

2 4-ounce logs goat cheese, crumbled

Preheat the oven to 400°F.

Place the bread in a medium mixing bowl and cover with water. Soak the bread for 3 to 5 minutes.

Heat a 10-inch nonstick skillet with oven-safe handle over medium to medium-high heat. To the hot pan, add 2 tablespoons of the EVOO (twice around the pan),

the broccoli florets, thyme, red pepper flakes, half of the onions, salt, and pepper. Cook for 6 to 7 minutes, until the broccoli starts to take on a little brown color and is tender.

Heat up another small skillet with about a tablespoon of EVOO. Add the chopped bacon and cook until crisp, about 2 to 3 minutes. Once crisp, remove from the pan and drain on a plate lined with a paper towel.

In small batches, remove the bread in handfuls from the water and wring it out without mashing or tearing the bread. You do not want wet bread, so wring it carefully. Place the softened bread in a salad bowl. Add the grape tomatoes, the remaining onions, the reserved crispy bacon, and the romaine lettuce. Dress with the red wine vinegar and 4 tablespoons of EVOO (4 times around the bowl). Season the salad with salt and pepper and toss to combine.

Beat the eggs with salt and pepper, the cream, and lemon zest. To the broccoli mixure in the skillet, add the crumbled goat cheese and the lemon juice. Follow directly with the seasoned beaten eggs. Lift and settle the eggs in the pan as they brown on the bottom. When the eggs are set but remain uncooked on top, transfer to the oven for 7 or 8 minutes, until the frittata is golden brown and puffy.

Serve the frittata in the hot pan and cut into wedges at the table. Serve the BLT bread salad alongside.

4 SERVINGS

☐ TRY THIS LATER

☐ IT'S A KEEPER

Also good for B, L, or D.

OMIT

> Broccoli
> Bacon
> Tomatoes

SWAP

> 5 cups trimmed, cleaned, and chopped arugula (2 bunches) for the romaine lettuce

ADD

> 1 fennel bulb, cored and very thinly sliced, plus a few fronds, chopped
> 2 navel oranges, peeled and chopped
> 1 pound small, raw deveined and peeled shrimp
> 1 6-ounce tub fresh lump crab meat, picked over

Sauté the shrimp as you would the broccoli until pink and firm. Add the crab, separating it into bits as you drop it into the pan. Season and proceed with the frittata according to the master recipe, #212.

Prepare the bread, as directed. Make the salad by tossing the bread with the remaining red onion, the fennel, oranges, and arugula, rather than the B, L, and T. Dress with the vinegar and EVOO.

Serve the frittata from the hot skillet and cut into wedges at the table. Serve the fennel, orange, and bread salad alongside.

4 SERVINGS

214

Thai-Style Shrimp and Veggies with Toasted Coconut Rice

2½ cups chicken stock or broth
1½ cups sweetened shredded coconut
1 cup long-grain rice
4 tablespoons vegetable oil
1½ pounds large shrimp, peeled and deveined
  Salt and freshly ground black pepper
1 small yellow onion, sliced
8 napa cabbage leaves, thinly shredded
1 cup store-bought shredded carrots,
  or 1 medium carrot, cut into matchsticks
1 teaspoon crushed red pepper flakes
  (⅓ palmful)
3 large garlic cloves, chopped
  3-inch piece of fresh ginger, peeled and grated
1 red bell pepper, cored, seeded, and thinly sliced
3 tablespoons tamari (dark aged soy sauce)
5 scallions, thinly sliced
20 fresh basil leaves, chopped or torn
¼ cup fresh cilantro leaves (a handful), chopped
  Juice of 1 lime

In a sauce pot, combine 1½ cups of the chicken stock with 1 cup of the sweetened shredded coconut; bring the mixture up to a simmer, and add the rice. Return to a simmer over low heat and place a tight-fitting lid on the pot. Cook the rice for 18 minutes.

Heat a small skillet over medium heat, add the remaining ½ cup of shredded coconut, stir frequently, and toast until golden, about 2 to 3 minutes. Heads up: Once the coconut starts to brown it will go from golden to burnt quickly, so keep an eye on it. Remove the toasted coconut from the pan and reserve.

Heat a large skillet over medium-high heat with 2 tablespoons of vegetable oil (twice around the pan). Season the shrimp with salt and pepper and add to the hot skillet. Sauté the shrimp for 2 minutes on each side, or until they turn pink but are not yet firm, then remove from the pan to a plate and reserve. Return the skillet to the heat and add the remaining 2 tablespoons of vegetable oil. Add the onions, napa cabbage, carrots, red pepper flakes, garlic, ginger, and red bell peppers to the pan. Cook, stirring frequently, for 3 to 4 minutes. Add the tamari and the remaining cup of stock, then toss the shrimp back into the pan and stir to combine. Cook the shrimp and veggies for 2 more minutes, or until the shrimp are cooked through. Add the scallions, basil, half of the cilantro, and lime juice and taste for seasoning, adding more tamari, salt, or pepper to taste.

Add the reserved toasted coconut to the cooked rice. Fluff the rice with a fork to distribute the toasted coconut. Serve the Thai shrimp on top of the toasted coconut rice, sprinkled with the remaining cilantro.

4 SERVINGS

TRY THIS LATER

IT'S A KEEPER

Chicken Breasts or Swordfish Steaks
with Raw Puttanesca Sauce and Roasted Capers

215

☐ TRY THIS LATER   ☐ IT'S A KEEPER

¼ cup drained capers
    Extra-virgin olive oil (EVOO), for drizzling
4   6-ounce chicken breast halves or 4 6-ounce
    portions of swordfish steak (1 inch thick),
    trimmed of skin
    Salt and freshly ground black pepper
4   plum tomatoes
3   garlic cloves, 2 chopped and 1 left whole but
    cracked away from its skin
¼ cup fresh flat-leaf parsley (a generous
    handful), chopped
1   small white onion, quartered and thinly sliced
4   large slices crusty semolina bread
½ lemon

Preheat the oven to 400°F. Scatter the capers on a rimmed cookie sheet. Drizzle with EVOO and roast for 5 to 6 minutes. Remove and set the oven to broil.

Heat a nonstick skillet over medium-high heat. Drizzle the chicken or swordfish with EVOO and season liberally with salt and pepper. Cook the chicken for 6 minutes on each side or the fish for 4 minutes on each side.

In a small bowl, mix the tomatoes with the chopped garlic, parsley, and onions. Drizzle EVOO over the raw sauce and season with salt and pepper.

Place the bread under the broiler and char on both sides. Rub the bread with the cracked garlic and drizzle with EVOO. Serve the chicken or fish on dinner plates with a squeeze of lemon juice, tons of tomato sauce, and roasted capers on top, and charred bread alongside.

4 SERVINGS

216
MASTER RECIPE
Chicken or Turkey Spanakopita Burgers

Serve these with olive oil and herb potato chips, available on the snack aisle of the market.

- 1 tablespoon extra-virgin olive oil (EVOO) (once around the pan), plus some for drizzling
- 1 tablespoon unsalted butter
- 2 garlic cloves, chopped
- 1 red onion, half chopped, and half thinly sliced
- 1 10-ounce box frozen spinach, defrosted
- 1 teaspoon dried oregano, lightly crushed in the palm of your hand
- ¼ pound feta crumbles
- 1 package (1⅓ pounds) ground chicken or ground turkey breast
- 1 tablespoon grill seasoning, such as McCormick's Montreal Steak Seasoning (a palmful)
- ⅓ seedless cucumber, thinly sliced lengthwise
- 2 plum tomatoes, thinly sliced lengthwise
  Salt and freshly ground black pepper

TOPPING

- 2 roasted red peppers, drained
- ¼ cup fresh flat-leaf parsley (a generous handful)
- ¼ cup pitted kalamata olives (10 to 12 olives)

- 4 crusty rolls, split
- 1 cup coarsely chopped or shredded arugula
  Hot pepper rings or pepperoncini (optional)

Heat a large nonstick skillet over medium heat. To one side, add the 1 tablespoon of EVOO and the butter. When the butter melts, add the garlic and all the onions and cook for 5 minutes. Transfer the garlic and onions to a bowl to cool. Return the pan to the heat.

Wring the defrosted spinach dry by twisting it in a clean kitchen towel over your sink. Separate the spinach as you add it to the bowl with the cooled onions and garlic, and season with the oregano. Add the feta crumbles, then the chicken or turkey, grill seasoning, and a drizzle of EVOO. Mix, score the meat into 4 equal sections, then form 4 patties, 1 inch thick. Raise the heat on the pan to medium high. Add the patties and cook for 6 minutes on each side.

Season the cucumbers and tomatoes with salt and pepper.

Place the topping ingredients in a food processor, season with salt and pepper, and process until a paste forms. Place the cooked burgers on the roll bottoms. Top with the sliced cucumbers, tomatoes, sautéed onions, shredded arugula, and hot peppers, if using. Slather the roll tops with the red pepper and olive paste and place atop the burgers. Serve with chips.

4 SERVINGS

NOW TRY... **Spanakopizza**

217

☐ TRY THIS LATER   ☐ IT'S A KEEPER

OMIT

Chicken or turkey
Grill seasoning
Cucumber
Crusty rolls

ADD

1 pizza dough, refrigerated or from your favorite pizzeria
Another 10-ounce box of frozen chopped spinach, defrosted and wrung dry in a clean kitchen towel
1 sack (10 ounces) or 2 cups shredded mozzarella cheese or shredded four-cheese blend of mozzarella, Parmesan, Provolone, and Asiago cheeses, any brand

PREP CHANGES

Thinly slice all of the red onion, rather than chopping half
Dice the tomatoes, rather than slicing them

Preheat the oven to 425°F.

Sauté the garlic and onions as directed in the master recipe, #216. Remove from the heat to cool.

Form the dough into a 12-inch pizza. Place on a pizza pan or large cookie sheet. Prepare the roasted pepper and olive topping and spread over the dough in a thin layer. Dot the pizza with the 2 boxes of defrosted and wrung spinach and the sautéed garlic and onions. Top with the shredded mozzarella or cheese blend and the feta crumbles. Sprinkle the oregano over the cheese. Bake the pizza until golden and bubbly all over, about 17 minutes.

Scatter the arugula, diced tomatoes, and, if using, the hot peppers (a must for me) over the pizza, cut into wedges, and serve.

4 SERVINGS

218
MASTER RECIPE
Spanish-Style Pork Chops with Chorizo
and Roasted Red Pepper Sauce and Green Beans

2 tablespoons extra-virgin olive oil (EVOO) (twice around the pan), plus some for drizzling

4 1½-inch-thick boneless center-cut pork chops

½ tablespoon paprika (half a palmful)
Salt and freshly ground black pepper

¼ pound chorizo, casing removed, finely chopped

2 garlic cloves, chopped

1 small yellow onion, chopped

1 tablespoon fresh thyme leaves, chopped (from 4 sprigs)

1 16-ounce jar roasted red peppers, drained

½ cup fresh flat-leaf parsley leaves (a couple of generous handfuls)

¼ cup dry sherry or dry white wine (eyeball it)

1 pound fresh green beans, trimmed (available ready-prepped in sacks at many markets)
Juice from 1 lemon
Crusty bread, to pass at the table

Preheat the oven to 375°F.

Heat a large skillet over medium-high to high heat. Add the 2 tablespoons of EVOO. Season the chops with the paprika, salt, and pepper. Place the chops in the skillet and sear the meat to caramelize, about 2 minutes each side. Transfer the chops to a rimmed cookie sheet and place in the oven to finish off, 8 to 10 minutes, until the meat is firm to the touch, but not tough. Remove from the oven and let the chops rest, covered with a piece of aluminum foil, for a few minutes.

While the chops are in the oven, return the skillet to medium heat. Add the diced chorizo and cook, stirring frequently, for 2 minutes. Add the garlic, onions, thyme, salt, and pepper. Cook the chorizo and onions for about 3 minutes.

Bring an inch or two of water to a boil in another skillet with a lid.

Process the roasted peppers and parsley in a food processor until smooth. Add the sherry to the chorizo and onions and stir, then pour in the roasted pepper puree. Cook for another minute or 2, until the pepper puree is heated through.

Place the green beans in the boiling water. Salt the water and cook for 4 to 5 minutes, until the beans are just tender. Drain and dress the beans with a drizzle of EVOO, the lemon juice, and salt and pepper.

Place a chop on each dinner plate, top with the chorizo and roasted red pepper sauce, and serve with green beans and crusty bread, for plate-mopping.

4 SERVINGS

NOW TRY... **Sliced Chicken Breast Subs**
with Italian Sausage, Roasted Pepper, and Onion Sauce

219

☐ TRY THIS LATER

☐ IT'S A KEEPER

OMIT

EVOO, for drizzling
Paprika
Thyme
Sherry—just use the dry white wine
Lemon juice
Green beans

SWAP

4 8-ounce boneless, skinless chicken breast halves for the pork chops

½ pound bulk Italian sweet sausage for the chorizo

4 10- to 12-inch sesame or plain sub rolls, top-split, for the crusty bread

ADD

8 deli-cut slices of Provolone cheese, halved

Brown and crumble the sausage for 5 to 6 minutes, then add the garlic and onions and proceed with the master recipe, #218, cooking the chicken just as you would the pork and making the sauce, using the dry white wine instead of sherry.

Remove the fully cooked chicken from the oven and switch the setting to preheat the broiler. Slice the chicken on an angle in thin slices and combine with the sausage and red pepper sauce. Build subs on the cookie sheet. Fill the sub rolls with sliced chicken and sauce and top each sub with 4 half-moon slices of cheese. Place the subs under the broiler and melt the cheese, about 1 minute, then serve.

4 SERVINGS

220 Charred Tomato Soup with Pesto and Prosciutto Stromboli

6 ripe plum tomatoes, cut in half lengthwise

1 small red onion, cut into chunks

2 tablespoons extra-virgin olive oil (EVOO), plus some for drizzling
Salt and freshly ground black pepper

1 tube refrigerated pizza dough, such as Pillsbury brand

1 tablespoon all-purpose flour or cornmeal

1/2 cup store-bought pesto (the good stuff they sell in the refrigerated case in tubs)

12 slices prosciutto di Parma

4 slices Provolone, deli sliced

2 tablespoons sesame seeds

2 teaspoons dried Italian seasoning blend (2/3 palmful)

1 teaspoon crushed red pepper flakes (1/3 palmful)

3 garlic cloves, chopped

1 quart chicken stock or broth

1 cup heavy cream

20 fresh basil leaves, shredded or torn

Preheat the broiler to high.

Arrange the plum tomato halves, skin side down, with the onions on a rimmed cookie sheet. Drizzle EVOO on the vegetables and season with salt and pepper. Broil for about 4 minutes, flip, and continue to broil for 3 minutes, or until the tomatoes and onions are slightly charred. Lower the oven setting to 400°F.

Dust your hands and the dough lightly with flour or cornmeal and unroll the dough out onto a work surface. Stretch out the dough, gently spreading its rec-tangle shape. Cut the dough into 4 equal pieces: Working across the dough, cut it in half and cut each half in half again. Cover each piece of dough with 2 table-spoons of the pesto.

Fold 3 slices of the prosciutto and 1 slice of the Pro-volone to fit each pesto-covered piece of dough, then roll each piece on an angle from corner to corner, mak-ing a long roll that is thicker in the middle and thinner on each end. Brush the rolls with EVOO, then mix the sesame seeds, dried Italian seasoning, and 1/2 tea-spoon of the red pepper flakes in a small cup. Sprinkle and pat the mixture onto the strombolis, place in the oven, and bake until evenly golden, 12 to 14 minutes.

Place the tomatoes and onions in a blender or food processor, and puree until somewhat smooth.

Preheat a soup pot over medium-high heat, add the 2 tablespoons of EVOO (twice around the pan), and add the garlic and the remaining 1/2 teaspoon of red pepper flakes. Sauté the garlic for a minute, then add the pureed veggies and the chicken stock. When the soup comes to a bubble, stir in the heavy cream, then season with salt and pepper. Simmer the soup for 8 to 10 minutes.

When ready to serve, turn off the soup and stir in the basil. Adjust the salt and pepper. Serve the soup alongside the pesto and prosciutto stromboli, dipping them into the soup as you eat them. YUMMO!

4 SERVINGS

Chunky Turkey, Potatoes, and Veggies
in Red Wine Sauce

1½ pounds small white boiling potatoes, cut in half
    Coarse salt

3 tablespoons extra-virgin olive oil (EVOO)

2 pounds turkey breast cutlets, cut into bite-size chunks
    Freshly ground black pepper

2 teaspoons poultry seasoning

2 tablespoons unsalted butter

1 medium yellow onion, chopped

2 cups baby carrots

2 celery ribs, cut into 2-inch lengths

12 cremini (baby portobello) mushrooms, sliced in half if large, left whole if small

1 tablespoon fresh thyme leaves, chopped (from 4 sprigs)

2 large garlic cloves, chopped

1 rounded tablespoon tomato paste

2 tablespoons all-purpose flour

1⅓ cups good dry red wine, such as Burgundy (eyeball it; about ¼ bottle)

2 cups chicken stock or broth

¼ cup fresh flat-leaf parsley leaves (a generous handful), chopped
    Crusty bread, to pass at the table

Place the potatoes in a sauce pot and cover with water. Add some salt and bring to a simmer. Cook for 12 minutes, or until fork tender. Drain the potatoes in a colander, then return the potatoes to the pan and let them dry out on the stovetop.

While the potatoes are cooking, preheat a large skillet with high sides or a soup pot over medium-high heat with about 2 tablespoons of the EVOO. Season the turkey cutlets with salt, pepper, and poultry seasoning, add to the hot skillet, and cook until lightly browned, about 3 to 4 minutes. Transfer the turkey to a plate and cover with aluminum foil to keep warm.

Return the skillet to medium-high heat and add the remaining tablespoon of EVOO and the butter. Add the onions, carrots, celery, mushrooms, thyme, garlic, and tomato paste and season with salt and pepper. Cook the veggies, stirring frequently, for 5 to 6 minutes. Sprinkle the vegetables with the flour and continue to cook for 1 minute. Whisk in the red wine and simmer for 2 minutes. Add the chicken stock and continue to simmer the mixture for 4 to 5 minutes, or until thickened. Add the cooked potatoes and the browned turkey pieces and continue to cook for about 2 to 3 more minutes, or until the turkey is cooked through. Add the parsley and taste for seasonings, adjusting with salt and pepper. Serve with the crusty bread.

4 SERVINGS

222 Oven-Baked Corn Dogs with O & V Slaw

2 8-ounce boxes corn muffin mix, such as Jiffy brand

2 eggs

1¼ to 1⅓ cups milk

4 tablespoons unsalted butter, melted

1 tablespoon chili powder (eyeball it in your palm)

2 teaspoons ground cumin (eyeball it)

2 teaspoons hot sauce, such as Tabasco or Frank's Red Hot

2 scallions, finely chopped

8 regular pork or beef franks

½ cup hamburger pickle relish

3 tablespoons vegetable oil (eyeball it)

2 tablespoons red wine vinegar (eyeball it)

1 sack (16 ounces) shredded cabbage mix for slaw salads
Salt and freshly ground black pepper

1 bag reduced-fat potato chips, such as Cape Cod brand or Terra brand garlic-and-onion-flavor Yukon chips

Preheat the oven to to 400°F.

In a shallow dish, combine the muffin mix with the eggs, milk, and melted butter. Season the mix with chili powder, cumin, hot sauce, and scallions. The batter will be thick like a wet dough. Place a hot dog into the bowlful of batter, swish it around to coat it, remove the coated dog to a nonstick cookie sheet, and use your fingers to spread batter on any exposed dog spots. Don't coat it too thickly, just shy of a half-inch should do the trick. If it is too thick, the batter will slide off the dog while it's baking, leaving the dog exposed. If that happens don't sweat it, they still taste great. Repeat until all 8 dogs are coated. Bake for 12 minutes or until evenly deep brown all over.

Mix the relish with the oil and vinegar. Add the shredded cabbage to the bowl, season with salt and pepper, and toss to coat the salad.

Serve the oven-baked corn dogs with your favorite hot dog condiments. Serve the slaw and chips alongside the dogs.

4 SERVINGS

TIDBITS

To serve these corn dogs on a stick, insert bamboo skewers into the bottom of the dogs. For parties, use mini dogs. You can coat up to 24 with one batch of batter. Serve them on 3-inch bamboo party skewers —TOO CUTE!

Bacon-Wrapped Beef Tenderloin and
Super-Stuffed Potatoes with Smoked Gouda and
Caramelized Mushrooms and Onions

223

☐ TRY THIS LATER

☐ IT'S A KEEPER

2 large Russet potatoes, cleaned and pricked
  with a fork several times each
4 tablespoons extra-virgin olive oil (EVOO)
1 pound button mushrooms, brushed clean and
  then thinly sliced
1 small yellow onion, sliced
2 large garlic cloves, chopped
1 tablespoon fresh thyme leaves, chopped
  (from 4 sprigs)
  Salt and freshly ground black pepper
4 slices center-cut bacon (look for the
  "center-cut" label on packaged bacon)
4 1½-inch-thick beef tenderloin steaks
¼ cup sour cream
⅓ pound smoked Gouda cheese, shredded

Preheat the broiler to high.

Place the potatoes on a microwave-safe plate and
microwave on High for 15 minutes, rotating once.
While the potatoes are cooking, make the stuffing for
the potatoes.

Preheat a skillet over medium-high heat with about 2
tablespoons of the EVOO (twice around the pan). Add
the mushrooms and cook until they start to brown,
about 4 to 5 minutes. Add the onions, garlic, thyme,
salt, and pepper. Continue to cook, stirring frequently,
for 4 to 5 minutes.

While all that is working, line the bacon slices up on a
meat-safe cutting board a few inches apart. Preheat a
second skillet over high heat with the remaining 2
tablespoons of EVOO. Season the steaks with salt and
pepper and center each steak atop a bacon slice. Wrap
the bacon over the steaks. Place seam side down in the
skillet and cook for 2 minutes on each side. Reduce the
heat to medium under the steaks after the first 2 minutes on each side. Cook the meat, turning occasionally,
for another 6 to 10 minutes for medium rare to
medium well.

Once the potatoes are cooked, cut them in half lengthwise and scoop out the flesh into a medium bowl, taking care not to rip the potato skins. Using a potato
masher, smash the potato flesh together with the sour
cream until combined. Stir in the sautéed mushrooms
and onions, shredded Gouda, salt, and pepper. Mound
the filling back into the potato skins. Place on a cookie
sheet and transfer to the broiler, 6 inches from the
heat, until lightly brown, 3 to 4 minutes.

Serve the bacon-wrapped beef tenderloin alongside
the super-stuffed potatoes.

4 SERVINGS

224 White Pita Pizzas
with Red and Green Prosciutto Salad

Extra-virgin olive oil (EVOO), for drizzling

4 10- to 12-inch pita breads, white or whole-wheat

1 large garlic clove, crushed

Salt and freshly ground black pepper

1½ cups whole-milk ricotta cheese

Zest of 1 lemon

1 sack (10 ounces) or 2 cups shredded mozzarella cheese

1 small fennel bulb

1 head of romaine lettuce

1 medium head of radicchio

8 slices prosciutto di Parma, cut into strips

20 fresh basil leaves, shredded or torn

A generous drizzle of balsamic vinegar

Preheat the oven to 400°F.

Drizzle EVOO over the pitas and rub them with the crushed clove of garlic. Season with a little salt and pepper and arrange on 2 cookie sheets or place directly on oven racks. Transfer the bread to the oven and toast for 2 to 3 minutes, or until the pitas start to flirt with being crispy.

While the pitas are in the oven, in a bowl combine the ricotta, lemon zest, salt, and pepper. Remove the slightly crispy seasoned pitas from the oven; spread the ricotta mixture over the bread, covering it from edge to edge. Sprinkle the ricotta with the shredded mozzarella and return the pitas to the oven for 4 to 5 minutes, or until the cheese melts and browns at the edges.

Trim the tops of the fennel bulb and quarter lengthwise. Remove the core from each quarter with an angled cut. Slice the fennel across into thin pieces and add to a salad bowl. Shred the romaine and the radicchio and add to the bowl. Add the prosciutto and basil, then drizzle balsamic vinegar and EVOO over the salad and season with a little salt and pepper. Toss the salad thoroughly.

To serve, remove the pitas from the oven, arrange them on 4 serving plates, and arrange a pile of the red and green salad on top. If eating pizza with a knife and fork isn't your style, then serve the salad on the side.

4 SERVINGS

Rosemary, Parmigiano, and Pine Nut Breaded Chicken Cutlets with Fennel Slaw

225

☐ TRY THIS LATER ☐ IT'S A KEEPER

2 fennel bulbs

1 red bell pepper, cored, seeded, and thinly sliced

1 cup shredded carrots (available on the produce aisle of the supermarket)

½ small red onion, thinly sliced

½ cup fresh flat-leaf parsley leaves (2 generous handfuls), chopped
   Salt and freshly ground black pepper

2 tablespoons balsamic vinegar (eyeball it)

3 tablespoons extra-virgin olive oil (EVOO) (eyeball it)
   Zest and juice of 1 lemon

1 cup Italian-style bread crumbs (eyeball it)

½ cup grated Parmigiano-Reggiano (a couple of generous handfuls)

1 teaspoon crushed red pepper flakes

2 sprigs fresh rosemary, leaves stripped off stems

1 garlic clove, peeled

3 ounces pine nuts (pignoli) (a generous handful)

2 eggs

1½ pounds chicken breast cutlets

3 to 4 tablespoons all-purpose flour
   Vegetable oil, for shallow frying

For the fennel slaw, cut both bulbs of fennel into quarters. Remove the core from each quarter with an angled cut into each piece. Slice the fennel across into super-thin pieces and add to a salad bowl. Add the bell peppers, carrots, onions, parsley, salt, pepper, balsamic vinegar, EVOO, and the juice of ½ lemon. Toss to coat and let the slaw marinate while you prepare the chicken.

Combine the bread crumbs, Parmigiano, red pepper flakes, rosemary, garlic, pine nuts, and lemon zest in a food processor and pulse to evenly distribute the flavors throughout the crumb and cheese mixture. Transfer the mixture to a plate. Beat the eggs in a separate shallow dish with a splash of water. Season the cutlets with salt and pepper on both sides and turn lightly in the flour.

Heat ½ inch of vegetable oil in a large skillet over medium to medium-high heat. Coat the seasoned and floured cutlets in eggs and then in breading and add to the hot oil. Cook the cutlets in a single layer, in 2 batches if necessary, for about 3 or 4 minutes on each side, until the juices run clear and the breading is evenly browned.

Squeeze the juice of the remaining ½ lemon over the cutlets. Serve the chicken cutlets with a generous portion of the fennel slaw on top or on the side.

4 SERVINGS

226
MASTER RECIPE
Chicken and Sweet Potato Curry-in-a-Hurry

1 cup white rice

2 tablespoons vegetable oil

1 medium-size sweet potato, peeled, cut in half lengthwise, then thinly sliced into half-moons

Salt and freshly ground black pepper

1 rounded tablespoon mild curry paste or 2 tablespoons curry powder (a generous palmful)

2 pounds chicken tenders, bite-size chunks

1 large yellow onion, thinly sliced

1 red bell pepper, cored, seeded, and thinly sliced

1 tablespoon all-purpose flour (1 palmful)

2½ cups chicken stock or broth

½ cup heavy cream or half-and-half

¼ cup prepared mango chutney (a couple of heaping tablespoons)

1 10-ounce box frozen peas

¼ cup fresh cilantro leaves (a generous handful), chopped

Heat 2 cups of water to a boil in a pot, then add the rice, stir, and return to a simmer. Reduce the heat to medium low and cook for 18 minutes, or until tender.

Preheat a large, deep skillet over medium-high heat with the vegetable oil. Add the sweet potatoes to the skillet, season with salt, pepper, and curry paste or powder, and cook, stirring frequently, for 3 to 4 minutes, or until lightly browned. Scoot the potatoes over to one side of the pan and add the chunks of chicken, season with salt and pepper, and cook, browning slightly, for 3 minutes. Add the onions and bell peppers and toss to combine. Add the flour and continue to cook for 1 minute. Add the chicken stock, cream, and mango chutney, bring to a simmer, and cook for 10 minutes, or until the chicken and potatoes are cooked through and the sauce has thickened.

Add the peas and cilantro and simmer for 1 minute to heat the peas through. Serve over the rice.

4 SERVINGS

NOW TRY... Eggplant, Mushroom, and Sweet Potato **227**
Indian-Spiced Stoup

OMIT

Rice
Chicken

SWAP

4 cups **vegetable stock** for the chicken stock
Coconut milk for the heavy cream

ADD

Extra **vegetable oil**
1 medium-firm **eggplant**, cut into large dice
3 **portobello mushroom caps**, diced
Warm **pita bread**, to pass at the table

Prepare just as you would the master recipe, #226, skipping the rice and adding a little extra oil to the skillet after you scoot over the sweet potatoes. Sauté the eggplant and mushrooms as you would the chicken. Follow the rest of the recipe, swapping the vegetable stock for the chicken stock and the coconut milk for cream. Serve with warm pita for dipping.

4 SERVINGS

☐ TRY THIS LATER   ☐ IT'S A KEEPER

TRY THIS LATER

IT'S A KEEPER

228
Chicken in Puttanesca Sauce over Creamy Polenta

2 cups chicken stock or broth

1 cup whole milk
Salt and freshly ground black pepper

5 tablespoons extra-virgin olive oil (EVOO)

2 packages (1¾ to 2 pounds) chicken tenders, cut into bite-size pieces

6 garlic cloves, chopped

1 tin flat anchovy fillets, drained (8 to 10 fillets)

1 teaspoon crushed red pepper flakes (⅓ palmful)

20 oil-cured black olives, cracked away from pits and coarsely chopped (½ cup)

3 tablespoons capers, drained

1 28-ounce can chunky-style crushed tomatoes, such as Furmano's brand

¼ cup fresh flat-leaf parsley leaves (a generous handful), chopped

1 cup quick-cooking polenta (found in Italian markets or specialty foods aisles)

2 tablespoons unsalted butter

½ cup grated Parmigiano-Reggiano (a few generous handfuls)

To start the creamy polenta, in a sauce pot over medium-high heat combine the chicken stock and milk and season with salt and pepper. Bring up to a simmer, then turn the heat down to low.

While the stock and milk are heating, heat a large skillet over medium-high heat and add 2 tablespoons of the EVOO (twice around the pan). Season the chicken chunks with salt and pepper. Add to the hot skillet and cook until lightly brown, about 3 to 4 minutes. Remove the chicken from the skillet to a plate, cover with aluminum foil, and reserve. Return the skillet to the cook top; add the remaining 3 tablespoons of EVOO. Add the garlic, anchovies, and red pepper flakes. Sauté the mixture until the anchovies melt into the oil and completely dissolve and the garlic becomes tender, about 3 minutes. Add the olives, capers, tomatoes, black pepper, and parsley. Bring the sauce to a bubble, add the chicken back to the pan, reduce the heat, and simmer for 5 minutes.

To the simmering chicken stock and milk add the polenta and whisk constantly until the cornmeal masses together, 2 minutes. Add the butter and grated cheese, stirring to combine. Keep in mind that polenta is very forgiving; if it becomes too thick, you can always add more stock or milk.

Serve the polenta in shallow bowls and top with a helping of the chicken and puttanesca sauce.

4 SERVINGS

The "greens of the first of May" are a spring treat I enjoy if I happen to be lucky enough to be wandering around Italy on the first of May. The mixture of spinach, anchovies, capers, and olives is stuffed and cooked inside a dough pocket, like an empanada. Here, I pile it atop a favorite of mine, creamy polenta.

OMIT

2 tablespoons of the EVOO (you'll still need 3 tablespoons)
Chicken
Tomatoes
Parsley

SWAP

20 chopped good-quality pitted green Sicilian olives (in bulk tubs near the deli) for the black olives

ADD

3 to 4 cups or baby spinach leaves, trimmed and coarsely chopped

3 to 4 cups fresh dandelion greens, trimmed and chopped (1 bunch)

¼ to ⅜ teaspoon freshly grated or ground nutmeg
Zest and juice of ½ lemon

Prepare the polenta exactly as directed in the master recipe, #228.

While the polenta cooks, heat a medium skillet over medium heat. Add the EVOO, the garlic, anchovies, and red pepper flakes and "melt" the anchovies into the oil. Add the spinach and the dandelion greens. Turn the greens to coat and wilt them together, season with black pepper and nutmeg, and mix in the olives. Remove the mixture from the heat and stir in the lemon zest and juice. Taste to adjust the seasonings.

Spoon the polenta into shallow bowls and top with the spring greens.

4 SERVINGS

☐ TRY THIS LATER

☐ IT'S A KEEPER

230 MASTER RECIPE
Sweet Prune and Sage Pork Chops with Potatoes

Serve with steamed green beans or broccoli, your choice, if you want to include a veggie on the menu.

2   pounds small **potatoes**, such as baby Yukons or red-skinned new potatoes
    Coarse salt
¾   cup **dry white wine**
1½ cups **chicken stock** or broth
1   tablespoon fresh **thyme** leaves, chopped (from 4 sprigs)
    Coarse black pepper
8   **pitted prunes**, cut in half
2   tablespoons **extra-virgin olive oil** (EVOO) (twice around the pan)
4   1½-inch-thick boneless center-cut **pork chops**
¼   cup fresh **sage** leaves (from 8 sprigs), finely chopped
4   tablespoons **unsalted butter**
3   large **shallots**, chopped
1   tablespoon all-purpose **flour**
¼   cup fresh **flat-leaf parsley** leaves (a generous handful), chopped
    Juice from ½ **lemon**
3   tablespoons chopped fresh **chives** (12 blades)

Preheat the oven to 375°F.

Place the potatoes in a medium sauce pot and cover with water, place the lid on the pot, and place over high heat. Bring the water to a boil, then remove the lid, salt the water and cook the potatoes until tender, about 12 minutes.

In a small sauce pot over medium-high heat combine the wine, chicken stock, thyme, salt, and pepper. Bring the liquids to a simmer and add the prunes, then turn the heat off and let them steep, covered in the hot liquid.

While the prunes are steeping, preheat a large skillet over medium-high heat with the EVOO. Season the chops with salt, pepper, and the sage. Place the chops in the skillet and sear on both sides to caramelize the chops. Transfer the chops to a rimmed cookie sheet and place in the oven to finish, 7 or 8 minutes, or until the meat is firm to the touch but not tough. Remove the chops from the oven and let them rest, covered with a piece of aluminum foil, for a few minutes.

Return the pork chop skillet to the heat and add 2 tablespoons of the butter. Once the butter has melted, add the shallots and season with salt and pepper. Cook, stirring frequently, for 2 minutes. Sprinkle the shallots with the flour and cook for 1 minute. Whisk in the steeped prunes and the liquid and cook until thickened, about 3 to 4 minutes. Add the parsley and lemon juice to the sauce and taste for seasoning. Turn off the heat.

Drain the potatoes and return to the hot pot. Add the remaining 2 tablespoons of butter and toss to coat. Season the potatoes with salt and pepper.

Transfer the chops to dinner plates and pour the sauce over them. Arrange a few potatoes alongside the chops and top liberally with the chopped chives.

4 SERVINGS

Sweet Date, Apricot, and Sage Veal Chops **231**
with Chive Potatoes

☐ TRY THIS LATER   ☐ IT'S A KEEPER

SWAP

  8 dried apricots, cut in half, for the prunes

  4 1½-inch-thick bone-in veal chops for the pork chops

ADD

12 pitted dates, coarsely chopped
     Zest of 1 orange

Prepare as for the master recipe, #230, just swapping the fruits, adding the zest with the dates, and roasting the chops up 4 to 5 minutes longer (because of the bone and the thickness of the chop). Again, the chops should feel firm but not tough. As similar as it is, this meal tastes entirely different from the original. (What a difference a *date* makes!)

4 SERVINGS

Chicken Sausage with Fennel and Onions **232**

☐ TRY THIS LATER   ☐ IT'S A KEEPER

¼ cup pine nuts (a generous handful)

  8 to 10 chicken sausages, any variety or brand

  4 tablespoons extra-virgin olive oil (EVOO)

  1 large fennel bulb, trimmed, cored, then thinly sliced

  1 large onion, thinly sliced
     Salt and freshly ground black pepper

¼ cup white vermouth or ⅓ cup dry white wine (eyeball it)
     A couple of handfuls of fresh flat-leaf parsley, coarsely chopped

Toast the nuts in a skillet over medium heat until golden, about 5 minutes. Remove them and reserve. Pierce the sausages with a fork and arrange in the skillet. Add ¼ inch water and 2 tablespoons of the EVOO (twice around the pan). Place the pan back on the heat and raise the temperature to medium-high. Allow the water to boil away completely, about 7 minutes. The EVOO left will coat and crisp the casings. Brown the sausages on all sides, 3 to 5 minutes.

While the sausages work, heat another medium skillet over medium-high heat and add the remaining 2 tablespoons of EVOO, the fennel, and the onions. Season with a little salt and pepper. Cook the vegetables, stirring and tossing frequently, for 5 minutes, or until just tender. Add the white vermouth and deglaze the pan. Add the toasted nuts and the parsley and cook for another minute, then turn off the heat.

Slice the sausages thick, on an angle. Pile one quarter of the fennel and onions on each dinner plate and top with sliced sausages.

4 SERVINGS

233 Chorizo and Butternut Soup with Herbed Tomato and Cheese Quesadillas

2 tablespoons extra-virgin olive oil (EVOO) (twice around the pan)

½ pound chorizo, casing removed, finely chopped

1 large yellow onion, chopped

3 large garlic cloves, chopped

1 tablespoon chili powder (a palmful)

1½ teaspoons ground cumin (half a palmful)
   Salt and freshly ground black pepper

1 10-ounce box frozen cooked butternut squash puree, defrosted

1 quart chicken stock or broth

4 12-inch flour tortillas

2 cups shredded Monterey Pepper Jack or smoked Cheddar cheese

4 scallions, finely chopped

½ cup fresh cilantro leaves (a generous handful), chopped

2 small plum tomatoes, seeded and chopped

Preheat a large soup pot over medium-high heat. Add the EVOO, then add the chopped chorizo and cook, stirring frequently, for 2 minutes. Add the onions, garlic, chili powder, cumin, salt, and pepper. Continue to cook for 3 minutes. Stir in the butternut squash puree. Add the chicken stock, bring to a simmer, and cook for 10 to 15 minutes.

While the soup is cooking, preheat a nonstick skillet or griddle pan to high heat. Blister a flour tortilla for 20 seconds, then flip. Cover half the tortilla surface with some of the shredded cheese, chopped scallions, cilantro, and tomatoes, and season with salt and pepper. Fold the tortilla in half and cook for a minute longer, 30 seconds on each side, pressing down gently with a spatula. Repeat with the remaining 3 flour tortillas. Cut the quesadillas into 4 wedges and serve alongside the soup.

4 SERVINGS

Big Beef and Garlic Italian Stir-Fry

234

TRY THIS LATER

IT'S A KEEPER

Coarse salt

1 bunch of broccoli rabe, coarsely chopped

4 tablespoons extra-virgin olive oil (EVOO) (4 times around the pan)

5 large garlic cloves, carefully cracked from the skins and very thinly sliced

2 pounds flank steak, thinly sliced against the grain

Coarse black pepper

1 medium yellow onion, thinly sliced

1 red bell pepper, cored, seeded, and thinly sliced

$\frac{1}{2}$ teaspoon crushed red pepper flakes

2 tablespoons balsamic vinegar (eyeball it)

A handful of fresh flat-leaf parsley, chopped

$\frac{1}{2}$ cup shaved Parmigiano-Reggiano, shaved from a wedge of Parm using a vegetable peeler

Crusty bread, warmed, to pass at the table

Bring a medium sauce pot of water to a boil, salt it, then add the broccoli rabe and cook for 5 minutes. Drain in a colander, scatter on a cookie sheet or large plate to quick-cool, then reserve.

Add the EVOO to a large nonstick skillet and arrange the sliced garlic in an even layer. Turn the heat on medium low and slowly brown the garlic, about 3 to 4 minutes. Keep an eye on it; the garlic can go from golden brown to burned very quickly. Once the garlic is golden brown, remove it with a slotted spoon to a plate lined with a paper towel.

Turn the heat up to high. Once the oil ripples and begins to smoke, add the beef to the pan in an even layer and season it with salt and pepper. Do not move the beef for at least 2 to 3 minutes. Give it time to caramelize. If you force it, you will rip the meat and make it tough. Once it is well browned on one side, stir the beef and continue to cook for 1 more minute. Remove the beef from the skillet with a slotted spoon and reserve it on a plate.

Return the skillet to the heat and add the onions, bell peppers, red pepper flakes, salt, and pepper. Cook, stirring frequently, for 3 minutes, or until the onions and peppers are tender. Add the reserved broccoli rabe, toss, and stir to combine. Season with salt and pepper and continue to cook for 2 minutes. Add the reserved beef and the golden garlic. Add the balsamic vinegar and cook for 1 to 2 more minutes to finish cooking the beef. Turn off the heat and add the parsley. Toss it all together and serve immediately, garnishing each serving with shaved Parmigiano curls. Serve with hot crusty bread.

4 SERVINGS

TRY THIS LATER ☐   IT'S A KEEPER ☐

235 Marinated Grilled Chicken Breasts
with Zippy Chunky Salad and Garlic Dill Fries

1   sack (16 to 18 ounces) crispy-style frozen French fries

4   6-ounce boneless, skinless chicken breast halves

2   tablespoons extra-virgin olive oil (EVOO) (eyeball it)
Zest and juice of 1 lemon

½   tablespoon dried oregano (half a palmful)

4   garlic cloves, chopped
Salt and freshly ground black pepper

1   seedless cucumber, cut in half lengthwise, then cut into ½-inch-thick half-moons

1   red bell pepper, cored, seeded, and chopped

1   green bell pepper, cored, seeded, and chopped

½   small red onion, finely chopped

10   radishes, thinly sliced

2   romaine lettuce hearts, chopped

½   cup plain yogurt

1   tablespoon red wine vinegar (eyeball it)

¼   cup fresh flat-leaf parsley leaves (a generous handful), chopped

3   tablespoons unsalted butter

4   tablespoons fresh dill, chopped (eyeball it)

Preheat the oven according to the package directions for the fries. Spread the fries out in a single layer on a rimmed cookie sheet. Place in the oven when it comes up to temp.

Heat an outdoor grill or grill pan on high.

In a shallow dish, combine the chicken with the EVOO, lemon juice, oregano, three fourths of the chopped garlic, salt, and pepper. Toss to coat evenly and marinate for 5 minutes.

In a salad bowl, combine the cucumbers, red and green bell peppers, onions, radishes, and romaine. To make the zippy dressing, in a small bowl combine the yogurt, lemon zest, red wine vinegar, parsley, salt, and pepper. Pour the dressing over the salad and toss together.

Transfer the marinated chicken to the grill and cook for 6 minutes on each side. Remove from the heat and let rest for 2 to 3 minutes.

A minute or two before the fries are finished cooking, combine in a small bowl or sauce pot the butter, dill, the remaining fourth of the chopped garlic, and some salt and pepper. Melt over low heat or in the microwave. Once the fries are done and very crisp, transfer to a large shallow bowl, drizzle with the melted garlic-dill butter, and toss to coat the fries evenly. Have a taste to check if they need more salt or pepper.

Serve the chicken with some of the chunky salad and the garlic-dill fries.

4 SERVINGS

Cornmeal-Crusted Catfish and Green Rice Pilaf

236

TRY THIS LATER

IT'S A KEEPER

5 tablespoons extra-virgin olive oil (EVOO)
1 tablespoon unsalted butter
1 large shallot, finely chopped
1 tablespoon fresh thyme leaves, chopped (from 4 sprigs)
Salt and freshly ground black pepper
1½ cups long-grain rice
½ cup dry white wine
3 cups chicken stock or broth
½ cup fresh flat-leaf parsley leaves (a couple of generous handfuls)
½ pound fresh spinach leaves, trimmed and cleaned
20 fresh basil leaves
1 lemon, ½ juiced, the other half cut into wedges
4 6- to 8-ounce catfish fillets
1 cup yellow cornmeal

Preheat the oven to 400°F.

Bring a medium sauce pot filled three-quarters full with water to a boil.

Heat a second medium saucepan or pot over moderate heat. Add 1 tablespoon of the EVOO (once around the pan), the butter, shallots, thyme, salt, and pepper. Sauté the shallots for 2 minutes, then add the rice and lightly brown, 3 to 5 minutes. Add the wine and allow it to evaporate entirely, 1 to 2 minutes. Add the chicken stock and bring to a boil. Cover the rice and reduce the heat. Cook for 18 to 20 minutes, until tender.

Salt the boiling water in the other pot and add the parsley, spinach, and basil. Stir to submerge the greens for 30 seconds, then carefully take the pot to the sink. Use a slotted spoon or a spider to remove the greens to a colander. Discard the water. Rinse the greens under slow-running cold water to stop the cooking process. Give the greens a gentle squeeze to get rid of the excess water. Transfer the cooled, drained greens to a blender or food processor. Add about 2 tablespoons of EVOO and the lemon juice. Puree until completely smooth. Reserve the puree for finishing the cooked rice.

Preheat a large oven-safe nonstick skillet over medium-high heat. Add the remaining 2 tablespoons of EVOO. Season the catfish with salt and pepper and coat evenly and completely in the cornmeal. Add the coated fish to the hot skillet and sear for 2 minutes on each side, then transfer the skillet with the fish to the oven and continue to cook for 8 to 10 minutes, until the fish is firm to the touch and opaque.

Once the rice is cooked, add the reserved greens puree and stir with a fork to combine and fluff the rice. Pile the rice onto dinner plates and serve the cornmeal-crusted catfish on top. Pass the lemon wedges at the table.

4 SERVINGS

237 Crispy Fried Sesame Shrimp, Zucchini, and Mushroom Caps with a Ginger-Soy Dipping Sauce

1/3 cup tamari (dark aged soy sauce)
1 garlic clove, crushed
  1-inch piece of fresh ginger, peeled and grated
1 tablespoon sugar
  Juice of 1 lime
  Toasted sesame oil, for drizzling
1 teaspoon hot sauce, such as Tabasco
  Vegetable oil, for frying
2½ cups complete pancake mix, any brand, divided
2 tablespoons sesame seeds
1 pound medium shrimp, peeled and deveined
1 medium zucchini, cut ½ inch thick on a bias
8 shiitake mushrooms, stems removed

In a small bowl, combine the tamari, ⅓ cup water, the garlic clove, ginger, sugar, lime juice, and a drizzle of sesame oil. Mix to dissolve the sugar, then add the hot sauce. Reserve the dipping sauce.

Heat a layer of vegetable oil, about 1½ inches deep, over medium to medium-high heat in a deep-sided skillet. To test the oil, add a 1-inch cube of bread to the hot oil. If it turns deep golden brown in color in a count of 40, the oil is ready.

While the oil is heating, in a wide mixing bowl combine 2 cups of the pancake mix, 1¼ cups water, and the sesame seeds. Place the remaining plain pancake mix in another wide mixing bowl. Arrange the batter and the bowl of plain pancake mix near the cooktop and the heating oil. Line a plate with a few sheets of paper towels and keep within reach.

Once the oil is ready, toss the shrimp, zucchini, and shiitake mushroom caps in the plain pancake mix, coat evenly, and shake off any excess. The plain dry pancake mix will help the batter stick to the shrimp and veggies. Plan to work in 3 to 4 batches to coat and fry the shrimp and veggies. Use a fork to toss some of the shrimp and veggies into the batter. Remove the first batch from the batter, shaking off some of the excess batter as you add the coated pieces to the hot oil. Fry for 2 to 3 minutes, or until deeply golden brown, then flip and fry for 2 minutes more. Remove from the oil and drain on the lined plate. Repeat with the remaining shrimp and veggies.

Arrange the shrimp and veggies on a platter along with the dipping sauce. Serve immediately.

4 SERVINGS

TIDBIT

If shrimp isn't your thing, try this same recipe using chicken tenders cut into bite-size pieces.

Sautéed Salmon with Spicy Fresh Mango-Pineapple Chutney

Serve with steamed asparagus, snap peas, or green beans.

- 3 tablespoons vegetable oil
- 1 small red onion, chopped
- 1 large jalapeño, seeded and chopped
  Salt and freshly ground black pepper
- 1 8-ounce can pineapple chunks in natural juices (such as Dole brand), drained
- 2 tablespoons honey (a couple of good drizzles)
- 4 6-ounce salmon fillets
- 1 tablespoon ground coriander
- 1 ripe mango, peeled and diced
  Juice of 1 lime
- ¼ cup fresh flat-leaf parsley leaves (a generous handful), chopped
- ¼ cup fresh cilantro (a generous handful), chopped

Heat a sauce pot over medium-high heat with 1 tablespoon of vegetable oil (once around the pan). Add the red onions and jalapeños and season with a little salt and pepper; cook for 3 to 4 minutes, or until the onions are slightly wilted. Add the pineapple, honey, and 1 cup water, turn the heat down to medium low, and gently simmer for about 5 minutes.

While the chutney is cooking, preheat a medium non-stick skillet over medium-high heat with the remaining 2 tablespoons of vegetable oil. Season the salmon with the coriander, salt, and pepper. Add the seasoned salmon to the hot pan and cook until just cooked through, about 3 to 4 minutes on each side.

While the salmon is cooking, finish the chutney: Add the mango, lime juice, parsley, and cilantro, stir to combine, and then turn off the heat.

Transfer the sautéed salmon to 4 serving plates and top each portion with some of the spicy mango-pineapple chutney.

4 SERVINGS

TRY THIS LATER

IT'S A KEEPER

239 MASTER RECIPE
Grilled Shrimp Scampi on Angel Hair Pasta

Coarse salt
1 pound angel hair pasta
6 garlic cloves, crushed
½ cup fresh flat-leaf parsley (a couple of generous handfuls), chopped
Coarse black pepper
¼ cup extra-virgin olive oil (EVOO) (eyeball it)
24 medium-size raw shrimp, peeled, deveined, and tails removed
1 teaspoon crushed red pepper flakes (⅓ palmful)
½ cup dry white wine (a couple of glugs; eyeball it)
Zest and juice of 1 lemon
5 tablespoons cold unsalted butter

Preheat a grill pan or outdoor grill on high.

Place a large pot of water over high heat to boil. Salt the water and cook the angel hair pasta until al dente, with a bite. Heads up: You will be using a couple of ladles of cooking water before draining the pasta.

While the pasta cooks, in a bowl combine the garlic, parsley, salt, pepper, and the EVOO. Place half of the garlic mixture with the shrimp in another bowl and toss to coat evenly. Transfer the shrimp to the hot grill and cook for about 2 to 3 minutes on each side, until the shrimp are firm and opaque.

While the shrimp are grilling, preheat a large skillet over medium-high heat. Add the reserved garlic mixture and the red pepper flakes; cook for 1 to 2 minutes, or until the garlic is lightly golden brown. Add the wine to the skillet and cook for 1 minute, then add 2 ladles of the pasta cooking water and the lemon zest and juice and continue to cook for 2 minutes. Add the butter and stir until melted. Add the grilled shrimp, toss to coat, add the drained angel hair pasta, and toss to coat again. Taste and adjust the seasoning with salt and pepper. Divide the pasta and shrimp among 4 serving plates.

4 SERVINGS

TIDBIT

If the fish folks at your market won't peel and tail the shrimp for you, ask for "easy-peels" (deveined raw shrimp in the shell) and just slide the shells off when you bring them home from the market.

NOW TRY... Grilled Chicken, Scampi Style, with Angel Hair Pasta

240

☐ TRY THIS LATER
☐ IT'S A KEEPER

SWAP

2 pounds chicken tenders for the shrimp

ADD

2 roasted red peppers, very thinly sliced

2 tablespoons chopped fresh chives (8 to 10 chives)

1½ teaspoons fresh oregano (from 2 sprigs), finely chopped, or 1 teaspoon dried oregano leaves

Prepare just as for the master recipe, #239, cooking the chicken tenders in the same way as the shrimp, but increase the grill cooking time to 3 to 4 minutes per side. Once the chicken is grilled, cut it into bite-size pieces and then continue as before. Toss the red pepper strips with the angel hair and they will thread through the pasta and really pump up the color. Garnish with chopped chives and oregano for a unique flavor finish.

4 SERVINGS

OR TRY... Grilled Scallops, Scampi Style, with Angel Hair Pasta

241

☐ TRY THIS LATER
☐ IT'S A KEEPER

SWAP

16 sea scallops for the shrimp

ADD

¼ pound prosciutto di Parma, cut into very thin strips

4 scallions, thinly sliced

Prepare just as for the master recipe, #239, cooking the scallops in the same way as the shrimp.

While tossing the angel hair, scatter in the prosciutto and scallions. The salt and onion flavors accent the sweetness of the scallops.

4 SERVINGS

PASTA NESTS

When I worked in a commercial kitchen, making different items for the prepared food counter, there were a few items that *always* "sold out." The best sellers, day to day, month to month, no matter the season, were apricot chicken tenders, sesame noodles, and pasta nests. Here are three pasta-licious nests, adapted for your home production kitchen.

242 MASTER RECIPE
Tomato-Basil Pasta Nests

A pretty basic version to get you started.

Coarse salt
1 pound angel hair pasta
3 tablespoons extra-virgin olive oil (EVOO) (3 times around the pan)
5 garlic cloves, minced
1 medium yellow onion, finely chopped
1 28-ounce can crushed tomatoes (look for San Marzano Italian tomatoes; when not available, use any brand)
Coarse black pepper
20 fresh basil leaves, shredded (chiffonade) or torn
3 rounded tablespoonfuls prepared, refrigerated pesto sauce
1 cup grated Parmigiano-Reggiano or Romano cheese (3 overflowing handfuls)
Crusty bread, to pass at the table

Bring a large pot of water to a boil for the pasta. Salt the water and cook the pasta al dente, with a bite to it.

While the water is heating, begin the sauce by heating a large, deep skillet over medium heat. Add the EVOO, garlic, and onions. Sauté for 8 to 10 minutes; reduce the heat a bit if the onions begin to brown. You want them to become sweet and soft, but not to caramelize.

Stir in the tomatoes and heat through. Season the sauce with salt and pepper. Wilt in the basil and turn off the heat. Stir in the pesto sauce.

Drain the pasta and add to the sauce. Toss in the pan to distribute. Sprinkle in the cheese, tossing to combine. Grab a meat fork. Stick the fork into the pasta and bring up a heaping forkful. Turn and twist the pasta, using your palm to guide the pasta a bit, to form a nest. The recipe should yield 8 small nests, 4 inches wide and 5 to 6 inches long.

Serve 2 nests per person with a small salad and crusty bread.

4 SERVINGS

NOW TRY... Roasted Garlic and Eggplant
Marinara Nests

OMIT

Pesto sauce

ADD

1 medium-size firm eggplant

½ teaspoon crushed red pepper flakes

¼ cup fresh flat-leaf parsley leaves (a generous handful)

Extra EVOO, for drizzling

PREP CHANGE

Leave the 5 garlic cloves whole and skins intact

Bring a large pot of water to a boil. Preheat the oven to 450°F.

Place the whole eggplant, skin and all, on a rimmed cookie sheet. Pierce the skin on the top of the eggplant several times with the tines of a fork. Drizzle a little EVOO on your hands and coat the garlic cloves well.

Wrap the garlic in a single layer of foil. Place the garlic packet next to the eggplant. Place the pan in the lower third of the hot oven and roast for 18 to 22 minutes, depending on the thickness of your eggplant; the eggplant will look weird, like a blown tire, when removed from the oven.

When the eggplant has been in the oven for 15 minutes add the pasta to the boiling water with the salt.

Sauté the red pepper flakes with the onions for 10 minutes, then stir in the tomatoes, season with salt and pepper, bring to a bubble, and reduce the heat to low.

Carefully cut the skin away from the cooked eggplant flesh; it will be hot. Use a sharp paring or boning knife and get messy—no contest for "best trimmed skin," you're just going to chuck it. Unwrap the garlic and pop the pulp from the skins. Place the eggplant and garlic in a food processor with the parsley. Season with salt and pepper and process until fairly smooth. Mix the hot eggplant and garlic into the hot tomato sauce and stir in the basil to wilt.

Drain the pasta, toss with the sauce and cheese, and roll into nests as directed in the master recipe, #242. Serve with salad and bread.

4 SERVINGS

(variations continue on page 216)

TRY THIS LATER

IT'S A KEEPER

OMIT

Prepared pesto sauce

Basil

ADD

1/2 pound ground beef

1/2 pound cremini (baby portobello) mushrooms

A couple of pinches of allspice

1/4 to 1/3 cup dry red wine (a good glug)

1/2 cup beef stock or broth

1/4 cup fresh flat-leaf parsley (a generous handful), finely chopped

Boil the water for the pasta as in the master recipe, #242, but wait until the sauce is simmering before you drop the angel hair into the salted boiling water.

For the sauce, heat a deep skillet over medium-high heat, then add the EVOO and the beef. Break into very tiny bits with a wooden spoon. Lightly brown the meat to caramelize it, then reduce the heat to medium and add the garlic and onions.

Finely chop the mushrooms in a food processor, then add the bits to the skillet and cook together with the meat, onions, and garlic for 10 minutes. Season the mixture with salt and pepper and a little allspice (the thing that makes them go, "Hummmmm"), then deglaze the pan with a glug of red wine. Cook the wine off, 30 seconds, then add the stock, parsley, and tomatoes. Heat to a bubble and reduce the heat to a simmer. Drop the pasta in the boiling water.

Drain the cooked pasta and toss with the sauce and cheese. Adjust the salt and pepper and roll the pasta into nests. Serve with salad and bread.

4 SERVINGS

Five-Spice Burgers
with Warm Mu Shu Slaw Topping, Pineapple, and Exotic Chips

MYOTO: MAKE YOUR OWN TAKE-OUT

245

TRY THIS LATER   IT'S A KEEPER

1½ pounds **ground chicken** or pork

2 teaspoons **Chinese five-spice powder** (⅔ palmful)

1 tablespoon **grill seasoning**, such as McCormick's Montreal Steak Seasoning (a palmful)

2 **garlic cloves**, minced
1-inch piece of fresh **ginger**, peeled and minced

5 **scallions**, 2 finely chopped, 3 cut into thirds then thinly sliced lengthwise

3 tablespoons **tamari** (dark aged soy sauce) (3 times around the bowl)

2 tablespoons **vegetable oil** (twice around the pan), plus more for drizzling

12 **shiitake mushrooms**, stems removed and thinly sliced

½ pound shredded **cabbage** (or buy a bag of cole slaw mix in the produce department)

3 tablespoons **hoisin sauce** (Chinese barbecue sauce, available on the international foods aisle)

4 cornmeal-dusted or sesame **kaiser rolls**, split and toasted

1 fresh **pineapple**, cored (available in the produce department), cut into chunks

1 package **exotic vegetable chips**, such as Terra brand

Heat a nonstick skillet or grill pan over medium-high heat. In a medium bowl, combine the meat with the five-spice powder, grill seasoning, garlic, ginger, finely chopped scallions, tamari, and a drizzle of vegetable oil. Mix and score the meat into quarters, then form 4 patties, 1 inch thick. Cook the burgers for 6 minutes on each side.

Heat a nonstick skillet over high heat. Add the 2 tablespoons of vegetable oil. Cook the shiitakes for 2 minutes, add the cabbage, and stir-fry for 3 minutes more. Add the sliced scallions and hoisin sauce, toss to combine, and remove from the heat.

Serve the burgers on the buns piled high with mu shu slaw on top. Serve with chunks of fresh pineapple and exotic chips alongside the burgers.

4 SERVINGS

365: NO REPEATS   217

246 MASTER RECIPE
Cod in a Sack

Serve with a green salad.

Parchment paper
1 pound cauliflower, cut into ½-inch-thick slices or florets
8 anchovy fillets
4 large garlic cloves, minced
½ cup pitted good-quality black olives, such as kalamata, chopped
2 pounds cod fillets, cut into 4 portions (buy thick pieces from the center rather than tail-end pieces)
Salt and freshly ground black pepper
4 scallions, chopped
¼ cup fresh flat-leaf parsley (a generous handful), chopped
Extra-virgin olive oil (EVOO), for generous drizzling
Zest and juice of 1 lemon
Crusty bread, to pass at the table

Preheat the oven to 400°F.

Rip off 4 sheets of parchment paper, each a little over a foot long. Place one fourth of the cauliflower in the center of each sheet of parchment, then top with 2 anchovy fillets, one fourth of the garlic and chopped olives, and 1 portion of cod. Season the cod with salt and pepper and top with equal amounts of the scallions and parsley. Drizzle EVOO liberally and sprinkle lemon zest and juice evenly over the fish portions. Fold the top and bottom edges of the parchment together and crease several times, then crease up the ends of the packets. Arrange the packets on a rimmed baking sheet and place in the center of the hot oven.

Bake the packets for 20 minutes. Serve each packet on a dinner plate and cut open at the table. Pass salad and bread to round out the meal.

4 SERVINGS

FISH IN A SACK

My mom made this for us as kids. It's really fancy and French in origin. It was her take on fish in parchment. I make mine in parchment, but Mom used a brown paper lunch sack, which I cannot even find in the stores these days. If you "brown bag it," brush the bag lightly with vegetable oil to keep it from burning in the oven. That's what Mama always did.

NOW TRY... French Fish in a Sack

247

☐ TRY THIS LATER

OMIT

Anchovies
Garlic
Olives

SWAP

Asparagus tips for the cauliflower
Fillet of sole for the cod
4 sprigs of fresh tarragon, stripped and chopped, for the parsley

Prepare just as for the master recipe, #246, but with swapped ingredients: a layer of asparagus tips, portions of sole, salt and pepper, scallions, tarragon, EVOO, lemon zest, and lemon juice. Bake for 14 to 15 minutes, rather than 20. Serve with salad and bread.

4 SERVINGS

☐ IT'S A KEEPER

- -

OR TRY... Spanish Fish in a Sack

248

☐ TRY THIS LATER

OMIT

Anchovies
Black olives

SWAP

Trimmed green beans, halved across, for the cauliflower
Red snapper fillets, for the cod

ADD

16 strips of thinly sliced pimiento or roasted red pepper

Prepare just as for the master recipe, #246, but with swapped ingredients: green beans, garlic, and pimiento or red pepper strips, snapper, salt and pepper, scallions, parsley, EVOO, lemon zest and juice. Roast for 17 to 18 minutes.

4 SERVINGS

☐ IT'S A KEEPER

The next three recipes are really unusual pestos (one of my favorite things!) and I eat so much of them, that all I serve with the pasta is a salad. Since I eat salad after dinner, it's rare that I even save room for it! If you like, you can beef up the protein (pun intended) by serving any of these pastas with grilled lamb chops, beef tenderloin steaks, chicken breasts, or pork loin chops alongside. Simply marinate any of the meats in just enough balsamic vinegar to coat, a healthy drizzle of EVOO, and salt and pepper, then broil to the desired doneness. With the Pistachio Pesto, scrod or haddock broiled with lemon and EVOO is lovely.

249 MASTER RECIPE
Pistachio Pesto

TRY THIS LATER

IT'S A KEEPER

Serve all of these variations with tomato and onion salad or mixed greens and some good bread.

Coarse salt
1 pound linguine or fettuccine
1 cup shelled pistachios (available in the bulk section of the market)
About ½ cup extra-virgin olive oil (EVOO)
1 medium zucchini, julienne cut (thick matchsticks)
Coarse black pepper
4 garlic cloves, chopped
1 cup fresh flat-leaf parsley leaves (a few generous handfuls)
½ cup fresh mint leaves (2 generous handfuls)
¼ to ⅓ cup grated Parmigiano-Reggiano (an overflowing handful), plus some to pass at the table

Heat a pot of water to boil for the pasta. When it boils, salt the water and add the pasta, cooking al dente, with a bite to it.

Heat a deep skillet over medium heat. Add the pistachios and toast for 5 minutes to develop their flavor. Remove the nuts from the pan and cool. Raise the heat a bit and return the pan to the stove. Add 2 tablespoons of the EVOO (twice around the pan), then the zucchini. Season the zucchini with salt and pepper. Cook, stirring frequently, for 2 minutes, then add the garlic and continue to cook for 3 minutes more.

While the zucchini cooks, grind half the nuts with the parsley, mint, and cheese in a food processor. Stream in about ⅓ cup of the EVOO and process until a paste forms, then season with salt and pepper.

Drain the pasta. Add the pistachio pesto to the zucchini. Add the pasta to the pesto and toss to coat evenly, then toss in the remaining whole toasted nuts. Adjust the seasonings and grated cheese and transfer to a serving platter or plates. Pass more cheese at the table.

4 SERVINGS

Pecan and Arugula Pesto

250

SWAP

Pecan pieces for the pistachios

½ pound haricots verts (or skinny green beans, halved) for the zucchini

2 cups arugula leaves for the parsley and mint

ADD

½ cup shredded carrots (available in the produce section) or 1 carrot cut into matchsticks

¼ teaspoon freshly grated or ground nutmeg

4 scallions, cut into thirds then thinly sliced lengthwise

Prepare the pasta just as for the master recipe, #249. Toast the nuts and reserve but, before sautéing the beans and carrots, first cook them for 2 to 3 minutes in an inch of boiling salted water. Drain the vegetables, then sauté in the 2 tablespoons of EVOO with the garlic for a couple of minutes. Make the pesto, adding the nutmeg when you season with salt and pepper. Add the scallions to the beans and carrots. Drain the pasta. Toss the pasta with the pesto and vegetables.

4 SERVINGS

Walnut-Parsley-Rosemary Pesto

251

SWAP

Penne rigate for the linguine or fettuccine

Walnuts for the pistachios

½ head of cauliflower, florets sectioned and cut into ½-inch slices, for the zucchini

3 tablespoons fresh rosemary leaves (from 4 sprigs) for the mint

Romano cheese for the Parmigiano cheese

ADD

Zest of 1 orange

Prepare the pasta just as for the master recipe, #249, cooking al dente, with a bite to it. Toast the nuts and reserve. Before sautéing the cauliflower, first cook it for 2 to 3 minutes in an inch of boiling salted water. Drain the cauliflower, then sauté in the 2 tablespoons of EVOO with the garlic for a couple of minutes. Make the pesto, adding in the orange zest with the herbs before processing the paste. Drain the pasta. Toss the pasta with the pesto and cauliflower.

4 SERVINGS

252 MASTER RECIPE
Croque
Monsieur with Greens

Ah, April in Paris! Word of advice: pack a parka! I have been in France twice in April, once to Paris, once to Bordeaux. Twice I froze. Oh, well. The hot ham and cheese tastes better then.

- 4 tablespoons softened unsalted butter
- 2 tablespoons all-purpose flour
- 1 cup half-and-half or whole milk
- 2 teaspoons Dijon mustard
- ⅛ teaspoon freshly grated or ground nutmeg (eyeball it)
  Salt and freshly ground black pepper
- 8 slices sandwich bread
- ¾ pound baked ham, thinly sliced
- 2 cups shredded Gruyère cheese (½ pound)
- 2 tablespoons white wine vinegar (a couple of splashes)
- 1 teaspoon apricot jam or orange marmalade
- 2 tablespoons fresh tarragon leaves, chopped (from 2 stems)
- 3 tablespoons extra-virgin olive oil (EVOO) (eyeball it)
- 6 cups mixed baby greens, any variety

Heat a heavy nonstick pan or a griddle over medium-low to medium heat.

Heat a small sauce pot over medium heat. Add 2 tablespoons of the butter and melt. Whisk the flour into the butter and cook for 1 minute, then whisk in the half-and-half. Season with 1 teaspoon of the Dijon mustard, the nutmeg, salt, and pepper and cook for 2 minutes to thicken. Remove from the heat. Spread the bread slices with the sauce and make sandwiches, using a couple of folded slices of ham per sandwich.

Spread the remaining 2 tablespoons of softened butter lightly across the outside faces of each sandwich. Spread the shredded cheese across a plate and gently press each side of the sandwiches into the cheese, then place on the hot pan or griddle. The cheese will brown and form a crisp coating as the sandwich cooks and heats through. Cook for 3 minutes on each side, or until evenly golden.

In a salad bowl, whisk together the remaining teaspoon of mustard, the vinegar, apricot jam, and tarragon. Whisk in the EVOO in a slow stream. Add the greens to the bowl and toss to dress. Season the salad with salt and pepper and serve on large plates with the hot sandwiches alongside.

4 SERVINGS

NOW TRY... **Ham and Asparagus Tartines**

253

TRY THIS LATER

IT'S A KEEPER

Tartines are open-face sandwiches that are especially popular in Belgium. This one is great for B or D: Brunch or Dinner.

OMIT

2 tablespoons of the butter (you'll still need 2 tablespoons

SWAP

4 large ¾-inch-thick hand-cut slices from a large loaf of farm-style bread for the 8 slices of sandwich bread

¾ pound Brie, sliced, for the shredded Gruyère cheese

ADD

16 asparagus tips, blanched for a minute or two then chilled in ice water and dried well

Prepare just as for the master recipe, #252, preheating the pan and making the white sauce. Lightly toast the bread under a hot broiler. Spread the toasted bread with the white sauce and top with a couple slices of ham, 4 asparagus tips, and the Brie. Melt the Brie under the broiler and serve with the dressed salad alongside.

4 SERVINGS

OR TRY... **Italian Open-Face Sandwiches**

254

TRY THIS LATER

IT'S A KEEPER

OMIT

2 tablespoons of the butter (you'll still need 2 tablespoons)

SWAP

4 large, ¾-inch-thick hand-cut slices from a loaf of semolina bread for the sandwich bread

½ pound prosciutto di Parma for the baked ham

¾ pound Fontina cheese, thinly sliced, for the Gruyère

12 fresh basil leaves for the tarragon

ADD

1 can artichoke hearts, drained and thinly sliced

Prepare just as for the master recipe, #252, preheating the pan and making the white sauce. Lightly toast the bread under a hot broiler. Spread the toasted bread with the white sauce. Top the bread with layers of prosciutto, sliced artichokes, and Fontina. Melt the cheese under the broiler and serve. Swap the basil for the chopped tarragon in the salad and serve alongside the open-face sandwiches.

4 SERVINGS

255 MASTER RECIPE
Wild Cream of Mushroom Egg Noodle Bake,
Hold the Canned Soup

Serve with a green salad.

CREAM OF MUSHROOM SAUCE

- 1 tablespoon extra-virgin olive oil (EVOO) (once around the pan)
- 2 tablespoons unsalted butter
- 12 button mushrooms, brushed off with a damp towel and chopped
- 2 tablespoons all-purpose flour
- 1 cup chicken stock or broth
- 1 cup whole milk or cream
- ⅛ teaspoon freshly grated or ground nutmeg
  Salt and freshly ground black pepper

CASSEROLE

- 2 tablespoons EVOO (twice around the pan)
- 1 shallot, thinly sliced
- 2 portobello mushroom caps, halved and thinly sliced
- ½ pound fresh mixed wild mushrooms, such as shiitakes, oysters, and wood-ears, stems trimmed and caps thinly sliced
- 1 tablespoon fresh thyme leaves, finely chopped (from 4 sprigs)
  Salt and freshly ground black pepper
- ⅓ cup dry white wine (eyeball it), or more stock
- 1 pound extra-wide egg noodles
- 1 to 2 tablespoons unsalted butter, softened
- ¾ pound Gruyère or Emmentaler cheese, shredded
- 3 tablespoons chopped fresh chives (12 to 15 chives)

Bring a large pot of water to a boil for the egg noodles.

To make the mushroom sauce, heat a medium sauce pot over medium heat. Add the EVOO and the butter. When the butter melts, add the chopped button mushrooms and cook for 5 minutes, until just tender. Sprinkle in the flour and cook for 1 minute. Whisk in the chicken stock and bring to a bubble, then stir in the whole milk. Reduce the heat to low and gently simmer. Season the sauce with nutmeg, salt, and pepper.

To make the casserole, heat a nonstick skillet over medium-high heat. Add the 2 tablespoons of EVOO, then the shallots and mushrooms. Cook the mushrooms for 8 minutes, or until tender. Season with the thyme, salt, and pepper, and deglaze the pan with the wine or a little stock. Reduce the heat to medium low and let the liquid cook off.

Preheat the broiler to high.

While the mushrooms cook, drop the egg noodles into the boiling water, salt the water, and cook the noodles al dente, with a bite to them. Drain the noodles and return them to the hot pot. Add the creamy sauce to the pot and toss the noodles to coat in the sauce.

Lightly coat a casserole dish with the softened butter, then transfer the cream of mushroom noodles to the dish and top with the mushroom ragout and the shredded cheese. Place the casserole under the broiler and melt and bubble the cheese until brown at the edges. Garnish with chives and serve.

4 SERVINGS

NOW TRY... Chicken Divan and Egg Noodle Bake

256

TRY THIS LATER ☐

IT'S A KEEPER ☐

OMIT

Both kinds of mushrooms

ADD

1 pound broccoli florets
1 pound chicken tenders, diced

Prepare the sauce and noodles as directed.

Cook the broccoli florets in salted boiling water for 5 minutes, then drain and reserve.

Prepare the casserole ingredients as in the master recipe, #255, adding the chicken after the shallots have cooked for one minute. Cook until lightly browned all over and firm, 6 to 7 minutes. Add the wine and stir to deglaze the pan.

Toss the noodles with the sauce. Transfer to the buttered casserole dish and top with chicken and broccoli. Proceed as in the original recipe.

4 SERVINGS

THEN TRY... Super Mashers with Chicken Cordon Bleu Hash

257

TRY THIS LATER ☐

IT'S A KEEPER ☐

OMIT

Shallot
Unsalted butter
Both kinds of mushrooms

SWAP

4 medium Idaho potatoes, peeled and cut into chunks, for the egg noodles

ADD

1 pound ham steak
1 pound chicken breast cutlets

Prepare the sauce as directed in the master recipe, #255.

Boil the potatoes until tender and return to the hot pot. Mash with the prepared sauce and salt and pepper.

While the potatoes cook, heat a nonstick skillet over medium-high heat. Add 1 tablespoon of the EVOO, then add the ham steak and cook for 3 minutes on each side to warm through. Remove the ham to a plate and add another tablespoon of the EVOO and the chicken to the pan. Season with salt and pepper and cook for 3 minutes on each side. Add the wine to the pan and deglaze it, then cook off the liquid. Cut the chicken and ham into thin strips. Sprinkle with chopped thyme leaves.

Pile the mashers onto heat-proof plates and top with ham and chicken strips and some shredded cheese. Place under the broiler just long enough to melt and lightly brown the cheese. Garnish with the chives.

4 SERVINGS

TRY THIS LATER ☐

IT'S A KEEPER ☐

258 Chicken Fingers with Honey Mustard Dipping Sauce and Spicy Chopped Salad

Yup, call the kids to the table for this one!

Vegetable oil, for frying
1½ pounds chicken tenders
Salt and freshly ground black pepper
1 cup all-purpose flour
3 tablespoons ground dry mustard
2 eggs
2 cups plain bread crumbs
½ cup mayonnaise
½ cup grainy Dijon mustard
3 tablespoons honey (3 gobs)
1 bunch of watercress, chopped
6 radishes, thinly sliced
1 seedless cucumber, cut lengthwise, then cut into half-moons
3 tablespoons fresh dill, chopped
½ cup fresh flat-leaf parsley leaves (a couple of generous handfuls), chopped
2 tablespoons red wine vinegar (eyeball it)
3 tablespoons extra-virgin olive oil (EVOO) (eyeball it)

In a large, deep skillet, heat 1½ inches vegetable oil over medium-high heat.

Season the chicken tenders with salt and pepper. Set out 3 shallow dishes: Mix the flour and dry mustard in one. Beat the eggs with a splash of water or milk in a second; and place the bread crumbs in the third dish. Coat the tenders in batches in the flour, then the eggs, and then the bread crumbs. Fry the tenders in small batches, 6 to 7 minutes. Drain on paper towels.

While the chicken is frying, in a bowl mix together the mayonnaise, grainy mustard, and honey to taste.

For the spicy chopped salad, combine the watercress, radishes, cucumbers, dill, and parsley in a large salad bowl or on a serving platter. Drizzle with the vinegar and EVOO and season with salt and pepper. Toss to coat.

Serve the chicken fingers with the honey mustard dipping sauce and spicy chopped salad.

4 SERVINGS

A Burger for Brad: Barbecue Burger Deluxe

259

TRY THIS LATER IT'S A KEEPER

Brad is one of my husband John's closest friends and fast becoming one of mine. He makes any situation into a party. He also claims to make the best burgers. Being Queen of burgers, I have taken him to task on this, but he never gives up the recipe. This is a tribute burger, for Brad.

Brad loves to make burgers with condiments mixed into them. This one tastes like it's made with spicy barbecue sauce and it's topped with beefy steak sauce. It's very Brad. Serve with fancy flavored potato chips, any brand.

1½ pounds ground sirloin
2 garlic cloves, minced
1 small red onion, half finely chopped, half thinly sliced
½ teaspoon liquid smoke (a few drops)
2 tablespoons Worcestershire sauce (eyeball it)
1 tablespoon hot sauce, such as Frank's Red Hot
3 tablespoons tomato paste (eyeball it)
2 tablespoons dark brown sugar
1 tablespoon grill seasoning, such as McCormick's Montreal Steak Seasoning (a palmful)
   Extra-virgin olive oil (EVOO), for drizzling
½ pound Cheddar cheese, sliced
4 crusty rolls, plain or onion flavor, split and toasted

TOPPINGS

   Leaf lettuce
   Sliced beefsteak tomatoes
1 cup steak sauce, such as A.1.

Heat a grill pan or outdoor grill over high heat.

Place the beef in a bowl with the garlic and the finely chopped onions. In a small bowl, mix the liquid smoke, Worcestershire, hot sauce, tomato paste, brown sugar, and grill seasoning. Pour the mixture over the meat and add a drizzle of EVOO. Combine the ingredients and form 4 1-inch-thick patties. Cook for 5 minutes on each side. Top with the cheese and let it melt during the last minute or two of cooking. Place the meat on the toasted roll bottoms and top with lettuce, tomato, and the thinly sliced red onions. Pour steak sauce on the roll tops and set into place. Serve the burgers with fancy chips.

   4 SERVINGS

260 Buffalo Turkey Burgers with Blue Cheese Dressing

Serve with barbecue chips and oil-and-vinegar dressed slaw. So much better for you than wings, you could eat two!

Vegetable oil, for drizzling
1 package (1⅓ pounds) ground turkey breast
1½ teaspoons poultry seasoning (half a palmful)
1 tablespoon grill seasoning, such as McCormick's Montreal Steak Seasoning (a palmful)
2 garlic cloves, chopped
4 scallions, finely chopped
1 celery rib from the heart, with greens, finely chopped
2 tablespoons unsalted butter
¼ cup hot sauce, such as Frank's Red Hot
Crusty rolls, split
1 cup sour cream, reduced-fat sour cream, or Ranch dressing
½ cup blue cheese crumbles
Salt and freshly ground black pepper
Leaf lettuce

Place a healthy drizzle of oil in a mixing bowl. Add the turkey, poultry seasoning, grill seasoning, garlic, scallions, and celery. Mix the burgers and form into 4 1-inch-thick patties.

Heat a nonstick skillet over medium-high heat and cook the burgers for 6 minutes on each side. Remove to a plate.

Wipe the pan clean and reduce the heat to low. Melt the butter in the pan. Add the hot sauce to the melted butter. Return the patties to the skillet and turn to coat in the hot sauce–butter mixture. Place the burgers on bun bottoms.

In a small bowl, mix the sour cream or Ranch dressing with the blue cheese crumbles and season with salt and pepper. Top the burgers with lettuce and blue cheese sauce, then set the bun tops in place.

4 SERVINGS

TIDBIT

I've made other versions of this—with chicken breasts and Buffalo-fied salads—but I think this is the tastiest takeoff on wings so far!

Baked Sesame Eggplant Subs
with Fire-Roasted Tomato and Red Pepper Sauce

261

1 cup Italian-style bread crumbs
   (3 overflowing handfuls)

½ cup grated Parmigiano-Reggiano (a couple of
   overflowing handfuls)

3 tablespoons sesame seeds

4 tablespoons extra-virgin olive oil (EVOO)

1 large firm eggplant, thinly sliced

½ cup all-purpose flour

2 eggs, beaten with a splash of water

2 garlic cloves, chopped

1 16-ounce jar roasted red peppers, drained

1 15-ounce can diced fire-roasted tomatoes,
   such as Muir Glen brand
   Salt and freshly ground black pepper

4 crusty sub rolls, tops split

1 pound smoked fresh mozzarella cheese,
   thinly sliced

Preheat the oven to 400°F. In a shallow bowl, combine the bread crumbs, Parmigiano, sesame seeds, and 2 tablespoons of the EVOO.

Dust the eggplant slices in the flour, then dip in the eggs and press into the breadcrumb mixture. Arrange the eggplant on a large nonstick cookie sheet and bake in the center of the oven until deep golden all over, 15 to 17 minutes.

While the eggplant cooks, in a medium sauce pot over medium heat, sauté the garlic in the remaining 2 tablespoons of EVOO. Puree the roasted peppers in a food processor. Add the peppers and tomatoes to the garlic, season with salt and pepper, and heat through.

Turn the oven from bake to broil. Fill the sub rolls with sauce, breaded sesame eggplant, and smoked mozzarella, then place the subs under the broiler. Brown the cheese until it bubbles, then serve up the subs nice and hot.

4 SERVINGS

262 Veal Saltimbocca
with Spinach Polenta

3 cups chicken stock or broth

8 veal cutlets
Salt and freshly ground black pepper

16 fresh sage leaves

8 slices prosciutto di Parma

2 tablespoons extra-virgin olive oil (EVOO)

4 tablespoons unsalted butter

1 cup instant or quick-cooking polenta (found in Italian foods or specialty foods aisles)

1 10-ounce box frozen chopped spinach, defrosted and wrung dry in a clean kitchen towel

½ cup grated Parmigiano-Reggiano or Romano cheese (a couple of generous handfuls)
Freshly grated or ground nutmeg, to taste

2 garlic cloves, chopped

1 shallot, thinly sliced

1 tablespoon all-purpose flour

½ cup dry white wine (a couple of glugs)

3 tablespoons fresh flat-leaf parsley leaves, chopped (a handful)

TIDBIT

You can also make this with thin chicken cutlets, cooking the saltimbocca a minute or two longer until opaque all the way through.

Heat the chicken stock to a boil in a medium sauce pot.

Heat a large nonstick skillet over medium to medium-high heat and heat a platter in a warm oven. Season the cutlets with salt and pepper and place 2 leaves of sage on each of the cutlets. Wrap each cutlet in prosciutto. Add a tablespoon of the EVOO (once around the pan) and 2 tablespoons of the butter to the pan. Fry the saltimbocca for 3 minutes on each side and transfer to the warm platter. Cover with loose foil to keep warm.

Add the remaining tablespoon of EVOO and the polenta to the simmering chicken stock. Stir to mass the polenta, 2 minutes, and add the spinach, separating it into small bits. Stir in the cheese and season the mixture with salt, pepper, and nutmeg.

Add another tablespoon of butter to the skillet, then add the garlic and shallots. Cook for 2 minutes, add the flour, and cook for a minute more. Whisk in the wine and the remaining tablespoon of butter. Remove from the heat and whisk in the parsley.

Place the polenta and spinach on plates and top with 2 pieces of saltimbocca. Spoon a healthy drizzle of sauce over the saltimbocca and serve.

4 SERVINGS

Grilled Swordfish Salad

263

☐ TRY THIS LATER

☐ IT'S A KEEPER

This one is especially good at summer's end.

- 2 lemons
- 6 tablespoons extra-virgin olive oil (EVOO)
- 2 pounds swordfish steaks, trimmed of dark connective tissue and skin, cut into 2- to 3-ounce chunks
  Salt and freshly ground black pepper
- 2 small to medium, firm zucchini, cut into bite-size chunks
- 2 roasted red peppers (homemade or jarred), drained and chopped
- 1 small red onion, chopped
- 3 vine-ripe tomatoes, diced
- ¼ cup fresh flat-leaf parsley (a generous handful), chopped
- 2 to 3 tablespoons fresh mint leaves (a small handful), chopped
- 2 small garlic cloves, minced
  Crusty bread, to pass at the table

Preheat a grill pan or outdoor grill to high heat.

Zest and juice 1 of the lemons into a shallow dish, then add about 3 tablespoons of the EVOO to the juice. Set the swordfish chunks into the lemon and oil and season with salt and pepper. Turn the fish to coat and let marinate for 10 minutes.

In a salad bowl, combine the zucchini, red peppers, onions, tomatoes, parsley, and mint. Add salt to the chopped garlic and mash it to a paste with the flat of your knife. Add the mashed garlic to the salad bowl. Add the juice of the remaining lemon to the salad with about 3 tablespoons of the EVOO (3 times around the bowl). Toss the salad to coat evenly and distribute the garlic. Season the salad with salt and pepper.

Grill the swordfish for 3 minutes on each side, until firm and cooked through.

Place the salad on dinner plates and top with grilled swordfish. Serve with the crusty bread.

4 SERVINGS

264 Warm and Cold Bordeaux Salad, Lamb Loins
with Red Wine, and Sweet Carrots and White Beans

This simple feast brings together all my favorite flavors from a short, sweet stay in Bordeaux.

1½ to 2 pounds lamb loins

9 large garlic cloves, 8 left whole in their skins, 1 cracked away from its skin

6 tablespoons extra-virgin olive oil (EVOO)

1 cup red Bordeaux wine, your pick

1 tablespoon unsalted butter, cut into small pieces
    Coarse sea salt and coarse black pepper

1 tablespoon fresh thyme leaves (from 4 sprigs)

2 carrots, cut into small dice

1 shallot, chopped

1 can small white beans or cannellini, drained and rinsed

½ cup chicken stock or broth

1 head of cauliflower, cut into small florets

4 thick slices good-quality bacon from the butcher counter, chopped

12 small radishes, halved

2 heads of frisée lettuce, cored and coarsely chopped or torn

3 tablespoons white wine or champagne vinegar (eyeball it)
    Crusty bread, for mopping

Heat a heavy ovenproof skillet over high heat. Preheat the oven to 325°F. Slather the lamb loins and the 8 whole garlic cloves in their skins with a couple of tablespoons of EVOO. Sear the loins in the screaming-hot pan and caramelize all over, 2 to 3 minutes. Add the garlic to the pan and transfer to the oven. Roast for 12 minutes (the loins should be firm but not hard), then remove the loins, place them on a carving board, and let stand, covered loosely with foil, for 5 to 10 minutes for the juices to redistribute. Place the garlic cloves in a small bowl. Return the pan to the stove over medium heat. Add the red wine and reduce for 2 to 3 minutes, scraping up the brown bits in the pan. Turn off the heat and stir in the butter. Slice the meat and season with lots of coarse sea salt and pepper and thyme. Set equal portions of lamb on the dinner plates and drizzle with the red wine sauce.

While the lamb cooks, place a medium skillet over medium heat. Add 1 tablespoon of the EVOO (once around the pan), the carrots, and the shallots. Cook gently for 10 minutes to soften, then add the beans and heat through. Season the vegetables and beans with salt and pepper, add the stock, and simmer for 5 minutes more for the beans to absorb the flavor.

While the beans cook, in a skillet, bring 1 inch of water to a boil. Add the cauliflower and some salt and cook for 2 to 3 minutes, then drain the florets, wipe the pan dry, and place the pan back on the stovetop over medium-high heat. Add 1 tablespoon of the EVOO, the chopped bacon, and the cracked clove of garlic. Cook for 5 minutes to lightly brown, then drain away some of the fat. Add the cooked cauliflower and the radishes and stir to combine. Remove the garlic clove. (I eat it.) Season the vegetables with salt and pepper. Arrange the frisée on a platter and top with the vegetables and bacon. Return the pan to the stove and deglaze it with the vinegar, then immediately turn off the heat. Whisk in the remaining 2 tablespoons EVOO and drizzle the dressing evenly over the salad.

Serve the loins with the roasted garlic, and with the beans and salad alongside plus plenty of crusty bread for mopping.

Vive la France!

4 SERVINGS

Columbus's Pork Chops

265

☐ TRY THIS LATER

☐ IT'S A KEEPER

When I worked at Macy's Marketplace in New York City years ago, we had a huge Italian import sale in honor of Columbus Day weekend. As part of the promotion, we handed out cookbooks entitled *Columbus's Menu*, given to us by the Italian Trade Commission. The book listed adaptations of recipes as old as Columbus sailing the ocean blue. One of my favorites was a roast pork loin with balsamic- and basil-macerated strawberries. Here's how you can make it in less than 30. Serve with salad and crusty bread.

4 1½-inch-thick boneless pork loin chops
   Salt and freshly ground black pepper
1 pint strawberries, sliced
1 cup basil leaves, shredded or torn
¼ cup aged balsamic vinegar (eyeball the amount)
2 tablespoons extra-virgin olive oil (EVOO) (twice around the pan)

Preheat the oven to 375°F. Season the chops with salt and pepper and let them come to room temperature, about 20 minutes.

In a medium bowl, toss the strawberries with the basil and vinegar and let stand for 15 to 20 minutes.

Heat an ovenproof skillet over medium-high heat. Add the EVOO to the skillet and sear and caramelize the meat for 2 to 3 minutes on each side. Transfer the skillet to the oven and roast for 10 to 12 minutes, until the juices run clear and the meat is firm but not hard. Let the meat rest for 5 minutes.

Mound the macerated berries on top of the chops and serve.

4 SERVINGS

TIDBIT

Look for balsamic vinegar that has been aged for at least 6 years. You can really taste the difference.

266 Grilled Halibut with Fennel, Orange, Red Onions, and Oregano

This dish is fast and healthy and incorporates a favorite Sicilian combo: oranges, red onions, and oregano.

2 tablespoons extra-virgin olive oil (EVOO), plus some for drizzling
4 6-ounce halibut fillets
  Salt and freshly ground black pepper
  Crusty bread, cut into thick slices
1 orange
1 fennel bulb, quartered, cored, and thinly sliced
1 red onion, thinly sliced
2 tablespoons red wine vinegar (a couple of splashes)
  A handful of fresh flat-leaf parsley, chopped
1 tablespoon chopped fresh oregano (from 2 sprigs)

Heat a grill pan over high heat. Drizzle EVOO over the fish and season with salt and pepper. Grill for 4 minutes on each side, or until the fish is firm and cooked through but not tough. Grill the bread alongside or char under a broiler, then dress with EVOO, salt, and pepper as well.

Preheat a skillet over medium-high heat.

While the fish cooks, grate the zest of the orange and reserve. Peel the orange as you would a melon: cut off the ends, stand it upright, and cut off the skin and pith in thin strips from top to bottom. Cut the orange into thin slices across.

To the preheated skillet, add the 2 tablespoons of EVOO (twice around the pan), the fennel, and onions, season with salt and pepper, and cook for 3 to 5 minutes, until seared and beginning to soften. Add the vinegar to the pan and give it a shake. Remove from the heat and toss in the oranges and zest, the parsley, and oregano. Adjust the seasoning and serve the salad on dinner plates topped with the fish. Serve the seasoned bread alongside.

4 SERVINGS

Pretzel-Crusted Chicken Breasts
with a Cheddar-Mustard Sauce

267

☐ TRY THIS LATER   ☐ IT'S A KEEPER

Yup, this was a really good idea. Serve with oil-and-vinegar dressed slaw salad.

- 4 medium (quart-size) plastic food storage bags
- 4 6- to 8-ounce boneless, skinless chicken breasts
- 1 5-ounce bag of salted pretzels, any shape
- 1 tablespoon fresh thyme leaves, chopped
  Freshly ground black pepper
- 2 eggs
  Vegetable oil, for frying
- 2 tablespoons unsalted butter
- 2 tablespoons all-purpose flour
- 2 cups milk
- 2 cups grated extra-sharp Cheddar cheese
- 2 heaping tablespoons spicy brown mustard, such as Gulden's
  Coarse salt
- ¼ cup fresh flat-leaf parsley leaves (a generous handful), chopped
- ¼ small yellow onion, finely chopped
- 1 large sour dill pickle, finely chopped
- 1 lemon, cut into wedges

Sprinkle a little water into the food storage baggies. Place 1 chicken breast in each bag and seal it up, pushing out excess air. Use a mallet or the bottom of a heavy pot or pan and pound each breast until flat, just shy of busting out of the bag. Repeat with the other 3 chicken breasts.

Place the pretzels in a food processor or blender and grind until fine. Transfer the ground pretzels to a shallow dish and add the thyme and some pepper. Crack and beat 2 eggs in a second shallow dish with a splash of water. Working with 1 pounded chicken breast at a time, coat the breast in the ground pretzels, then in the eggs, then in the pretzels again. Preheat a large skillet with ¼ inch of vegetable oil; add the pretzel-coated chicken breasts to the hot oil. Cook in a single layer, in 2 batches if necessary, about 3 or 4 minutes on each side, until the cutlets' juices run clear and the breading is evenly browned.

While the chicken is frying, in a medium sauce pot over medium heat, melt the butter and add the flour to it. Cook for 1 minute, then whisk in the milk. When the milk comes to a bubble, stir in the cheese and mustard with a wooden spoon. Season with a little salt and pepper and remove the cheese sauce from the heat.

Transfer the fried pretzel-crusted chicken breasts to serving plates, drizzle with the cheddar–mustard sauce, and then sprinkle with a little parsley, finely chopped onions, and finely chopped pickles. Serve immediately, with lemon wedges alongside

4 SERVINGS

SPAGHETTI AND MEATBALLS

Sure it's a classic, but don't get stuck in a rut; here I give 3 ways to make the meatballs, 3 ways to serve them.

TRY THIS LATER

IT'S A KEEPER

268 MASTER RECIPE
Veal Polpette with Thin Spaghetti and Light Tomato and Basil Sauce

Polpette are baby meatballs and these are stuffed with a pine nut (buttery, slightly crunchy surprise) and a currant or raisin (to keep the meat moist).

Coarse salt

¾ pound thin spaghetti (vermicelli)

1 pound ground veal

4 garlic cloves, 2 cloves minced, 2 cloves chopped

1 egg

½ to ⅔ cup Italian-style bread crumbs (a couple of overflowing handfuls)

½ cup grated Parmigiano-Reggiano, plus some to pass at the table

¼ teaspoon freshly grated or ground nutmeg (eyeball it)

Coarse black pepper

3 tablespoons extra-virgin olive oil (EVOO), plus some for drizzling

¼ cup pine nuts (a handful)

¼ cup small raisins or currants

1 small to medium yellow onion, finely chopped

½ cup dry white wine (a couple of glugs)

1 28-ounce can diced tomatoes, San Marzano variety if available

1 8-ounce can tomato sauce

20 fresh basil leaves, torn

Preheat the oven to 400°F. Heat a large pot of water to a boil. When it boils, salt it and add the pasta.

While the water boils, in a large bowl, mix the meat with the minced garlic, egg, bread crumbs, cheese, nutmeg, salt, pepper, and a generous drizzle of EVOO. Roll small meatballs with a pine nut and raisin in the center of each, and arrange them on a rimmed nonstick cookie sheet. Bake the meatballs for 10 minutes, or until cooked through.

Heat a deep skillet over medium heat. Add the 3 tablespoons of EVOO (3 times around the pan). Add the chopped garlic and the onions and cook for 5 minutes, or until soft and sweet. Add the wine, reduce for a minute, then stir in the diced tomatoes and tomato sauce and simmer for 5 minutes. Fold in the basil to wilt it.

Cook the pasta al dente, drain, and toss with half of the sauce. Take the meatballs from the oven and carefully loosen them from the cookie sheet with a thin spatula, then add them to the remaining sauce to coat.

Top the pasta with the polpette and serve with extra grated cheese to pass at the table and a green salad.

4 SERVINGS

□ TRY THIS LATER

□ IT'S A KEEPER

OMIT

Pine nuts
Raisins

SWAP

1½ pounds ground sirloin for the ground veal
Ground allspice for the nutmeg
½ cup fresh flat-leaf parsley leaves, chopped,
   for the basil
1 pound bucatini (thick, hollow spaghetti) for
   the vermicelli
½ cup dry red wine for the white wine
Crushed tomatoes for the diced tomatoes

ADD

2 more garlic cloves, chopped
3 tablespoons capers, drained and chopped
2 tablespoons chopped fresh sage
   (from 4 to 6 sprigs)
¼ pound pancetta, chopped
12 cremini (baby portobello) mushroom caps,
   chopped
½ cup beef stock or broth

Heat a deep skillet over medium heat. Cook the onions in 1 tablespoon of the EVOO (once around the pan) for 5 minutes. Remove the onions and set them aside to cool.

In a large bowl, mix the meat with half the onions, 3 cloves of the chopped garlic, the egg, bread crumbs, cheese, allspice, capers, sage, a handful of the chopped parsley, salt, pepper, and a healthy drizzle of EVOO. Score the meat into 4 sections and make 3 very large balls from each section. Arrange the 12 balls on a non-stick cookie sheet and roast for 15 minutes until firm but not hard.

Drop the bucatini in the salted boiling water and cook until al dente. Drain the pasta.

While the pasta and meatballs are cooking, heat another tablespoon of EVOO in the skillet in which the onions were cooked. Add the pancetta and cook for 3 to 4 minutes, then add the remaining garlic and the mushrooms and cook for 5 minutes. Season the mushrooms with salt and pepper. Add the remaining onions back and deglaze the pan with the red wine, cook for 1 minute, add the beef stock, and whisk up any brown bits. Stir in the tomatoes and season the sauce with salt and pepper. Stir in the remaining parsley. Simmer for 5 minutes.

Toss the pasta with half the sauce. Remove the meatballs from the oven and add to the remaining sauce, turning to coat. Serve 3 meatballs per person alongside the pasta. Spoon any remaining sauce over the pasta. Pass extra cheese at the table. Serve with a green salad.

4 SERVINGS

(variations continue on page 238)

270

OR TRY... Sausage Meatballs with Peppers, Onions, and a Side of Penne

OMIT

Egg
Bread crumbs
Pine nuts
Raisins

SWAP

1½ pounds ground pork for the ground veal
Ground allspice for the nutmeg

1 pound penne rigate for the vermicelli

1 large onion, thinly sliced, for the medium onion
Crushed tomatoes for the diced tomatoes

ADD

2 more garlic cloves, chopped

1 teaspoon fennel seeds

½ teaspoon crushed red pepper flakes

1 red bell pepper, cored, seeded, and thinly sliced

1 cubanelle pepper (mild Italian pepper), seeded and thinly sliced

In a large bowl, mix the pork with 3 cloves of chopped garlic, the cheese, allspice, fennel seeds, red pepper flakes, salt and black pepper, and a healthy drizzle of EVOO. Divide the mixture into 4 sections, and form 4 meatballs per section. Arrange the meatballs on a rimmed nonstick cookie sheet and bake as directed, up to 18 minutes, to make sure the pork is cooked through.

Drop the pasta into the salted boiling water to cook.

While the meatballs and pasta cook, heat a deep skillet over medium to medium-high heat. Add 2 tablespoons of the EVOO, a couple times around the pan, then add the remaining garlic, the sliced onions, and the bell and cubanelle peppers. Sauté the onions and peppers for 5 minutes, then deglaze the pan with the wine. Stir in the crushed tomatoes and tomato sauce. Simmer for 5 minutes, then wilt in the basil.

Toss the drained pasta with half the sauce and peppers and onions. Remove the sausage meatballs from the oven and toss with the remaining sauce. Top the pasta with the meatballs and serve with extra cheese and a green salad.

4 SERVINGS

Mixed Wild Mushroom Sauté on Toast Points
with Gruyère

TRY THIS LATER   IT'S A KEEPER

2 tablespoons extra-virgin olive oil (EVOO)
(twice around the pan)

2 tablespoons unsalted butter, cut into pieces

4 garlic cloves, finely chopped

2 shallots, thinly sliced

1½ pounds assorted mushrooms, such as cremini
(baby portobello), portobello, shiitake, or
fresh porcini, thinly sliced

2 tablespoons chopped fresh thyme plus a few
sprigs for garnish
Salt and freshly ground black pepper

3 tablespoons all-purpose flour

½ cup dry sherry or dry white wine

1 cup beef stock or broth

½ cup cream or half-and-half

8 slices wheat, whole-grain, or white sliced
bread, toasted

2 cups shredded Gruyère cheese (½-pound
brick)

Heat a large nonstick skillet over medium to medium-high heat. Add the EVOO and butter. When the butter melts, add the garlic and shallots and swish around for 30 seconds, then add the mushrooms and combine. Sprinkle the chopped thyme over the mushrooms. Cook the mushrooms, stirring frequently, until they brown. Add salt and pepper to taste. (Do not season mushrooms before they brown. Salt draws out liquid and will make the mushrooms wet and as a result, they will actually take longer to brown.) Sprinkle the flour over the mushrooms and cook for 1 to 2 minutes more, stirring to evenly distribute. Whisk the sherry into the pan first and cook it off for a minute, then whisk in the stock. Thicken the stock for a minute, then add the cream and simmer over low heat for 5 minutes.

Cut the toasted bread from corner to corner. Arrange 4 triangles of toast on each dinner plate. Pour one quarter of the mushrooms across each portion and top with lots of Gruyère and with thyme sprigs. Serve with a tossed green salad or baby spinach salad.

4 SERVINGS

(variations continue on page 240)

TIDBIT

You can make this dish (and variations, #273 or #274) vegetarian by substituting vegetable broth for the stock.

272

NOW TRY... Mushroom Sauté on Charred Polenta and Seared Spicy Ham

OMIT

Cream

SWAP

Dry red wine for the sherry or white wine

1   24-ounce tube of prepared polenta for the 8 slices of bread

1   10-ounce sack of Italian cheese blend or shredded Provolone for the Gruyère cheese

ADD

¼   cup EVOO, for brushing the polenta and ham

12   slices deli-sliced capocolla (Italian spicy ham), cut as thick as a slice of bacon

1   15-ounce can (about 2 cups) crushed fire-roasted tomatoes, such as Muir Glen brand

Preheat a grill pan or large nonstick skillet to high. Cut the polenta into 12 disks. Pour the EVOO into a small dish. Using a pastry or grill brush, paint the polenta with EVOO and char the disks on each side, 5 or 6 minutes total. Remove the polenta and cover with foil to keep warm. Brush the capocolla ham with EVOO and sear on both sides, 2 to 3 minutes total.

Preheat the broiler to high.

Prepare the mushrooms in the same manner as for the master recipe, #271, swapping the red wine for the sherry or white wine. Add the tomatoes to the skillet when you would have added the cream in the original recipe.

In a shallow casserole, layer the polenta with ham. Top with the mushroom–tomato sauce and cover with the cheese. Place under the hot broiler 6 inches from the heat to melt and brown the cheese. Serve with a green salad.

4 SERVINGS

OR TRY... Creamed Mushroom Sauté
with Artichoke Hearts, Spinach, and Penne

273

OMIT

Sherry (the dry white wine remains)
Gruyère cheese

SWAP

Chicken stock for the beef stock

ADD

1 pound penne pasta
1 15-ounce can quartered artichoke hearts, drained well
1 10-ounce box frozen chopped spinach, defrosted and wrung dry in a kitchen towel
¼ teaspoon grated or ground nutmeg

½ cup grated Parmigiano-Reggiano (a couple of handfuls)

Bring a large pot of water to a boil. Add the pasta and salt and cook until al dente.

Prepare the mushrooms and sauce just as for the master recipe, #271, using dry white wine and chicken stock. When the sauce is completed, stir in the artichoke hearts. Break up the spinach and add to the sauce. Stir to heat through and add the nutmeg. Adjust the salt and pepper to taste. Add the drained penne and cheese to the pan and toss to combine.

4 SERVINGS

THEN TRY... Creamed Mushroom Sauté
with Hearts of Palm, Arugula, and Pappardelle

274

OMIT

Sherry (the dry white wine remains)
Gruyère cheese

SWAP

3 tablespoons chopped fresh chives, plus additional for garnish, for the thyme
Chicken stock for the beef stock

ADD

1 15-ounce can hearts of palm, drained and sliced
2 cups stemmed and chopped arugula leaves
1 pound pappardelle (wide ribbon pasta)

Bring a large pot of water to a boil. Add the pasta and salt and cook until al dente.

Prepare the mushrooms and sauce just as for the master recipe, #271, using chives, white wine, and chicken stock rather than the thyme, sherry, and beef stock. When completed, stir in the hearts of palm and heat through. Adjust salt and pepper to taste. Fold in the arugula leaves and toss with the pasta or egg noodles to combine. Top with additional chives for garnish.

4 SERVINGS

275 Lamb "Stew" (Wink, Wink)

2 tablespoons extra-virgin olive oil (EVOO)
(twice around the pan)

1 large yellow onion, chopped

6 medium red bliss potatoes, cut in half and
then sliced

1 tablespoon chopped fresh thyme
(from 3 to 4 sprigs)

3 garlic cloves, chopped

1 bay leaf, fresh or dried
Salt and freshly ground black pepper

2 large carrots, peeled and thinly sliced

2 celery ribs, chopped into 1-inch pieces

2 rounded tablespoons tomato paste

2 tablespoons all-purpose flour

½ cup dry red wine (a couple of glugs)

2½ cups of chicken stock (eyeball it: just over
half a quart-size carton)

12 rib lamb chops (3 chops per person)

¼ cup fresh flat-leaf parsley leaves (a generous
handful), chopped

Preheat the broiler.

To make the "stew," preheat a large skillet over medium-high heat with the EVOO; add the onions, potatoes, thyme, garlic, bay leaf, salt, and pepper. Cook until the onions start to brown, about 6 to 7 minutes. Add the carrots, celery, and tomato paste and continue to cook for 2 to 3 minutes. Sprinkle with the flour, cook for 1 more minute, and then whisk in the red wine. Cook for 1 minute, then add the chicken stock and bring the mixture up to a bubble. Turn the heat down to medium low and simmer for 10 minutes.

While the "stew" is simmering, start the lamb chops. Arrange the chops on a broiler pan and season both sides with salt and pepper. Broil the chops for 3 to 4 minutes on each side for medium rare, up to 5 minutes on each side for medium well.

To serve, add the parsley to the "stew," remove and discard the bay leaf, taste, and adjust the seasoning with salt and pepper. Divide the stew among 4 shallow serving bowls and arrange 3 chops atop each portion.

4 SERVINGS

Veal Chops and Balsamic–Thyme Roasted
Tomatoes and Mushrooms

276

☐ TRY THIS LATER   ☐ IT'S A KEEPER

- 4 portobello mushroom caps
- 5 plum tomatoes, cut in half lengthwise
  Salt and freshly ground black pepper
- 3 tablespoons balsamic vinegar (eyeball it)
- 4 tablespoons extra-virgin olive oil (EVOO)
- 1 tablespoon fresh thyme leaves, chopped
  (from 4 sprigs)
- 4 1- to 1½-inch-thick bone-in rib veal chops
- 1 large shallot, chopped
- ½ cup dry white wine (a couple of glugs)
- ½ cup chicken stock or broth
- 2 tablespoons cold unsalted butter
- ¼ cup fresh flat-leaf parsley leaves (a generous
  handful), chopped
  Crusty bread

Preheat the oven to 450°F.

Place the portobello mushrooms and plum tomatoes on a rimmed cookie sheet. Season with salt, pepper, balsamic vinegar, 2 tablespoons of the EVOO, and the thyme; toss in the seasonings to coat thoroughly. Arrange the mushrooms gill side up and the tomatoes flesh side up. Put them in the oven and roast for 12 minutes, or until cooked through. Once roasted, remove from the oven, thinly slice the mushrooms, and cut the plum tomatoes in half again. Reserve any pan juices.

While the mushrooms and tomatoes are roasting, start the veal chops. Heat a large skillet over medium-high heat with the remaining 2 tablespoons of EVOO (twice around the pan). Liberally season the veal chops with salt and pepper. Once the skillet is screaming hot and you see the first wafts of smoke rising, add the chops to the hot skillet and cook on the first side for 5 minutes. Resist the temptation to move the chops around in the pan; you want a nice brown crust on them and messing with them won't help you get there. Before flipping the chops, reduce the heat to medium. Flip, and cook them on the second side for 8 to 10 minutes, or until the desired doneness. Remove the chops from the pan and let them rest, tented with aluminum foil, for about 5 minutes.

While the veal chops are resting, return the skillet to medium-high heat, add the shallots, and cook for 1 minute. Add the wine and the chicken stock. Bring up to a simmer and reduce by half, about 2 to 3 minutes. Turn the heat off and add the butter, stirring with a spoon until the butter has completely melted. Add the parsley and the roasted sliced mushrooms and roasted chopped tomatoes along with any pan juices, and stir to combine. Serve the chops with the balsamic–thyme roasted tomatoes and mushrooms, and with some crusty bread.

4 SERVINGS

277

Chorizo-Tomato Stew on Garlic Croutons
with Zesty Parsley Sprinkle

2 tablespoons extra-virgin olive oil (EVOO) (twice around the pan), plus some for drizzling

¾ pound chorizo sausage, thinly sliced

3 garlic cloves, 2 chopped and 1 crushed

1 large yellow onion, chopped

2 celery ribs, chopped

1 large carrot, peeled and chopped

6 medium red potatoes, cut in half and then thinly sliced

1 tablespoon fresh thyme leaves, chopped (from 4 sprigs)

Salt and freshly ground black pepper

1 15-ounce can diced fire-roasted tomatoes, such as Muir Glen brand

2 cups chicken stock or broth

4 thick slices crusty country-style bread

½ cup fresh flat-leaf parsley leaves (two large handfuls)

Zest of 1 lemon

Zest of 1 orange

Preheat a large soup pot over medium-high heat with the 2 tablespoons of EVOO. Add the chorizo and cook, stirring frequently, for 3 minutes. Add the 2 cloves of chopped garlic, the onions, celery, carrots, potatoes, thyme, salt, and pepper, and cook for 3 to 4 minutes. Add the tomatoes and chicken stock and bring up to a bubble, then turn the heat down to medium low and simmer for 10 minutes, or until slightly thickened.

While the stew is simmering, toast the bread in the broiler or in a toaster oven. Rub with the crushed garlic clove and then drizzle EVOO over it and reserve.

Pile the parsley leaves, lemon zest, and orange zest on a cutting board. Run your knife through the pile until the parsley is finely chopped and the zests are completely incorporated into the parsley; reserve.

To serve, arrange the garlic croutons in the bottom of 4 shallow soup bowls, ladle some of the chorizo-tomato stew on top of the garlic croutons, toss a little of the zesty parsley sprinkle over the stew, and serve.

4 SERVINGS

Serve with Sangria.

ADD

2 tablespoons white wine vinegar (eyeball it)
4 eggs

Prepare just as for the master recipe, #277. Once the chorizo-tomato stew is all put together and simmering, fill a medium skillet with warm water and bring to a gentle simmer over medium-low heat. As the water is coming up to a simmer, proceed with making the garlic croutons and the zesty parsley sprinkle. Pour the vinegar into the simmering water. Crack an egg into a small bowl. Gently pour the egg into the simmering water. Repeat with the remaining 3 eggs. Cook the eggs for about 2 minutes for runny yolks. Carefully remove the eggs with a slotted spoon to a towel-lined plate to drain, and serve atop the chorizo-tomato stew.

4 SERVINGS

Everything-Crusted Chicken Rolls 279
Stuffed with Scallion Cream Cheese

You've heard of everything bagels—why not everything chicken! These are great hot or cold, for picnics or tailgate parties with cut raw veggies.

Vegetable oil, for frying
1 pound cream cheese, softened
4 scallions, chopped
2 pounds chicken breast cutlets
Salt and freshly ground black pepper
1½ cups bread crumbs (6 overflowing handfuls)
2 teaspoons granulated garlic
2 tablespoons poppy seeds
3 tablespoons dehydrated onion flakes
3 tablespoons sesame seeds
½ cup all-purpose flour (eyeball it)
2 eggs, beaten with a splash of water

Heat an inch of vegetable oil in a large frying pan over medium to medium-high heat.

In a small bowl, mix the cream cheese with the scallions. Spread the chicken cutlets with the cheese and roll into tight, small bundles. Wash up. Season the bundles liberally with salt and pepper.

Mix the bread crumbs with the garlic, poppy seeds, onion flakes, and sesame seeds in a shallow dish. Coat the bundles in flour, dip them in the eggs, and then roll in the flavored bread crumbs. Fry until evenly golden all over and serve hot, or chill and serve cold.

4 SERVINGS

TRY THIS LATER
IT'S A KEEPER

TRY THIS LATER
IT'S A KEEPER

TRY THIS LATER

IT'S A KEEPER

280 Pasta with a Lot of Mussel

Coarse salt
1 pound spaghetti
2 tablespoons extra-virgin olive oil (EVOO) (twice around the pan)
½ pound chorizo, cut in half lengthwise, then sliced into half-moons
1 small red onion, chopped
3 garlic cloves, chopped
1 celery rib, finely chopped
1 small carrot, peeled and finely chopped
1 tablespoon fresh thyme leaves, chopped
Coarse black pepper
1 cup dry white wine
1 15-ounce can diced fire-roasted tomatoes, such as Muir Glen brand
1 pound mussels (ask at the seafood counter to check that they have been scrubbed)
½ cup fresh flat-leaf parsley leaves (two handfuls), coarsely chopped
Crusty bread

Bring a large pot of water up to a boil to cook the spaghetti. Add salt to the boiling water, add the pasta, and cook al dente.

Heat a large, deep skillet with a tight-fitting lid over medium heat with the EVOO. Add the chorizo and cook for 2 minutes, add the onions, garlic, celery, carrots, and thyme, and season with salt and pepper. Cook for 5 minutes, add the wine and fire-roasted tomatoes, and bring up to a bubble. Add the mussels and cover with the tight-fitting lid or some aluminum foil; cook until the mussels open, 4 to 6 minutes.

Discard any unopened shells. Using a slotted spoon, transfer the mussels to a bowl and cover with foil to keep warm. Add the drained cooked pasta and the parsley to the skillet with the chorizo and tomatoes, toss to coat in the sauce, and cook for 1 minute.

Divide the pasta among 4 serving plates and top each bowl of pasta with a portion of the mussels. Serve immediately with some crusty bread.

4 SERVINGS

Big Bistro Burgers with Caramelized Shallots
on Grilled Bread with Beet and Goat Cheese Salad

5 tablespoons extra-virgin olive oil (EVOO), plus some for drizzling

4 large shallots, thinly sliced
Salt and freshly ground black pepper

4 tablespoons sherry vinegar

2 pounds ground sirloin

2 tablespoons fresh thyme leaves, chopped (from 4 sprigs)

2 tablespoons Worcestershire sauce (eyeball it)

1 tablespoon grill seasoning, such as McCormick's Montreal Steak Seasoning (a palmful)

2 tablespoons Dijon mustard

4 thick slices crusty country-style bread

1 8¼-ounce can sliced beets, drained and slices cut into sticks

6 cups frisée, arugula, watercress, or baby spinach, your favorite

1 cup crumbled goat cheese

Preheat a grill pan or outdoor grill to high.

Preheat a small skillet over medium-high heat with 2 tablespoons of EVOO. Add the shallots, season with salt and pepper, and cook, stirring frequently, for 5 to 6 minutes, or until lightly brown. Add 2 tablespoons of the sherry vinegar and continue to cook for 1 minute, then remove from the heat and reserve.

While the shallots are getting brown, in a large bowl, combine the beef, thyme, Worcestershire, grill seasoning, and Dijon mustard. Divide the meat into 4 por-

tions. Form large patties about 1¼ inches thick. Coat the beef patties with a good drizzle of EVOO. Grill for 5 to 6 minutes per side for medium rare, 7 to 8 minutes per side for medium well to well.

Drizzle or brush EVOO onto both sides of the bread slices, season with salt and pepper, and add to the grill. Cook until well marked on both sides, remove from the grill, and wrap in foil to keep warm.

In a bowl, combine the beets and greens and drizzle with the remaining 2 tablespoons of sherry vinegar, the remaining 3 tablespoons of EVOO, and a little salt and pepper. Toss to coat; add the crumbled goat cheese and toss to distribute.

To serve, divide the grilled bread among 4 serving plates. Top the bread with the beet and goat cheese salad, letting it overflow onto the plates. Transfer the burgers to top the salad and then pile each burger with some of the caramelized shallots. Attack your big bistro burger with a fork and knife, please. This *is* a bistro!

4 SERVINGS

TIDBIT

For the large slices of country-style bread, cut a rectangular loaf lengthwise or a round loaf from the center.

282 Ginger-Lime Chicken with String Beans and Wasabi Smashed Potatoes

My favorite ginger-lime chicken was had at a bistro in Montreal, Canada, of all places. This is the at-home version.

2-inch piece of fresh ginger, peeled and grated
Zest and juice of 1 lime
3 tablespoons tamari (dark aged soy sauce, found on the international aisle)
3 tablespoons vegetable oil
Coarse black pepper
4 6-ounce skinless, boneless chicken breast halves
2 to 2¼ pounds baby Yukon Gold potatoes, cut in half
½ cup milk
1 to 1½ tablespoons prepared wasabi paste, depending on how spicy you like it
5 tablespoons unsalted butter
Coarse salt
1 medium red onion, sliced
2 garlic cloves, chopped
1¼ pounds string beans, trimmed of stem ends
1½ cups chicken stock or broth (eyeball it)

In a shallow dish, combine the ginger, lime juice (make sure you remove the zest first!), tamari, 2 tablespoons of the vegetable oil, and pepper. Add the chicken breasts and toss to coat in the mixture; let marinate for about 5 minutes.

Fill a large sauce pot with water, add the potatoes, place over high heat, and bring up to a boil. Reduce the heat to a simmer for 10 minutes, or until the potatoes are tender. Drain and return the potatoes to the hot pot. Smash the potatoes with a masher and combine with the milk, wasabi paste, and 3 tablespoons of the butter. Add salt and pepper to taste.

While the potatoes are cooking, preheat a large non-stick skillet over medium-high heat, add the marinated chicken, and cook on both sides for 5 to 6 minutes, or until cooked through. Remove the cooked chicken from the skillet to a plate and cover with aluminum foil to keep warm.

Return the skillet to the heat with the remaining tablespoon of vegetable oil (once around the pan), add the onions and garlic, and cook for 3 minutes. Add the string beans, toss to distribute, add the chicken stock, and bring up to a simmer. Cook for 3 to 4 minutes, or until the beans are tender. Turn the heat off and add the lime zest and the remaining 2 tablespoons of butter, stirring until the butter has melted completely.

Divide the string beans and the sauce among 4 serving plates. Slice the chicken on an angle and place atop the beans, then spoon a big helping of wasabi smashed potatoes alongside.

4 SERVINGS

Broiled Lamb Chops
with Sweet Pea and Spinach Couscous

283

☐ TRY THIS LATER

☐ IT'S A KEEPER

2 cups chicken stock or broth
3 tablespoons extra-virgin olive oil (EVOO)
1½ cups plain couscous
1 large red onion, chopped
4 garlic cloves, chopped
  Salt and freshly ground black pepper
  2-pound rack of lamb cut into 12 chops
  (3 chops per person)
1 10-ounce box frozen peas
4 cups baby spinach
10 fresh basil leaves, chopped or torn
10 fresh mint leaves, chopped

Preheat the broiler.

Place about 1½ cups of the chicken stock and 1 tablespoon of the EVOO in a medium sauce pot over medium heat. Cover the pot and raise the heat; bring the broth to a boil. Remove the pot from the heat. Add the couscous, cover, and let stand for 10 minutes.

While the chicken stock is heating up, preheat a medium skillet over medium-high heat with the remaining 2 tablespoons of the EVOO (twice around the pan). Add the onions, garlic, salt, and pepper and cook, stirring frequently, for 3 to 4 minutes, or until the onions are tender.

While the onions are cooking, arrange the chops on a slotted broiler pan and season both sides with salt and pepper. Broil the chops for 3 to 4 minutes on each side for medium rare, 5 to 6 for medium well.

To the onions and garlic, add the frozen peas and the remaining ½ cup of chicken stock. Heat for 2 minutes, then add the baby spinach and wilt. Add the basil and mint and remove from the heat.

Fluff the cooked couscous with a fork. Add the veggies and herbs to the couscous on a large platter, toss to distribute, and adjust the seasonings with salt and pepper.

Serve the lamb chops on top of the sweet pea and spinach couscous.

4 SERVINGS

284 MASTER RECIPE
For Neil Diamond: Tangy Cherry Chicken

You got the way to move me, Baby! Serve with a green salad and boiled baby potatoes.

- 3 tablespoons extra-virgin olive oil (EVOO)
- 4 6-ounce boneless, skinless chicken breast halves
- 1 tablespoon fresh thyme leaves, chopped (from 4 sprigs)
  Salt and freshly ground black pepper
- 1 small red onion, finely chopped
- 2 celery ribs, finely chopped
- ¼ teaspoon crushed red pepper flakes (a couple of pinches)
- ¼ teaspoon freshly grated or ground nutmeg (eyeball it)
- ½ cup dry white wine (a couple of glugs)
- 1 cup chicken stock or broth
- ½ cup dried cherries (a couple of handfuls)
- 3 tablespoons cold unsalted butter

Preheat a large nonstick skillet over medium-high heat with 2 tablespoons of the EVOO (twice around the pan). Season the chicken liberally with half of the thyme and salt and pepper and add to the hot skillet. Cook the chicken for 5 to 6 minutes on each side until cooked through. Remove the chicken from the pan and cover with foil to keep warm.

Return the skillet to the burner over medium-high heat, add the remaining 1 tablespoon of EVOO, and add the onions, celery, red pepper flakes, nutmeg, salt, and pepper. Cook for 3 to 4 minutes, or until the celery and onions are tender. Add the white wine and cook until the pan is almost dry, 1 minute. Add the chicken stock, dried cherries, and remaining thyme and continue to cook for about 4 to 5 minutes, or until there is only about ¼ cup of liquid left in the pan. Turn the heat off under the pan. Add the butter and whisk until it has completely melted.

Serve the chicken breasts whole or sliced with cherry sauce poured over them.

4 SERVINGS

NOW TRY... # Golden Raisin and Almond Chicken

285

☐ TRY THIS LATER   ☐ IT'S A KEEPER

SWAP

Golden raisins for the cherries

ADD

4 ounces sliced or slivered almonds (available on the baking aisle)

1 additional tablespoon unsalted butter

1 tablespoon chopped fresh chives

Prepare just as for the master recipe, #284, adding the raisins when you would have added the cherries. Toast the nuts in a small skillet over medium heat. Add 1 tablespoon butter to the toasted nuts; melt and toss to coat. Add the chives and toss to combine.

Top the whole or sliced chicken breasts with the raisin sauce and the buttered, toasted almonds, then serve with salad and potatoes or bread.

4 SERVINGS

OR TRY... # For Almodovar: Spicy Spanish Raisin and Olive Chicken, Olé!

286

☐ TRY THIS LATER   ☐ IT'S A KEEPER

Pedro Almodovar is my favorite foreign film director—I have his whole library. My favorite film and the one I most relate to: *Woman on the Verge of a Nervous Breakdown.*

SWAP

Paprika for the nutmeg

⅓ cup dry sherry for the white wine (eyeball it)

Golden raisins for the cherries

ADD

¼ pound chorizo, finely chopped

¼ cup large Spanish green olives with pimientos, drained and coarsely chopped

Zest and juice of ½ lemon

¼ cup fresh flat-leaf parsley leaves (a generous handful), finely chopped

Prepare just as for the master recipe, #284, adding the chorizo at the same time you add the onions. Add the raisins when you would have added the cherries. Finish the sauce with the olives and parsley, and toss to combine. Serve the chicken breasts, whole or sliced, with the raisin and olive sauce.

4 SERVINGS

287 Grilled Skirt Steak and Orzo with the Works

1½ to 2 pounds skirt steak
3 tablespoons balsamic vinegar (eyeball it)
2 tablespoons extra-virgin olive oil (EVOO),
  plus some for drizzling
  Coarse black pepper
  Coarse salt
½ pound orzo
1 large red onion, chopped
4 garlic cloves, chopped
1 fennel bulb, quartered, cored, and thinly
  sliced
¼ teaspoon crushed red pepper flakes
  (a couple of pinches)
1 cup chicken stock or broth
1 pint grape tomatoes
10 fresh basil leaves, chopped or torn
½ cup fresh flat-leaf parsley leaves (a couple
  of generous handfuls), chopped
½ cup grated Parmigiano-Reggiano (a couple of
  overflowing handfuls)

Coat the skirt steak in balsamic vinegar, a good drizzle of EVOO, and a lot of freshly ground black pepper and marinate in a nonreactive dish for 5 to 10 minutes.

Preheat an outdoor grill or ridged grill pan to high.

Bring a large sauce pot of water to a boil to cook the orzo. Once boiling, salt the water and add the orzo. Cook until al dente, with a bite to it, about 12 minutes.

While the water is coming up to a boil, preheat a large skillet over medium-high heat with the 2 tablespoons of EVOO (twice around the pan); add the onions, garlic, fennel, red pepper flakes, salt, and pepper and cook, stirring frequently, for 4 to 5 minutes, or until the veggies are slightly tender.

Season the steak with salt and grill for 3 to 4 minutes on each side. Remove the meat to a plate, tent loosely with foil, and let it rest for 5 minutes to allow the juices to redistribute.

To the veggies, add the chicken stock and grape tomatoes, bring up to a bubble, and cook for 2 minutes, or until the grape tomatoes begin to burst. Add the cooked orzo, basil, parsley, and grated Parmigiano cheese and stir to combine.

Slice the meat very thin on a sharp angle. Serve alongside the orzo with the works.

4 SERVINGS

Lime-and-Honey Glazed Salmon with Warm Black Bean and Corn Salad

288

☐ TRY THIS LATER   ☐ IT'S A KEEPER

4 tablespoons extra-virgin olive oil (EVOO)

1 medium red onion, chopped

2 large garlic cloves, chopped

½ to 1 teaspoon crushed red pepper flakes (medium heat to extra spicy)

1 teaspoon ground cumin (⅓ palmful)
Salt and freshly ground black pepper
Juice of 2 limes

3 tablespoons honey (3 gobs)

1 teaspoon chili powder (⅓ palmful)

4 6-ounce salmon fillets

1 red bell pepper, cored, seeded, and chopped

1 10-ounce box frozen corn kernels, defrosted

½ cup chicken stock or broth

1 15-ounce can black beans, rinsed and drained

2 to 3 tablespoons fresh cilantro leaves (a handful), chopped

6 cups baby spinach

Preheat a medium skillet over medium heat with 2 tablespoons of the EVOO (twice around the pan). Add the onions, garlic, red pepper flakes, cumin, salt, and pepper. Cook, stirring occasionally, for 3 minutes.

While the onions are cooking, preheat a medium non-stick skillet over medium-high heat with the remaining 2 tablespoons of EVOO. In a shallow dish, combine the juice of 1 lime, honey, chili powder, salt, and pepper. Add the salmon fillets to the lime–honey mixture and toss to coat thoroughly. Add the seasoned salmon to the hot skillet and cook until just cooked through, about 3 to 4 minutes on each side.

To the cooked onions, add the bell peppers and corn kernels and cook for 1 minute. Add the chicken stock and continue to cook for another 2 minutes. Add the black beans and cook until the beans are just heated through. Remove the skillet from the heat and add the juice of the second lime, the cilantro, and spinach. Toss to wilt the spinach and then taste and adjust the seasoning. Serve the lime-and-honey-glazed salmon on top of the warm black bean and corn salad.

4 SERVINGS

TIDBIT

If fresh corn is in season, by all means cut the kernels from 4 fresh ears instead of using frozen.

289 Sage and Balsamic Pork Chops
with Creamy Pumpkin Polenta

Serve with steamed broccoli or cauliflower.

- 3 tablespoons extra-virgin olive oil (EVOO)
- 2 tablespoons balsamic vinegar (enough to just coat the pork chops; eyeball it)
- 5 fresh sage leaves, chopped
- ¼ cup fresh flat-leaf parsley leaves (a handful), chopped
- 1 large garlic clove, chopped
  Salt and freshly ground black pepper
- 4 1½-inch-thick boneless center-cut pork chops
- 2½ cups chicken stock or broth
- 1 cup milk
- 1 cup canned pumpkin puree
  Freshly grated or ground nutmeg, about ⅛ teaspoon
- ¾ cup quick-cooking polenta (found in Italian foods or specialty foods aisles)
- ½ cup grated Parmigiano-Reggiano (a few handfuls), plus some for garnish
- 2 tablespoons unsalted butter

Preheat the oven to 375°F.

Preheat a large, oven-proof skillet over medium-high heat with 2 tablespoons of the EVOO (twice around the pan). In a shallow dish, combine the balsamic, sage, parsley, garlic, the remaining 1 tablespoon of EVOO, salt, and pepper. Coat the pork chops and then place them in the skillet and sear the meat on both sides to caramelize, about 2 minutes on each side. Transfer the skillet to the oven to finish off, about 8 minutes, or until the meat is firm to the touch but not tough.

While the chops are cooking, in a sauce pot combine the chicken stock, milk, and pumpkin and season with the nutmeg, salt, and pepper. Place over high heat and bring up to a simmer. Whisk in the polenta and stir until it begins to mass together. Add the grated cheese and butter, stirring to combine. Keep in mind that polenta is very forgiving. If it becomes too thick, not smooth and creamy, you can always add more warm chicken stock or milk.

Serve the polenta alongside the sage and balsamic pork chops with steamed vegetables. Garnish the polenta with a little extra grated or shaved cheese.

4 SERVINGS

Chili–Sweet Potato Hash with Fried Eggs
and Fresh Tomato Salsa

290

☐ TRY THIS LATER ☐ IT'S A KEEPER

Another B, L, or D meal: good for Breakfast, Lunch, or Dinner.

- 2 tablespoons extra-virgin olive oil (EVOO) (twice around the pan)
- ½ pound bulk breakfast sausage, such as maple sausage
- 1 medium sweet potato, scrubbed clean, cut in half lengthwise, and thinly sliced into half-moons
- 1 large red onion, finely chopped
- 2 teaspoons chili powder (⅔ palmful)
- 1 teaspoon ground cumin (⅓ palmful)
- 2 teaspoons ground coriander (⅔ palmful)
  Salt and freshly ground black pepper
- 3 vine-ripe yellow tomatoes, seeded and diced
- 1 small jalapeño pepper, seeded and chopped
- 2 to 3 tablespoons chopped fresh cilantro (a palmful)
  Juice of 1 lime
- ½ cup fresh flat-leaf parsley leaves (a few handfuls), chopped
- 1 cup grated Manchego or extra-sharp Cheddar cheese
- 1 tablespoon unsalted butter
- 4 large eggs

Preheat a large nonstick skillet over medium-high heat with the EVOO. Add the breakfast sausage and break it up with the back of a wooden spoon into little chunks; brown the sausage for 3 minutes. Add the sweet potatoes and three fourths of the chopped red onions to the sausage, season with chili powder, cumin, coriander, salt, and pepper, stir frequently, and cook for 10 to 12 minutes, or until the potatoes are nice and tender.

While the hash is cooking, in a small bowl, combine the tomatoes, jalapeños, the remaining chopped red onions, the cilantro, lime juice, and a little salt and pepper.

Once the hash is cooked, add the chopped parsley, stir to combine, and transfer the hash to a serving platter. Sprinkle with the cheese and cover with aluminum foil; the cheese will melt while you make the fried eggs.

Wipe clean the skillet you made the hash in, return it to the cooktop over medium-high heat, and add the butter. Once the butter has melted, crack each of the eggs into the skillet, season with a little salt and pepper, and fry to desired doneness. The eggs may, of course, be scrambled as well. As you like it!

Transfer the fried eggs to the top of the hash, sprinkle with the fresh tomato salsa, and serve.

4 SERVINGS

291 Spinach and Goat Cheese Chicken Rolls in a Pan Sauce

Serve with buttered and parslied orzo or small potatoes or with lots of crusty bread.

- 4 6-ounce chicken breast halves
- 1 10-ounce box frozen chopped spinach, defrosted
- ½ cup crumbled goat cheese or goat cheese with herbs, or crumbled Boursin (garlic and herb cow's-milk cheese)
  Zest and juice of 1 lemon
  Salt and freshly ground black pepper
  Toothpicks
- 3 tablespoons sesame seeds
  All-purpose flour, for dredging, plus 1 tablespoon
- 4 tablespoons extra-virgin olive oil (EVOO)
- 3 garlic cloves
- 1 small yellow onion, finely chopped
- 1 tablespoon fresh thyme leaves, chopped (from 4 sprigs)
- ½ teaspoon crushed red pepper flakes
- 2 cups chicken stock or broth
- ¼ cup fresh flat-leaf parsley leaves (a generous handful), chopped
- 3 tablespoons diced roasted red peppers

Preheat the oven to 325°F.

Sprinkle a little water in food storage bags. Place 1 chicken breast in each bag, and seal it up, pushing out excess air. Using a mallet or a small, heavy pot or pan, pound each breast until flat and just shy of busting out of the bag.

Wring the spinach dry in a kitchen towel. Separate it and add it to a bowl. Add the goat cheese and the lemon zest, season with salt and pepper, and mix until combined.

Lay the 4 pounded chicken breasts out on a cutting board. Season them with salt and pepper. Place one fourth of the spinach–goat cheese filling on each breast, along one long edge of the cutlet. Roll the chicken breast to enclose the filling, creating a cigar shape, and secure with toothpicks. Season the outside of the chicken with salt and pepper and then dredge in the sesame seeds and flour.

Preheat a large skillet over medium to medium-high heat with 2 tablespoons of the EVOO. Shake the excess flour from the chicken and then add to the hot skillet and sauté on all sides for about 5 minutes, or until golden brown all over. Transfer to a rimmed cookie sheet and place in the oven to finish cooking through, another 5 to 7 minutes, until the juices run clear.

TIDBIT

Use this method of pounding chicken portions in plastic storage bags to store the meat as well. You can transfer the food bags to the freezer and have single-portion servings of chicken cutlets for quick defrosting, anytime. It's a great way to take full advantage of a terrific sale on chicken.

Place the skillet back over medium-high heat, add the remaining 2 tablespoons of EVOO, and add the garlic, onions, thyme, red pepper flakes, and some salt. Cook for about 3 minutes, then sprinkle the mixture with 1 tablespoon flour and continue to cook for about 1 minute. Whisk in the chicken stock and thicken the sauce, 3 to 4 minutes. Finish the sauce with the lemon juice, the parsley, and the diced roasted peppers.

Ladle some sauce onto each dinner plate. Slice the chicken rolls on an angle, and serve atop the sauce.

4 SERVINGS

Lemon and Brown Butter Fish Fillets
with Seared Red and Yellow Grape Tomatoes

292

☐ TRY THIS LATER ☐ IT'S A KEEPER

4 tablespoons extra-virgin olive oil (EVOO)
½ pint red grape tomatoes
½ pint yellow grape tomatoes
½ cup fresh flat-leaf parsley leaves (a couple of handfuls), chopped
Salt and freshly ground black pepper
4 6-ounce tilapia, skate, or Dover sole fillets
All-purpose flour, for dredging
4 tablespoons cold unsalted butter
Juice of 1 lemon
Crusty bread

Preheat a large skillet over high heat with 2 tablespoons of the EVOO (twice around the pan). Add the grape tomatoes in an even layer and let them sear for 2 minutes without moving them. Add half of the parsley and season with salt and pepper, then continue to cook for 1 to 2 more minutes, or until all of the tomatoes start to burst. Remove them from the pan to a plate and cover with some aluminum foil to keep warm.

Thoroughly wipe out the skillet and return to the cooktop over medium-high heat. Season the fish with salt and pepper and then dredge in the flour. Add the remaining 2 tablespoons EVOO to the skillet. Once the oil is hot, shake the excess flour from the fish and add to the skillet. Cook the fish for 4 to 5 minutes on each side, or until firm to the touch and cooked through. Once cooked, transfer the fish to a serving platter and cover with aluminum foil to keep warm.

Wipe the skillet clean again and return to the cooktop over medium-high heat. Melt the butter; but keep your eye on it. It will go from melted to brown pretty quickly. Once the butter is brown and smells slightly nutty, add the lemon juice and the remaining parsley. Pour the brown butter over the fish and then top with the seared grape tomatoes. Serve with crusty bread, for mopping.

4 SERVINGS

MORE CHICKEN?

The chicken recipes here through page 260 will quickly become your "go to" recipes. (Next year, these will be the chicken recipes you become bored with. God help us!) So, you need to know how flexible this sauce is. Say you don't have any sour cream or plain yogurt in the house. No sweat! You can substitute half-and-half or heavy cream. Or, let's say you don't have those either. Well, you need a little trip to the grocery store! However, until then, add 1 to 2 more minutes of cooking time to the sauce to really reduce the chicken stock. Turn the heat off and whisk in 2 tablespoons of cold butter and you are in business! (If you don't have butter, give up and call for pizza.)

TRY THIS LATER · IT'S A KEEPER

293 MASTER RECIPE
Chicken No. 14,752—Chicken in Mustard Sauce

As many chicken recipes as I write, as many as other chefs have piled up in books, people still ask "Do you have any new chicken recipes?" Those poor birds— they can't even fly! Clearly, it's all anyone wants to eat anymore!

- 4   6-ounce boneless, skinless chicken breast halves
- 1   tablespoon fresh thyme leaves, chopped (from 4 sprigs)
     Juice of 1 lemon
     Salt and freshly ground black pepper
- 2   tablespoons extra-virgin olive oil (EVOO) (twice around the pan)
- ¾   cup chicken stock or broth
- 3   super-heaping tablespoons good-quality Dijon mustard
- 3   super-heaping tablespoons sour cream

Season the chicken with the thyme, lemon juice, salt, and pepper. Heat a large nonstick skillet over medium-high heat with the EVOO. Add the seasoned chicken breasts and cook for 5 to 6 minutes on each side, or until cooked through. Remove the chicken from the pan and cover with foil. Turn up the heat on the skillet to high and add the chicken stock and mustard, whisking to combine. Bring up to a boil, reduce the heat, and simmer for 3 minutes.

Whisk in the sour cream and continue to cook until slightly thickened, about 2 more minutes. Serve the sauce over the chicken and accompany with a simple salad and something to sop up the sauce, like couscous or bread.

4 SERVINGS

294

ADD

- 2 10-ounce boxes frozen broccoli spears
  A few pieces of lemon peel
- 2 teaspoons hot sauce
- 2 cups shredded Gruyère or Swiss cheese such as Emmentaler

Cook the broccoli in boiling water in a shallow pan with the lemon peel. Cook to just heat through—you want the broccoli spears to retain their bright color. Drain well.

Preheat the broiler.

Prepare the chicken and sauce as directed in the master recipe, #293, adding the hot sauce to the finished sauce (to "Devil" it). Place the cooked chicken breasts and broccoli in a shallow casserole and top with the deviled sauce and the cheese. Broil until the cheese is brown and bubbly. Serve with crusty bread.

4 SERVINGS

· ·

OR TRY... **Chicken No. 14,754–Chicken Bustard**
(in Basil-Mustard Sauce)

295

ADD

- 1 small yellow onion, finely chopped
- 2 garlic cloves, chopped
- 2 rounded spoonfuls good-quality prepared pesto sauce
- 15 to 20 fresh basil leaves, chopped or torn

Prepare the chicken and sauce as in the master recipe, #293. Once you have turned the chicken in the pan and it is starting to cook on the second side, scoot the chicken over slightly and make a little room for the onions and garlic. Cook for 6 minutes, occasionally stirring the onions and garlic. Once the chicken is cooked, remove it from the pan, leaving the onions and garlic behind. Proceed with the sauce according to the master recipe.

Add the pesto and chopped basil to the fully prepared sauce and remove from the heat. Serve the sauce over the chicken.

4 SERVINGS

(variations continue on page 260)

296 OR TRY... Chicken No. 14,755—Chicken in Mustard-Tarragon Sauce

Hey, you asked for more! This is a favorite of my mom's, so I had to include it!

SWAP

½ cup heavy cream for the sour cream

ADD

1 more tablespoon EVOO

3 shallots, finely chopped

1 tablespoon all-purpose flour

3 tablespoons fresh tarragon, chopped (from 4 sprigs)

1 pound asparagus, trimmed

Prepare the chicken just as for the master recipe, #293. Once the chicken has been cooked and removed from the pan, add the extra tablespoon of EVOO and the chopped shallots. Cook the shallots for about 2 minutes, stirring occasionally. Add the flour and cook for a minute more. Add the stock and mustard and thicken, then add the cream and tarragon. Bring an inch of water to a boil in a sauce pot. Steam the asparagus just until tender, 3 or 4 minutes.

Slice the chicken and layer it with the asparagus. Serve the sauce over the chicken and asparagus and pass some crusty bread.

4 SERVINGS

297 AND THEN TRY... Chicken No. 14,756—Chicken in "Lighter" Mustard and Lemon Sauce

SWAP

3 tablespoons plain yogurt for the sour cream

ADD

3 tablespoons fresh flat-leaf parsley (a small handful), chopped

1 cup couscous, plain or flavored

PREP CHANGE

Zest the lemon before juicing it

Prepare just as for the master recipe, #293. Once the chicken is cooked, add the chicken stock and mustard to the pan and cook for 5 minutes. Prepare the couscous according to the package instructions. Let stand for 10 minutes, then fluff with a fork. Finish the sauce by whisking in the yogurt, then the lemon zest and parsley. Serve the sauce over the sliced chicken and couscous.

4 SERVINGS

TRY THIS LATER · IT'S A KEEPER

Grilled Steak Sandwich . . . I Mean, Salad—No! Sandwich!

298

☐ TRY THIS LATER

☐ IT'S A KEEPER

I imagine eating this meal on a farm table, outside, in Tuscany—maybe it's early fall. I have a glass of Rosso di Montalcino. Where will you be for your first bite?

½ pound day-old chewy farm-style bread, cubed

5 tablespoons balsamic vinegar (eyeball it)

¼ cup plus 2 tablespoons extra-virgin olive oil (EVOO)

2 tablespoons chopped fresh rosemary leaves (from 2 sprigs)
Coarse black pepper

1½ to 2 pounds skirt steaks

4 small vine-ripe tomatoes, chopped

1 small red onion, chopped

8 ounces fresh or smoked mozzarella, cubed

1 cup loosely packed fresh basil leaves, torn or shredded
Coarse salt

Preheat a grill pan or outdoor grill to high.

Place the bread in a medium mixing bowl and cover with water. Soak the bread for 3 to 5 minutes.

In a shallow dish, combine about 3 tablespoons of the balsamic vinegar with about 2 tablespoons of the EVOO, the rosemary, and a liberal amount of black pepper. Add the steaks to the dish and coat thoroughly, then marinate for 5 to 10 minutes.

After the bread has soaked, working in small batches, remove it in handfuls from the water and wring it out without mashing or tearing it. You do not want wet bread, so wring it carefully, then place in a salad bowl. Add the tomatoes, onions, mozzarella, and basil. Toss a few times and then dress with the remaining 2 tablespoons of Balsamic vinegar, about ¼ cup of the EVOO (3 to 4 times around the bowl), salt, and pepper. Adjust the seasonings and let the salad sit for the flavors to come together.

Season the steak with salt and grill the meat for 3 to 4 minutes on each side. Remove the meat and let it rest for 5 minutes to allow the juices to redistribute.

Slice the meat very thin on a sharp angle against the grain. Divide the bread salad among 4 serving plates and top with a few slices of the balsamic steak.

4 SERVINGS

299
MASTER RECIPE
Chipotle Chicken Rolls with Avocado Dipping Sauce

TRY THIS LATER   IT'S A KEEPER

CHIPOTLE CHICKEN ROLLS

- 1 package (1⅓ pounds) ground chicken breast
- 6 scallions, thinly sliced, then chopped
- 1½ cups grated sharp Cheddar cheese
- 1 garlic clove, finely chopped
- 1 chipotle pepper in adobo sauce, finely chopped, or 3 tablespoons of a chipotle-flavored salsa
  Salt and freshly ground black pepper
- 6 sheets frozen phyllo dough, defrosted
- 4 tablespoons unsalted butter, melted

DIPPING SAUCE

- 1 ripe Hass avocado
  Juice of 3 limes
  A handful of fresh cilantro leaves (2 tablespoons)
- 1 teaspoon coarse salt
- 3 tablespoons extra-virgin olive oil (EVOO) (eyeball it)

  Bibb lettuce, to serve rolls on

Preheat the oven to 400°F.

In a bowl, combine the ground chicken, scallions, Cheddar cheese, garlic, and chipotles and season with salt and pepper. Transfer the mixture to a sealable plastic bag. To turn the sealable plastic bag into a homemade pastry bag, trim 1½ inches off one of the bottom corners of the plastic bag. Push the chicken mixture to the cut corner without pushing it through the hole. Reserve while you prepare the phyllo.

Arrange 1 sheet of phyllo dough with the long side closest to you on your kitchen counter, brush liberally from edge to edge with the melted butter, and season with salt and pepper. Place another sheet of phyllo on top, again brush liberally with butter, and season with salt and pepper. Repeat with the third sheet of phyllo.

Place the trimmed end of the pastry bag ½ inch in from the left side and ½ inch up from the bottom of the phyllo sheet. Squeeze half of the chicken mixture from the bag while moving along in a straight line from left to right. Roll the front edge of the phyllo sheet away from you, encasing the chicken mixture. Continue until you have completed a long roll. Tuck the ends in and then brush the entire outside of the phyllo log with more melted butter. Transfer the first log to a rimmed cookie sheet, putting the seam side down. Repeat this process to make the second log with the remaining half of the chicken mixture. Bake for 15 minutes, or until the logs feel firm to the touch.

While the phyllo-wrapped chicken is in the oven, cut the avocado in half lengthwise, cutting around the pit. Separate the halves and scoop out the pit with a spoon, then use the spoon to scoop the avocado from

TIDBIT

Chipotles in adobo sauce are sold in 7-ounce cans in the international foods aisle.

its skin. Place the avocado in a food processor bowl and combine with the lime juice, cilantro, coarse salt, and about 3 tablespoons of water. Process until the avocado mixture is smooth, then stream the EVOO into the dressing. Taste and adjust the seasonings.

Once the chipotle chicken rolls are cooked, remove from the oven and let them cool just enough to handle. Cut each roll in half, then cut each half into 3 equal pieces. Serve 3 chicken rolls per person on a bed of Bibb lettuce with a small bowl or ramekin of the dipping sauce.

4 SERVINGS

NOW TRY... Turkey and Sage Rolls
with Cranberry Dipping Sauce

300

☐ TRY THIS LATER

☐ IT'S A KEEPER

OMIT FROM THE ROLLS

Chipotle in adobo sauce

SWAP INGREDIENTS FOR THE ROLLS

Ground turkey breast for the ground chicken
Swiss cheese for the Cheddar cheese

ADDITIONAL INGREDIENTS FOR THE ROLLS

1   tablespoon poultry seasoning
1   tablespoon Worcestershire sauce (eyeball it)
4   fresh sage leaves, chopped

OMIT

Avocado dipping sauce

NEW DIPPING SAUCE

$1\frac{1}{2}$ cups mayonnaise
$\frac{1}{2}$ cup whole-berry cranberry sauce, such as
Ocean Spray brand
Juice of 1 lime

Prepare the rolls in the same way as described in the master recipe, #299, adding the additional ingredients to the filling mixture.

Combine all the ingredients for the dipping sauce in a bowl; serve the cranberry dipping sauce alongside the turkey and sage rolls on a bed of Bibb lettuce.

4 SERVINGS

(variations continue on page 264)

301

OR TRY... Lamb and Feta Rolls with
Cucumber-Mint-Yogurt Dipping Sauce

SWAP INGREDIENTS FOR THE ROLLS

Ground lamb for the ground chicken
Crumbled feta for the Cheddar cheese
1 jalapeño, finely chopped, for the chipotle in adobo sauce

OMIT

Avocado dipping sauce

NEW DIPPING SAUCE

1½ cups plain yogurt
½ seedless cucumber, peeled and grated

¼ medium yellow onion, grated
1 garlic clove, finely chopped
10 fresh mint leaves, finely chopped

Prepare the rolls in the same way as described in the master recipe, #299, making the ingredient swaps listed.

Combine the dipping sauce ingredients in a bowl; serve the cucumber-mint-yogurt dipping sauce alongside the lamb and feta rolls on a bed of Bibb lettuce.

4 SERVINGS

- -

302

OR TRY... Wingless Buffalo Chicken Rolls
with Blue Cheese Dip

Serve with celery sticks, of course!

OMIT FROM THE ROLLS

Cheddar cheese
Chipotle in adobo sauce

ADDITIONAL INGREDIENTS FOR THE ROLLS

3 to 4 tablespoons of your favorite kind of hot sauce

OMIT

Avocado dipping sauce

NEW DIPPING SAUCE

1 cup crumbled domestic blue cheese
1½ cups sour cream

ADD

12 fresh celery sticks, for dipping

Prepare the rolls in the same way as described in the master recipe, #299, adding in the hot sauce to the filling mixture.

For the dipping sauce, in a bowl combine the blue cheese and the sour cream. Smash the blue cheese with a fork to break it up, then stir to thoroughly combine with the sour cream. Serve the blue cheese dip alongside the wingless buffalo chicken rolls and some celery sticks.

4 SERVINGS

London Broil with Buttered Potatoes and Caramelized Zucchini and Mushrooms

303

☐ TRY THIS LATER ☐ IT'S A KEEPER

1 tablespoon Worcestershire sauce (eyeball it)

1 tablespoon red wine vinegar (eyeball it)

2 teaspoons hot sauce, such as Tabasco

1½ pounds 1½-inch-thick shoulder steak (London broil)
   Coarse black pepper

2 pounds very small red or white bliss potatoes
   Coarse salt

½ cup fresh flat-leaf parsley leaves (a couple of handfuls), chopped

3 tablespoons fresh dill, chopped

3 tablespoons cold unsalted butter

3 tablespoons extra-virgin olive oil (EVOO) (3 times around the pan)

12 cremini (baby portobello) mushrooms, brushed, cleaned, and cut in half

¼ teaspoon crushed red pepper flakes

3 garlic cloves, chopped

1 large zucchini, cut into quarters lengthwise, then cut into chunks about the same size as the mushrooms

Preheat the broiler.

In a small bowl, combine the Worcestershire, red wine vinegar, and hot sauce. Brush the steak with the mixture and sprinkle liberally with coarse black pepper. Let the steak marinate for 5 to 10 minutes.

Place the potatoes in a sauce pot and cover with cold water. Place the pot over high heat and bring up to a boil, add some salt, and cook until the potatoes are tender, about 10 to 12 minutes. Drain the potatoes, return to the hot pan, and let sit for 1 to 2 minutes to dry. Add half of the parsley, the dill, butter, salt, and pepper.

Preheat a large skillet over medium-high heat with the EVOO. Add the mushrooms and cook, stirring every now and then, for 4 to 5 minutes, or until nice and brown. Add the red pepper flakes, garlic, and zucchini, and season with a little salt; continue to cook until the zucchini are tender and starting to get a little brown.

While the zucchini are browning up with the mushrooms, broil the steak on the top rack for 6 minutes on each side, for medium rare to medium doneness.

Remove the meat from the broiler and let it rest for a few minutes.

Very thinly slice the meat on an angle against the grain. The degree to which you can slice thinly will determine how tender the meat is to cut and chew, so make sure the carving knife is sharp: The thinner the better!

Add the remaining parsley to the mushrooms and zucchini, stir to combine, and transfer to a serving platter. Serve the sliced London broil alongside the buttered potatoes and the caramelized zucchini and mushrooms.

4 SERVINGS

304 MASTER RECIPE
Zucchini and Bow Ties

Serve with tomato salad.

Coarse salt
1 pound bow-tie pasta
¼ cup extra-virgin olive oil (EVOO) (4 times around the pan)
6 garlic cloves, minced
2 medium zucchini, cut into matchsticks
Coarse black pepper
1 cup grated Parmigiano-Reggiano or Romano cheese
1 cup fresh basil leaves, torn or shredded (20 leaves)

Bring a large pot of water to a boil and salt it. Cook the bow ties al dente, with a bite. Heads up: You will need a couple of ladles of starchy cooking water.

Heat a large, deep skillet over medium heat. Add the EVOO and the garlic. Cook for 2 minutes, then add the zucchini. Cook gently for 8 to 10 minutes. Season with salt and pepper and add a couple of ladles of cooking water. Drain the pasta and add to the zucchini. Toss with the cheese and turn off the heat. Toss for 2 minutes, until the liquids are absorbed. Serve in shallow bowls with lots of shredded basil on top.

4 SERVINGS

- -

305 NOW TRY... Springtime Bows with Asparagus, Ham, and Peas

OMIT

4 cloves of garlic

SWAP

1 pound asparagus for the zucchini

ADD

1 shallot, thinly sliced
1 cup frozen peas, defrosted
¼ pound prosciutto, chopped or shredded

Cook the pasta as directed for the master recipe, #304.

Halve each stalk of asparagus lengthwise, then cut into 2-inch pieces. Sauté the shallot with the garlic as above, then add the asparagus and cook for 5 minutes. Add the cooking water, drained pasta, and cheese. Add the peas and prosciutto as you toss. The peas will heat through quickly. Season with salt and pepper and serve in shallow bowls with lots of basil on top.

4 SERVINGS

Incredible French Crunchy Salad

TRY THIS LATER

IT'S A KEEPER

That's what Mom and I called it, this light, delicious midday meal in Saint-Émilion, France. It's a wonderful light supper in warm months and a good lunch in any season. To make this salad into a movable feast, serve with French ham, sausage, or pâté, cheese, and a baguette. Oh, and plenty of Saint-Émilion wine.

Coarse salt
¾ cup long-grain rice
1 green apple, peeled and quartered, cored, and finely diced
½ small red or green bell pepper, cored, seeded, and finely chopped
¼ medium red onion, minced
6 young radishes—not so red—finely chopped
2 tablespoons plus about 2 teaspoons fresh lemon juice (eyeball the amounts)
2 tablespoons white wine vinegar (eyeball it)
1 garlic clove, chopped
1 teaspoon Dijon mustard
Coarse black pepper
¼ cup extra-virgin olive oil (EVOO)
3 slices toasting bread
Softened unsalted butter, to spread on the toast
1 small head of red leaf lettuce, chopped
1 small head of green leaf lettuce, chopped
1 head of frisée, trimmed and separated

Heat 1⅓ cups water in a small pot. When it comes to a boil, salt it and add the rice. Cover and reduce to a simmer and cook the rice for 18 minutes, or until just tender, with a bite remaining. Remove the lid and fluff the rice, then spread it on a rimmed cookie sheet to quick-cool. Heads up: This meal is a great use for cold leftover rice as well.

While the rice cooks, combine the apples, bell peppers, onions, and radishes in a small bowl, adding them to it as you chop. Dress them with about 2 tablespoons of the fresh lemon juice and lightly toss the crunchy mixture with your fingertips.

In a blender, combine the remaining 2 teaspoons of lemon juice, the white wine vinegar, the chopped garlic, mustard, and some salt and pepper. Turn the blender on the "puree" setting and stream in the EVOO through the top. When the dressing emulsifies and is smooth, stop.

Toast the bread lightly in a toaster, and let it pop up. Let the bread stand for 5 minutes, then lightly toast it again. The bread should be dry yet remain quite pale. Lightly butter the bread and cut it into tiny cubes.

Arrange the lettuces on a large platter. Scatter the frisée like lace across the lettuce. Scatter the cool rice across the salad and top with the crunchy apple mixture. Drizzle the dressing in a slow, even stream back and forth all over the salad. Serve the homemade baby croutons at the table to top and toss as you eat.

4 SERVINGS

TRY THIS LATER

IT'S A KEEPER

307 MASTER RECIPE
Triple-Onion Soup with Triple-Cheese Toast

1 tablespoon extra-virgin olive oil (EVOO) (once around the pan)

2 tablespoons unsalted butter

2 softball-size firm yellow onions, sliced

2 shallots, thinly sliced

2 leeks, trimmed, cut into half-moons, then washed and drained

2 tablespoons chopped fresh thyme (from 5 to 6 sprigs)

Salt and white pepper

1 cup white wine (eyeball it)

6 cups beef stock or broth

8 1-inch-thick pieces of crusty bread

1 cup shredded Gruyère cheese

1 cup shredded sharp Cheddar cheese

1 cup shredded smoked Gouda cheese

Heat a medium soup pot over medium to medium-high heat. Add the EVOO, then the butter. Slice and drop the onions, shallots, and leeks into the pot as you work. Add the thyme, salt, and white pepper. Cook for 20 minutes, or until the yellow onions are soft, lightly golden all over, and sweet. Add the wine and cook for 1 minute, then add the stock and bring to a boil. Reduce the heat to low.

Preheat the broiler.

Char the bread under the broiler on each side. Mix the grated cheeses and cover the bread with the cheese. Return to the broiler and melt. Serve shallow bowls of soup with a gooey, cheesy floater on top and a second piece of cheese toast alongside, for the second half of the bowl.

4 SERVINGS

308 NOW TRY... Sausage, Fennel, and Tomato Soup
with Triple-Cheese Toast

TRY THIS LATER

IT'S A KEEPER

OMIT

Leeks

Butter

Thyme

SWAP

1 thinly sliced fennel bulb for 1 of the yellow onions

4 crushed garlic cloves for the shallots

1 28-ounce can crushed tomatoes for 4 cups of the beef stock

Shredded Fontina for the Gruyère

Shredded Provolone for the Cheddar

Shredded Scamorza (smoked, firm mozzarella) for the smoked Gouda

ADD

1 pound bulk sweet Italian sausage

Heat a medium soup pot over medium-high heat. Add the EVOO and brown the sausage. Remove with a slotted spoon. Add the onions, fennel, and garlic and cook for 10 minutes. Add the sausage back, deglaze the pan with the wine, add the tomatoes and 2 cups beef stock, and bring to a boil. Season with salt and pepper to taste and serve with the cheese toasts, made just as for the master recipe, #307, using the cheesy combo listed.

4 SERVINGS

Turkey Tacos

309

TRY THIS LATER □ IT'S A KEEPER □

This one is fun for kids, like me. Serve as is, or accompany with black beans or refried beans and plain or flavored rice, prepared according to the package directions.

1 package super-size taco shells, such as Old El Paso or Ortega brands
2 tablespoons extra-virgin olive oil (EVOO) (twice around the pan)
1 package (1⅓ pounds) ground turkey breast Salt and freshly ground black pepper
2 teaspoons poultry seasoning (⅔ palmful)
3 garlic cloves, chopped
1 medium onion, chopped
¼ cup golden raisins, chopped
2 tablespoons chili powder (a couple of palmfuls)
2 teaspoons cumin (⅔ palmful)
½ cup beer or chicken stock
1 cup tomato sauce
2 cups shredded Pepper Jack cheese (8- to 10-ounce brick)
1 romaine lettuce heart, shredded
2 firm plum tomatoes, diced
½ cup green olives with pimiento
1 cup salsa verde, green chili salsa, or your choice of salsa or taco sauce

Preheat the oven to 325°F. Place 8 large taco shells on a rimmed cookie sheet and bake for 6 to 7 minutes, until crisp but not brown. Remove.

Meanwhile, heat a large nonstick skillet over medium-high heat. Add the EVOO. Add the turkey and break up with a wooden spoon. Season the meat with salt and pepper and poultry seasoning. Add the garlic, onions, and raisins to the meat, then season with the chili powder and cumin. Cook for 5 minutes, then stir in the beer or stock and deglaze the pan. Stir in the tomato sauce and simmer over low heat for 5 minutes.

Fill the shells with a couple of spoonfuls each of meat sauce. Top with the cheese and return to the oven to melt, 3 minutes. Top with the lettuce, tomatoes, olives, and salsa verde, green chili salsa, or your pick of salsa or taco sauce. Serve.

4 SERVINGS, 2 TACOS EACH

TIDBIT

The golden raisins keep the meat moist and balance the spice. You don't even notice them once they are plumped and cooked.

TRY THIS LATER

IT'S A KEEPER

310

MASTER RECIPE
Mexican Pasta with Tomatillo Sauce
and Meatballs

Tomatillos look like green tomatoes, but they're not. They are related to gooseberries and they are sour to taste. This dish is a funky, fun twist on spaghetti and meatballs. It's crazy–crazy good!

Coarse salt
1 pound fettuccine

MEATBALLS

Extra-virgin olive oil (EVOO), for drizzling
1 pound ground pork or chicken
1 egg
½ cup plain bread crumbs
2 tablespoons fresh cilantro, finely chopped
2 tablespoons finely chopped fresh thyme (from 5 to 6 sprigs)
3 scallions, finely chopped
1 teaspoon allspice
A few dashes of hot sauce
Coarse black pepper

SAUCE

2 tablespoons EVOO
4 garlic cloves, crushed
1 large yellow onion, finely chopped
2 jalapeños, fully seeded and very thinly sliced
1 cup Mexican beer or chicken stock
20 tomatillos, peeled and coarsely chopped
2 tablespoons fresh cilantro, finely chopped
Salt and freshly ground black pepper
1 cup grated Manchego cheese

Crusty bread

Preheat the oven to 400°F. Bring a large pot of water to a boil for the pasta. Salt the water and cook the pasta al dente.

While the pasta works, add a generous drizzle of EVOO to a mixing bowl. Place the meat in the bowl. Add the egg, bread crumbs, cilantro, the thyme, scallions, allspice, hot sauce, salt, and pepper, and mix to combine. Form 2-inch meatballs and arrange on a rimmed nonstick cookie sheet. Bake for 15 minutes.

While the meatballs bake, make the sauce. Heat a deep-sided skillet over medium-high heat. Add the 2 tablespoons of EVOO (twice around the pan), the garlic, onions, and jalapeños. Cook for 5 minutes, add the beer or stock, and cook for 1 minute. Add the tomatillos and the cilantro, season with salt and pepper, and cook until tender and saucy, about 10 minutes.

To serve, toss the drained pasta with the sauce and meatballs and the Manchego cheese. Olé! Pass crusty bread for mopping.

4 SERVINGS

NOW TRY... **Mexican Tomatillo Stoup with Chorizo** **311**

☐ TRY THIS LATER   ☐ IT'S A KEEPER

A stoup is thicker than soup and thinner than stew.

OMIT

> Fettuccine
> Ingredients for meatballs
> Crusty bread

ADD

> ¾ pound chorizo, casings removed, diced
> 1¼ to 1½ pounds diced peeled Idaho potatoes (2 large potatoes)
> 1 leek, sliced, washed, and drained
> 1 quart chicken stock or broth
> Coarse black pepper
> 2 cups crushed tortilla chips, any flavor

Sauté the chorizo in a tablespoon of EVOO to start the stoup. Remove with a slotted spoon and cook the potatoes, onions, and leeks in the renderings. Add the garlic and jalapeños and cook for another minute or two. Add the beer or first cup of stock and cook off. Add the tomatillos, cilantro, just a little salt (you'll get a lot from the chorizo), and pepper and cook for 10 minutes. Place the chorizo back in the pot. Add the remaining quart of stock and crank up the heat to a boil, then reduce to low and adjust the seasonings. Serve with the crushed chips and grated Manchego to garnish.

4 SERVINGS

TRY THIS LATER

IT'S A KEEPER

312 MASTER RECIPE
Boo-sotto

This is a risotto my mom and I created for my dog Boo. As she got older, she needed a careful balance of carbs and meat: mostly carbs (that's my girl!). Mom and I would eat as much as Boo. Now that she has gone on, we eat this in her honor.

Serve with a dark green salad.

2 tablespoons extra-virgin olive oil (EVOO) (twice around the pan)
3 crushed garlic cloves (Boo loved garlic!)
1 medium onion, finely chopped (we grated a little onion for Boo; she didn't like pieces of it in her food)
2/3 cup Arborio rice
2/3 cup barley
Salt and freshly ground black pepper
1/2 cup dry white wine
4 cups warm chicken stock (keep over low heat on the stovetop)

1 pound ground veal or turkey (we used 1/3 this amount for Boo, but she wished she had all this meat!)
1 cup grated Parmigiano-Reggiano (a few good handfuls)
A handful of fresh flat-leaf parsley, finely chopped

Preheat a deep, sloped skillet over medium-high heat. Add the EVOO, garlic, and onions. Cook for 2 to 3 minutes, add the rice and barley, season with salt and pepper, then cook for 2 to 3 minutes more. Add the wine and cook away, 1 minute. Add a few ladles of the warm stock, just to cover the rice and barley, then drop the ground meat in small bits. Wash up. Stir frequently and continue to ladle in stock until the meat is cooked, the rice and barley are cooked al dente, and the risotto is very starchy, about 22 minutes total cooking time. Stir in the cheese, adjust the pepper, and serve with the chopped parsley.

4 SERVINGS

TRY THIS LATER

IT'S A KEEPER

313 AND TRY... Scotch and Wild Mushroom Risotto

John, my sweetie, loves my wild mushroom risotto, which I used to make with a little brandy in it. John loves Johnny Walker like a brother, so I make his risotto with Scotch—more than a little, too. (Sadly for him, the alcohol cooks off. However, the smoky flavor left behind is great with the earthy mushrooms. To the wise: The better the Scotch, the deeper the effect.)

OMIT

Meat
Barley

SWAP

3 jiggers (just over ⅓ cup) really good Scotch
for the wine
Beef stock for the chicken stock

ADD

⅓ cup additional Arborio rice
2 ounces dried porcini mushrooms
1 portobello mushroom cap, finely chopped
16 shiitake mushroom caps, finely chopped
2 tablespoons chopped fresh thyme leaves
(from 5 to 6 sprigs)

Steep the dried porcini mushrooms in the warm beef stock to reconstitute.

Sauté the garlic, onions, and portobello and shiitake mushrooms in 2 tablespoons EVOO over medium-high heat until the mushrooms darken, then season with salt and pepper. Add the rice and cook for another minute or two.

Add and cook off the Scotch, then cook the risotto just as for the master recipe, #312. When all is added, the beef stock, remove the tender porcini mushrooms, coarsely chop the porcini mushrooms, and stir into the risotto. Stir in the cheese, thyme, and parsley and serve.

4 SERVINGS

NOW TRY... Lemon and Artichoke Risotto with Shrimp

314

OMIT

Barley

SWAP

1 pound small peeled, deveined shrimp for the ground veal or turkey

ADD

⅓ cup additional Arborio rice (1⅓ cups total)
Zest of 1 large lemon
1 15-ounce can quartered artichoke hearts, drained well and chopped

2 sprigs fresh rosemary, leaves stripped and finely chopped
1 cup frozen green peas

Cook as for the master recipe, #312, adding the shrimp a little later than you would the meat—wait until you add the third dose of liquids to your risotto, about 15 minutes into the cooking process. Stir in the lemon zest, artichokes, and rosemary with the shrimp. Add the peas in the last minute or two.

4 SERVINGS

(variations continue on page 274)

TRY THIS LATER

IT'S A KEEPER

315

THEN TRY... Cream Risotto with White Asparagus and Andouille

OMIT

Barley

SWAP

3 cups vegetable broth for 3 cups of the chicken stock

1½ cups heavy cream, for the rest of the chicken stock

2 andouille sausages (for the veal)

ADD

⅓ cup additional Arborio rice

8 spears white asparagus

3 tablespoons chopped chives

A handful of fresh flat-leaf parsley, finely chopped

Prepare the risotto according to the master recipe, #312, swapping the vegetable broth and 1 cup of the cream for the stock (reserve ½ cup cream).

Peel the asparagus ends and steam the spears for 6 to 7 minutes. Grill the sausages on a hot grill pan or in a large skillet to heat through. Remove the sausages and sear the asparagus on the grill or in the skillet. Slice both the asparagus and andouille into small disks on a slight angle.

Stir the remaining ½ cup heavy cream, the chives, and parsley into the risotto. Serve the risotto with the white asparagus and sausages on top.

4 SERVINGS

- -

316

OR TRY... Spinach and Hazelnut Risotto

TRY THIS LATER

IT'S A KEEPER

OMIT

Meat

SWAP

Vegetable or wild mushroom stock (available on the soup aisle) for the chicken stock

ADD

2 10-ounce boxes frozen chopped spinach, drained and wrung dry in a kitchen towel

Freshly grated or ground nutmeg, to taste

1 cup chopped hazelnuts, toasted

1 cup Gorgonzola crumbles

Sauté the garlic and onions, then add the Arborio and barley as directed in the master recipe, #312, and cook for another minute or two. Add the wine or first cup of stock, then cook until starchy and almost al dente, ladling in the stock as necessary. Add the spinach, separating it as you drop it into the pot, and season with salt, pepper, and nutmeg. Stir in the grated cheese and adjust the seasonings. Serve the risotto in shallow bowls with toasted hazelnuts, Gorgonzola crumbles, and parsley on top.

4 SERVINGS

Zucchini Pizza

317

TRY THIS LATER ☐   IT'S A KEEPER ☐

This is a pizza I discovered on a trip to Rome as I wandered the side streets with my mom. It became such a favorite of mine that, on a return trip I made in the cold late fall, I think I ate hot, half-kilo blocks of it every day for a week. This is my at-home version. I love the feeling of giant slices of this hanging from my mouth. It really brings me back to Roman Holidays.

Extra-virgin olive oil (EVOO), for drizzling
2   pizza dough rolls from a tube, such as Pillsbury brand
Coarse salt and coarse black pepper
2   cups ricotta cheese
8   garlic cloves, minced
4   cups shredded mozzarella cheese
2   medium to large zucchini

Preheat the oven to 400°F. Drizzle EVOO on one large or two small cookie sheets, then roll out the dough. It's already in a rectangular shape; just pat it out a bit. Poke with the tines of a fork, season with salt and pepper, and place in the oven for 5 to 6 minutes.

In a medium bowl, mix the ricotta with the garlic. When you remove the dough, cover it evenly with the ricotta cheese. Top the ricotta with a layer of mozzarella cheese, then return it to the oven on the center rack and cook until golden, 12 to 13 minutes more.

Heat a large nonstick griddle or skillet over medium-high heat. Trim the ends off the zucchini. Cut the zucchini into thin strips lengthwise, no more than $1/4$ inch thick. Trim a sliver off the skin on one side if you need to make the zucchini more stable while you slice it. Fill the dry skillet with a single layer of the zucchini strips and cook for 5 minutes, turning once. Remove to a cutting board and repeat. When all of the zucchini is cooked, pile a few slices at a time into stacks. Cut the cooked zucchini across into thin sticks. Pile the sticks together and season with salt and pepper. Scatter the sticks across the pizzas in the last 2 to 3 minutes of cooking time.

Serve large squares of the pizza hot from the oven. Ah, Roma!

4 SERVINGS, $1/2$ PIZZA EACH

318 MASTER RECIPE
Bacon-Wrapped
Beef Supper Salads

4 slices bacon
4 1-inch-thick beef tenderloin steaks
  Salt and freshly ground black pepper
  Extra-virgin olive oil (EVOO), for drizzling
  the steaks

SALAD

3 tablespoons EVOO, plus some for drizzling
1 small shallot, finely chopped
1 teaspoon Dijon mustard
2 tablespoons balsamic vinegar (eyeball it)
1 romaine lettuce heart, chopped
2 cups chopped arugula (1 large bunch)
4 plum tomatoes, halved and cut into
  half-moons
1 15-ounce can artichoke hearts, drained and
  thinly sliced

16 caper berries, for garnish
16 large good-quality olives, for garnish
  Crusty bread

Heat a large nonstick skillet over medium-high heat.

Line up the bacon on a meat-safe cutting board and center a steak across each slice of bacon. Season the meat with salt and pepper, then wrap the steaks in the bacon. Do not overlap the bacon, just let it travel around the meat like a stripe on a barber pole. Add a generous drizzle of EVOO to the pan and add the steaks. Cook the bacon-wrapped steaks for 4 minutes on each side, or until the bacon is crisp and the meat feels like it is just beginning to firm up. Let the meat rest for 5 minutes.

While the meat is working, in a salad bowl, combine the shallots with the mustard and vinegar and let sit for 10 minutes. Whisk in the 3 tablespoons of EVOO in a slow stream. Add the lettuce, arugula, tomatoes, and artichokes and toss to combine. Season the salad with salt and pepper and divide among 4 plates.

Slice the meat on an angle into 4 slices per steak. Arrange the meat on the salad and serve with the caper berries, olives, and bread.

4 SERVINGS

NOW TRY... Pancetta-Wrapped Shrimp Supper Salad

My mom created the pancetta-wrapped shrimp years ago. I love her SOOOOO much!

SWAP

- 12 jumbo (6- to 8-count) shrimp, peeled and deveined, for the steaks
- 12 slices pancetta for the bacon
  Juice of 1 lemon for the balsamic vinegar

ADD

- 12 fresh sage leaves

Place a piece of sage with each shrimp, nesting it in the space where the shrimp has been deveined, along the back. Line up the 12 slices of pancetta on a cutting board, unrolling them a bit as you set them out. Place

SUPER SUPPER SALAD

319

a shrimp on each piece of pancetta and season the shrimp with salt and pepper. Wrap the pancetta around each shrimp, using the barber-pole technique, being careful not to overlap. Add a generous drizzle of EVOO to a hot nonstick skillet over medium-high heat. Cook the shrimp for 3 minutes on each side, or until the pancetta is crisp and the shrimp are pink and firm.

Prepare the salad as directed in the master recipe, #318, swapping the lemon juice for the vinegar. Serve the shrimp on the salad with the caper berries, olives, and bread alongside.

4 SERVINGS

☐ TRY THIS LATER   ☐ IT'S A KEEPER

Lamb and Scallion Burgers with Fried Asparagus 320

The fried asparagus is a perfect use for the thick stalks that you find from time to time in the market.

- 1 package (1½ pounds) ground lamb
- 2 large garlic cloves, finely chopped
- 4 scallions, chopped
  Zest of 1 lemon
- 2 tablespoons chopped fresh thyme (from 4 sprigs)
  Salt and freshly ground black pepper

- 3 tablespoons extra-virgin olive oil (EVOO) (3 times around the pan), plus some for drizzling
- 8 thick asparagus spears, minimum ½ inch in diameter
  All-purpose flour, for dredging
  Leaf lettuce, green or red, for garnish
- ½ cup Dijon mustard
- 4 large slices sourdough or farmhouse bread, cut in half to fit the burgers

(continued on the next page)

☐ TRY THIS LATER   ☐ IT'S A KEEPER

Heat a grill pan or large nonstick skillet over medium-high heat. In a large bowl, mix the meat with the garlic, scallions, lemon zest, thyme, salt, pepper, and a drizzle of EVOO. Form 4 1-inch-thick patties and cook for 3 to 4 minutes on each side for medium, 5 minutes for medium well.

Heat a second skillet over medium-high heat. Trim the tough ends of the asparagus. Cut the stalks in half across, then thinly slice them lengthwise. Dredge the thinly sliced asparagus in the flour. Add the 3 tablespoons of EVOO to the skillet and fry the asparagus until deeply golden, a couple of minutes on each side. Drain on paper towels. Season the fried asparagus with salt.

Toast the bread slices. Serve the burgers topped with crisp lettuce and Dijon mustard on toast, with fried asparagus alongside.

4 SERVINGS

TRY THIS LATER

IT'S A KEEPER

321 Sweet Sea Scallops in a Caper-Raisin Sauce

Serve with a green salad.

- 3 tablespoons extra-virgin olive oil (EVOO)
- 2 shallots, chopped
  Salt and freshly ground black pepper
- ¼ cup fresh flat-leaf parsley leaves (a generous handful), chopped
- 3 tablespoons capers, drained
- ¾ cup dry white wine (eyeball it)
- ½ cup golden raisins
- 16 sea scallops, drained and trimmed
  Juice of 1 lemon
  2 tablespoons unsalted butter
  Crusty bread, to pass at the table

Heat a large nonstick skillet over medium-high heat. Add 2 tablespoons of the EVOO (twice around the pan) and the chopped shallots. Cook the shallots for a minute or so, season with salt and pepper, and combine with the parsley and capers. Add the wine and golden raisins. Simmer for 3 minutes, then transfer to a bowl and reserve.

Wipe out the pan and return to the heat, raising the heat to high. Season the scallops with salt and pepper. Add the remaining tablespoon of EVOO to the very hot pan and immediately place the scallops in the pan. Sear the scallops in a single layer, allowing them to caramelize, 2 minutes on each side. Add the reserved caper-raisin mixture along with the lemon juice. Turn the heat back a bit and cook for 1 to 2 minutes. Remove the scallops from the pan and arrange on a serving platter. Remove the pan from the stove, add the butter, and shake the skillet until the butter has completely melted. Pour the sauce over the scallops and serve with the bread.

4 SERVINGS

Veal, Chicken, or Fish Francese with Lemon and Wine

This meal is a combo of two favorite preparations: francese and piccata. Francese are egg-battered cutlets or fillets, and piccata are simply flour-dredged or plain cutlets or fillets sautéed with lemon and wine. I was never good at making decisions, especially regarding dinner, so I made up this two-for-one dinner. Serve with wilted fresh spinach or green salad.

- 2 tablespoons extra-virgin olive oil (EVOO) (twice around the pan)
- 5 tablespoons unsalted butter
- 1½ pounds your choice: very thin veal or chicken cutlets or flounder fillets
   Salt and freshly ground black pepper
   All-purpose flour, for dredging
- 4 eggs, beaten until frothy
- 2 pinches of freshly grated or ground nutmeg
- 1 lemon
- ½ cup dry white wine (a couple of glugs)
- 2 tablespoons capers, coarsely chopped
- 3 tablespoons (a small handful) fresh flat-leaf parsley leaves, chopped
   Crusty bread

Place a platter in a low oven to warm. Heat a **very large** nonstick skillet over medium heat. Add 1 tablespoon of the EVOO and 2 tablespoons of the butter to the skillet.

Season the meat or fish with salt and pepper. Coat half the meat at a time in flour, then in the eggs, adding each piece directly to the hot fat in the pan. Sauté the cutlets or fillets for 2 to 3 minutes on each side, until golden and puffy. Transfer the cooked meat or fish to the warm platter and repeat with the remaining cutlets or fillets, using the remaining tablespoon of EVOO and 2 more tablespoons of the butter.

Once all of the meat or fish has been cooked, add the nutmeg, the juice of half of the lemon, and the white wine to the pan. Scrape up the pan drippings with a whisk. Slice the remaining half lemon into thin disks and add to the sauce. Stir the capers and parsley and the remaining tablespoon of butter into the sauce. Turn off the heat. Shake the pan to combine the sauce. Arrange the lemon slices over the platter, then spoon the sauce evenly over the cutlets or fillets. Serve immediately with crusty bread and greens or spinach.

4 SERVINGS

323 Mushroom-Veggie Sloppy Sandwiches

4 portobello mushrooms, stems removed
Coarse salt and freshly ground black pepper
2 limes
4 tablespoons vegetable oil
5 garlic cloves, chopped
3 tablespoons chili powder
1 medium yellow onion, chopped
1 large red bell pepper, cored, seeded, and chopped
1 large jalapeño pepper, seeded and chopped
1 small zucchini or yellow squash, cut in half lengthwise, then sliced into half-moons
1 tablespoon ground cumin (a palmful)
1 tablespoon hot pepper sauce (eyeball it)
1 cup pale beer or vegetable stock or broth
1 15-ounce can crushed tomatoes
1 14-ounce can dark red kidney beans, rinsed and drained
1 cup spicy vegetarian refried beans
¼ cup fresh cilantro leaves (a generous handful), chopped
4 sandwich-size English muffins
1 ripe avocado
2 cups (8 to 10 ounces) shredded spicy Monterey Jack or smoked Cheddar cheese

Preheat the oven to 450°F.

Place the portobello mushrooms on a rimmed cookie sheet. Season the mushrooms with salt, pepper, the juice of 1 lime, about 2 tablespoons of the vegetable oil, half the chopped garlic, and 1 tablespoon of the chili powder, tossing them around in the seasonings to coat thoroughly. Arrange the mushrooms gill side up.

Put them in the oven and roast for 12 minutes, or until cooked through. Remove from the oven and cover with foil to keep warm.

Preheat a large soup pot over medium-high heat and add the remaining 2 tablespoons of vegetable oil. Add the onions, bell peppers, jalapeños, zucchini or yellow squash, and the remaining garlic. Season the veggies with the cumin, the remaining 2 tablespoons of chili powder, the hot pepper sauce, and 1 teaspoon of salt and sauté for 5 to 6 minutes, to soften and lightly brown the vegetables. Deglaze the pan with the beer or stock. Add the tomatoes and red kidney beans to the vegetable chili and stir to combine. Thicken the chili by stirring in the refried beans. Simmer over low heat for about 10 minutes longer. Finish with the cilantro.

While the sloppy chili is simmering, toast the English muffins.

Prepare the avocado: Cut all around the circumference of the ripe avocado, lengthwise and down to the pit. Twist and separate the halved fruit. Remove the pit with a spoon, then scoop the flesh out in one piece from both halves and slice the flesh lengthwise. Squeeze the juice of the second lime over the avocado to season it and prevent it from discoloring. Place 1 roasted mushroom on the bottom half of each muffin. Place a large helping of chili on top of the mushroom, sprinkle with the shredded cheese, and arrange some of the slices of avocado on top of that. Finish with the English muffin tops. Live on the edge and eat it with your hands. Have napkins handy.

4 SERVINGS

Pork Loin Chops with Golden Delicious Apples
and Onions on Polenta with Honey

324

☐ TRY THIS LATER   ☐ IT'S A KEEPER

2 tablespoons extra-virgin olive oil (EVOO)
(twice around the pan)

8 thin-cut boneless pork loin chops
Salt and freshly ground black pepper

3 cups chicken stock or broth

4 tablespoons unsalted butter

1 medium yellow onion, thinly sliced

2 crisp Golden Delicious apples, quartered,
cored, and thinly sliced
Juice of ¼ lemon

2 shots brandy

2 tablespoons chopped fresh thyme
(from 4 sprigs)

1 cup quick-cooking (sometimes called
"instant") polenta (found in Italian foods or
specialty foods aisle)

¼ cup honey (eyeball it)

Place a platter in the oven on the lowest setting to keep warm. Preheat a large nonstick skillet over medium-high heat. Add the EVOO, then the chops. Season the chops with salt and pepper and cook for 3 to 4 minutes on each side, until golden and firm but not hard. Remove the platter from the oven. Place the meat on the warm platter and cover loosely with foil.

Place the chicken stock in a medium pot and bring to a boil.

Return the pork chop skillet to the stovetop and reduce the heat to medium. Melt 2 tablespoons of the butter, then add the onions and cook for 2 minutes. Add the apple slices and lemon juice and cook for 5 minutes more, or until the onions are soft and the apples are tender but not falling apart. Add the brandy to the pan and cook it off, 1 minute. Toss the apples and onions with the thyme, salt, and pepper and turn off the heat.

Stir the polenta into the stock and let it mass while stirring constantly, 2 minutes. Stir in the 2 remaining tablespoons of butter and the honey, then salt to taste.

Pile some polenta on each dinner plate and top with 2 chops and one fourth of the apples and onions.

4 SERVINGS

325 Creamy Chicken and Asparagus on Toast

4 tablespoons extra-virgin olive oil (EVOO)

1 large yellow onion, thinly sliced

1 tablespoon fresh thyme leaves, chopped (from 4 sprigs)

3 garlic cloves, chopped
Salt and freshly ground black pepper

6 tablespoons softened unsalted butter

4 6-ounce boneless, skinless chicken breast halves

1 French baguette

1 cup fresh flat-leaf parsley leaves (a few really big handfuls), chopped

2 tablespoons all-purpose flour

½ cup dry white wine (a couple of glugs)

1 cup chicken stock or broth

¼ cup half-and-half or cream

1 bunch of thin "pencil" asparagus, ends trimmed off, then cut into 1-inch lengths

1 cup grated Gruyère cheese

2 tablespoons plain bread crumbs

4 thin slices Black Forest ham or other good-quality ham, chopped

Preheat the oven to 400°F.

Preheat a large skillet over medium-high heat with 2 tablespoons of the EVOO (twice around the pan). Add the onions, thyme, and garlic, season with salt and pepper, and cook, stirring frequently, until nice and brown, about 5 to 8 minutes. Remove the onions from the pan, add the remaining 2 tablespoons of EVOO and 1 tablespoon of the butter, add the chicken, season with salt and pepper, and cook until lightly browned, about 3 to 4 minutes on each side.

While the chicken is cooking, split the French bread in half lengthwise, just shy of cutting it completely through. Dig out some of the insides of the bread and discard. Push the bread open and flatten out to keep it open. In a small bowl, combine the remaining 5 tablespoons of butter, a little salt and pepper, and 3 tablespoons of the parsley, and evenly spread the butter mixture on the inside of the bread. Cut the buttered loaf into 4 portions, arrange on a cookie sheet, and transfer to the oven and bake until golden brown, about 5 minutes. Remove the toasted bread from the oven, set aside on the cookie sheet, and switch the broiler on.

Add the browned onions back to the skillet with the chicken, dust with the flour, and continue to cook for 1 minute. Whisk in the white wine, stock, and half-and-half and bring up to a simmer. Add the asparagus and continue to cook for 2 to 3 minutes, or until the asparagus are tender and the sauce is thick. In a small bowl, combine the grated Gruyère with the bread crumbs; toss to coat the cheese evenly with the bread crumbs. Stir the remaining chopped parsley and the chopped ham into the chicken and sauce. Divide the creamy chicken into 4 portions in the pan, then transfer each portion to top the toasted bread. Sprinkle a little of the cheese on top of the chicken, then transfer the cookie sheet to the broiler to melt and brown the cheese.

4 SERVINGS

Simple and Delicious Chicken with Potatoes and Asparagus
326

TRY THIS LATER ☐

IT'S A KEEPER ☐

French and fantastique, this will become a real favorite.

3 tablespoons extra-virgin olive oil (EVOO)
4 6- to 8-ounce boneless, skinless chicken breast halves
1 tablespoon fresh thyme leaves, chopped (from 4 sprigs)
  Salt and freshly ground black pepper
2 tablespoons unsalted butter
6 medium red bliss potatoes, cut in half and then thinly sliced
1 medium yellow onion, thinly sliced
½ cup dry white wine (a couple of glugs)
1 heaping tablespoon Dijon mustard
1½ cups chicken stock or broth (eyeball it)
1 pound thin asparagus, trimmed and cut into 2-inch pieces
¼ cup fresh flat-leaf parsley leaves (a generous handful), chopped

Preheat a large nonstick skillet over medium-high heat with 2 tablespoons of the EVOO (twice around the pan). Season the chicken liberally with half of the thyme and salt and pepper, then add to the hot skillet. Cook the chicken for 5 to 6 minutes on each side until cooked through. Remove the chicken to a plate and cover it with foil to keep it warm.

Return the skillet to the burner over medium-high heat; add the remaining tablespoon of EVOO and the 2 tablespoons of butter. Add the sliced potatoes, the remaining half of the thyme, salt, and pepper and cook until lightly browned, about 5 minutes. Add the sliced onions and continue to cook for 3 minutes, stirring occasionally.

Add the wine, mustard, and chicken stock and bring up to a bubble, then add the asparagus and continue to cook for 4 to 5 minutes, until the asparagus and potatoes are both tender. Add the parsley and stir to combine. Serve the chicken breasts whole or sliced, on top of the potatoes and asparagus.

4 SERVINGS

327 MASTER RECIPE
Mushroom Bisque

1 tablespoon extra-virgin olive oil (EVOO) (once around the pan)

2 tablespoons unsalted butter, plus more for buttering the bread

1 pound cremini (baby portobello) mushrooms, brushed clean and chopped

1 tablespoon fresh thyme leaves, chopped (from 4 sprigs)

1 large onion, chopped

3 garlic cloves, chopped
Salt and freshly ground black pepper

¼ cup cognac

3 cups chicken stock or broth

½ cup heavy cream
A few dashes of hot sauce, such as Tabasco

3 slices toasting bread

¼ cup fresh flat-leaf parsley leaves, chopped, or 3 tablespoons chopped fresh chives

Preheat a large soup pot over high heat with the EVOO and the butter. Add the mushrooms and thyme and cook for 6 to 7 minutes. Add the onions, garlic, salt, and pepper and continue to cook for 5 more minutes. Add the cognac, stir for 1 minute, then add ½ cup of the chicken stock and cook for 1 minute more.

Transfer the mushrooms and the liquid to a blender or food processor and puree until really smooth. Return the puree to the soup pot and add the remaining 2½ cups of stock and the cream. Add a few dashes of hot sauce and bring up to a simmer, then cook for 5 more minutes.

Toast the bread dark and extra crisp. Butter the toast and cut it into very small cubes. Ladle the soup into 4 bowls and top with croutons and parsley or chives.

SERVES 4

328 NOW TRY... Pasta with Mushroom Cream Sauce

OMIT

2 of the 3 cups of chicken stock (use 1 cup stock, total)
Bread

ADD

1 pound linguine or fettuccine
Coarse salt

¾ cup grated Parmigiano-Reggiano (a few large handfuls), plus some to pass at the table

Bring a large pot of water to a boil. Add the pasta and salt and cook all dente. Follow the directions for the master recipe, #327, to the point where the mushroom puree is transferred back to the soup pot. At this stage, add the cream, ½ cup more chicken stock, and the hot sauce. Bring up to a bubble, add the cooked pasta, and turn the heat off. Toss to coat; add the parsley and the Parmigiano. Serve immediately.

4 SERVINGS

Ham and Spinach Hash with Fried Eggs

329

☐ TRY THIS LATER ☐ IT'S A KEEPER

This is a B, L, or D: Breakfast, Lunch, or Dinner recipe.

- 2 tablespoons extra-virgin olive oil (EVOO) (twice around the pan)
- 4 tablespoons unsalted butter
- 8 small red potatoes
  Salt and freshly ground black pepper
- 1 tablespoon fresh thyme leaves, chopped (from 4 sprigs)
- ¼ teaspoon crushed red pepper flakes
- 1 medium red onion, chopped
- 1 large ham steak, finely chopped
- 4 extra-large eggs
- 2 cups baby spinach leaves, chopped
- 10 fresh basil leaves, chopped or torn
- ½ cup grated Parmigiano-Reggiano (a couple of generous handfuls)
- 2 plum tomatoes, seeded and chopped

Preheat a large nonstick skillet over medium-high heat with the EVOO and 2 tablespoons of the butter. While the pan is getting hot and the butter is melting, cut the potatoes in half and then thinly slice them. Add them to the hot skillet and season with salt, pepper, the thyme, and the red pepper flakes. Cook, stirring every now and then, for about 10 minutes, or until the potatoes have browned and are tender. Add the onions and ham and continue to cook for 3 to 4 minutes.

Preheat another skillet over medium-high heat with the remaining 2 tablespoons of butter. Once the butter has melted and the bubbles have subsided, crack the eggs into the pan, season with salt and pepper, and fry to the desired doneness.

While the eggs are frying, finish off the hash by adding the spinach and basil to the potatoes. Toss to wilt the spinach. Sprinkle the hash with the cheese and remove from the heat. Transfer the ham and spinach hash to plates. Top each portion with some tomatoes and a single fried egg.

4 SERVINGS

330 French Onion Sliced Steak Croissant Sandwich

You won't find this at the drive-thru! Serve with a mixed green or spinach salad.

- 2 **garlic cloves**, finely chopped
- 2 tablespoons **grill seasoning**, such as McCormick's Montreal Steak Seasoning (2 palmfuls)
- 1 teaspoon **hot sauce**, such as Tabasco (eyeball it)
- 2 tablespoons **Worcestershire sauce** (eyeball it)
- 2 tablespoons **red wine vinegar**
- 5 tablespoons **extra-virgin olive oil** (EVOO)
- 2 pounds **flank steak**
- 2 large **yellow onions**, thinly sliced
- 1 tablespoon fresh **thyme** leaves, chopped (from 4 sprigs)
  Salt and freshly ground black pepper
- 1 cup **chicken stock** or broth
- 4 large **croissants**
- 4 slices **Gruyère** or Emmentaler cheese

Heat a grill pan or outdoor grill to high heat. Preheat the broiler.

In a small bowl, mix the garlic, grill seasoning, hot sauce, Worcestershire sauce, and vinegar. Whisk in about 3 tablespoons of the EVOO. Place the flank steak in a shallow dish and pour the marinade over. Toss to coat thoroughly and marinate for 5 to 10 minutes.

While the steak is marinating, heat a large skillet over medium-high heat with the remaining 2 tablespoons of EVOO (twice around the pan). Add the onions, thyme, salt, and pepper, and cook, stirring frequently, for 7 to 8 minutes, until the onions are deep golden brown. Add the chicken stock and continue to cook for 2 to 3 more minutes, until the chicken stock has almost completely cooked away but the onions are still a little wet with the stock. Remove from the heat and reserve.

Remove the flank steak from the marinade and pat dry.

Grill the flank steak for 6 to 7 minutes on each side. Remove the steak from the grill to a cutting board to rest for about 5 minutes, covered loosely with foil. Thinly slice the flank steak on an angle, against the grain.

Split the croissants in half and arrange on a cookie sheet, cut sides up. Pile some of the onions on the bottoms of each croissant. Arrange a pile of the sliced steak on top of the onions and then follow that with some more onions. Place slices of Gruyère or Emmentaler cheese on top and transfer both the croissant bottoms and tops to the broiler. Melt the cheese and toast the cut sides of the tops, 1 to 2 minutes. Place the croissant tops on the melted cheese. Serve immediately.

4 SERVINGS

Rosemary Lemon–Pepper Pork Tenderloin with Creamy Lemon-Parmigiano Dressed Greens and Garlic Croutons

331

TRY THIS LATER

IT'S A KEEPER

2¼ pounds pork tenderloins (1 package with 2 tenderloins)
Zest and juice of 2 lemons

½ tablespoon coarsely ground black pepper, plus some for seasoning

4 garlic cloves, chopped

2 sprigs fresh rosemary, leaves stripped and finely chopped

7 tablespoons extra-virgin olive oil (EVOO)
Coarse salt

3 thick slices country-style bread, cut into 1-inch cubes

3 heaping tablespoons mayonnaise

½ cup grated Parmigiano-Reggiano (a few handfuls)

2 large romaine lettuce hearts, chopped, or 8 to 10 cups mixed greens

Preheat the oven to 500°F.

Trim the silver skin or connective tissue off the tenderloins with a very sharp thin knife.

Place the tenderloins on a rimmed nonstick cookie sheet. In a bowl, mix together all of the lemon zest, the juice of 1 lemon, the coarse ground black pepper, 3 cloves of the chopped garlic, the rosemary, 2 table-spoons of the EVOO, and some salt. Thoroughly coat the tenderloins in the rosemary–lemon–pepper mixture, rubbing it into the meat. Roast in the hot oven for about 20 to 22 minutes. Once roasted, remove from the oven to a cutting board to rest for a few minutes, loosely tented with aluminum foil.

To make the croutons, preheat a medium skillet over medium-high heat with 2 tablespoons of the EVOO and add the cubed bread; toss to coat in the oil. Add the remaining 1 clove of chopped garlic, salt, and pepper and toast the bread cubes, stirring frequently, until golden brown, about 4 to 5 minutes. Remove from the heat and reserve.

While the croutons are toasting, in a bowl, combine the mayo and the juice of the remaining lemon. Whisk in 3 tablespoons of EVOO, season with pepper, and stir in the grated cheese.

Once the pork is out of the oven and resting, put the salad together. In a salad bowl, combine the home-made garlic croutons with the greens. Pour the dressing over the salad and toss to coat. Thinly slice the rested pork tenderloin and serve alongside the salad.

4 SERVINGS

332 Bacon-Wrapped Meatloaf Patties with Pan Gravy
and Sour Cream–Tomato Smashed Potatoes

Serve with steamed broccoli or asparagus.

- 2 pounds small red-skinned potatoes, quartered
- 1⅓ pounds ground sirloin (90-percent lean ground beef)
- ¼ cup plain bread crumbs (a generous handful)
- ½ cup milk, plus a splash
- 1 egg
- 2 teaspoons grill seasoning, such as McCormick's Montreal Steak Seasoning, or coarse salt and black pepper combined
- ½ teaspoon ground allspice
- 1 rounded tablespoon tomato paste
- 1 medium onion, finely chopped (reserve one fourth)
- 8 slices bacon
- 2 tablespoons extra-virgin olive oil (EVOO) (twice around the pan)
- 3 tablespoons unsalted butter
- 2 rounded tablespoons sour cream
  Salt and freshly ground black pepper
- 2 plum tomatoes, seeded and chopped
- 2 tablespoons all-purpose flour
- 1 to 1½ cups chicken stock or broth
- 1 rounded teaspoon spicy brown mustard
- 1 tablespoon Worcestershire sauce (eyeball it)
- ¼ cup fresh flat-leaf parsley (a generous handful), chopped

Cover the potatoes in water in a medium saucepan. Bring the water to a boil and cook the potatoes for 10 minutes, or until fork tender.

Place the meat in a large mixing bowl and create a well in the center of the meat. Fill the well with the bread crumbs and dampen them with a splash of milk. Add the egg, grill seasoning, allspice, tomato paste, and three quarters of the onions to the bowl. Combine the mixture and form into 4 large ¾-inch-thick oval patties. Arrange 2 slices of bacon in an X on a cutting board; repeat with the other 6 slices of bacon so that you have a total of 4 X's. Place a meatloaf patty on the center of each X. Fold the bacon around each patty. Preheat a large nonstick skillet over medium-high heat with the EVOO. Transfer the bacon-wrapped patties, bacon seam side down, to the hot skillet. Fry the meatloaf patties for 7 minutes on each side under a loose aluminum-foil tent. The tent will reflect heat and allow steam to escape the pan.

Check on the potatoes. When they are tender, turn the heat off; drain the potatoes and return them to the hot pan and warm stovetop to dry them out. Add 2 tablespoons of the butter, the sour cream, and the ½ cup of milk to the potatoes and smash to the desired consistency. Season the potatoes with salt and pepper, then fold in the chopped plum tomatoes. Cover the potatoes to keep warm until you are ready to serve.

Remove the meatloaf patties to a platter and return the pan to the heat. Reduce the heat to medium and add the remaining tablespoon of butter and the remaining onions to the skillet. Cook the onions for 2 minutes and sprinkle the pan with the flour. Cook the flour for 1 minute, then whisk in 1 cup of the chicken stock. Bring the broth to a bubble. If the gravy is too thick, thin with additional stock. Stir in the mustard, Worcestershire sauce, and parsley and taste to see if the sauce needs salt and pepper.

Drizzle the bacon-wrapped meatloaf patties with the gravy. Pile smashed potatoes alongside and make a well in the center for extra sour cream or gravy.

4 SERVINGS

Sweet and Spicy Pineapple Pork

333

TRY THIS LATER

IT'S A KEEPER

Serve with white or flavored rice, cooked according to the package directions, or with sweet rolls.

- 3 tablespoons extra-virgin olive oil (EVOO)
- 4 1½-inch-thick boneless center-cut pork chops
  Salt and freshly ground black pepper
- 1 large red onion, chopped
- 2 garlic cloves, chopped
- 1 red bell pepper, cored, seeded, and chopped
- 1 jalapeño pepper, seeds removed, finely chopped
- 1 8-ounce can pineapple chunks in juice
- ½ cup chicken stock or broth
- ¼ cup fresh flat-leaf parsley leaves (a generous handful)

Preheat the oven to 375°F.

Heat a large skillet over medium-high to high heat with 2 tablespoons of the EVOO (twice around the pan). Season the chops with salt and pepper. Place the chops in the skillet and sear for about 2 minutes on each side to caramelize. Transfer the chops to a rimmed cookie sheet and place in the oven to finish off, 8 to 10 minutes, until the meat is firm to the touch, but not tough. Remove from the oven and let the chops rest, covered with a piece of aluminum foil, for a few minutes.

While the chops are in the oven, return the skillet to medium-high heat and add the remaining tablespoon of EVOO. Add the onions, garlic, bell peppers, jalapeños, salt, and pepper and cook for 3 to 4 minutes or until the veggies start to wilt. Add the chunked pineapple and its juice and the chicken stock. Continue to cook the sauce for 3 to 4 minutes. Add the parsley and stir to combine, then pour the sweet and spicy pineapple sauce over the pork chops.

4 SERVINGS

334 Chili-Spiced Grilled Halibut with Grilled-Corn Saucy Salsa

4 ears of corn, shucked

5 tablespoons vegetable oil, plus some for drizzling
Salt and freshly ground black pepper

1 large red onion, chopped

3 garlic cloves, chopped

1 jalapeño, seeded and chopped

1 red bell pepper, cored, seeded, and chopped

1 tablespoon dark brown sugar

1½ cups vegetable or chicken stock or broth

1 tablespoon chili powder (a palmful)

4 6-ounce 1-inch-thick halibut fillets (1½ pounds)

¼ cup fresh cilantro leaves (a generous handful), chopped
Juice of 2 limes

Preheat a grill pan or outside grill to high.

Drizzle the shucked corncobs with a little of the vegetable oil and season with salt and pepper. Place the shucked corn on the grill. Turn the corn and char on all sides, about 4 to 5 minutes. Remove from the grill and let cool enough so that you can handle them.

While the corn is grilling, preheat a medium skillet over medium-high heat with 2 tablespoons of the vegetable oil (twice around the pan). Add the onions, garlic, jalapeños, bell peppers, and brown sugar, and season with salt and pepper. Cook, stirring frequently, for about 3 minutes. Add the vegetable or chicken stock and continue to cook for about 4 minutes.

For the halibut, in a shallow dish combine the remaining 3 tablespoons of vegetable oil with the chili powder and a little salt. Add the fish and coat thoroughly. Place the seasoned halibut on the grill and cook for 4 to 5 minutes on each side.

With a knife, cut the charred corn kernels from the cobs. Add the corn kernels to the skillet with the onion mixture, stir, and continue to cook for about 2 to 3 more minutes, or until the corn is cooked through. Add the cilantro and lime juice and stir to combine. Taste and adjust the seasonings with salt and pepper.

Serve the grilled halibut with some of the grilled-corn saucy salsa over the top.

4 SERVINGS

Chicken Topped with Caponata and Mozzarella **335**

TRY THIS LATER ☐   IT'S A KEEPER ☐

Caponata is an eggplant dish normally served as a relish or appetizer, but I am so fond of it that I keep reinventing ways to add it to each cookbook I write. I've topped polenta with it, tossed it with pasta, packed it into sub sandwiches, and now, here we go again . . .

4 tablespoons extra-virgin olive oil (EVOO)
4 garlic cloves, chopped
½ teaspoon crushed red pepper flakes
1 cubanelle pepper (long, light green Italian), seeded and diced
1 small sweet onion, chopped
1 celery rib, chopped
¼ cup large green olives, pitted and chopped
¼ cup black kalamata olives, pitted and chopped
2 tablespoons capers, drained
1 2-ounce box (¼ cup) golden raisins
   Coarse salt
3 baby eggplant or 1 small eggplant (about ½ pound firm eggplant), diced
1 8-ounce can tomato sauce
   A handful of fresh flat-leaf parsley, chopped
4 6-ounce boneless, skinless chicken breast halves
   Freshly ground black pepper
2 to 3 cups shredded mozzarella cheese (it depends on how cheesy you like it)
   Crusty bread, to pass at the table

Place the cutting board near the stovetop. Preheat a deep skillet over medium heat. Add 2 tablespoons of the EVOO (twice around the pan) along with the garlic and red pepper flakes. As you chop the vegetables (cubanelle, onions, and celery), add them to the pot. Once the vegetables are in there, increase the heat a bit.

Stir in the olives, capers, and raisins. Salt the diced eggplant and stir into the pot. Add the tomato sauce to the pot and stir the caponata well to combine. Cover the pot and cook the caponata for 15 to 20 minutes, until the vegetables are tender. Stir in the parsley and remove the pan from the heat.

Preheat the broiler.

While the caponata is cooking, preheat a large nonstick skillet over medium-high heat with the remaining 2 tablespoons of EVOO. Season the chicken breasts with salt and pepper. Add the chicken to the hot skillet and cook on each side for 5 to 6 minutes, until cooked through. Cut the breasts into large chunks and arrange in a heat-safe baking dish. Top the chicken with the caponata, then scatter the mozzarella over the top. Transfer to the broiler to melt and lightly brown the cheese, 3 to 4 minutes. Serve with lots of crusty bread.

4 SERVINGS

Sweet Lemon Salmon with Mini Carrots and Dill

TRY THIS LATER

IT'S A KEEPER

3 tablespoons light brown sugar
  Zest and juice of 1 lemon
2 tablespoons vegetable oil (twice around the pan)
4 6-ounce salmon fillets
  Salt and freshly ground black pepper
1 18-ounce bag of "baby" carrots (really, these are big carrots cut by machine into baby carrots), the larger babies cut in half on a long diagonal
2 tablespoons unsalted butter
¼ cup fresh dill (a generous handful), chopped

Preheat the oven to 400°F.

For the mini carrots with dill, fill a medium skillet with 1½ inches of water and bring up to a simmer.

For the sweet lemon salmon, in a small sauce pot, combine the brown sugar, 2 tablespoons water, and the lemon juice. Place over medium heat and bring up to a simmer while stirring to dissolve the sugar. Once at a simmer, cook for 1 minute, then reserve in a warm place.

To cook the salmon, preheat an ovenproof nonstick skillet over medium-high heat with the vegetable oil. Season the salmon fillets with salt, pepper, and the lemon zest. Add to the hot skillet, and cook for 3 to 4 minutes on the first side. Flip the salmon over, brush with the brown sugar–lemon mixture, transfer to the oven, and cook for 4 to 5 more minutes, or until cooked through.

While the salmon is cooking, add the baby carrots to the boiling water, season with salt, and simmer for 3 to 4 minutes, or until tender. Drain the carrots, then return them to the skillet and place back over the heat. Add the butter, dill, salt, and pepper and stir the carrots until the butter has melted. Transfer the carrots to a serving platter and serve alongside the sweet lemon salmon.

4 SERVINGS

Mediterranean Chicken and Saffron Couscous

337

☐ TRY THIS LATER

☐ IT'S A KEEPER

4 tablespoons extra-virgin olive oil (EVOO)

½ cup all-purpose flour

4 6-ounce boneless, skinless chicken breast halves

Salt and freshly ground black pepper

½ teaspoon cayenne pepper (eyeball it)

3 cups chicken stock or broth

1 pinch of saffron, or 1 single-use packet saffron powder (available at many fish markets)

4 garlic cloves, 1 crushed, 3 chopped

1 cup couscous

1 large red onion, chopped

1 tablespoon fresh thyme leaves, chopped (from 4 sprigs)

1 15-ounce can quartered artichoke hearts, drained

1 cup dry white wine (3 or 4 glugs)

10 kalamata olives, pitted, cut in half

½ pint grape or cherry tomatoes

½ cup fresh flat-leaf parsley leaves (a couple of generous handfuls), coarsely chopped

20 fresh basil leaves, coarsely chopped

Preheat a large skillet over medium-high heat with 2 tablespoons of the EVOO (twice around the pan). Place the flour in a shallow dish, season the chicken breasts with salt, pepper, and the cayenne, then transfer the seasoned chicken to the dish with the flour, toss around in the flour, then shake off the excess. Add the chicken to the skillet and cook for 5 to 6 minutes on each side. While the chicken is cooking, make the saffron couscous.

In a sauce pot, bring 2 cups of the chicken stock up to a boil with the saffron, the crushed clove of garlic, salt, and pepper. When the stock is at a boil, add the couscous, cover with a lid, and turn the heat off. Let the couscous stand for 10 minutes.

Once the chicken is done, remove it from the pan and cover with a piece of aluminum foil to keep warm. Return the skillet to the heat and add the remaining 2 tablespoons of EVOO. Add the onions, the 3 cloves of chopped garlic, the thyme, salt, and pepper. Cook, stirring frequently, for 4 minutes. Add the artichokes and wine to the pan, bring up to a simmer, then add the remaining 1 cup of chicken stock, olives, and grape tomatoes. Return the liquids to a simmer and cook for 2 to 3 minutes, or until the grape tomatoes start to burst and the sauce has reduced by half. Give the sauce a taste to see if it needs more salt and pepper. Add the chicken back to the skillet and warm through. Add the parsley and basil to the completed dish and stir to distribute the herbs.

To serve, fluff the couscous with a fork, remove and discard the crushed garlic clove, and transfer the couscous to serving plates. Serve the chicken whole or sliced on top of the saffron couscous. Top the chicken with some of the sauce and vegetables.

4 SERVINGS

338 MASTER RECIPE
Thai-Style Steak Salad

3 garlic cloves, chopped

2-inch piece of fresh ginger, peeled and grated

2 tablespoons tamari (dark aged soy sauce, found on the international aisle)

2 teaspoons hot sauce, such as Tabasco

6 tablespoons vegetable oil

2 pounds flank steak

1 cup sweetened shredded coconut

1 tablespoon sugar

3 tablespoons rice wine vinegar (eyeball it)

Salt and freshly ground black pepper

½ English or seedless cucumber, thinly sliced

1 red bell pepper, cored, seeded, and thinly sliced

5 radishes, thinly sliced

2 cups shredded carrots (available in pouches in the produce department)

½ small red onion, thinly sliced

10 fresh mint leaves, chopped

¼ cup fresh cilantro leaves (a generous handful), chopped

10 fresh basil leaves, chopped or torn

1 sack (12 ounces) baby spinach or ¾ pound from bulk bins, washed and patted dry

¼ cup unsalted roasted peanuts, chopped

Heat a grill pan or outdoor grill to high heat.

In a small bowl, mix the garlic, three fourths of the grated ginger, the tamari, and hot sauce. Whisk in about 3 tablespoons of the vegetable oil. Place the meat in a shallow dish and coat it evenly in marinade. Let stand for 10 minutes.

In a small skillet, toast the shredded coconut until lightly golden, about 2 to 3 minutes. Keep an eye on it; the coconut can go from golden brown to burnt, quickly. Remove the toasted coconut from the skillet and reserve.

In a small bowl, whisk together the remaining ginger, the sugar, rice wine vinegar, salt, and pepper. Whisk in the remaining 3 tablespoons of vegetable oil in a slow, steady stream.

In a salad bowl, combine the cucumbers, bell peppers, radishes, shredded carrots, onions, mint, cilantro, and basil. Pour the dressing over the veggies, toss to coat, and let sit while you cook the steak.

Grill the flank steak for 6 to 7 minutes on each side. Remove the flank steak from the grill and let the juices redistribute before slicing, 5 to 10 minutes. Thinly slice the meat on an angle, cutting the meat against the grain. To the dressed veggies, add the spinach, sliced steak, toasted coconut, and chopped peanuts, toss thoroughly, and serve.

4 SERVINGS

Thai-Style Pork and Noodle Salad

339

☐ TRY THIS LATER

☐ IT'S A KEEPER

SWAP

1½ pounds thin-cut boneless pork loin chops (no more than ½ inch thick) for flank steak

ADD

1 8-ounce package rice stick noodles

Marinate and cook the pork as you would the beef in the master recipe, #338, but reduce the cooking time to just 3 minutes on each side.

Cook the noodles in a large pot of boiling water according to the package directions. Drain and rinse the noodles under cold water to stop the cooking. Cut the pork into very thin strips. Make and dress the salad as before, adding the cooled cooked noodles to the salad when you add the sliced pork. Garnish and serve.

4 SERVINGS

Gnocchi with Sausage and Swiss Chard

340

☐ TRY THIS LATER

☐ IT'S A KEEPER

Coarse salt
1-pound package potato gnocchi
2 tablespoons extra-virgin olive oil (EVOO) (twice around the pan)
1 pound bulk sweet Italian sausage
1 large red onion, chopped
3 garlic cloves, chopped
1 teaspoon crushed red pepper flakes
Freshly ground black pepper
1 bunch of red Swiss Chard, chopped
½ cup white wine (a couple of glugs)
2 cups chicken stock or broth
¾ cup grated Parmigiano-Reggiano (a few large handfuls)

Bring a large pot of water to a boil, salt the water, and cook the gnocchi according to the package directions.

While the water for the gnocchi is coming up to a boil, preheat a large skillet over medium-high heat with the EVOO. Add the sausage and break it up into small pieces with the back of a wooden spoon; cook until the sausage is browned all over, about 5 minutes. Add the onions, garlic, red pepper flakes, salt, and pepper. Continue to cook for 4 to 5 more minutes. Add the Swiss chard; toss to wilt it into the pan. Add the wine, cook for 1 minute, then add the chicken stock and continue to cook for 3 to 4 more minutes.

Add the cooked and drained gnocchi, toss to coat and distribute, and cook for 1 minute. Turn the heat off and add the cheese; stir to combine. Serve immediately.

4 SERVINGS

341 Turkey Stroganoff Noodle Toss

Coarse salt

¾ pound extra-wide **egg noodles** (save the rest for a soup)

3 tablespoons **unsalted butter**

2 tablespoons all-purpose **flour**

2 cups **chicken stock** or broth

2 teaspoons Dijon **mustard**

¼ cup **sour cream** (eyeball it)

1 tablespoon fresh **tarragon** leaves, chopped (from 2 sprigs)

Freshly ground black pepper

1 tablespoon **extra-virgin olive oil** (EVOO) (once around the pan)

2 pounds **turkey breast cutlets**, cut into thin strips

1 small **onion**, sliced

⅓ cup coarsely chopped **cornichons** or baby gherkin pickles

½ cup fresh **flat-leaf parsley** leaves (a couple of generous handfuls), chopped

Thickly sliced **pumpernickel bread**

Bring a large pot of water to a boil over high heat for the egg noodles. Salt the boiling water and cook the noodles al dente.

While the water comes to a boil and the noodles cook, heat a medium skillet over medium heat. Melt 2 tablespoons of the butter and cook with the flour for 1 minute. Whisk in the chicken stock. Thicken for 1 minute. Stir in the mustard and sour cream, and thicken for 2 to 3 minutes. Add the tarragon, remove from the heat, and season with salt and pepper.

Heat a large skillet over high heat. Add the EVOO and the remaining tablespoon of butter. Add the turkey strips and onions and cook over high heat until the turkey is brown on both sides, 4 to 5 minutes. Add the chopped cornichons and stir to combine.

Add the thickened sauce to the skillet with the turkey. Drain the cooked noodles and add to the skillet with the parsley. Stir thoroughly. Serve with thickly sliced pumpernickel bread.

4 SERVINGS

Spiced Grilled Chicken and Veggie Pockets

342

☐ TRY THIS LATER

☐ IT'S A KEEPER

1 cup plain yogurt

½ teaspoon ground cinnamon

1 tablespoon ground cumin (a palmful)

1 tablespoon ground coriander

½ teaspoon crushed red pepper flakes
   Juice of 1 lemon

¼ cup fresh cilantro leaves (a handful), finely
   chopped

2 pounds chicken tenders

½ English or seedless cucumber, finely
   chopped

3 plum tomatoes, finely chopped

½ cup crumbled feta cheese

10 kalamata olives, pitted and coarsely chopped

4 scallions, thinly sliced

1 red or yellow bell pepper, cored, seeded, and
   finely chopped

2 cups shredded carrots (available in pouches
   in the produce department)

½ cup fresh flat-leaf parsley leaves (a couple of
   generous handfuls), chopped

2 tablespoons fresh dill, chopped

2 cups shredded red leaf lettuce

1 heaping tablespoon Dijon mustard

2 tablespoons red wine vinegar (eyeball it)

¼ cup extra-virgin olive oil (EVOO) (eyeball it)

4 pita pockets
   Salt and freshly ground black pepper

Preheat a grill pan or outdoor grill to high.

In a shallow bowl, combine the yogurt, cinnamon, cumin, coriander, red pepper flakes, lemon juice, and cilantro. Add the chicken tenders and coat evenly in the yogurt marinade. Marinate for 10 minutes. Shake off any excess marinade, then grill the chicken for about 4 to 5 minutes on each side, until charred at the edges and firm and cooked through.

While the chicken is working, in a large bowl combine the cucumbers, tomatoes, feta cheese, olives, scallions, bell peppers, carrots, parsley, dill, and shredded red leaf lettuce.

For the dressing, in a small bowl, combine the mustard and red wine vinegar. In a slow, steady stream, whisk in the EVOO.

When you remove the chicken from the grill, place the pitas on the grill to blister and warm through. Chop the grilled chicken into bite-size pieces and add to the veggies along with the dressing; season with salt and pepper, and toss to coat thoroughly. Cut the pitas in half; fill the pockets with the chicken and veggies.

4 SERVINGS

343 MASTER RECIPE
Sausage and Mushroom Polenta "Lasagna"

Okay, this one could take 35 minutes; but the results taste far more time-consuming.

  2 tablespoons extra-virgin olive oil (EVOO), plus more for drizzling
  2 tablespoons unsalted butter
  ½ pound bulk sweet Italian sausage
  1 portobello mushroom, stem removed
  1 small yellow onion, chopped
  4 large garlic cloves, chopped
  2 fresh rosemary sprigs, leaves stripped and finely chopped
  ½ teaspoon crushed red pepper flakes
    Salt and freshly ground black pepper
  ½ cup chicken stock or broth
    Zest and juice of 1 lemon
  2 cups ricotta cheese
  1 egg
  ½ cup grated Parmigiano-Reggiano (a couple of generous handfuls)
  ½ cup plain bread crumbs
  1 24-ounce tube prepared polenta, plain or flavored, cut into 21 disks about ¼ inch thick
  1 cup shredded mozzarella

Preheat the oven to 450°F.

Preheat a large skillet over medium-high heat with the 2 tablespoons of EVOO (twice around the pan) and the butter. Once the butter has melted, add the sausage, breaking it up with the back of a wooden spoon. While the sausage is starting to brown, cut the portobello mushroom in half and then thinly slice and add to the sausage. Chop and add to the pan as you go the onions, garlic, and rosemary. Season the sausage and mushrooms with the red pepper flakes, salt, and pepper. Once everything is in the pan, the sausage is lightly browned, and the mushrooms and onions have wilted, add the chicken stock and lemon juice. Continue to cook over high heat until the liquids have evaporated, about 2 to 3 minutes.

While the sausage and mushrooms are cooking down in the liquid, in a bowl, combine the ricotta cheese with the egg, lemon zest, Parmigiano, and bread crumbs.

Brush an 8-inch springform pan or an 8 x 8-inch baking dish with a little EVOO and place 7 disks of the polenta on the bottom of the dish. If they overlap a little that's fine; it will vary depending on what kind of dish you are using. Divide the sausage and mushroom mixture into 3 even portions. Do the same with the ricotta mixture.

Using the back of a spoon, spread one third of the ricotta mixture on top of the polenta. Don't make yourself crazy doing this—just mush it out over the polenta. Top the ricotta with one third of the sausage and mushrooms. Repeat the layers two more times, starting with the polenta and finishing with a sausage and mushroom layer. Sprinkle the top with the mozzarella. Cover the baking dish with aluminum foil, transfer to the oven, and bake for 15 to 18 minutes. To make sure it is cooked through, insert a knife into the center of the dish, wait a few seconds, and then remove it. Touch the knife with your fingertips and if it is hot, the lasagna is done. Remove from the springform (or cut loose from the baking dish) and serve.

4 SERVINGS

NOW TRY... **Sweet and Savory Polenta "Lasagna"** # 344

What a difference a little fruit and nuts can make!

ADD

- ½ cup golden raisins
- ½ cup pine nuts

Prepare just as for the master recipe, #343, adding the raisins and pine nuts at the same time you add the chicken stock and lemon juice to the sausage and onions.

4 SERVINGS

OR TRY... **Sausage, Mushroom, and Olive Polenta "Lasagna"** # 345

Again, this dish has a totally different flavor, with only one additional ingredient.

ADD

- 4 rounded tablespoons store-bought black or green olive tapenade

Prepare just as for the master recipe, #343, adding the tapenade to the ricotta cheese along with the egg, lemon zest, Parmigiano, and bread crumbs.

4 SERVINGS

THEN TRY... **Sausage, Mushroom, and Pesto Polenta "Lasagna"** # 346

I hate to beat a point to death, but this tastes totally different from all of the above, with only one change. Space these lasagnas out over the seasons of the year.

ADD

- 4 tablespoons store-bought good-quality pesto

Prepare just as for the master recipe, #343, adding the pesto to the ricotta cheese along with the egg, lemon zest, Parmigiano, and bread crumbs.

4 SERVINGS

(one more variation on page 300)

TRY THIS LATER

IT'S A KEEPER

TRY THIS LATER

IT'S A KEEPER

TRY THIS LATER

IT'S A KEEPER

347

AND NOW TRY... Super Mushroom Polenta "Lasagna"

This is the vegetarian version.

OMIT

Sweet Italian sausage

SWAP

Dry white wine for the chicken stock or broth

ADD

2 additional portobello mushrooms
1 jarred roasted red pepper, drained and chopped

Prepare according to the directions in the master recipe, #343, adding the 2 extra mushrooms along with the original mushroom quantity. Add the roasted red pepper to the ricotta mixture.

4 SERVINGS, FOR VEGETARIANS OR CARNIVORES ALIKE

TRY THIS LATER

IT'S A KEEPER

348

MASTER RECIPE
Turkey, Tomatillo, and Bean Burritos

TRY THIS LATER

IT'S A KEEPER

4 12-inch flour tortillas
2 tablespoons vegetable oil (twice around the pan)
1 package (1⅓ pounds) ground turkey breast
1 large onion, chopped
3 garlic cloves, chopped
1 red bell pepper, cored, seeded, and chopped
Salt and freshly ground black pepper
1 cup chicken stock or broth
1 15-ounce can pinto beans, rinsed and drained
1 16-ounce jar tomatillo salsa
2 tablespoons fresh cilantro leaves (a handful), chopped

1 10-ounce package (2½ cups) shredded Monterey Jack cheese (available on the dairy aisle)

Preheat the oven to 275°F. Wrap the flour tortillas in foil and warm in the oven.

Preheat a large nonstick skillet with the vegetable oil. Add the ground turkey and break it up with the back of a spoon as it cooks and browns, about 4 minutes. Add the onions, garlic, bell peppers, salt, and pepper. Continue to cook for 3 minutes. Add the chicken stock, pinto beans, and 1½ cups of the tomatillo salsa—that's about three quarters of the jar. Turn the heat up to high and continue to cook for 5 to 6 minutes, or until the mixture is thickened. Remove from the heat and add the cilantro, stirring to distribute.

Remove the flour tortillas from the oven and switch the broiler on.

Pile the turkey mixture into the warm flour tortillas, sprinkle each with ¼ cup of cheese, and then roll them up. Line a casserole or baking dish with the burritos, seam side down. Top each burrito with a little bit of the remaining ½ cup of tomatillo salsa, spreading it over the burritos with the back of a spoon. Sprinkle with the remaining cheese and place the dish under the hot broiler, 6 inches from the heat source. Broil for 5 minutes to melt and brown the cheese. Serve immediately.

4 SERVINGS

NOW TRY... Pork, Chipotle, and Bean Burritos 349

Awesome tasting and so different from the previous recipe, you could eat these two nights in a row and not feel redundant (as long as you go for Mexican food!).

SWAP

Ground pork for the ground turkey
Chipotle salsa for the tomatillo salsa

Prepare according to the directions in the master recipe, #348, swapping the pork for the turkey and the chipotle salsa for the tomatillo salsa.

4 SERVINGS

350 Crispy Horseradish-Battered Fried Fish
with Watercress-Cucumber Tartar Sauce

The English have nothing on this fish! Serve with store-bought frozen waffle-cut fries, prepared to package directions, and oil-and-vinegar-dressed slaw. Also, try skipping the tartar sauce one time and serve with malt vinegar instead—it takes even less time and effort and tastes great!

Vegetable oil, for frying

2½ cups complete pancake mix (the kind that needs only water)

1 heaping tablespoon prepared horseradish

2 pounds fresh cod, cut into 4- to 6-ounce pieces

Salt and freshly ground black pepper

1¼ cups mayonnaise (eyeball it)

2 rounded tablespoons sweet pickle relish

1 half-sour pickle, finely chopped

2 tablespoons finely chopped onions

2 tablespoons chopped fresh dill

Juice of ½ lemon

1 bunch of watercress, finely chopped

¼ large English or seedless cucumber, finely chopped

A few drops of hot pepper sauce

Pour about 2 inches of vegetable oil into a large skillet. Place the skillet over a large burner and heat the oil over medium-high heat. To check if the oil is hot enough, drop in a 1-inch cube of white bread. The bread should brown in a 40 count.

While the oil is heating up, make the batter for the fish. In a wide mixing bowl, combine 2 cups of the pancake mix, 1¼ cups water, and the horseradish. Place the remaining ½ cup of pancake mix in another wide mixing bowl. Arrange the batter and the bowl of dry pancake mix near the cooktop and the heating oil. Line a plate with a few sheets of paper towels and keep it within reach.

Season the fish with salt and pepper, then toss it in the dry pancake mix, coat evenly, and shake off the excess. The pancake mix will help the batter stick to the fish. Add the fish to the batter, flipping it around in the batter with a fork. You want the fish to be completely coated. Remove the fish from the batter, carefully place it in the hot oil, and fry for 4 to 5 minutes on each side, until deep golden. Remove from the oil and drain on the paper towels.

While the fish is frying, make the watercress–cucumber tartar sauce. In a bowl, combine the mayonnaise, pickle relish, chopped pickle, onions, dill, lemon juice, watercress, chopped cucumbers, salt, pepper, and some hot pepper sauce.

To serve, top the crispy horseradish-battered fried fish with the watercress–cucumber tartar sauce.

4 SERVINGS

Pork Chops in a Sweet Chili and Onion Sauce
with Creamy Cilantro Potato Salad

2½ pounds russet potatoes (3 medium-large potatoes), peeled and cubed
     Coarse salt
4   tablespoons extra-virgin olive oil (EVOO)
4   1½-inch-thick boneless center-cut pork chops
     Freshly ground black pepper
1   large red onion, finely chopped
1   heaping tablespoon chili powder (a heaping palmful)
½   tablespoon ground cumin (half a palmful)
3   garlic cloves, chopped
2   tablespoons dark brown sugar
2   cups chicken stock or broth
2   tablespoons cold unsalted butter
⅓   cup mayonnaise
½   cup fresh cilantro leaves (a couple of handfuls), chopped
2   tablespoons red wine vinegar (eyeball it)
3   celery ribs, finely chopped
2   red bell peppers, cored, seeded, and chopped

Preheat the oven to 375°F.

Place the potatoes in a sauce pot and cover with water. Place over high heat and bring up to a boil, add some salt, and simmer for 10 to 12 minutes, or until just tender. Drain the potatoes and spread out onto a rimmed cookie sheet to cool quickly, about 10 minutes.

While the potatoes are working, preheat a large skillet over medium-high heat with 2 tablespoons of the EVOO (twice around the pan). Season the pork chops liberally with salt and pepper. Place the chops in the skillet and sear for about 2 minutes on each side to caramelize. Transfer the chops to a rimmed cookie sheet and place in the oven to finish off, 7 or 8 minutes, until the meat is firm to the touch, but not tough. Remove from the oven and let the chops rest, covered with a piece of aluminum foil, for a few minutes.

While the chops bake, return the skillet to the heat and add the remaining 2 tablespoons of EVOO, three quarters of the chopped onions, the chili powder, cumin, two thirds of the chopped garlic, the brown sugar, salt, and pepper. Cook the mixture, stirring frequently, for 2 to 3 minutes. Add the chicken stock and simmer until reduced by half. Once reduced, turn off the heat and whisk in the cold butter.

While the sweet chili-onion sauce is cooking, in a large bowl, combine the mayonnaise, cilantro, the remaining chopped onions, the remaining chopped garlic, the red wine vinegar, salt, and pepper. Add to the dressing the chopped celery and red bell peppers. When you are ready to serve, add the cooled potatoes. Stir the potatoes to combine, and check the seasoning.

Pour the sweet chili-onion sauce over the rested pork chops; serve the creamy cilantro potato salad alongside.

4 SERVINGS

352 Asian Pinwheel Steaks with Noodle and Cabbage Sauté

Coarse salt

$\frac{1}{2}$ pound angel hair pasta

$\frac{1}{3}$ cup roasted unsalted peanuts

2 cups fresh baby spinach leaves

$\frac{1}{2}$ cup fresh flat-leaf parsley leaves (a couple of generous handfuls)

$\frac{1}{4}$ cup cilantro leaves (half as much as the parsley)

3 garlic cloves, chopped

Zest and juice of 1 lemon

3-inch piece of fresh ginger, peeled and grated

4 tablespoons tamari (dark aged soy sauce, found on the international aisle)

6 scallions, chopped

Salt and freshly ground black pepper

Pinch of cayenne pepper or a dash of hot sauce, such as Tabasco

$\frac{1}{4}$ cup plus 2 tablespoons vegetable oil, plus some for drizzling

2 $\frac{3}{4}$-inch-thick New York strip steaks

Metal skewers

1 sack (16 ounces) shredded cabbage "slaw mix" (on the produce aisle)

2 tablespoons rice wine vinegar (eyeball it)

1 cup chicken stock or broth

Preheat the oven to 500°F.

Bring a large pot of water to a boil, add salt and the pasta, and cook until al dente, with a bite to it. Drain and run under cold water to stop the cooking process.

While the water is heating, in the bowl of a food processor, place the peanuts, spinach, parsley, cilan-tro, three fourths of the garlic, the lemon zest and juice, one third of the ginger, 1 tablespoon of the tamari, one fourth of the chopped scallions, a little salt and pepper, and the cayenne and pulse-grind the ingredients to form a paste. While the machine is still running, slowly pour in the $\frac{1}{4}$ cup of vegetable oil. Taste and adjust the seasonings; reserve.

Place the steaks several inches apart between layers of wax paper. With a meat mallet or a heavy-bottomed pan, pound the steaks to half their thickness. Season each steak with salt and pepper on both sides. Cover each steak with a thin layer of the peanut filling. Roll the steaks tightly and cut each in half across. Secure the pinwheels with a carefully placed skewer and set the 4 pinwheels on a rimmed baking sheet. Drizzle with a little oil and roast for 12 to 15 minutes.

While the pinwheels are cooking, heat a large skillet over medium-high heat with the remaining 2 table-spoons of vegetable oil (twice around the pan). Add the cabbage, the remaining ginger, and the remaining garlic and cook for 2 minutes. Add the remaining 3 tablespoons of tamari, the rice wine vinegar, and chicken stock. Bring up to a simmer and add the reserved noodles and the remaining scallions. Toss to coat and continue to cook for 1 minute to heat the noo-dles through. Taste to adjust the seasoning with more tamari or salt and pepper.

To serve, remove the skewers and transfer the pin-wheels to dinner plates. Serve some of the noodle and cabbage sauté alongside.

4 SERVINGS

Crispy Rosemary–Orange Chicken
with Parmigiano String Beans

353

- 3 tablespoons extra-virgin olive oil (EVOO)
- 4 6-ounce boneless, skinless chicken breast halves, cut into bite-size pieces
- 2 sprigs fresh rosemary, leaves removed and chopped
  Salt and freshly ground black pepper
- 1 large yellow onion, sliced
- 2 large carrots, thinly sliced
- 2 large garlic cloves, chopped
- 2 tablespoons all-purpose flour
  Zest and juice of 1 orange
- 2½ cups chicken stock or broth
- 10 pitted kalamata olives, coarsely chopped
- 1 cup plain bread crumbs (eyeball it)
- ½ cup fresh flat-leaf parsley leaves (a couple of handfuls), chopped
- ¾ cup grated Parmigiano-Reggiano (a few overflowing handfuls), divided
- 1½ to 2 pounds string beans, stem ends trimmed
- 2 tablespoons cold unsalted butter

Preheat the broiler.

Preheat a large skillet over medium-high heat with 2 tablespoons of the EVOO (twice around the pan). Add the chicken, rosemary, salt, and pepper. Cook and stir for 3 to 4 minutes, or until lightly browned, then add the onions, carrots, and garlic. Continue to cook for 2 minutes.

While the chicken is cooking with the veggies, place another skillet with 2 inches of water in it over high heat and bring up to a boil.

Dust the chicken and vegetables with the flour and cook for 1 minute more. Stir in the orange juice and chicken stock. Bring up to a simmer and cook until the liquid has reduced by half, then add the olives.

While the liquid is reducing, make the bread-crumb topping. In a small bowl, combine the bread crumbs, orange zest, parsley, and ¼ cup of the Parmigiano.

Transfer the chicken and vegetables to a baking dish and top with the bread-crumb mixture, covering from edge to edge. Place under the broiler until the topping is brown and crispy, 2 to 3 minutes.

While the chicken is under the broiler, add the string beans and a little salt to the skillet with the boiling water. Simmer the beans for just 2 minutes, then drain them in a colander and return the skillet to the cook-top over medium-high heat. Add the remaining table-spoon of EVOO and the butter. Once the butter has melted, add the beans back to the skillet, season with salt and pepper, toss to coat in the butter. Cook for 1 minute, add the remaining ½ cup of grated Parmi-giano, and toss to coat. Transfer the cheesy string beans to a serving platter. Serve the string beans alongside the crispy-topped rosemary–orange chicken.

4 SERVINGS

354 Chicken Cutlets on Buttermilk-Cheddar-Chorizo Biscuits with Tomato–Olive Salsa Mayo

This one is good for B, L, D: brunches, lunches, or dinners.

1 8-ounce package buttermilk biscuit mix, such as Jiffy brand

½ cup shredded extra-sharp Cheddar cheese

¼ pound packaged (not fresh) Spanish chorizo, casing removed, finely chopped

2 plum tomatoes, seeded and chopped

3 tablespoons fresh flat-leaf parsley or cilantro leaves (a handful), finely chopped

¼ small red onion, finely chopped

10 large green olives, cracked away from the pits and coarsely chopped
Juice of 1 lime

1 to 2 dashes of hot sauce, such as Tabasco

½ cup mayonnaise
Salt and freshly ground black pepper

2 tablespoons vegetable oil (twice around the pan)

4 thin-cut chicken cutlets, 3 to 4 ounces each

½ tablespoon ground coriander (half a palmful)

4 romaine lettuce leaves

Preheat the oven to 450°F.

Place the buttermilk biscuit mix in a bowl. Add the shredded Cheddar and the chorizo and mix with a fork to distribute. Add water according to the package directions. Once combined, dump the biscuit mix out on a lightly floured cutting board. Using your fingertips, press out the dough into a 1-inch-thick square. Divide the square with a knife into 4 squares. Arrange the jumbo-size biscuits on a foil-lined cookie sheet and bake for 12 to 15 minutes, or until the biscuits are cooked through and the bottoms are golden brown. Remove from the oven and let cool.

To make the tomato, olive, and salsa mayo, in a bowl, combine the tomatoes, parsley or cilantro, onions, olives, half of the lime juice, dash of hot sauce, and the mayonnaise. Season with salt and pepper and reserve.

Preheat a large skillet over medium-high heat with the vegetable oil. Season the chicken with salt, pepper, coriander, and the remaining half of the lime juice. Add the seasoned chicken to the skillet and cook on each side for 3 to 4 minutes, or until cooked through.

Split the cheddar–chorizo biscuits in half. Slather the tops and bottoms of the biscuits with the tomato, olive, and salsa mayo. Cut each cooked chicken cutlet in half; arrange the halved cutlets on the bottoms of the biscuits, garnish with a folded leaf of romaine lettuce, and finish with the biscuit top. Open wide!

4 SERVINGS

TIDBIT

Spanish-style chorizo is made with smoked pork and comes already cooked in the package. Mexican-style chorizo is made with fresh (uncooked) pork and must be thoroughly cooked.

Spinach and Spicy Ham Pasta Bake

355

☐ TRY THIS LATER

☐ IT'S A KEEPER

Coarse salt

1 pound cavatappi (ridged corkscrew pasta) or ridged macaroni

3 tablespoons extra-virgin olive oil (EVOO)

2 tablespoons unsalted butter

1 medium onion, chopped
Coarse black pepper

3 tablespoons all-purpose flour

1½ cups whole or 2-percent milk

½ pound sliced capocollo (spicy ham), halved, then sliced into thin ribbons

1 10-ounce box frozen chopped spinach, defrosted and wrung out in a clean kitchen towel

1 cup grated Parmigiano-Reggiano (a few large handfuls)

½ teaspoon ground or freshly grated nutmeg (eyeball it)

¼ teaspoon ground cayenne pepper (a couple pinches)

1-pound ball of fresh mozzarella (buy a piece wrapped, not packed in water, then cut into ½-inch cubes)

1 cup plain or Italian-style bread crumbs

Preheat the broiler.

Bring a large pot of water to a boil over high heat. Salt the water, add the pasta, and cook al dente, with a bite.

While the water is coming up to a boil for the pasta, heat a medium, deep skillet over medium heat. Add 1 tablespoon of the EVOO (once around the pan), and the butter. When the butter melts into the oil, add the onions and season with salt and pepper. Cook, stirring frequently, for 2 minutes, then dust the onions with the flour and continue to cook for 1 minute. Slowly whisk in the milk. Gently bring the milk to a bubble, allow the mixture to thicken a bit, then stir in the capocollo, spinach, and ½ cup of the grated Parmigiano. Season the sauce with nutmeg and cayenne and remove from the heat. Taste and add a little salt, if you like.

Combine the cooked pasta and the cubed mozzarella with the sauce, then stir to coat completely by turning over and over. Transfer the dressed pasta to a baking dish.

To make the bread-crumb topping, in a small bowl, combine the bread crumbs, the remaining 2 table-spoons of EVOO, and the remaining ½ cup of Parmi-giano. Sprinkle the bread-crumb mixture over the top to cover the pasta from edge to edge. Transfer the baking dish under the broiler and broil until golden brown and crispy. What a gut-buster! YUMMO!

4 SERVINGS AMONG BIG EATERS LIKE ME
AND MY FAMILY

356 Honey Chicken over Snow Pea Rice

3 tablespoons vegetable oil

1 tablespoon unsalted butter

1½ cups long-grain rice

Salt and freshly ground black pepper

½ cup dry white wine (a couple of glugs)

4½ cups chicken stock or broth

Zest and juice of 1 lemon

2 large handfuls snow peas, thinly sliced across the width

2 pounds chicken tenders, cut into bite-size pieces

½ teaspoon crushed red pepper flakes

1 large onion, sliced

3 large garlic cloves, chopped

3-inch piece of fresh ginger, peeled and grated

3 tablespoons honey (3 gobs)

1 tablespoon cornstarch

5 scallions, thinly sliced

Heat a medium saucepan or pot over medium-high heat. Add 1 tablespoon of the vegetable oil and the butter to the pot. Once the butter melts, add the rice, season with salt and pepper, and lightly brown the rice for 3 to 5 minutes. Add the wine and allow it to evaporate entirely, 1 to 2 minutes. Add 3 cups of the chicken stock and the lemon zest to the rice. Bring the liquid to a boil. Cover and reduce the heat. Cook the rice for 18 to 20 minutes, or until tender. Once the rice only has about 3 more minutes of cook time, remove the lid and add the sliced snow peas. Don't stir the rice; just add the snow peas on top and put the lid on. The steam will lightly cook the snow peas. Once cooked, fluff the rice with a fork and stir in the snow peas. They should still have some crunch to them.

While the rice is cooking, preheat a large skillet over medium-high heat with the remaining 2 tablespoons of vegetable oil (twice around the pan). Add the chicken, season with salt and pepper, and brown for about 3 minutes. Add the red pepper flakes, onions, garlic, ginger, and honey. Stir frequently and continue to cook for 3 to 4 minutes, or until the onions are tender. Add the remaining 1½ cups of chicken stock to the pan and bring up to a simmer. Once at a simmer, combine the cornstarch with a splash of water, and mix to create a thin paste. Add the cornstarch mixture to the simmering chicken, mix thoroughly, and continue to cook for 2 minutes, or until the liquid is thickened. Add the sliced scallions and the lemon juice to the chicken and stir to combine.

Serve the honey chicken over the snow pea rice.

4 SERVINGS

Crispy Turkey Cutlets with Bacon-Cranberry Brussels Sprouts

2 tablespoons vegetable oil (twice around the pan), plus some for shallow frying

5 slices bacon, chopped

1 large onion, chopped

1 tablespoon fresh thyme leaves, chopped (from 4 sprigs)

Salt and freshly ground black pepper

2 pounds turkey breast cutlets

½ tablespoon poultry seasoning (half a palmful)

3 to 4 tablespoons all-purpose flour

2 cups plain bread crumbs

1 lemon, zested, then cut into wedges

2 eggs

2 10-ounce boxes frozen Brussels sprouts, defrosted

½ cup dried cranberries

¾ cup chicken stock or broth

½ cup fresh flat-leaf parsley leaves (a few handfuls), chopped

Start the bacon-cranberry Brussels sprouts by preheating a nonstick skillet over medium-high heat with the 2 tablespoons of vegetable oil. Add the chopped bacon and cook until crispy, about 2 to 3 minutes. Add the onions and thyme, season with salt and pepper, and cook for 3 to 4 more minutes.

While the onions are cooking with the bacon, season the cutlets with the poultry seasoning, salt, and pepper on both sides, and dredge in the flour. Combine the bread crumbs and lemon zest in a shallow dish. Beat the eggs in a separate shallow dish with a splash of water.

Heat ½ inch of vegetable oil in a large skillet over medium to medium-high heat. Coat the cutlets in eggs, then in breading, and add to the hot oil. Cook the cutlets in a single layer, in 2 batches if necessary, for about 3 or 4 minutes on each side, until their juices run clear and the breading is evenly browned.

While the first batch of cutlets is cooking, add the defrosted Brussels sprouts to the bacon and onions, toss, and stir to combine. Add the dried cranberries and the chicken stock to the pan and continue to cook for 3 to 4 minutes, or until the Brussels sprouts are heated through and the cranberries have plumped. Finish the sprouts with the chopped parsley.

Serve the turkey cutlets alongside the bacon-cranberry Brussels sprouts. Pass the lemon wedges; squeeze the juice over the cutlets at the table.

4 SERVINGS

358 Fresh Tomato and Basil Chicken
over Super Creamy Polenta

4 cups chicken stock or broth

2 tablespoons extra-virgin olive oil (EVOO) (twice around the pan)

4 6-ounce boneless, skinless chicken breast halves
Salt and freshly ground black pepper

¼ teaspoon crushed red pepper flakes

1 large red onion, thinly sliced

5 garlic cloves, chopped

1 cup quick-cooking polenta (found in Italian or specialty foods aisles)

½ cup mascarpone cheese

¼ cup grated Parmigiano-Reggiano (a handful)

½ pint yellow grape tomatoes

½ pint red grape tomatoes

20 fresh basil leaves, chopped or torn

For the super creamy polenta, bring 3 cups of the chicken stock to a boil in a sauce pot. If the chicken stock is at a boil before you are ready to add the polenta, just turn it down to low and let it wait for you.

While the stock is coming to a boil, start the fresh tomato and basil chicken. Heat a large nonstick skillet over medium-high heat with the EVOO. Season the chicken with salt, pepper, and red pepper flakes, add to the hot skillet, and cook for about 3 to 4 minutes, or until the chicken is lightly browned. Scoot the chicken over to the edges of the skillet, then add the onions and garlic, continuing to cook for 3 minutes more. Add the remaining cup of chicken stock and cook until reduced by half, another 3 to 4 minutes.

While the sauce is reducing, whisk the quick-cooking polenta into the boiling chicken stock in the sauce pot until it masses. Stir in the mascarpone cheese and the Parmigiano and season with salt and pepper. You want the polenta to be slightly loose. If it gets too tight, stir in some more stock to loosen it up a little.

To finish the chicken, add the yellow and red grape tomatoes, stir to combine, and continue to cook for about 1 to 2 minutes, or until the tomatoes are heated through and starting to burst. Add the basil and toss with the chicken and tomatoes.

Serve the polenta in shallow bowls and top with the fresh tomato and basil chicken.

4 SERVINGS

Roast Crispy Mushrooms and Grilled Tenderloin Steaks with Green Onions

359

In France, I had some cèpes (wild mushrooms) cooked in duck fat—yummo! Being that I don't kill many ducks and that I like wearing small sizes, I make these with EVOO at home. (Man, nothing beats that duck fat though! You should taste the potatoes boiled in it!)

- 8 portobello mushroom caps, cut into large chunks
- 8 large garlic cloves, cracked from the skins
- ½ cup fresh flat-leaf parsley leaves (a couple of generous handfuls)
- ½ cup extra-virgin olive oil (EVOO), plus some for drizzling
  Sea salt and coarse black pepper
- 4 1½-inch-thick beef tenderloin steaks
- 8 scallions, split lengthwise
  Crusty bread

Preheat the oven to 500°F. Preheat a grill pan or outdoor grill to high.

Place the mushroom chunks in a large bowl. Combine the garlic and parsley in a food processor and finely chop. Add the garlic and parsley to the mushrooms.

Pour about ½ cup EVOO over the bowl and toss vigorously to coat the mushrooms with oil and garlic. Arrange the mushrooms in a single layer on a rimmed cookie sheet and roast for 20 minutes, or until crisp, dry, and dark brown. RESIST the devil on your shoulder that wants you to open the oven because things smell good in there. If you let the heat out, the 'shrooms will not crisp.

Also, season with salt and pepper *after* removing from the oven—salting too soon will cause the mushrooms to give off their juices and not crisp.

Grill the steaks for 4 minutes on each side for medium rare, 5 to 6 for medium to medium well. Season the steaks with salt and pepper and let them rest for 5 to 10 minutes for the juices to redistribute. Coat the scallions in EVOO and season with salt and pepper. Grill to mark, 2 minutes on each side.

Serve the steaks with grilled scallions on top and crispy mushrooms on the side. Low-carbers can skip the bread.

4 SERVINGS

360 Incredible French Endive Salad
with Aged Herb Goat Cheese Toasts

This is the at-home version of another perfect meal from France. To make this more of a meal, serve with sliced French sausages and ham.

- 1 garlic clove
  Juice of ½ lemon
  Coarse salt
  A few sprigs of fresh flat-leaf parsley leaves
- ¼ cup extra-virgin olive oil (EVOO) (eyeball it)
- 12 heads of endive (look for the whitest heads you can find, free of scars)
- 8 slices white toasting bread
- 2 8-ounce logs aged goat cheese
- 3 tablespoons Herbes de Provence (dried French herb blend, available on the spice aisle)

Heat a grill pan to medium high. Turn on the broiler and place a rack at least 10 inches from the heat.

In a blender, combine the garlic, lemon juice, a little salt, and the parsley. Turn the blender on the "puree" setting. Stream the EVOO into the blender and puree the dressing until smooth and emulsified.

Trim the endives of tough ends and peel away any dry or badly scarred outer leaves. Place the endives in a shallow dish and pour the dressing over them. Turn them in the dressing to coat them evenly. Place on the hot grill pan and gently cook the endives for 6 to 7 minutes, until tender, turning frequently.

Lightly toast the bread under the broiler on each side and remove. Cut the bread corner to corner to make 16 triangles. Trim the ends off the logs of cheese and cut each log into 8 disks. (Cut across the middle of each log, then keep halving the sections until you have 16 equal disks from the 2 logs.) Scatter the Herbes de Provence onto the cutting board. Gently turn each disk of cheese in the dried herbs and situate a disk on each toast. Return the toasts to the oven and broil for 2 to 3 minutes to warm the cheese through and darken the toast to a light, even golden brown.

Remove the endives 3 at a time to a plate. Carefully halve them lengthwise with a small sharp knife and fan the halved grilled endives across the plate. Add 4 triangles of toast with warm goat cheese to the same plate and serve. Repeat with the remaining portions.

4 SERVINGS

This is a special end-of-the-year section of the absolute easiest meals I can think of, today anyway. At the end of every year, I am at my busiest. I am up at all hours, wrapping, writing, cleaning, working, and cooking for others. Whenever I am done, I make—for myself and whoever is left standing—a meal of whatever I have on hand, stuffed in or piled on bread. (I always have bread, always. Keep a well-wrapped baguette in the freezer and you'll always be ready to crisp and fill at will.) These recipes are based on the things I usually have on hand, in the cupboard, fridge, or freezer. Feel free to swap away based on the things you keep around. They all make great meals for any too-tired night of the year.

Tuna with Everything-but-the-Kitchen-Sink, Hold-the-Mayo, Stuffed Bread

361

☐ TRY THIS LATER

☐ IT'S A KEEPER

1 baguette or other crusty loaf (day-old is fine)
1½ cups (2 small cans) Italian tuna in oil, drained
1 15-ounce can artichoke hearts, whole or quartered, drained and chopped or sliced
6 soft sun-dried tomatoes, dry or drained if packed in oil, thinly sliced
A handful of fresh flat-leaf parsley, chopped
A handful of olives, any or all varieties are fine, chopped
¼ red onion, chopped or thinly sliced
3 tablespoons capers or a couple of caper berries, drained and chopped
2 cups arugula or other greens, chopped
4 anchovy fillets, finely chopped, or a little anchovy paste (optional but recommended)
A couple of sprigs of fresh herbs: rosemary, thyme, tarragon, or basil—whichever you have—chopped

Coarse black pepper
Zest and juice of 1 lemon
3 tablespoons extra-virgin olive oil (EVOO) (eyeball it)

Preheat the oven to 200°F.

Crisp the bread in the oven. Remove, split, and hollow out some of the soft insides.

Place the tuna in a bowl and flake it with a fork. Add the remaining salad ingredients, dress with pepper, lemon zest and juice, and EVOO, and work the salad together with a rubber spatula. Overfill the bottom of the loaf, mounding the salad. Set the top in place and press down to set the creation. Cut into quarters. Wrap each sandwich in wax paper or paper towels at one end to limit dripping as you crunch and munch.

4 SERVINGS

362 Chopped Antipasto Stuffed Bread

1 baguette, semolina round loaf, or other crusty bread

¾ pound mixed assorted Italian ham and salami (choose from Genoa salami, capocollo spicy ham, prosciutto, prosciutto cotto, sweet or hot sopressata, mortadella, hard salami, pepperoni, abruzzese salami, calabrese salami)

⅓ pound Italian table cheeses (choose from Provolone, Pecorino, Asiago, Fontina, Scamorza, or mozzarella)

1 cup giardiniera (Italian jarred hot pickled vegetables), drained

A handful of fresh flat-leaf parsley leaves, chopped

A handful of olives, pitted and chopped

1 celery rib with the greens, chopped

2 cups shredded romaine lettuce hearts

Juice of 1 lemon

3 tablespoons extra-virgin olive oil (EVOO) (eyeball it)

Coarse black pepper

Shredded or torn fresh basil, if you have it, or a few spoonfuls of prepared pesto will do

Preheat the oven to 200°F.

Crisp the bread in the low oven and cool. Split and hollow out the bread.

Chop and add the meats, cutting them into bite-size pieces or strips and place in a large bowl. Dice or slice the cheeses and add to the meats. Finely chop the pickled vegetables and add to the bowl. Add the parsley, olives, celery, and lettuce to your antipasto salad and dress with the lemon juice, EVOO, and pepper.

Fill the bottom of the bread with salad, mounding and packing it in there with a rubber spatula to help. Top with the basil leaves or spread the top with a layer of pesto, and set the top into place, pressing down on the stuffed bread. Cut a baguette into 4 pieces across, or cut a round loaf into 4 wedges. Wrap the ends of the sandwiches with wax paper or paper towels to control drips. How wide can you open your mouth?

4 SERVINGS

Quick Cassoulet Stuffed Bread Melts

363

☐ TRY THIS LATER   ☐ IT'S A KEEPER

- 1 baguette (day-old is fine)
- ½ pound sausage (choose from andouille, chorizo, Italian bulk hot or sweet, kielbasa)
- 2 tablespoons extra-virgin olive oil (EVOO) (twice around the pan)
- 1 carrot, chopped
- 1 small yellow onion, chopped
- 2 large garlic cloves, chopped
- 1 bay leaf
- 1 teaspoon dried thyme or 1 tablespoon fresh thyme leaves (a couple of sprigs)
- 1 can small white beans or cannellini, rinsed and drained
   Salt and freshly ground black pepper
- ½ cup white wine or chicken stock
- 4 slices deli Swiss cheese or thinly sliced Cheddar, Fontina, Gouda, or Gruyère
   A handful of chopped fresh flat-leaf parsley

Preheat the oven to 200°F.

Crisp the bread in the low oven, remove, and split lengthwise. Hollow it out and cut each half in half again across, making 4 bread boats. Switch the broiler on and place a rack 8 inches or so from the heat.

If you are using cooked sausage, finely chop it. For raw Italian, cut open a couple of links. Heat a large non-stick skillet over medium-high heat. Add the EVOO and the sausage; brown cooked sausage for 2 minutes, and brown and break up raw sausage into small bits, 5 minutes. Add the carrots, onions, garlic, bay leaf, and thyme and cook for 5 minutes more. Add the beans and stir to combine. Season the quick cassoulet with salt and pepper. Deglaze the pan with the wine or stock, scraping up the good bits. Reduce the heat to low and simmer over very low heat for 2 to 3 minutes to combine the flavors. If the mixture sticks at all, add a bit more wine or stock, but do not make the mixture wet. It should be starchy and thick.

Fill the bread boats with the cassoulet. Top with cheese, folding the slices to fit. Melt the cheese under the broiler and garnish each open-face stuffed sandwich with a little parsley. Serve with a fork and knife.

4 SERVINGS

364 Nacho Bread Pizza

1 baguette or semolina bread (day-old is fine)

1 tablespoon vegetable oil (once around the pan)

2 garlic cloves, chopped

1 jalapeño, seeded and chopped, or 1 pickled hot pepper of any kind, chopped

1 15-ounce can refried beans, black beans, or red beans

2 teaspoons hot sauce

1 teaspoon chili powder or ground cumin ($^1/_3$ palmful)

Salt and freshly ground black pepper

1 cup prepared salsa, any variety

2 cups shredded Cheddar, smoked Cheddar, Monterey Jack, or Pepper Jack cheese

1 romaine lettuce heart or $^1/_2$ head of iceberg lettuce, shredded

$^1/_2$ cup green olives with or without pimiento, chopped

$^1/_4$ red onion or 2 to 3 scallions, chopped

2 plum or vine-ripe tomatoes, seeded and diced

Preheat the oven to 200°F.

Crisp the bread in the low oven and split lengthwise. Hollow the bread out and cut each half in half across, making 4 boats. Switch the broiler on.

Heat a small nonstick skillet over medium heat. Add the oil, garlic, and jalapeños. Add the refried beans or, if you are using whole beans, drain, add half of the beans, then mash the remainder of the beans in the can using a fork. Add the mashed beans to the pan and combine with the whole beans. Season the beans with hot sauce, chili powder or cumin, salt, and pepper. When the spicy beans are hot through, spread them evenly across all of the bread. Top the beans liberally with the salsa, then the cheese, covering the bread to all edges. The boats will only be half full. Melt the cheese under the broiler until it bubbles and begins to brown.

Fill the nacho bread pizzas with the lettuce, olives, onions, and tomatoes and serve. You can pick them up with your hands, but eat over the plate—or over the kitchen sink, like me.

4 SERVINGS

Hamburger and
Onion Stuffed Bread

365

1 baguette (day-old is fine)
1 tablespoon extra-virgin olive oil (EVOO)
   (once around the pan)
1 pound ground beef
   Salt and freshly ground black pepper
2 medium yellow onions, finely chopped
1 tablespoon Worcestershire sauce
   Dijon or spicy brown mustard, to dress the
   bread
4 slices deli Swiss cheese, folded to cover the
   bread, or 6 ounces Gouda or smoked Gouda,
   sliced to fit the bread
   Chopped fresh chives or flat-leaf parsley, for
   garnish

Preheat the oven to 200°F.

Crisp the bread in the low oven, split lengthwise, then cut in half again to make 4 bread boats and hollow out the bread. Switch the broiler on.

Heat a nonstick skillet over medium-high heat. Add the EVOO. Add the meat, season liberally with salt and pepper, and brown and crumble it, 3 minutes. Add the onions and cook for 10 minutes more, stirring frequently. Add the Worcestershire and remove from the heat.

Spread a little Dijon or spicy brown mustard across the bottoms of the breads. Fill with the meat and onions and top the filled breads with the cheese. Melt the cheese under the broiler and garnish with the chives or parsley.

4 SERVINGS

366 AND LAST BUT NOT LEAST...Christmas Pasta

I make this dinner every Christmas. I have included it in other books, but I cannot finish any year without it. I have made some small improvements in the recipe over the years, so it's faster and easier to make than ever. You can eat it all year long as do I. For Italians, after all those fishes on Christmas Eve, this dish, with four different meats in it, is especially nice on Christmas night.

This is the greatest gift I can give to myself and those I love: a big bowl of pasta with the works. Have a great year!

Serve with tomato, basil, and mozzarella salad (the colors of the season and the Italian flag).

Salt
1 pound rigatoni
2 tablespoons extra-virgin olive oil (EVOO) (2 turns of the pan)
¼ pound pancetta, chopped
¼ pound bulk hot Italian sausage (No bulk? Split a link open)
¼ pound bulk sweet Italian sausage
½ pound ground sirloin
½ pound ground veal
½ teaspoon allspice, eyeball it in your palm
Coarse black pepper
1 carrot, peeled and finely chopped
1 medium yellow onion, peeled and finely chopped
4 garlic cloves, crushed
½ cup dry red wine, a couple of glugs
1 cup beef stock or broth
1 28-ounce can crushed tomatoes
¼ cup flat-leaf parsley (a generous handful), finely chopped
½ cup grated Romano cheese (a couple of handfuls), plus some to pass at the table

Bring a large pot of water to a boil and salt it. Add the pasta and cook to al dente, with a bite to it.

While the water and pasta work, heat a large nonstick skillet over medium-high heat. Add 1 tablespoon EVOO (1 turn of the pan). Add the pancetta to one half of the pan, the sausage, both hot and sweet, to the other. Break up the sausage into bits and brown while the pancetta renders, then combine and cook together another minute or so. Remove to a plate with a slotted spoon. Add the remaining tablespoon of EVOO, then the beef and veal. Brown and crumble the meat into tiny bits and season with allspice, salt, and pepper. Add the carrots, onions, and garlic and cook another 5 to 6 minutes to soften the vegetables, then add sausage and pancetta back into the pan, draining away some of the fat. Deglaze the pan with the wine, scraping up all the good bits with a wooden spoon. Stir in the stock, then the tomatoes. Check the seasoning. Simmer over low heat until ready to serve, at least 10 minutes. Stir in half the parsley to finish.

Drain the pasta and add back to the hot pot. Ladle a few spoonfuls of the sauce over the pasta and add a couple of handfuls of cheese to the pot. Stir to coat the pasta evenly. Transfer to a large serving dish or individual bowls and top with the remaining sauce and parsley. Pass plenty of extra cheese at the table.

6 SERVINGS

Index

A

Artichoke(s)
  Italian Open-Face Sandwiches, 223
  Pizza Capricciosa, 162–63
  Salad Capricciosa, 163
  Spinach, and Tortellini, About-15-Minute Soup with, 172
  and Spinach Calzones, 123
  and Walnut Pesto Pasta, 122
Arugula and Pecan Pesto, 221
Asparagus
  and Chicken, Creamy, on Toast, 282
  Ham, and Peas, Springtime Bows with, 266
  and Ham Tartines, 223
  White, and Andouille, Cream Risotto with, 274

B

Bean(s)
  Black, Chicken, and Corn Stoup, 89
  Black, Stoup and Southwestern Monte Cristos, 18
  Fall Minestrone, 177
  and Greens Soup, 125
  Mushroom-Veggie Sloppy Sandwiches, 280
  Nacho Bread Pizza, 316
  Peasant Soup, 105
  Pork, and Chipotle Burritos, 301
  Quick Cassoulet Stuffed Bread Melts, 315
  and Tomato Soup, My Mom's 15-Minute, 158
  Uptown Down-Home Chili, 58
  White, Pancetta, and Pasta, 173
Beef
  Asian Pinwheel Steaks with Noodle and Cabbage Sauté, 304
  Aussie Meat Pies, Made Quick, 176
  Bacon-Wrapped, Supper Salads, 276
  Bacon-Wrapped Meatloaf Patties with Pan Gravy and Sour Cream–Tomato Smashed Potatoes, 288–89
  Balls, Big, with Bucatini, 237
  Big Bistro Burgers with Caramelized Shallots on Grilled Bread with Beet and Goat Cheese Salad, 247
  Boneless Rib-Eye Steaks with Killa' Chimichurri and Mushrooms with Smoky Chipotle and Wilted Spinach, 106–7

A Burger for Brad: Barbecue Burger Deluxe, 227
Burger Stack-Ups, Big, with Mushrooms, Peppers, and Onions, 105
Cheddar-Studded Tex-Mex Meatloaf Patties, Scallion Smashed Potatoes, and Spicy Pan Gravy, 91
and Chicken Fajita Burgers with Seared Peppers and Onions, 25
Christmas Pasta, 318
Couple-of-Minute Steaks and Potato Ragout, 43
Fiery Hot Texas T-Bones with Chipotle Smashed Potatoes and Hot and Sweet Pepper Sauté, 12
French Onion Sliced Steak Croissant Sandwich, 286
and Garlic Italian Stir-Fry, Big, 207
Goulash, 3
Gravy-Smothered Cajun-Style Meatloaf Patties with Maple Pecan–Glazed String Beans, 90
Grilled Flank Steak Sandwich with Blue Cheese Vinaigrette–Dressed Arugula and Pears, 34
Grilled Skirt Steak and Orzo with the Works, 252
Grilled Steak Sandwich...I mean, Salad–No! Sandwich!, 261
Hamburger and Onion Stuffed Bread, 317
Involtini all'Enotec'Antica with Gnocchi, 166
London Broil with Buttered Potatoes and Caramelized Zucchini and Mushrooms, 265
London Broil with Mushroom Vinaigrette, 146
London Broil with Parsley-Horseradish Chimichurri, 83
Mashed Plantains with Oh, Baby! Garlic-Tomato Shrimp on Top, Grilled Flank Steak with Lime and Onions, and Quick Rice with Black Beans, 72–73
Mega Meatball Pizza and Zippy Italian Popcorn, 6
Mix-n-Match Lettuce Tacos, 124
and Mushroom Nests, 216
Pie, Fajita, 65
Roast Crispy Mushrooms and Grilled Tenderloin Steaks with Green Onions, 311

Ropa Vieja Josés (Cuban Sloppy Joes) with Smashed Yucca, Sliced Tomatoes, Plantain Chips, and Mojo Sauce, 74–75
Shrimp Martinis and Manhattan Steaks, 141
Sirloin Burgers with Gorgonzola Cheese and Mediterranean Slaw, 60
Sliced Grilled Steak on Blue Cheese Biscuits with Watercress, Sour Cream, and Sliced Tomatoes, 85
Sliced Herb and Garlic Tagliata over Shaved Portobello, Celery, and Parmigiano-Reggiano Salad, 116
Smoky Chipotle Chili Con Queso Mac, 137
Steak Sandwich...Knife and Fork Required, 165
Steaks with Horseradish Cream Sauce, Watercress Salad, and Crusty Bread, 111
Steaks with Two Tapenades, Arugula Salad, and Crusty Bread, 110
Strip Steaks with a Side of Blue Cheese Spaghetti, 181
Super-Grilled Steak Sandwich with Horseradish-Dijon Cream and Spicy Greens, 143
Super Mashers with Steak and Pepper Hash, 128–29
Taco Chili-Mac, 22
Tenderloin, Bacon-Wrapped, and Super-Stuffed Potatoes with Smoked Gouda and Caramelized Mushrooms and Onions, 197
Tenderloin Steaks, Olive and Anchovy–Slathered, with Caramelized Onion Orzo and Sliced Tomatoes, 183
Thai-Style Steak Salad, 294
Uptown Down-Home Chili, 58
Broccoli
  Frittata with Goat Cheese and BLT Bread Salad, 186
  Soup, Creamy, with Cheddar and Chive Toast, 149
Burgers and patties
  Bacon-Wrapped Meatloaf Patties with Pan Gravy and Sour Cream–Tomato Smashed Potatoes, 288–89
  Beef and Chicken Fajita Burgers with Seared Peppers and Onions, 25
  Big Beef Burger Stack-Ups with Mushrooms, Peppers, and Onions, 105

Burgers and Patties (*continued*)
Big Bistro Burgers with Caramelized Shallots on Grilled Bread with Beet and Goat Cheese Salad, 247
Boo's Smoky Chicken Patties on Buttered Toast, 21
Buffalo Turkey Burgers with Blue Cheese Dressing, 228
A Burger for Brad: Barbecue Burger Deluxe, 227
Burly-Man-Size Chicken–Cheddar Barbecued Burgers with Spicy Coleslaw, 142
Cacciatore Burgers, 104
Cheddar-Studded Tex-Mex Meatloaf Patties, Scallion Smashed Potatoes, and Spicy Pan Gravy, 91
Chicken Chimichurri Burgers with Exotic Chips, 107
Chicken or Turkey Spanakopita Burgers, 190
Chicken Sausage on a Roll with Egg and Fontina, 180
Chili Dog Bacon Cheeseburgers and Fiery Fries, 155
Five-Spice Burgers with Warm Mu Shu Slaw Topping, Pineapple, and Exotic Chips, 217
Garlic and Mint Lamb or Chicken Patties on Lentil Salad, 62
Gravy-Smothered Cajun-Style Meatloaf Patties with Maple Pecan–Glazed String Beans, 90
Italian Sweet Chicken Sausage Patties with Peppers and Onions on Garlic Buttered Rolls, 178
Jambalaya Burgers and Cajun Corn and Red Beans, 103
Jumbo Chicken, Spinach, and Herb Burgers with Mushrooms and Swiss, 50
Lamb and Scallion Burgers with Fried Asparagus, 277–78
Lamb Patties with Garlic and Mint over Mediterranean Chopped Salad, 80
Paella Burgers and Spanish Fries with Pimiento Mayonnaise, 26–27
Ricotta Smothered Mushroom "Burgers" with Sweet Onion–Olive Topping, Prosciutto, and Arugula, 40
Salmon Burgers with Ginger-Wasabi Mayo and Sesame-Crusted French Fries, 93
Scallop Burgers, 160–61

Sirloin Burgers with Gorgonzola Cheese and Mediterranean Slaw, 60
Super Marsala Burgers and Arugula-Tomato Salad, 169
Super Tuscan Burgers and Potato Salad with Capers and Celery, 13
Swordfish Burgers with Lemon, Garlic, and Parsley, 160
Turkey Chili–Topped Turkey Chili Burgers with Red Pepper Slaw and Funky Fries, 8–9
Burritos, Pork, Chipotle, and Bean, 301
Burritos, Turkey, Tomatillo, and Bean, 300–301

C
Calamari, Venetian, with Spicy Sauce and Egg Fettuccine, 162
Calzones, Spinach and Artichoke, 123
Cheddar
Boo's Butternut Squash Mac-n-Cheese, 20
Mac-n- , Smoky Chipotle, with Tomato and Chorizo, 5
Mac-n- , Tex-Mex, with Beef and Peppers, 5
Mac-n- , with Broccoli, 4
Salsa Stoup and Double-Decker Baked Quesadillas, 22
Southwestern Pasta Bake, 136
Triple-Onion Soup with Triple-Cheese Toast, 268
Cheese. *See also* Cheddar; Ricotta
Caprese Hot-or-Cold Pasta Toss, 70
Croque Monsieur with Greens, 222
Ham and Asparagus Tartines, 223
Ham and Swiss Crepes with Chopped Salad, 153
Italian Open-Face Sandwiches, 223
Mac-n-Smoked Gouda with Cauliflower, 4
Salsa Stoup and Double-Decker Baked Quesadillas, 22
Triple- , Toast, Sausage, Fennel, and Tomato Soup with, 268–69
Triple- , Toast, Triple-Onion Soup with, 268
White Pita Pizzas with Red and Green Prosciutto Salad, 198
Chicken. *See also* Chicken Sausage(s)
and Asparagus, Creamy, on Toast, 282
and Baby and Big Bella Mushroom Stew, 135
Balsamic-Glazed, with Smoked Mozzarella and Garlic Rice Pilaf, 55

BBQ Sloppy, Pan Pizza, 64
and Beef Fajita Burgers with Seared Peppers and Onions, 25
Big, Thick, Hearty Thighs...and That's a Compliment!, 46
Big, Thick, Hearty Thighs Spanish Style, 46
Breast, Sliced, Subs with Italian Sausage, Roasted Pepper, and Onion Sauce, 193
Breasts, Garlic-Parsley Pan-Roasted Garlic and Herb, with Chopped Salad and Creamy Caper Dressing, 147
Breasts, Marinated Grilled, with Zippy Chunky Salad and Garlic Dill Fries, 208
Breasts, Pretzel-Crusted, with a Cheddar-Mustard Sauce, 235
Breasts, Sautéed Sweet, with a Spicy Fresh Tomato Chutney and White Rice, 32
Breasts with Raw Puttanesca Sauce and Roasted Capers, 189
Cacciatore Burgers, 104
Cacciatore Stoup, 61
Caesar, Orange and Herb, 145
Caesar, Tex-Mex Grilled, 144
Cashew, Asian-Style, 99
Cashew, Park City, 98
–Cheddar Barbecued Burgers, Burly-Man-Size, with Spicy Coleslaw, 142
Chili Mac, Chipotle, 59
Chimichurri Burgers with Exotic Chips, 107
Cider Vinegar, with Smashed Potatoes and a Watercress and Cucumber Salad, 38–39
Citrus-Marinated, and Orange Salad, 19
Cordon Bleu Hash, Super Mashers with, 225
Corn, and Black Bean Stoup, 89
Croquettes with Spinach Mashers and Pan Gravy, 66
Curry, Fruited, in a Hurry, 152
Curry, Mostly Green, over Coconut Jasmine Rice, 36
Cutlets, Lemony Crispy, and Roasted Tomato Salad with Pine Nuts and Blue Cheese, 95
Cutlets, Rosemary, Parmigiano, and Pine Nut Breaded, with Fennel Slaw, 199

Cutlets, Sicilian-Style, with Chopped Caprese Salad for Two, 70
Cutlets on Buttermilk-Cheddar-Chorizo Biscuits with Tomato-Olive Salsa Mayo, 306
Cutlets with the Works! Breaded Meat with Mushroom and Onion Gravy, Bacon, and Cornichons, 119
Divan and Egg Noodle Bake, 225
Fingers with Honey Mustard Dipping Sauce and Spicy Chopped Salad, 226
Five-Spice Burgers with Warm Mu Shu Slaw Topping, Pineapple, and Exotic Chips, 217
Francese and Wilted Spinach, 76
Francese with Lemon and Wine, 279
in a Fresh Tomato and Eggplant Sauce with Spaghetti, 157
Garlic and Herb, with Romesco Sauce on Spicy Greens, 94
Ginger-Lime, with String Beans and Wasabi Mashed Potatoes, 248
Ginger-Soy, on Shredded Lettuce, 102
Ginger Vegetable Noodle Bowl, 75
Golden Raisin and Almond, 251
and Green Chili Hash, Super Mashers with, 129
Grilled, Paillard with Grilled Red Onion and Asparagus Salad, 92
Grilled, Scampi Style, with Angel Hair Pasta, 213
Grilled Chicken and Tangerine Salad, Warm, served on Grilled Garlic Crisps, 140
Honey, over Snow Pea Rice, 308
in a Horseradish Pan Sauce over Orange and Herb Couscous, 53
Jambalaya Burgers and Cajun Corn and Red Beans, 103
Mamacello and Asparagus Tips, 77
Mediterranean, and Saffron Couscous, 293
Mexican Pasta with Tomatillo Sauce and Meatballs, 270
Mix-n-Match Lettuce Tacos, 124
No. 14,752–Chicken in Mustard Sauce, 258
No. 14,753–Deviled Divan, 259
No. 14,754–Chicken Bustard (in Basil-Mustard Sauce), 259
No. 14,755–Chicken in Mustard-Tarragon Sauce, 260
No. 14,756–Chicken in "Lighter" Mustard and Lemon Sauce, 260
Paella Burgers and Spanish Fries with Pimiento Mayonnaise, 26–27

and Pasta, Bel Aria, 78–79
Patties, Boo's Smoky, on Buttered Toast, 21
Patties, Garlic and Mint, on Lentil Salad, 62
Pineapple-Rum, 86
Prosciutto, Garlic, and Herb Cheese–Stuffed, with Tarragon Pan Sauce, 42
in Puttanesca Sauce over Creamy Polenta, 202
and Rice Stoup, 109
Rolls, Chipotle, with Avocado Dipping Sauce, 262–63
Rolls, Everything-Crusted, Stuffed with Scallion Cream Cheese, 245
Rolls, Spinach and Goat Cheese, in a Pan Sauce, 256–57
Rolls, Wingless Buffalo, with Blue Cheese Dip, 264
Rosemary-Orange, Crispy, with Parmigiano String Beans, 305
Saucy BBQ, Sammies with Pepper and Scallion Potato Salad, 11
Schnitzel with Red Caraway Cabbage, 118
Simple and Delicious, with Potatoes and Asparagus, 283
Some, 3 Beans and, 30
Southwestern Pasta Bake, 136
Spanakopita Burgers, 190
Spiced Grilled, and Veggie Pockets, 297
in Spicy and Sweet Onion Sauce with Goat Cheese Smashed Potatoes and a Watercress and Cucumber Salad, 39
Spicy Spanish Raisin and Olive, Olé!, 251
Spinach, and Herb Burgers, Jumbo, with Mushrooms and Swiss, 50
Spring, with Leeks and Peas Served with Lemon Rice, 108
Sticks, Honey Nut, 15
Super Marsala Burgers and Arugula-Tomato Salad, 169
and Sweet Potato Curry-in-a-Hurry, 200
with Sweet Raisins and Apricots on Toasted Almond Couscous, 52
Tangy Cherry, 250
Thai, with Basil, 102
30-Minute, Under a Brick, 164
Tomato and Basil, Fresh, over Super Creamy Polenta, 310

Topped with Caponata and Mozzarella, 291
Tortilla Soup with Lime, 87–88
Warm Lemon, Sandwich with Arugula and Pears, 34
with White and Wild Rice Soup, 161
with Wild Mushroom and Balsamic Cream Sauce, 47
Chicken Sausage(s)
with Fennel and Onions, 205
with Hot and Sweet Peppers, Rosemary Corn Cakes with Prosciutto and, 17
Mini Meatballs with Gnocchi and Tomato Sauce, 179
Patties, Italian Sweet, with Peppers and Onions on Garlic Buttered Rolls, 178
on a Roll with Egg and Fontina, 180
Chili, Uptown Down-Home, 58
Chili Dog Bacon Cheeseburgers and Fiery Fries, 155
Chorizo(s)
and Butternut Soup with Herbed Tomato and Cheese Quesadillas, 206
Eggs-traordinary Spanish-Style Stuffed Toasty Baskets with Lemony Greens, 49
and Fish Stoup, Spanish, 130–31
Mexican Tomatillo Soup with, 271
and Saffron Rice, Big Mussels with, 175
and Shrimp Hash, Super Mashers with, 130
-Tomato Stew on Garlic Croutons with Zesty Parsley Sprinkle, 244
Corn
Chicken, and Black Bean Stoup, 89
Chowder, Bacon-Makes-It-Better, with Tomato and Ricotta Salata Salad, 127
and Crab Chowda, 120
Crab
and Corn Chowda, 120
Frutti di Mare and Linguine, 113
Salad Lettuce Wraps, 71
Seafood Frittata with Fennel, Orange, and Arugula Bread Salad, 187
and Shrimp Fritters with Chopped Salad and Roasted Red Pepper and Pickle Vinaigrette, 114
Tortilla (Egg Pie) and Shredded Plantain Hash Browns, 126
Crepes, Ham and Swiss, with Chopped Salad, 153

E

Eggplant
  Chicken Topped with Caponata and Mozzarella, 291
  and Fresh Tomato Sauce, Chicken in a, with Spaghetti, 157
  Mushroom, and Sweet Potato Indian-Spiced Stoup, 201
  Roasted, Sauce and Ricotta Salata, Pasta with, 35
  and Roasted Garlic Marinara Nests, 215
  Subs, Baked Sesame, with Fire-Roasted Tomato and Red Pepper Sauce, 229
Egg(s)
  Anyone for Brunch? B,L, or D Adaptation, 245
  Broccoli Frittata with Goat Cheese and BLT Bread Salad, 186
  Eggs-traordinary Spanish-Style Stuffed Toasty Baskets with Lemony Greens, 49
  Eggs-traordinary Stuffed Toasty Baskets with Lemony Greens, 48
  Fried, and Fresh Tomato Salsa, Chili–Sweet Potato Hash with, 255
  Fried, Ham and Spinach Hash with, 285
  and Ham, Fried Greens with, 159
  Pie (Crab Tortilla) and Shredded Plantain Hash Browns, 126
  Scramblewiches, 1
  Seafood Frittata with Fennel, Orange, and Arugula Bread Salad, 187
  Endive Salad, Incredible French, with Aged Herb Cheese Toasts, 312

F

Fish
  Baked Sole and Roasted Asparagus with Sesame, 117
  Balsamic-Glazed Swordfish with Capers and Grape Tomato–Arugula Rice, 55
  Chili-Spiced Grilled Halibut with Grilled-Corn Saucy Salsa, 290
  and Chorizo Stoup, Spanish, 130–31
  Cod Croquettes and Red Bell Pepper Gravy with Spinach Mashers, 67
  Cod in a Sack, 218
  Cornmeal-Crusted Catfish and Green Rice Pilaf, 209
  Crunchy Japanese, with Vegetable and Noodle Toss, 168
  Fillets, Lemon and Brown Butter, with Seared Red and Yellow Grape Tomatoes, 257
  Flounder Francese with Toasted Almonds, Lemons, and Capers, 77
  Francese with Lemon and Wine, 279
  Fried, Crispy Horseradish-Battered, with Watercress-Cucumber Tartar Sauce, 302
  Grilled Halibut with Fennel, Orange, Red Onions, and Oregano, 234
  Grilled Swordfish Salad, 231
  Halibut Soup, 49
  Indian-Asian Seared Cod with Cilantro-Mint Chutney and Sweet Pea and Coconut Jasmine Rice, 138
  Lime-and-Honey Glazed Salmon with Warm Black Bean and Corn Salad, 253
  Pesce Spada Pasta, 79
  in a Sack, French, 219
  in a Sack, Spanish, 219
  Salmon Burgers with Ginger-Wasabi Mayo and Sesame-Crusted French Fries, 93
  Sardine and Bread Crumb Pasta with Puttanesca Salad, 63
  Sautéed Salmon with Spicy Fresh Mango-Pineapple Chutney, 211
  Seafood Newburg Stoup with Cayenne-Chive-Buttered Corn Toasties, 120
  Sicilian-Style Swordfish Rolls with Fennel and Radicchio Salad, 68
  Sweet Lemon Salmon with Mini Carrots and Dill, 292
  Swordfish Burgers with Lemon, Garlic, and Parsley, 160
  Swordfish Cutlets with Tomato and Basil Salad, 69
  Swordfish Steaks with Raw Puttanesca Sauce and Roasted Capers, 189
  Tuna with Everything-but-the-Kitchen-Sink, Hold-the-Mayo, Stuffed Bread, 313
  Whole, with Ginger and Scallions, 57

G

Gnocchi
  Involtini all'Enotec'Antica with, 166
  with Sausage and Swiss Chard, 295
  and Tomato Sauce, Mini Chicken Sausage Meatballs with, 179

Greens. *See also specific greens*
  and Beans Soup, 125
  Fried, with Ham and Eggs, 159
  Incredible French Crunchy Salad, 267
  Ribollita con Verdure, 29
  Seared, with Cheese Ravioli and Sage Butter, 158–59
  Verdure di Primo Maggio con Polenta (Mixed Greens on the First Day of May with Polenta), 203

H

Ham
  Asparagus, and Peas, Springtime Bows with, 266
  and Asparagus Tartines, 223
  Black Bean Stoup and Southwestern Monte Cristos, 18
  Charred Tomato Soup with Pesto and Prosciutto Stromboli, 194
  Chopped Antipasto Stuffed Bread, 314
  Croque Monsieur with Greens, 222
  and Eggs, Fried Greens with, 159
  Italian Open-Face Sandwiches, 223
  Scramblewiches, 1
  Seared Spicy, and Charred Polenta, Mushroom Sauté on, 240
  Spicy, and Spinach Pasta Bake, 307
  and Spinach Hash with Fried Eggs, 285
  Steaks, Honey-Orange–Glazed, with Spicy Black Bean, Zucchini, and Corn Salad, 96
  and Swiss Crepes with Chopped Salad, 153
Hot dogs
  Chicago Dog Salad, 99–100
  Chili Dog Bacon Cheeseburgers and Fiery Fries, 155
  Oven-Baked Corn Dogs with O & V Slaw, 196

I

Ice Cream, Boo's Vanilla, with Chunky Peanut Butter Sauce and Gingersnaps, 21

L

Lamb
  Chops, Broiled, with Sweet Pea and Spinach Couscous, 249
  Chops, Olive-Butter–Slathered Broiled, with Caramelized Zucchini Orzo, 182

Chops, Spiced, on Sautéed Peppers and Onions with Garlic and Mint Couscous, 10
Chops and Early Spring Salad, 145
and Feta Rolls with Cucumber-Mint-Yogurt Dipping Sauce, 264
Goulash, 3
Loins with Red Wine, Warm and Cold Bordeaux Salad, and Sweet Carrots and White Beans, 232–33
Patties, Garlic and Mint, on Lentil Salad, 62
Patties with Garlic and Mint over Mediterranean Chopped Salad, 80
and Scallion Burgers with Fried Asparagus, 277–78
"Stew" (Wink, Wink), 242
Lasagna. See Polenta "Lasagna"

M
Meatballs
Big Beef Balls with Bucatini, 237
Florentine, 23
Involtini all'Enotec'Antica with Gnocchi, 166
Lion's Head (Pork Meatballs and Napa Cabbage), 56
Mexican Pasta with Tomatillo Sauce and, 270
Mini Chicken Sausage, with Gnocchi and Tomato Sauce, 179
Sausage, with Peppers, Onions, and a Side of Penne, 238
Veal Polpette with Thin Spaghetti and Light Tomato and Basil Sauce, 236
Mushroom(s)
Bisque, 284
"Burgers," Ricotta Smothered, with Sweet Onion–Olive Topping, Prosciutto, and Arugula, 40
Cream Sauce, Pasta with, 284
Polenta "Lasagna," Sausage and, 298
Polenta "Lasagna," Sausage and Olive, 299
Polenta "Lasagna," Sausage and Pesto, 299
Polenta "Lasagna," Super, 300
Polenta "Lasagna," Sweet and Savory, 299
Sauté, Creamed, with Artichoke Hearts, Spinach, and Penne, 241
Sauté, Creamed, with Hearts of Palm, Arugula, and Pappardelle, 241
Sauté on Charred Polenta and Seared Spicy Ham, 240

-Veggie Sloppy Sandwiches, 280
Wild, and Scotch Risotto, 272–73
Wild, Sauté on Toast Points with Gruyère, 239
Wild Cream of, Egg Noodle Bake, Hold the Canned Soup, 224
Mussels
Big, with Chorizo and Saffron Rice, 175
Frutti di Mare and Linguine, 113
a Lot of, Pasta with, 246

Onion, Triple-, Soup with Triple-Cheese Toast, 268

P
Pasta
Angel Hair, Grilled Chicken, Scampi Style, with, 213
Angel Hair, Grilled Shrimp Scampi on, 212
Artichoke and Walnut Pesto, 122
Bake, BLT: Bacon, Leeks, and Tomatoes, 33
Bake, Southwestern, 136
Bake, Spinach and Spicy Ham, 307
Big Beef Balls with Bucatini, 237
Boo's Butternut Squash Mac-n-Cheese, 20
Chicken and, Bel Aria, 78–79
Chicken in a Fresh Tomato and Eggplant Sauce with Spaghetti, 157
Chipotle Chicken Chili Mac, 59
Christmas, 318
Creamed Mushroom Sauté with Artichoke Hearts, Spinach, and Penne, 241
Creamed Mushroom Sauté with Hearts of Palm, Arugula, and Pappardelle, 241
Frutti di Mare and Linguine, 113
Italian-Style Garlic Shrimp with Cherry Tomatoes and Thin Spaghetti, 132
with a Lot of Mussel, 246
Mac-n-Cheddar with Broccoli, 4
Mac-n-Smoked Gouda with Cauliflower, 4
Mexican, with Tomatillo Sauce and Meatballs, 270
with Mushroom Cream Sauce, 284
Nests, Beef and Mushroom, 216
Nests, Roasted Garlic and Eggplant Marinara, 215
Nests, Tomato-Basil, 214
Olive and Anchovy–Slathered Beef Tenderloin Steaks with Caramelized Onion Orzo and Sliced Tomatoes, 183

Pecan and Arugula Pesto, 221
Pesce Spada, 79
Pistachio Pesto, 220
Pumpkin, with Sausage and Wild Mushrooms, 24
Ricotta, with Grape Tomatoes, Peas, and Basil, 170
Ricotta, with Sausage, 170
Ricotta, with Spinach, 172
Ricotta, with Tomatoes al Forno, 171
Ricotta, with Zucchini, Garlic, and Mint, 171
with Roasted Eggplant Sauce and Ricotta Salata, 35
Sardine and Bread Crumb, with Puttanesca Salad, 63
Sausage Meatballs with Peppers, Onions, and a Side of Penne, 238
Seared Greens with Cheese Ravioli and Sage Butter, 158–59
Smoky Chipotle Chili Con Queso Mac, 137
Smoky Chipotle Mac-n-Cheddar with Tomato and Chorizo, 5
Spaghetti con Aglio e Olio with Tomato and Onion Salad, 121
Spicy Shrimp and Penne with Puttanesca Sauce, 112–13
with Spinach, Mushrooms, Pumpkin, and Hazelnuts, 24
Springtime Bows with Asparagus, Ham, and Peas, 266
with Swiss Chard, Bacon, and Lemony Ricotta Cheese, 45
Taco Chili-Mac, 22
Tex-Mex Mac-n-Cheddar with Beef and Peppers, 5
Toss, Caprese Hot-or-Cold, 70
Veal Polpette with Thin Spaghetti and Light Tomato and Basil Sauce, 236
Venetian Calamari with Spicy Sauce and Egg Fettuccine, 162
Walnut-Parsley-Rosemary Pesto, 221
White Beans, Pancetta, and, 173
Zucchini and Bow Ties, 266
Pea, Sweet, Soup with Parmigiano Toast, 148
Pecan and Arugula Pesto, 221
Pesto
Pecan and Arugula, 221
Pistachio, 220
Walnut-Parsley-Rosemary, 221
Pistachio Pesto, 220
Pizza
BBQ Sloppy Chicken Pan, 64

Pizza (*continued*)
  Capricciosa, 162–63
  Nacho Bread, 316
  Spanakopizza, 191
  White Pitas, with Red and Green
    Prosciutto Salad, 198
  Zucchini, 275
Polenta
  Pumpkin, Vegetarian, with Spinach
    and White Beans, 185
  Pumpkin, with Chorizo and Black
    Beans, 184
  Pumpkin, with Italian Sausage and
    Fennel, 184–85
  Verdure di Primio Maggio con (Mixed
    Greens on the First Day of May with
    Polenta), 203
Polenta "Lasagna"
  Sausage, Mushroom, and Olive, 299
  Sausage, Mushroom, and Pesto, 299
  Sausage and Mushroom, 298
  Super Mushroom, 300
  Sweet and Savory, 299
Pork. *See also* Chorizo(s); Ham;
    Sausage(s)
  Chipotle, and Bean Burritos, 301
  Chops, Balsamic-Glazed, with
    Arugula-Basil Rice Pilaf, 54
  Chops, Columbus's, 233
  Chops, Ham and Cheese–Stuffed, with
    Lot-o'-Mushrooms Sauce, 88
  Chops, Oregon-Style, with Pinot Noir
    and Cranberries; Oregon Hash with
    Wild Mushrooms, Greens, Beets,
    Hazelnuts, and Blue Cheese;
    Charred Whole-Grain Bread with
    Butter and Chives, 14–15
  Chops, Rosemary-Orange, and Lemon-
    Butter Broccolini, 84
  Chops, Sage and Balsamic, with
    Creamy Pumpkin Polenta, 254
  Chops, Spanish-Style, with Chorizo
    and Roasted Red Pepper Sauce and
    Green Beans, 192
  Chops, Sweet Prune and Sage, with
    Potatoes, 204
  Chops in a Sweet Chili and Onion
    Sauce with Creamy Cilantro Potato
    Salad, 303
  Chops with Grainy Mustard and Raisin
    Sauce, 100
  Cutlets with the Works! Breaded Meat
    with Mushroom and Onion Gravy,
    Bacon, and Cornichons, 119

Five-Spice Burgers with Warm Mu Shu
    Slaw Topping, Pineapple, and Exotic
    Chips, 217
Lion's Head (Pork Meatballs and Napa
    Cabbage), 56
Loin Chops with Golden Delicious
    Apples and Onions on Polenta with
    Honey, 281
Mexican Pasta with Tomatillo Sauce
    and Meatballs, 270
and Noodle Salad, Thai-Style, 295
Pineapple, Sweet and Spicy, 289
Sausage Meatballs with Peppers,
    Onions, and a Side of Penne, 238
Schnitzel with Red Caraway Cabbage,
    118
Super Tuscan Burgers and Potato
    Salad with Capers and Celery, 13
Tenderloin, Cumin and Lime Roasted,
    with Spicy Creamed Corn, 150
Tenderloin, Rosemary Lemon–Pepper,
    with Creamy Lemon-Parmigiano
    Dressed Greens and Garlic Croutons,
    287
Thai, with Basil, 102
Potato(es). *See also* Gnocchi; Sweet
    Potato(es)
  Fancy-Pants Bangers 'n' Mash, 82
  Salad, German, Salad with Kielbasa,
    134
  Turkey Club Super Mashers, 97
Pumpkin
  Pasta with Sausage and Wild
    Mushrooms, 24
  Polenta, Vegetarian, with Spinach and
    White Beans, 185
  Polenta with Chorizo and Black Beans,
    184
  Polenta with Italian Sausage and
    Fennel, 184–85
  Spinach, Mushrooms, and Hazelnuts,
    Pasta with, 24
Rice. *See also* Risotto
  Incredible French Crunchy Salad, 267
Ricotta
  Cheese, Lemony, Swiss Chard, and
    Bacon, Pasta with, 45
  Pasta with Grape Tomatoes, Peas, and
    Basil, 170
  Pasta with Sausage, 170
  Pasta with Spinach, 172
  Pasta with Tomatoes al Forno, 171
  Pasta with Zucchini, Garlic, and Mint,
    171

White Pita Pizzas with Red and Green
    Prosciutto Salad, 198
Risotto
  Boo-sotto, 272
  Cream, with White Asparagus and
    Andouille, 274
  Lemon and Artichoke, with Shrimp,
    273
  Scotch and Wild Mushroom, 272–73
  Spinach and Hazelnut, 274

S
Salads (main-dish)
  Bacon-Wrapped Beef Supper, 276
  Capricciosa, 163
  Chicago Dog, 99–100
  Chicken Caesar, Orange and Herb, 145
  Chicken Caesar, Tex-Mex Grilled, 144
  Citrus-Marinated Chicken and Orange,
    19
  Endive, Incredible French, with Aged
    Herb Cheese Toasts, 312
  French Salade Superb, 134
  German Potato, with Kielbasa, 134
  Greek Bread, with Grilled Shrimp, 154
  Grilled Steak Sandwich...I mean,
    Salad–No! Sandwich!, 261
  Grilled Swordfish, 231
  Pancetta-Wrapped Shrimp Supper, 277
  Tangerine and Grilled Chicken, Warm,
    served on Grilled Garlic Crisps, 140
  Thai-Style Pork and Noodle, 295
  Thai-Style Steak, 294
Sandwiches. *See also* Burgers and
    patties
  Baked Sesame Eggplant Subs with
    Fire-Roasted Tomato and Red
    Pepper Sauce, 229
  Black Bean Stoup and Southwestern
    Monte Cristos, 18
  Charred Tomato Soup with Pesto and
    Prosciutto Stromboli, 194
  Chopped Antipasto Stuffed Bread, 314
  Croque Monsieur with Greens, 222
  French Onion Sliced Steak Croissant,
    286
  Grilled Flank Steak, with Blue Cheese
    Vinaigrette–Dressed Arugula and
    Pears, 34
  Ham and Asparagus Tartines, 223
  Hamburger and Onion Stuffed Bread,
    317
  Italian Open-Face, 223
  Mushroom-Veggie Sloppy, 280

Quick Cassoulet Stuffed Bread Melts, 315

Ropa Vieja Josés (Cuban Sloppy Joes) with Smashed Yucca, Sliced Tomatoes, Plantain Chips, and Mojo Sauce, 74–75

Saucy BBQ Chicken Sammies with Pepper and Scallion Potato Salad, 11

Scramblewiches, 1

Sliced Chicken Breast Subs with Italian Sausage, Roasted Pepper, and Onion Sauce, 193

Spiced Grilled Chicken and Veggie Pockets, 297

Steak...Knife and Fork Required, 165

Super-Grilled Steak, with Horseradish-Dijon Cream and Spicy Greens, 143

Tuna with Everything-but-the-Kitchen-Sink, Hold-the-Mayo, Stuffed Bread, 313

Warm Lemon Chicken, with Arugula and Pears, 34

Sausage(s). *See also* Chorizo(s)
Christmas Pasta, 318
Fancy-Pants Bangers 'n' Mash, 82
Fennel, and Tomato Soup with Triple-Cheese Toast, 268–69
and Fennel Ragout with Creamy Polenta, 41
German Potato Salad with Kielbasa, 134
Italian Sub Stoup and Garlic Toast Floaters, 9
Meatballs with Peppers, Onions, and a Side of Penne, 238
Mushroom, and Olive Polenta "Lasagna," 299
Mushroom, and Pesto Polenta "Lasagna," 299
and Mushroom Polenta "Lasagna," 298
Quick Cassoulet Stuffed Bread Melts, 315
and Spinach Pastry Squares with Cherry Tomato–Arugula Salad, 44
Sweet, Braised in Onions with Horseradish Smashed Potatoes, 31
Sweet and Savory Polenta "Lasagna," 299
and Swiss Chard, Gnocchi with, 295

Sausages, chicken. *See* Chicken Sausage(s)

Scallop(s)
Burgers, 160–61
Grilled, Scampi-Style, with Angel Hair Pasta, 213
Sweet Sea, in a Caper-Raisin Sauce, 278

Shellfish. *See also* Crab; Shrimp
Big Mussels with Chorizo and Saffron Rice, 175
Frutti di Mare and Linguine, 113
Grilled Scallops, Scampi-Style, with Angel Hair Pasta, 213
Pasta with a Lot of Mussels, 246
Scallop Burgers, 160–61
Sweet Sea Scallops in a Caper-Raisin Sauce, 278
Venetian Calamari with Spicy Sauce and Egg Fettuccine, 162

Shrimp
and Bok Choy Noodle Bowl, Spicy, 65
and Chorizo Hash, Super Mashers with, 130
and Crab Fritters with Chopped Salad and Roasted Red Pepper and Pickle Vinaigrette, 114
Frutti di Mare and Linguine, 113
Garlic, and Orzo, Greek-Style, 133
Garlic, and Rice, Spanish-Style, 132–33
Garlic, Italian-Style, with Cherry Tomatoes and Thin Spaghetti, 132
Garlic-Parsley, Lemon-Thyme Succotash with, 174
Grilled, Greek Bread Salad with, 154
Grilled, Scampi on Angel Hair Pasta, 212
Lemon and Artichoke Risotto with, 273
Martinis and Manhattan Steaks, 141
Mix-n-Match Lettuce Tacos, 124
Pancetta-Wrapped, Supper Salad, 277
and Penne, Spicy, with Puttanesca Sauce, 112–13
Piña Colada, 87
Seafood Frittata with Fennel, Orange, and Arugula Bread Salad, 187
Seafood Newburg Stoup with Cayenne-Chive-Buttered Corn Toasties, 120
Sesame, Zucchini, and Mushroom Caps, Crispy Fried, with a Ginger-Soy Dipping Sauce, 210
Thai, with Basil, 102
and Veggies, Thai-Style, with Toasted Coconut Rice, 188

Soup. *See also* Stew; Stoup
About-15-Minute, with Spinach, Artichokes, and Tortellini, 172
Bacon-Makes-It-Better Corn Chowder with Tomato and Ricotta Salata Salad, 127
Beans and Greens, 125
Charred Tomato, with Pesto and Prosciutto Stromboli, 194
Chicken Tortilla, with Lime, 87–88
Chicken with White and Wild Rice, 161
Chorizo and Butternut, with Herbed Tomato and Cheese Quesadillas, 206
Crab and Corn Chowda, 120
Creamy Broccoli, with Cheddar and Chive Toast, 149
Creamy Spinach, with Fontina Toast, 149
Fall Minestrone, 177
Halibut, 49
Mushroom Bisque, 284
Papa al Pomodoro, 28
Peasant, 105
Ribollita con Verdure, 29
Sausage, Fennel, and Tomato, with Triple-Cheese Toast, 268–69
Sweet Pea, with Parmigiano Toast, 148
Triple-Onion, with Triple-Cheese Toast, 268

Spinach
and Artichoke Calzones, 123
Chicken or Turkey Spanakopita Burgers, 190
Florentine Meatballs, 23
and Ham Hash with Fried Eggs, 285
and Hazelnut Risotto, 274
and Sausage Pastry Squares with Cherry Tomato–Arugula Salad, 44
Soup, Creamy, with Fontina Toast, 149
Spanakopizza, 191
and Spicy Ham Pasta Bake, 307
and Tofu, Indian, over Almond Rice, 156

Squash. *See also* Pumpkin
Butternut, Mac-n-Cheese, Boo's, 20
Chorizo and Butternut Soup with Herbed Tomato and Cheese Quesadillas, 206
Zucchini and Bow Ties, 266
Zucchini Pizza, 275

Stew. *See also* Stoup
Baby and Big Bella Mushroom and Chicken, 135
Chorizo-Tomato, on Garlic Croutons with Zesty Parsley Sprinkle, 244

"Stew," Lamb (Wink, Wink), 242
Stoup
  Black Bean, and Southwestern Monte
    Cristos, 18
  Chicken, Corn, and Black Bean, 89
  Chicken and Rice, 109
  Chicken Cacciatore, 61
  Eggplant, Mushroom, and Sweet
    Potato Indian-Spiced, 201
  Fish and Chorizo, Spanish, 130–31
  Italian Sub, and Garlic Toast Floaters,
    9
  Meat Dumpling, Swedish, 111–12
  Mexican Tomatillo, with Chorizo, 271
  Salsa, and Double-Decker Baked
    Quesadillas, 22
  Seafood Newburg, with Cayenne-
    Chive-Buttered Corn Toasties, 120
  Tomato and Bean, My Mom's 15-
    Minute, 158
Sweet Potato(es)
  and Chicken Curry-in-a-Hurry, 200
  –Chili Hash with Fried Eggs and Fresh
    Tomato Salsa, 255
  Eggplant, and Mushroom Indian-
    Spiced Stoup, 201

T
Tacos, Mix-n-Match Lettuce, 124
Tacos, Turkey, 269
Tofu and Mostly Green Curry Veggies
  over Coconut Jasmine Rice, 37
Tofu and Spinach, Indian, over Almond
  Rice, 156
Tomato(es)
  and Bean Stoup, My Mom's 15-Minute,
    158
  Charred, Soup with Pesto and
    Prosciutto Stromboli, 194
  –Chorizo Stew on Garlic Croutons with
    Zesty Parsley Sprinkle, 244
  Christmas Pasta, 318
  Papa al Pomodoro, 28
  Salsa Stoup and Double-Decker Baked
    Quesadillas, 22

Sausage, and Fennel Soup with Triple-
    Cheese Toast, 268–69
Tortilla(s)
  Chicken Soup with Lime, 87–88
  Chorizo and Butternut Soup with
    Herbed Tomato and Cheese
    Quesadillas, 206
  Pork, Chipotle, and Bean Burritos, 301
  Salsa Stoup and Double-Decker Baked
    Quesadillas, 22
  Turkey, Tomatillo, and Bean Burritos,
    300–301
Turkey
  Black Bean Stoup and Southwestern
    Monte Cristos, 18
  Burgers, Buffalo, with Blue Cheese
    Dressing, 228
  Chili-Topped Turkey Chili Burgers with
    Red Pepper Slaw and Funky Fries,
    8–9
  Chunky, Potatoes and Veggies in Red
    Wine Sauce, 195
  Club Super Mashers, 97
  Croquettes with Spinach Mashers and
    Pan Gravy, 66
  Cutlet Parmigiano with Warm, Fresh
    Grape Tomato Topping, Pesto, and
    Mozzarella, 51
  Cutlets, Crispy, with Bacon-Cranberry
    Brussels Sprouts, 309
  Cutlets, Grilled, with Warm Cranberry
    Salsa and Sautéed Sweet Potatoes,
    81
  Cutlets with Sautéed Brussels Sprouts
    with Pancetta and Balsamic Vinegar,
    151
  Florentine Meatballs, 23
  Noodle Casserole, 7
  and Sage Rolls with Cranberry
    Dipping Sauce, 263
  Saltimbocca Roll-Ups, Mushroom and
    White Bean Ragout, and Spinach
    with Pancetta and Onions, 16
  Smoky, Shepherd's Pie, 2–3

Spanakopita Burgers, 190
Stroganoff Noodle Toss, 296
Tacos, 269
Tomatillo, and Bean Burritos, 300–301

V
Veal
  Boo-sotto, 272
  Chops, Sweet Dates, Apricot, and
    Sage, with Chive Potatoes, 205
  Chops and Balsamic-Thyme Roasted
    Tomatoes and Mushrooms, 243
  Christmas Pasta, 318
  Cutlets with the Works! Breaded Meat
    with Mushroom and Onion Gravy,
    Bacon, and Cornichons, 119
  Francese with Lemon and Wine, 279
  Polpette with Thin Spaghetti and Light
    Tomato and Basil Sauce, 236
  Rolls, Sweet and Savory Stuffed, with
    a Mustard Pan Sauce, 139
  Saltimbocca with Spinach Polenta, 230
  Scallopine with Dijon Sauce,
    Asparagus, and Avocados, 167
  Schnitzel with Red Caraway Cabbage,
    118
  Super Marsala Burgers and Arugula-
    Tomato Salad, 169
  Swedish Meat Dumpling Stoup, 111–12
Vegetable(s). See also specific vegetables
  Fall Minestrone, 177
  Indian Spiced, 101
  Mushroom-Veggie Sloppy
    Sandwiches, 280
  Veggie Fritters and Asian Salad, 115

W
Walnut and Artichoke Pesto Pasta, 122
Walnut-Parsley-Rosemary Pesto, 221

Z
Zucchini and Bow Ties, 266
Zucchini Pizza, 275